SECOND EDITION

From Master Student to Master Employee

Doug Toft
Contributing Editor

Houghton Mifflin Company Boston New York

Publisher: Patricia A. Coryell
Sponsoring Editor: Shani B. Fisher
Marketing Manager: Edwin Hill
Discipline Product Manager: Guiseppina Daniel
Development Editor: Julia Giannotti
Senior Project Editor: Cathy Labresh Brooks
Senior Media Producer: Philip Lanza
Content Manager: James Edmonds
Art and Design Manager: Jill Haber
Cover Design Director: Tony Saizon
Senior Photo Editor: Jennifer Meyer Dare
Composition Buyer: Chuck Dutton
New Title Project Manager: Patricia O'Neill
Editorial Assistant: Amanda Nietzel
Marketing Assistant: Bettina Chiu

Cover credits: (Mechanic) © Manchan/GettyImages; (nurse, office worker, Keyboarder, carpenter, teacher) © Masterfile Royalty Free

College Survival
2075 Foxfield Drive, Suite 100
St. Charles, IL 60174
1-800-528-8323
collegesurvival@hmco.com

Photo and illustration credits appear on page 349.

Printed in the U.S.A.

Library of Congress Control Number: 2007927639

Student Edition
ISBN-13: 978-0-618-95160-4
ISBN-10: 0-618-95160-1

Annotated Instructor's Edition
ISBN-13: 978-0-618-95032-4
ISBN-10: 0-618-95032-X

3 4 5 6 7 8 9 – WC – 12 11 10 09 08

advisory board

Justina Boyd
Colorado University

Jodi Caldwell
Georgia Southern University

Marla Cartwright
Kaplan University

Jennifer Combs
Fullerton College, CA

Carol Forrey
Kaplan University

James George
Westwood College, Chicago Loop, IL

Paul Gore
University of Utah

Anne Gupton
Mott Community College, MI

Jane Jepson
Cypress College, CA

Jill Jurgens
Old Dominion University, VA

Patsy Krech
University of Memphis, TN

Stephen Lewis
Westwood College, O'Hare Campus, IL

Susan Loffredo
Northeastern University, MA

Carole Mackewich
Clark College, WA

Dean Mancina
Golden West College, CA

Eldon L. McMurray
Utah Valley State College

Amanda Millard
Westwood College, Chicago Loop, IL

Sharon Occipinti
Florida Metropolitan University, Tampa

Keri O'Malley
ECPI Technical College at Greensboro, NC

Margaret Puckett
North Central State College, OH

Deidre Sepp
Marist College, NY

Linda Nelson
Davenport University, IN

Valerie Smolek
Westwood College, Torrance, IL

Jake Sneva
University at Buffalo, NY

David Southwell
Westwood College, O'Hare Campus, IL

Pat Twaddle
Moberly Area Community College, MO

Debra Watson
Mississippi Gulf Coast Community College

Diane Williams
PIMA Medical Institute, AZ

Eric S. Wormsley
PIMA Community College

past advisory board members

Judy Brandon
Clovis Community College, NM

Carl Bridges
Career Education Corporation, IL

Julie Brown
Corinthian Colleges, Inc., CA

David Cooper
Northwest Business College, IL

Katharine Davis
Mississippi Delta Community College

Sylvia Edwards-Borens
Texas State Technical College, Waco

Steven Epstein
SUNY—Suffolk Community College, NY

Mary Etter
Davenport University, MI

Marie Feuer
Mt. Sierra College, CA

Richard Gargan
Florida Metropolitan University, Orlando

Vicki Gidney
International Business College, TX

Dorothy Herndon
National College of Business and Technology, VA

Pat Hunnicutt
ITT-Technical Institutes, Little Rock, AR

Martha Johnson
Texas A&M University

Linda Kester
Erie Institute of Technology, PA

Blake Mackesy
Wilkes University, PA

Diane Noraas
Baker College, MI

Nancy Porretto
Katherine Gibbs Schools, Melville, NY

Diane Savoca
St. Louis Community College, MO

Kathlene Scholljegeredes
Bethel College, MN

Jeffrey Swanberg
Rockford Business College, IL

Jean Wisuri
American Education Centers, KY

brief table of contents

table of contents

Mastering Transitions

1 Discovering Yourself

2 Discovering Careers

3 Time

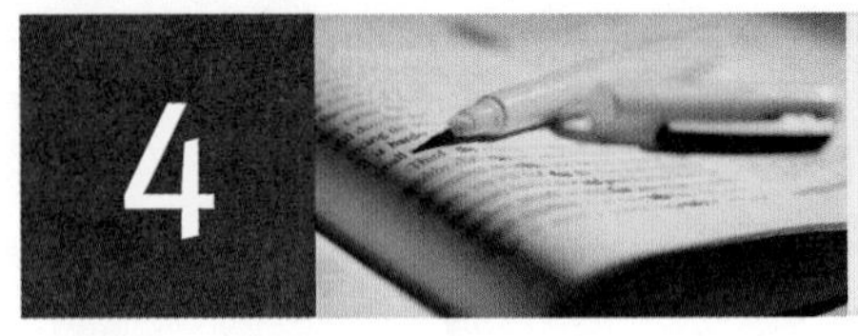

4 Reading

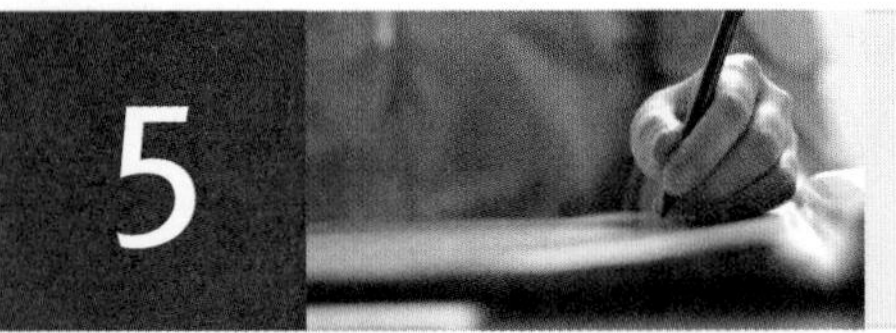

5 Notes

6 Tests

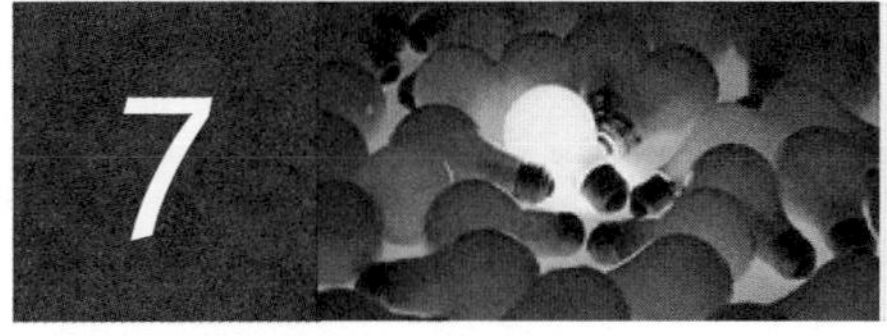

7 Thinking

8 Communicating

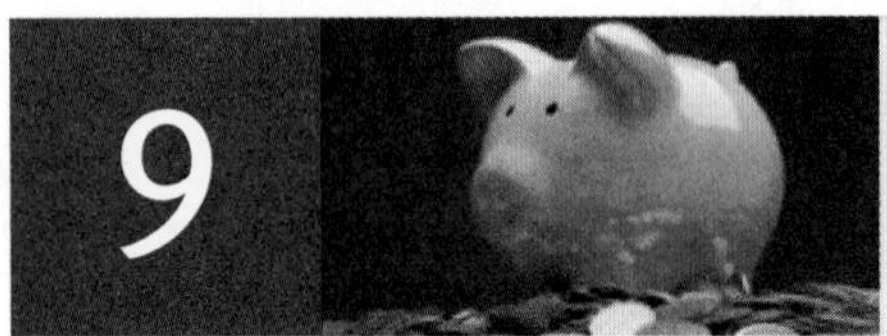

9 Money

10 Working

INTRODUCTION

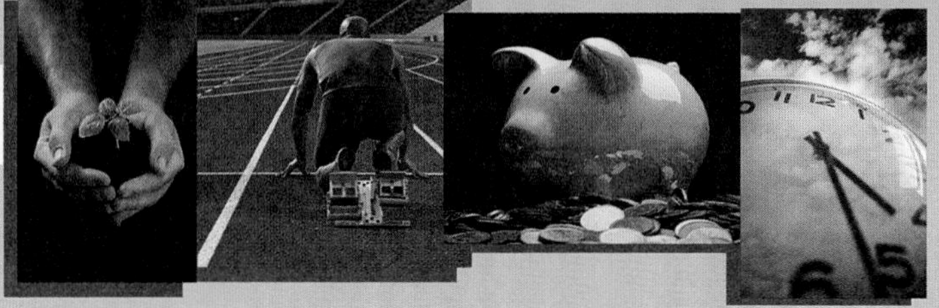

Mastering Transitions

MASTER STUDENT MAP

why the Introduction matters . . .

Gain learning strategies that will help you make a successful transition to higher education.

how you can use this Introduction . . .

Keep a journal that translates insights into new behaviors.

Learn to approach higher education in a way that can help you succeed in the work force.

As you read, ask yourself what if . . .

I could use the strategies that help me succeed in school to also succeed in the workplace?

what is included . . .

FROM THE DESK OF . . .

The first and most important thing college does is it shifts all the responsibility for getting ahead to you. If you don't want to do your homework or class work or even show up to class, you fail. End of story. You don't get called into the principal's office. College is like the minor leagues for the corporate world. Obviously you gain the knowledge and skills you need; you also gain this intangible social quality that allows you to interact with your coworkers and bosses on the proper level.

—STUART SHOSTAK, STRUCTURED FINANCE ANALYST

From master student to master employee

Once upon a time, people thought of education as an enterprise set apart from the business of daily life. The halls of colleges, universities, and other schools were described as ivory towers—places where scholars retreated from the world of work to pursue knowledge.

Today, a different point of view prevails. The boundaries between classroom, office, and factory floor are fluid and flexible. Some people earn a high school diploma, enter the work force, and then enroll in higher education to expand their career options. Other people continue directly from high school to college. Even so, their learning includes practicum experience, internships, work-study assignments, and other career-related experiences. Many students work full-time while attending classes.

Instead of competing, workplaces and classrooms can now complement each other. This development mirrors some key discoveries in the psychology of learning: that we learn by immersing ourselves in concrete experiences, reflecting on them, constructing theories, and then testing those theories in action.

Pioneers of both liberal education and modern work methods would agree. In his classic book *The Idea of a University,* John Henry Newman wrote that "all Knowledge is a whole and the separate Sciences parts of one"—leaving no room to divorce theory from practice or knowledge from application. And he wrote this even though he completed only eight years of formal schooling.[1] Henry Ford said, "The only real security that a person can have in this world is a reserve of knowledge, experience, and ability. Without these qualities, money is practically useless."[2]

The purpose of this book is to build two kinds of bridges between your classroom experiences and your career. One is the bridge of skills—your ability to perform tasks that are valued by employers. Second is the bridge of learning—the ability to update your skills and acquire new ones any time you choose.

As a student, you are now involved in a multimillion-dollar enterprise called higher education. By focusing on the skills you acquire and the results you create, you can move between the role of employee and the role of student as easily as you change clothes. As a student, you are also at work, performing in ways that produce measurable results. This is natural because both roles draw on a common set of skills. The phrases *master student* and *master employee* are terms for qualities that live inside you, waiting only to be discovered.

critical thinking exercise 1

TEXTBOOK RECONNAISSANCE

Start becoming a master student this moment by doing a 15-minute "textbook reconnaissance." Here's how.

First, read the table of contents. Do it in three minutes or less. Next, look at every page in the book. Move quickly. Scan headlines. Look at pictures. Notice forms, charts, and diagrams. Don't forget the last few pages in back, which include extra copies of planning forms that you might find useful.

A textbook reconnaissance shows you where a course is going. It gives you the big picture. That's useful because brains work best when going from the general to the specific. Getting the big picture before you start makes it easier to recall and understand details later on.

Your textbook reconnaissance will work even better if, as you scan, you look for ideas you can use. When you find one, write the page number and a short description of it in the space below. If you run out of room, just continue your list on a separate sheet of paper. Or use Post-it Notes to flag the pages that look useful. You could even use notes of different colors to signal priority, such as green for ideas to use right away and yellow for those to apply later. The idea behind this technique is simple: It's easier to learn when you're excited, and it's easier to get excited about a course if you know it's going to be useful, interesting, or fun.

Remember, look at every page, and do it quickly. And here's another useful tip for the master student: Do it now.

Page number	*Description*

This book is worthless— if you just read it

From Master Student to Master Employee is worthless—*if* reading it is all you do. Until you take action and use the ideas to change your behavior, this book will make little difference in your life.

The purpose of this book is to help you make successful transitions to higher education and to your chosen career by setting up a pattern of success that will last the rest of your life. You probably won't take action and use the ideas in this book until you are convinced that you have something to gain. That's one reason for this Introduction—to persuade you to use this book actively.

Before you stiffen up and resist this sales pitch, remember that you have already bought the book. Now you can get something for your money by committing yourself to take action—in other words, by committing yourself to success. Here's what's in it for you.

Pitch #1: You can save money now and make more later. Start with money. Your college education is one of the most expensive things you will ever buy. Typically, it costs students $30 to $70 an hour to sit in class. Unfortunately, many students think their classes aren't worth even 50 cents an hour.

As a master student, you control the value you get out of your education, and that value can be considerable. The joy of learning aside, college graduates make more money during their lifetimes than their nondegreed peers. According to the U.S. Department of Labor, college graduates over age 25 earn nearly twice as much as people who stop their education at high school.[3] It pays to be a master student.

Pitch #2: You can rediscover the natural learner in you. Joy is important, too. As you become a master student, you will learn to gain knowledge in the most effective way possible by discovering the joyful, natural learner within you.

Children are great natural students. They quickly master complex skills, such as language, and they have fun doing it. For them, learning is a high-energy process involving experimentation, discovery, and sometimes broken dishes. Then comes school. For some students, drill and drudgery replace discovery and dish breaking. Learning can become a drag. You can use this book to reverse that process and rediscover what you knew as a child—that laughter and learning go hand in hand.

Sometimes learning does take effort, especially in higher education. As you become a master student, you will learn many ways to get the most out of that effort.

Pitch #3: You can choose from hundreds of techniques. This book is packed with hundreds of practical, nuts-and-bolts techniques. And you can begin using them immediately. For example, during the textbook reconnaissance on page 1, you can practice three powerful learning techniques in one 15-minute exercise. Even if you doze in lectures, drift during tests, or dawdle on term papers, you'll find ideas in this book that you can use to become a more effective student.

Not all of these ideas will work for you. That's why there are so many of them in this book. You can experiment with the techniques. As you discover what works, you will develop a unique style of learning that you can use for the rest of your life.

Pitch #4: You get the best suggestions from thousands of students. The concepts and techniques in this book are here not because learning theorists, educators, and psychologists say they work. They are here because thousands of students from all kinds of backgrounds have tried them and say that they work. These are people who dreaded giving speeches, couldn't read their own notes, and fell behind in their course work. Then they figured out how to solve these problems. Now you can use their ideas.

Pitch #5: You can learn about you. The process of self-discovery is an important theme throughout this book. You can use Discovery and Intention Statements explained in this chapter for everything from organizing your desk to choosing long-term goals. Studying for an organic chemistry quiz is a lot easier with a clean desk and a clear idea of the course's importance to you.

Pitch #6: You can use a proven product. This book works. Student feedback has been positive. In particular, students with successful histories have praised the techniques included in this book.

Pitch #7: You can learn the secret of student success. If this sales pitch still hasn't persuaded you to use this book actively, maybe it's time to reveal the secret of student success. (Provide your own drum roll here.) The secret is . . . that there are no secrets. Perhaps the ultimate formula is to give up formulas and keep inventing.

The strategies and tactics that successful students use are well known. You have hundreds of them at your fingertips right now, in this book. Use them. Modify them. Invent new ones. You're the authority on what works for you.

However, what makes any technique work is commitment—and action. Without them, the pages of *From Master Student to Master Employee* are just two pounds of expensive mulch. Add your participation to the mulch, and these pages are priceless.

This book is worth $1,000

Houghton Mifflin Student Success is proud to present three students each year with a $1,000 scholarship for tuition reimbursement. Any post-secondary school in the United States and Canada can nominate one student for the scholarship. To be considered, students must write an essay that answers the question: "How do you define success?"

For more details, go to the Student Website. ***Student Website***

Get the **most** out of this book

1. Rip 'em out. The pages of this book are perforated because some of the information here is too important to leave in the book and some your instructor might want to see. For example, Journal Entry #2 on page 20 asks you to list some important things you want to get out of your education. To keep yourself focused, you could rip that page out and post it on your bathroom mirror or some other place where you'll see it several times a day.

You can reinsert the page later by sticking it into the spine of the book. A piece of tape will hold it in place.

2. Skip around. You can use this book in several different ways. Read it straight through. Or pick it up, turn to any page, and find an idea you can use. Look for ideas you can use right now. For example, if you are about to choose a major, skip directly to the article on this topic in Chapter Two.

3. If it works, use it. If it doesn't, lose it. If there are sections of the book that don't apply to you at all, skip them—unless, of course, they are assigned. Then see if you can gain value from these sections anyway. When you are committed to getting value from this book, even an idea that seems irrelevant or ineffective at first can turn out to be a powerful tool.

4. Put yourself into the book. As you read about techniques in this book, create your own scenarios, starring yourself in the title role. For example, when reading through Critical Thinking Exercise #1: "Textbook reconnaissance," picture yourself using this technique on your world history textbook.

5. Listen to your peers. Chapters in this book open with quotations from people who provide models of success. As you dig into the following chapters, think about what you would say if you could add your voice to theirs. Look for tools and techniques that can make a huge difference in your life.

6. Own this book. Right now, put your name, address, and related information on the inside cover of this book, and don't stop there. Determine what you want to get out of school and create a record of how you intend to get it by reading the Power Process and completing the Journal Entries in this Introduction. Every time your pen touches a page, you move closer to mastery of learning.

7. Do the exercises. Action makes this book work. Throughout this book are exercises designed to promote critical thinking. These exercises reinforce contemplation, creativity, analysis, decision making, and problem solving. To get the most out of an exercise, read the instructions carefully before you begin. To get the most out of this book, do most of the exercises. More important, avoid feeling guilty if you skip some. And by the way, it's never too late to go back and do the ones you skipped.

These exercises invite you to write, touch, feel, move, see, search, ponder, speak, listen, recall, choose, commit, and create. You might even sing and dance. Learning often works best when it involves action.

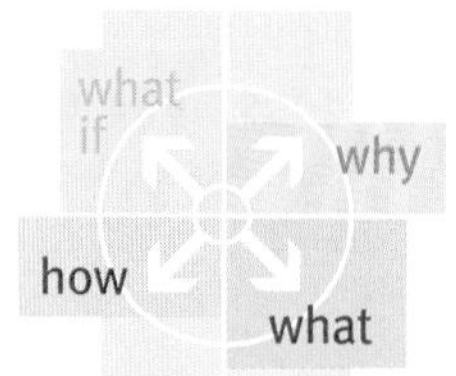

8. Learn about learning styles. Check out the Learning Styles Application near the end of each chapter. These exercises are included to increase your awareness of your preferred learning styles and to help you explore new styles. Each application will guide you through experiencing four specific modes of learning as applied to the content of the chapter. The modes can be accessed by asking four basic questions: *Why? What? How?* and *What if?* You'll find more details in the Learning Style Inventory in Chapter One.

9. Navigate through learning experiences with the Master Student Map. You can orient yourself for maximum learning every time you open this book by asking those same four questions. That's the idea behind the Master Student Map included on the first page of each chapter. Eventually, you'll be able to use the four-part structure of this map to guide yourself in effectively learning anything.

10. Link to the Web. Throughout this book, you'll notice reminders to visit the Website for *From Master Student to Master Employee* through the use of an icon.

Check regularly for articles, online exercises, and links to other useful Websites.

11. Sweat the small stuff. Look for sidebars—short bursts of words and pictures placed between longer articles—throughout this book. These short pieces might offer an insight that transforms your experience of higher education. And remember this related point: Shorter chapters in this book are just as important as longer chapters.

12. Take it to work now. You can apply nearly all of the techniques in this book to your current job or next career. Starting in Chapter Two and then throughout the rest of the book, you'll find information about *transferable skills*, such as communicating effectively and thriving with cultural diversity. Begin to identify skills you already have and uncover ways to develop new ones. To stimulate your thinking, see the Career Application at the end of each chapter. These case studies can help you identify skills for making successful transitions from school to the workplace.

13. Get used to a new look and tone. This book looks different from traditional textbooks. Each chapter presents major ideas in magazine-style articles. You will discover lots of lists, blurbs, one-liners, pictures, charts, graphs, illustrations, and even a joke or two.

Even though this book is loaded with special features, you'll find some core elements. For example, the two pages that open each chapter include a lead article and an introductory Journal Entry. And at the end of each chapter you'll find a Power Process, Career Application, chapter quiz, Learning Styles Application, and Master Student Profile—all noted in a toolbar at the top of the page.

Note: As a strategy for avoiding sexist language, this book alternates the use of feminine and masculine pronouns.

critical thinking exercise 2

COMMITMENT

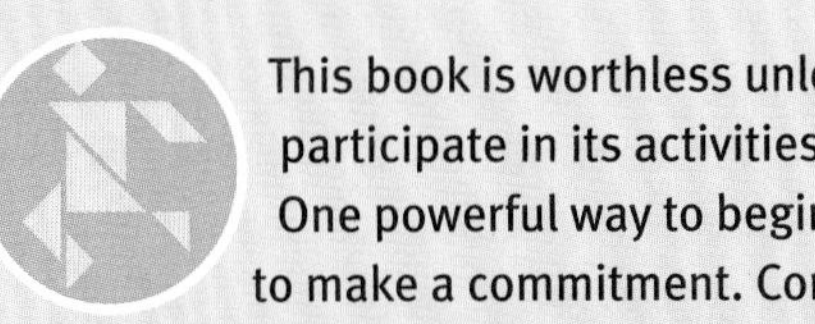

This book is worthless unless you actively participate in its activities and exercises. One powerful way to begin taking action is to make a commitment. Conversely, without commitment, sustained action is unlikely, and the result is again a worthless book. Therefore, in the interest of saving your valuable time and energy, this exercise gives you a chance to declare your level of involvement up front. From the choices below, choose the sentence that best reflects your commitment to using this book. Write the number in the space provided at the end of the list.

1. "Well, I'm reading this book right now, aren't I?"
2. "I will skim the book and read the interesting parts."
3. "I will read the book and think about how some of the techniques might apply to me."
4. "I will read the book, think about it, and do the exercises that look interesting."
5. "I will read the book, do some exercises, and complete some of the Journal Entries."
6. "I will read the book, do some exercises and Journal Entries, and use some of the techniques."
7. "I will read the book, do most of the exercises and Journal Entries, and use some of the techniques."
8. "I will study this book, do most of the exercises and Journal Entries, and use some of the techniques."
9. "I will study this book, do most of the exercises and Journal Entries, and experiment vigorously with most of the suggestions in order to discover what works best for me."
10. "I promise myself to get value from this book, beginning with Critical Thinking Exercise #1: 'Textbook reconnaissance,' even if I have to rewrite the sections I don't like and invent new techniques of my own."

Enter your commitment level and today's date here:

Commitment level 6 Date 9/10/10

If you selected commitment level 1 or 2, you might consider passing this book on to a friend. If your commitment level is 9 or 10, you are on your way to terrific success in school. If your level is somewhere in between, experiment with the techniques and learning strategies in this book. If you find that they work, consider returning to this exercise and raising your level of commitment.

Complete this exercise online.

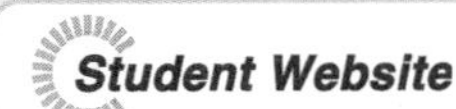

LINK *to the work* WORLD

One theory of education separates life into two distinct domains: work and school. One is the "real" world. The other is the place where you attend classes to prepare for the real world.

Consider another point of view: Success in higher education promotes success on the job. You can link school experiences to the work world, starting today.

When you graduate from school, you don't leave your capacity for mastery locked inside a classroom. Excellence in one setting paves the way for excellence in other settings. A student who knows how to show up for class on time is ready to show up for work on time. And a student who's worked cooperatively in a study group brings people skills to the table when joining a project team at work.

To stimulate your thinking, experiment with this strategy: Whenever you go to class, imagine that you're actually at work. Then act accordingly. When you read, think like an employee who's gathering information to include in a bid for a multimillion-dollar project. When you take notes, imagine that you're documenting the results of a corporate board meeting. Whenever you complete a class assignment, imagine that you're about to be paid for the quality of your work.

This is not a far-fetched idea. In some career and technical schools, students are required to dress as they would in the workplace. They know that *dressing* the part of an employee makes it easier for them to *act* the part.

Psychologist William James promoted this strategy nearly a century ago. He wrote that when you act repeatedly in a new and constructive way, you're likely to stimulate new feelings and gain new habits in the process.[4] Another name for this is the "act as if" technique. In other words, act as if you are a master employee right now.

Starting with this page, read this book with a mental filter in place. Ask yourself:

- How can I use these ideas to meet my career goals?
- How can I use these techniques at my current job?
- How can these strategies help me to get a better job—one with more pay, more recognition, and more opportunities to do what I love to do?

For example, suggestions from ***Making the transition to higher education*** (page 13) can also help you make the transition to a new career.

The techniques presented in ***Setting and achieving goals*** (page 81) can help you plan and complete work-related projects on time.

The article ***20 memory techniques*** (page 187) will come in handy as you learn the policies and procedures for a new job.

Use the techniques presented in Chapter Four, starting with ***How Muscle Reading works*** (page 128), to keep up with journals and books in your career field. This set of techniques can also help you extract valuable information from Websites, keep up with ever-increasing volumes of e-mail, and reduce mountains of interoffice memos to manageable proportions.

Adapt the ideas mentioned in ***Cooperative learning—working in teams*** (page 185) in order to collaborate more effectively with coworkers.

Ideas from ***Managing conflict*** (page 256) can help you defuse tensions among coworkers.

And the suggestions in ***Communicating across cultures*** (page 253) can assist you in adapting to the culture of a new company.

These are just a few examples. Take any idea that you gain from this book and put it to the test. Use it, modify it, expand it, or replace it with one of your own. When you start looking for ways to break down the barriers between higher education and higher achievement on the job, there's no limit to the possibilities.

The Discovery and Intention Journal Entry system

One way to become a better student is to grit your teeth and try harder. There is another way. Using familiar tools and easily learned processes, the Discovery and Intention Journal Entry system can help increase your effectiveness by showing you how to focus your energy.

The Discovery and Intention Journal Entry system is a little like flying a plane. Airplanes are seldom exactly on course. Human and automatic pilots are always checking positions and making corrections. The resulting flight path looks like a zigzag. The plane is almost always flying in the wrong direction, but because of constant observation and course correction, it arrives at the right destination.

A similar system can be used by students. Journal Entries throughout this book are labeled as Discovery Statements, Intention Statements, or Discovery/Intention Statements. Each Journal Entry will contain a short set of suggestions that involve writing.

Through Discovery Statements, you can assess "where you are." These statements are a record of what you are learning about yourself as a student—both strengths and weaknesses. Discovery Statements can also be declarations of your goals, descriptions of your attitudes, statements of your feelings, transcripts of your thoughts, and chronicles of your behavior.

Sometimes Discovery Statements chronicle an "aha!" moment—a flash of insight that results when a new idea connects with your prior experiences, preferred styles of learning, or both. Perhaps a solution to a long-standing problem suddenly occurs to you. Or a life-changing insight wells up from the deepest recesses of your mind. Don't let such moments disappear. Capture them in Discovery Statements.

Intention Statements can be used to alter your course. They are statements of your commitment to do a specific task. An intention arises out of your choice to direct your energy toward a particular goal. While Discovery Statements promote awareness, Intention Statements are blueprints for action. The two processes reinforce each other.

The purpose of this system is not to get you pumped up and excited to go out there and try harder. Rather, Discovery and Intention Statements are intended to help you focus on what you want and how to achieve it. By staying focused, you can work smarter rather than harder.

AIRPORT

The Journal Entry process is a cycle. First, you write Discovery Statements about where you are now and where you want to be. Next, you write Intention Statements about the specific steps you will take to get there. Then you follow up with Discovery Statements about whether you completed those steps and what you learned in the process, followed by more Intention Statements, and so on.

Sometimes a statement will be long and detailed. Usually, it will be short—maybe just a line or two. With practice, the cycle will become automatic.

Don't panic when you fail to complete an intended task. Straying off course is normal. Simply make the necessary corrections. Mastery is not an end state or final goal. Rather, mastery is a process that never ends, a path that you can travel for the rest of your life. The process of becoming more effective never ends.

Miraculous progress might not come immediately. Do not be concerned. Stay with the cycle. Use Discovery Statements to get a clear view of your world and what you want out of it. Then use Intention Statements to direct your actions. When you notice progress, record it.

The following statement might strike you as improbable, but it is true: It can take the same amount of energy to get what you *don't* want in school as it takes to get what you *do* want. Sometimes getting what you don't want takes even more effort. An airplane burns the same amount of fuel flying away from its destination as it does flying toward it. It pays to stay on course.

You can use the Discovery and Intention Journal Entry system to stay on your own course and get what you want out of school. This system will allow you to generate many of the success strategies in this text—and more of your own. Go beyond the Journal Entries included in the text. Write Discovery and Intention Statements of your own at any time, for any purpose.

Also use the system for the rest of your life. As you grow and change, your discoveries and intentions will change. Strategies that work for you today might not work as well in the future. With the Discovery and Intention Journal Entry system, you can create new strategies at any time, based on your current situation.

Consider the guidelines for Discovery and Intention Statements that follow, and then develop your own style. Once you get the hang of it, you might discover you can fly.

Hello Author
I Agree

Rewrite this book

Some books should be preserved in pristine condition. This book isn't one of them.

Something happens when you interact with your book by writing in it. Learning is an active pursuit, not a passive one. When you make notes in the margin, you can hear yourself talking with the author. When you doodle and underline, you can see the author's ideas taking shape. You can even argue with the author and come up with your own theories and explanations. In all of these ways, you become a coauthor of this book. You rewrite it to make it yours.

While you're at it, you can create symbols or codes that will help when reviewing the text later on, such as "Q" for questions or exclamation points for important ideas. You can also circle words to look up in a dictionary.

Remember, if any idea in this book doesn't work for you, you can rewrite it. Change the exercises to fit your needs. Create a new technique by combining several others. Create a technique out of thin air!

Find something you agree or disagree with on this page and write a short note in the margin about it. Or draw a diagram. Better yet, do both. Let creativity be your guide. Have fun.

Begin rewriting now.

Discovery and Intention Statement guidelines

Discovery statements

1 Record the specifics about your thoughts, feelings, and behavior. Thoughts include inner voices. We talk to ourselves constantly in our heads. When internal chatter gets in the way, write down what you are telling yourself. If this seems difficult at first, just start writing. The act of writing can trigger a flood of thoughts.

Thoughts also include mental pictures. These are especially powerful. Picturing yourself flunking a test is like a rehearsal to do just that. One way to take away the power of negative images is to describe them in detail.

Also notice how you feel when you function well. Use Discovery Statements to pinpoint exactly where and when you learn most effectively.

In addition, observe your actions and record the facts. If you spent 90 minutes chatting online with a favorite cousin instead of reading your anatomy text, write about it and include the details, such as when you did it, where you did it, and how it felt. Record your observations quickly, as soon as you make them.

2 Use discomfort as a signal. When you approach a daunting task, such as a difficult accounting problem, notice your physical sensations—a churning stomach, perhaps, or shallow breathing or yawning. Feeling uncomfortable, bored, or tired might be a signal that you're about to do valuable work. Stick with it. Tell yourself you can handle the discomfort just a little bit longer. You will be rewarded.

You can experience those rewards at any time. Just think of a problem that poses the biggest potential barrier to your success in school. Choose a problem that you face right now, today. (Hint: It might be the thing that's distracting you from reading this article.) If you have a lot of emotion tied up in this problem, that's even better. Write a Discovery Statement about it.

3 Suspend judgment. When you are discovering yourself, be gentle. Suspend self-judgment. If you continually judge your behaviors as "bad" or "stupid" or "galactically imbecilic," sooner or later your mind will revolt. Rather than put up with the abuse, it will quit making discoveries. For your own benefit, be kind.

4 Tell the truth. Suspending judgment helps you tell the truth about yourself. "The truth will set you free" is a saying that endures for a reason. The closer you get to the truth, the more powerful your Discovery Statements will be. And if you notice that you are avoiding the truth, don't blame yourself. Just tell the truth about it.

Intention statements

1 Make intentions positive. The purpose of writing intentions is to focus on what you want rather than what you don't want. Instead of writing "I will not fall asleep while studying accounting," write "I intend to stay awake when studying accounting." Also avoid the word *try*. Trying is not doing. When we hedge our bets with *try*, we can always tell ourselves, "Well, I *tried* to stay awake." We end up fooling ourselves into thinking we succeeded.

2 Make intentions observable. Experiment with an idea from educational trainer Robert Mager, who suggests that goals be defined through behaviors that can be observed and measured.[5] Rather than writing "I intend to work harder on my history assignments," write "I intend to review my class notes, and I intend to make summary sheets of my reading." Then, when you review your progress, you can determine more precisely whether you have accomplished what you intended.

3 Make intentions small and achievable. Give yourself opportunities to succeed by setting goals you can meet. Break large goals into small, specific tasks that can be accomplished quickly. Small and simple changes in behavior—when practiced consistently over time—can have large and lasting effects. If you want to get an A in biology, ask yourself: "What can I do today?" You might choose to study biology for an extra hour. Make that your intention.

When setting your goals, anticipate self-sabotage. Be aware of what you might do, consciously or unconsciously, to undermine your best intentions. If you intend to study differential equations at 9 p.m., notice when you sit down to watch a two-hour movie that starts at 8 p.m.

Also, be careful of intentions that depend on others. If you write that you intend for your study group to complete an assignment by Monday, then your success depends on the other students in the group.

4 Set timelines that include rewards. Timelines can focus your attention. For example, if you are assigned to write a paper, break the assignment into small tasks and set a precise due date for each one. You might write "I intend to select a topic for my paper by 9 a.m. Wednesday."

Timelines are especially useful when your intention is to experiment with a technique suggested in this book. The sooner you act on a new idea, the better. Consider practicing a new behavior within four hours after you first learn about it.

Remember that you create timelines for your own benefit, not to set yourself up to feel guilty. And you can always change the timeline.

When you meet your goal on time, reward yourself. Rewards that are an integral part of a goal are powerful. For example, your reward for earning a degree might be the career you've always dreamed of. External rewards, such as a movie or an afternoon in the park, are valuable, too. These rewards work best when you're willing to withhold them. If you plan to take a nap on Sunday afternoon whether or not you've finished your English assignment, the nap is not an effective reward.

Another way to reward yourself is to sit quietly after you have finished your task and savor the feeling. One reason why success breeds success is that it feels good. ☒

journal entry 1

Discovery Statement

Welcome to the first Journal Entry in this book. You'll find Journal Entries in every chapter, all with a similar design that allows space for you to write.

In the space below, write a description of a time in your life when you learned or did something well. This experience does not need to be related to school. Describe the details of the situation, including the place, time, and people involved. Describe how you felt about it, how it looked to you, how it sounded. Describe the physical sensations you associate with the event. Also describe your emotions.

I discovered that . . .

The value of higher education

When you're waist-deep in reading assignments, writing papers, and studying for tests, you might well ask yourself, "Is all this effort going to pay off someday?"

That's a fair question. And it addresses a core issue—the value of getting an education beyond high school.

Be reassured. The potential benefits of higher education are enormous. To begin with, there are economic benefits. Over their lifetimes, college graduates on average earn much more than high school graduates.

That's just one potential payoff. Consider the others explained below.

Gain a broad vision

It's been said that a large corporation is a collection of departments connected only by a plumbing system. This quip makes a point: As workers in different fields become more specialized, they run the risk of forgetting how to talk to each other.

Higher education can change that. One benefit of studying the liberal arts is the chance to gain a broad vision. People with a liberal arts background are aware of the various kinds of problems tackled in psychology and theology, philosophy and physics, literature and mathematics. They understand how people in all of these fields arrive at conclusions and how these fields relate to each other.

Master the liberal arts

According to one traditional model of education, there are two essential tasks for people to master—the use of language and the use of numbers. To acquire these skills, students once immersed themselves in seven subjects: grammar, rhetoric, logic, arithmetic, geometry, music, and astronomy. These subjects were called the liberal arts. They complemented the fine arts, such as poetry, and the practical arts, such as farming.

This model of liberal arts education still has something to offer. Today we master the use of language through the basic processes of communication: reading, writing, speaking, and listening. In addition, courses in mathematics and science help us understand the world in quantitative terms. The abilities to communicate and calculate are essential to almost every profession. Excellence at these skills has long been considered an essential characteristic of an educated person.

The word *liberal* comes from the Latin verb *libero*, which means "to free." Liberal arts are those that promote critical thinking. Studying them can free us from irrational ideas, half-truths, racism, and prejudice. The liberal arts grant us freedom to explore alternatives and create a system of personal values. These benefits are priceless, the very basis of personal fulfillment and political freedom.

Discover your values

We do not spend all of our waking hours at our jobs. That leaves us with a decision that affects the quality of our lives: how to spend leisure time. By cultivating our interest in the arts and community affairs, the liberal arts provide us with many options for activities outside work. These studies add a dimension to life that goes beyond having a job and paying the bills.

Practical people are those who focus on time and money. And managing these effectively calls for a clear sense of values. Our values define what we commit our time and money to. Higher education offers the opportunity to question and refine our values.

Vocational education is about *how to do* things that we can get paid for. Through a liberal arts education, we discover *what's worth doing*—what activities are worthy of our energy and talents. Both types of education are equally important. No matter where they've attended school, liberally educated people can state what they're willing to bet their lives on.

Discover new interests

Taking a broad range of courses has the potential to change your direction in life. A student previously committed to a career in science might try a drawing class and eventually switch to a degree in studio arts. Or a person who swears that she has no aptitude for technical subjects might change her major to computer science after taking an introductory computer course.

To make effective choices about your long-term goals, base those choices on a variety of academic and personal experiences. Even if you don't change majors or switch career directions, you could discover an important avocation or gain a complementary skill. For example, science majors who will eventually write for professional journals can benefit from taking English courses.

Hang out with the great

Today we enjoy a huge legacy from our ancestors. The creative minds of our species have given us great works of art, systems of science, and technological advances that defy the imagination. Through higher education we can gain firsthand knowledge of humanity's greatest creations. The poet Ezra Pound defined literature as "news that stays news." Most of the writing in newspapers and magazines becomes dated quickly. In contrast, many of the books you read in higher education have passed the hardest test of all—time. Such works have created value for people for decades, sometimes for centuries. These creations are inexhaustible. We can return to them time after time and gain new insights. These are the works we can justifiably deem great. Hanging out with them transforms us. Getting to know them exercises our minds, just as running exercises our bodies.

By studying the greatest works in many fields, we raise our standards. We learn ways to distinguish what is superficial and fleeting from what is lasting and profound.

The criteria for a great novel, poem, painting, or piece of music or dance might vary among individuals. Differences in taste reflect the differences in our backgrounds. The point is to discover those works that have enduring value—and enjoy them for a lifetime.

Learn skills that apply across careers

Jobs that involve responsibility, prestige, and higher incomes depend on self-management skills. These include knowing ways to manage time, resolve conflicts, set goals, learn new skills, and relate to people of diverse cultures. Higher education is a place to learn and practice such skills.

Judging by recent trends, most of us will have multiple careers in our lifetimes. In this environment of constant change, it makes sense to learn skills that apply across careers.

Join the conversation

Long ago, before the advent of printing presses, televisions, and computers, people educated themselves by conversing with each other. Students in ancient Athens were often called *peripatetic* (a word that means "walking around") because they were frequently seen strolling around the city, engaged in heated philosophical debate.

Since then, the debate has deepened and broadened. The world's finest scientists and artists have joined voices in a conversation that spans centuries and crosses cultures. This is a conversation about the nature of truth and beauty, knowledge and compassion, good and evil—ideas that form the very basis of human society.

Robert Hutchins, former president of the University of Chicago, called this the "great conversation."[6] By studying this conversation, we take on the most basic human challenges: coping with death and suffering, helping create a just global society, living with meaning and purpose.

Our greatest thinkers have left behind tangible records. You'll find them in libraries, concert halls, museums, and scientific laboratories across the world. Through higher education, you gain a front-row seat for the great conversation—and an opportunity to add your own voice. ☒

You share one thing in common with other students at your vocational school, college, or university: Entering higher education represents a major change in your life. You've joined a new culture with its own set of rules, both spoken and unspoken.

Making the transition to higher education

Whether they've just graduated from high school or have been out of the classroom for decades, students new to higher education immediately face many differences between secondary and post-secondary education. The sooner you understand such differences, the sooner you can deal with them. Some examples include:

- *New academic standards.* Once you enter higher education, you'll probably find yourself working harder in school than ever before. Instructors will often present more material at a faster pace. Often there are fewer tests in higher education than in high school, and the grading might be tougher. Compared to high school, you'll have more to read, more to write, more problems to solve, and more to remember.
- *A new level of independence.* College instructors typically give less guidance about how or when to study. You may not get reminders about when assignments are due or when quizzes and tests will take place. Overall, you might receive less consistent feedback about how well you are doing in each of your courses. Don't let this tempt you into putting off work until the last minute. You will still be held accountable for all course work. And anything that's said in class or included in assigned readings might appear on an exam.
- *Differences in teaching styles.* Instructors at colleges, universities, and vocational schools are often steeped in their subject matter. Many did not take courses on how to teach and might not be as interesting as some of your high school teachers. And some professors might seem more focused on research than on teaching.
- *A larger playing field.* The institution you've just joined might seem immense, impersonal, and even frightening. The sheer size of the campus, the variety of courses offered, the large number of departments—all of these can add up to a confusing array of options.

- *More students and more diversity.* The school you're attending right now might enroll hundreds or thousands more students than your high school. And the range of diversity among these students might surprise you.

In summary, you are now responsible for structuring your time and creating new relationships. Perhaps more than ever before, you'll find that your life is your own creation. You are free to set different goals, explore alternative ways of thinking, change habits, and expand your circle of friends. All this can add up to a new identity, a new way of being in the world.

At first, this world of choices might seem overwhelming or even frightening. You might feel that you're just going through the motions of being a student or playing a role that you've never rehearsed.

That feeling is understandable. Use it to your advantage. Consider that you *are* assuming a new role in life—that of being a student in higher education. And just as actors enter the minds of the characters that they portray, you can take on the character of a master student.

When you're willing to assume responsibility for the quality of your education, you can create the future of your dreams. Keep the following strategies in mind.

Decrease the unknowns. To reduce surprise, anticipate changes. Before classes begin, get a map of the school property and walk through your first day's schedule, perhaps with a classmate or friend. Visit your instructors in their offices and introduce yourself. Anything you can do to get familiar with the new routine will help.

Admit your feelings—whatever they are. School can be an intimidating experience for new students. People of diverse cultures, adult learners, commuters, and people with disabilities can feel excluded. Anyone can feel anxious, isolated, homesick, or worried about doing well academically.

Those emotions are common among new students, and there's nothing wrong with them. Simply admitting the truth about how you feel—to yourself and to someone else—can help you cope. And you can almost always do something constructive in the present moment, no matter how you feel.

If your feelings about this transition make it hard for you to carry out the activities of daily life—going to class, working, studying, and relating to people—then get professional help. Start with a counselor at the student health service on your campus. The mere act of seeking help can make a difference.

Allow time for transition. You don't have to master the transition to higher education right away. Give it some time. Also plan your academic schedule with your needs for transition in mind. Balance time-intensive courses with others that don't make as many demands.

Access resources. A supercharger increases the air supply to an internal combustion engine. The resulting difference in power can be dramatic. You can make just as powerful a difference in your education by using all of the resources available to students. In this case, your "air supply" includes people, campus clubs and organizations, and school and community services.

Of all resources, people are the most important. You can isolate yourself, study hard, and get a good education. However, this is not the most powerful use of your tuition money. When you establish relationships with teachers, staff members, fellow students, and employers, you can get a *great* education. Build a network of people who will personally support your success in school.

Accessing resources is especially important if you are the first person in your family to enter higher education. As a first-generation student, you are having experiences that people in your family may not understand. Talk to them about your activities at school. If they ask how they can help you, give specific answers. Also ask your advisor about programs for first-generation students on your campus.

Meet with your academic advisor. One person in particular can help you access resources and make the transition to higher education—your academic advisor. Meet with this person regularly. Advisors generally have a big picture of course requirements, options for declaring majors, and the resources available at your school. Peer advisory programs might also be available.

When you work with an advisor, remember that you're a paying customer and have a right to be satisfied with the service you get. Don't be afraid to change advisors when that seems appropriate.

Learn the language of higher education. Terms such as *grade point average (GPA), prerequisite, accreditation, matriculation, tenure,* and *syllabus* might be new to you. Ease your transition to higher education by checking your school catalog for definitions of these words and others that you don't understand. Also ask your academic advisor for clarification.

Attend class. In higher education, teachers generally don't take attendance. Yet you'll find that attending class is essential to your success. The amount that you pay in tuition and fees makes a powerful argument for going to classes regularly and getting your money's worth. In large part, the material that you're tested on comes from events that take place in class.

Showing up for class occurs on two levels. The most visible level is being physically present in the classroom. Even more important is showing up mentally. This includes taking detailed notes, asking questions, and contributing to class discussions.

Manage out-of-class time. For students in higher education, time management takes on a new meaning. What you do *outside* class matters as much as—or even more than—what you do in class. Instructors give you the raw materials for understanding a subject while a class meets. You then take those materials, combine them, and *teach yourself* outside class.

To allow for this process, schedule two hours of study time for each hour that you spend in class. Also get a calendar that covers the entire academic year. With the syllabus for each of your courses in hand, note key events for the entire term—dates for tests, papers, and other projects. Getting a big picture of your course load makes it easier to get assignments done on time and erases the need for all-night study sessions.

Don't assume that you already know how to study. You can cope with increased workloads and higher academic expectations by putting all of your study habits on the table and evaluating them. Don't assume that the learning strategies you used in the past—in high school or the workplace—will automatically transfer to your new role in higher education. Keep the habits that serve you, drop those that hold you back, and adopt new ones to promote your success. On every page of this book, you'll find helpful suggestions.

Take the initiative in meeting new people. Promise yourself to meet one new person each week, then write an Intention Statement describing specific ways to do this. Introduce yourself to classmates and instructors. Just before or after class is a good time to do this. Realize that most of the people in this new world of higher education are waiting to be welcomed. You can help them and help yourself at the same time.

You might envision higher education as a hotbed of social activity—and then find yourself feeling lonely and disconnected from campus during your first weeks of school. Your feelings are common. Remember that plugging into the social networks at any school takes time. And it's worth the effort. Connecting to school socially as well as academically promotes your success and your enjoyment.

Become a self-regulated learner. Reflect on your transition to higher education. Think about what's working well, what you'd like to change, and ways to make those changes.

Psychologists use the term *self-regulation* to describe this kind of thinking.[7] Self-regulated learners set goals, monitor their progress toward those goals, and change their behavior based on the results they get.

From Master Student to Master Employee promotes self-regulation through the ongoing cycle of discovery, intention, and action. Write Discovery Statements to monitor your behavior and evaluate the results you're currently creating in any area of your life. Write about your level of commitment to school, your satisfaction with your classes and grades, your social life, and your family's support for your education.

Based on your discoveries, write Intention Statements about your goals for this term, this year, next year, and the rest of your college career. Describe exactly what you will do to create new results in each of these time frames. In this way, you can take charge of your transition to higher education, starting now. ☒

For more strategies on mastering the art of transition, visit the *From Master Student to Master Employee* Website.

Connect to **resources**

As a student in higher education, you can access a world of student services and community resources. Any of them can help you succeed in school. Many of them are free.

Name a problem that you're facing right now or that you anticipate facing in the future: finding money to pay for classes, resolving conflicts with a teacher, lining up a job after graduation. Chances are that a school or community resource can help you. The ability to access resources is a skill that will serve you long after you stop being a student.

Resources often go unused—even when people pay taxes and tuition to fund them. Following are examples of what you can find. Check your school and city Websites for more options.

Academic advisors can help you with selecting courses, choosing majors, planning your career, and adjusting in general to the culture of higher education.

Arts organizations energize local museums, concert venues, clubs, and stadiums.

Athletic centers often open weight rooms, swimming pools, indoor tracks, basketball courts, and racquetball and tennis courts to all students.

Childcare is sometimes made available to students at a reasonable cost through the early childhood education department on campus or through community agencies.

Churches, synagogues, mosques, and temples have members happy to welcome fellow worshippers who are away from home.

Computer labs on campus are places where students can go 24 hours a day to work on projects and access the Internet. Instruction on computer use might also be offered.

Computer access is often available off-campus as well. Check public libraries for this service. Some students get permission to use computers at their workplace after hours.

Consumer credit counseling can help even if you've really blown your budget. And it's usually free. Remember, no matter how bad your financial picture, you are probably in better shape than most governments. Do your research and choose a reputable and not-for-profit consumer credit counselor.

Counseling centers in the community can assist you with a problem when you can't get help at school. Look for job and career planning services, rehabilitation offices, veteran's outreach programs, church and social service agencies, and mental health clinics.

The ***financial aid office*** assists students with loans, scholarships, work study, and grants. To find ways to finance your education, visit this office.

Governments (city, county, state, and federal) often have programs for students. Check the government listings in your local telephone directory.

Job placement offices can help you find part-time employment while you are in school and a job after you graduate.

Legal aid services provide free or inexpensive assistance to low-income people.

Libraries are a treasure on campus and in any community. Most employ people who are happy to help you locate information.

Newspapers published on campus and in the local community list events and services that are free or inexpensive.

The ***school catalog*** lists course descriptions and tuition fees, requirements for graduation, and information on everything from the school's history to its grading practices.

School security agencies can tell you what's safe and what's not. They can also provide information about parking, bicycle regulations, and traffic rules. Some offer safe escorts at night for female students.

Special needs/disability services assist college students who have learning disabilities or other disabilities.

Student health clinics often provide free or inexpensive counseling and other medical treatment.

Student organizations present opportunities for extracurricular activities. Explore student government, fraternities, sororities, service clubs, veteran's organizations, religious groups, sports clubs, and political groups. Find women's centers; multicultural student centers; and organizations for international students, disabled students, and gay and lesbian students.

Student unions are hubs for social activities, special programs, and free entertainment.

Support groups exist for people with almost any problem, from drug addiction to cancer. You can find people with problems who meet every week to share suggestions, information, and concerns. Some examples are groups for single parents, newly widowed people, alcoholics or drug addicts, breast cancer survivors, and parents who have lost a child.

Tutoring is usually free and is available through academic departments or counseling centers. ✕

More resources are available for adult learners on the *From Master Student to Master Employee* Website.

Extracurricular activities: Reap the benefits

Many students in higher education are busier than they've ever been before. Often that's due to the variety of extracurricular activities available for them: athletics, fraternities, sororities, student newspapers, debate teams, study groups, political action groups, and many more.

With this kind of involvement come potential benefits. People involved in extracurricular activities are often excellent students. Such activities help them bridge the worlds inside and outside the classroom. Through student organizations, they develop new skills, explore possible careers, build contacts for jobs, and build a lifelong habit of giving back to their communities. They make new friends among both students and faculty, work with people from other cultures, and sharpen their skills at conflict resolution.

Getting involved in such organizations comes with some risks as well. When students don't balance extracurricular activities with class work, their success in school can suffer. They can also compromise their health by losing sleep, neglecting exercise, skipping meals, or relying on fast food. These costs are easier to avoid if you keep a few suggestions in mind:

- *Make conscious choices* about how to divide your time between schoolwork and extracurricular activities. Decide up front how many hours each week or month you can devote to a student organization. Leave room in your schedule for relaxing and for unplanned events. For more ideas, see Chapter Three: Time.
- *Look to the future* when making commitments. Write down three or four of the most important goals you'd like to achieve in your lifetime. Then choose extracurricular activities that directly support those goals.
- *Create a career plan* that includes a list of skills needed for your next job. Then choose extracurricular activities to develop those skills. If you're unsure of your career choice, then get involved in campus organizations to explore your options.
- *Whenever possible, develop leadership experience* by holding an office in an organization. If that's too much of a commitment, then volunteer to lead a committee or plan a special event.
- *Get involved in a variety of extracurricular activities.* This demonstrates to future employers that you can work with a variety of people in a range of settings.
- *Recognize reluctance* to follow through on a commitment. You might agree to attend meetings and find yourself forgetting them or consistently showing up late. If that happens, write a Discovery Statement about the way you're using time. Follow that with an Intention Statement about ways to keep your agreements—or consider renegotiating your agreements.
- *Say no* to activities that fail to create value for you. Avoid joining groups only because you feel guilty or obligated to do so.
- *Check out the rules* before joining any student organization. Ask about dues and attendance requirements.
- *Do a trial run* by attending one or two meetings of an organization. Explain that you want to find out what the group is about before making a commitment.

If you're returning to school after a long break from the classroom, there's no reason to feel out of place. Returning adults and other nontraditional students are already a majority in some schools.

Succeeding in higher education—at any age

Being an adult learner puts you on strong footing. With a rich store of life experiences, you can ask meaningful questions and make connections between course work and daily life.

Following are some suggestions for adult learners who want to ease their transition to higher education. If you're a younger student, commuting student, or community college student, look for useful ideas here as well.

Get clear about why you're back in school. Deborah Davis, author of *The Adult Learner's Companion*, suggests that you state your reason for entering higher education in a single sentence or phrase.[8] For example:

- To be a role model for my family.
- To finish a degree that I started work on years ago.
- To advance in my current job.
- To increase my income and career prospects over the long term.

Make your statement brief, memorable, and personally inspiring. Recall it whenever you're buried in the details of writing papers, reading textbooks, and studying for tests.

Ease into it. If you're new to higher education, consider easing into it. You can choose to attend school part-time before making a full-time commitment. If you've taken college-level classes in the past, find out if any of those credits will transfer into your current program.

Plan your week. Many adult learners report that their number one problem is time. One solution is to plan your week. By planning ahead a week at a time, you get a bigger picture of your multiple roles as a student, an employee, and a family member. With that awareness, you can make conscious adjustments in the number of hours you devote to each domain of activity. For many more suggestions on this topic, see Chapter Three: Time.

Delegate tasks. Consider hiring others to do some of your household work or errands. Yes, this costs money. It's also an investment in your education and future earning power.

If you have children, delegate some of the chores to them. Or start a meal co-op in your neighborhood. Cook dinner for yourself and someone else one night each week. In return, ask that person to furnish you with a meal on another night. A similar strategy can apply to childcare and other household tasks.

Get to know other returning students. Introduce yourself to other adult learners. Being in the same classroom gives you an immediate bond. You can exchange work, home, or cell phone numbers and build a network of mutual support. Some students adopt a buddy system, pairing up with another student in each class to complete assignments and prepare for tests.

Find common ground with traditional students. You share a central goal with younger students: succeeding in school. It's easier to get past the generation gap when you keep this in mind. Traditional and nontraditional students have many things in common. They seek to gain knowledge and skills for their chosen careers. They desire financial stability and personal fulfillment. And, like their older peers, many younger students are concerned about whether they have the skills to succeed in higher education.

Consider pooling resources with younger students. Share notes, edit papers, and form study groups. Look for ways to build on each other's strengths. If you want help with using a computer for assignments, you might find a younger student to help. In group projects and case studies, expand the discussion by sharing insights from your experiences.

Enlist your employer's support. Employers often promote continuing education. Further education can increase your skills in a specific field while enhancing your ability to work with people. That makes you a more valuable employee or consultant.

Let your employer in on your educational plans. Point out how the skills you gain in class will help you meet work objectives. Offer informal seminars at work to share what you're learning in school.

Get extra mileage out of your current tasks. You can look for specific ways to merge your work and school lives. Some schools offer academic credit for work and life experience. Your company might reimburse its employees for some tuition costs or even grant time off to attend classes.

Experiment with combining tasks. For example, when you're assigned a research paper, choose a topic that relates to your current job tasks.

Look for childcare. For some students, returning to class means looking for childcare outside the home. Many schools offer childcare facilities at reduced rates for students.

Review your subjects before you start classes. Say that you're registered for trigonometry and you haven't taken a math class since high school. Consider brushing up on the subject before classes begin. Also talk with future instructors about ways to prepare for their classes.

Be willing to adopt new study habits. Rather than returning to study habits from previous school experiences, many adult learners find it more effective to treat their school assignments exactly as they would treat a project at work. They use the same tactics in the library as they do on the job, which often helps them learn more actively.

Integrate class work with daily experiences. You can start by remembering two words: *why* and *how.*

Why prompts you to look for a purpose and benefit in what you're learning. Say that your psychology teacher lectures about Abraham Maslow's ideas on the hierarchy of human needs. Maslow stated that the need for self-actualization is just as important as the need for safety, security, or love.[9]

As you learn what Maslow meant by *self-actualization,* ask yourself why this concept would make a difference in your life. Perhaps your reason for entering higher education is connected to your own quest for self-actualization, that is, for maximizing your fulfillment in life and living up to your highest potential. The theory of self-actualization could clarify your goals and help you get the most out of school.

How means looking for immediate application. Invent ways to use and test concepts in your daily life—the sooner, the better. For example, how could you restructure your life for greater self-actualization? What would you do differently on a daily basis? What would you have that you don't have now? And how would you be different in your moment-to-moment relationships with people?

"Publish" your schedule. After you plan your study and class sessions for the week, hang your schedule in a place where others who live with you will see it.

Enroll family and friends in your success. The fact that you're in school will affect the key relationships in your life. Attending classes and doing homework could mean less time to spend with others. You can prepare family members by discussing these issues ahead of time. For ways to prevent and resolve conflict, see Chapter Eight: Communicating.

You can also involve your spouse, partner, children, or close friends in your schooling. Offer to give them a tour of the campus and encourage them to attend social events at school with you.

Take this process a step further and ask the key people in your life for help. Share your reason for getting a degree, and talk about what your whole family has to gain from this change in your life. Ask them to think of ways that they can support your success in school. Make your own education a joint mission that benefits everyone. ☒

Discovery Statement

Success is a choice—your choice. To *get* what you want, it helps to *know* what you want. That is the purpose of this Journal Entry, which has two parts.

You can begin choosing success right now by setting a date, time, and place to complete this Journal Entry. Write your choices here, then block out the time on your calendar.

Date: ____________________

Time: ____________________

Place: ____________________

Part 1

Select a time and place when you know you will not be disturbed for at least 20 minutes. (The library is a good place to do this.) Relax for two or three minutes, clearing your mind. Next, complete the following sentences—and then keep writing.

When you run out of things to write, stick with it just a bit longer. Be willing to experience a little discomfort. Keep writing. What you discover might be well worth the extra effort.

What I want from my education is . . .

____

____

____

When I complete my education, I want to be able to . . .

____

____

____

I also want . . .

____

____

____

____

____

Part 2

After completing Part 1, take a short break. Reward yourself by doing something that you enjoy. Then come back to this Journal Entry.

Now, review the above list of things that you want from your education. See if you can summarize them in a one-sentence, polished statement. This will become a statement of your purpose for taking part in higher education.

Allow yourself to write many drafts of this mission statement, and review it periodically as you continue your education. With each draft, see if you can capture the essence of what you want from higher education and from your life. State it in a vivid way—a short sentence that you can easily memorize, one that sparks your enthusiasm and makes you want to get up in the morning.

You might find it difficult to express your purpose statement in one sentence. If so, write a paragraph or more. Then look for the sentence that seems most charged with energy for you.

Following are some sample purpose statements:

- My purpose for being in school is to gain skills that I can use to contribute to others.
- My purpose for being in school is to live an abundant life that is filled with happiness, health, love, and wealth.
- My purpose for being in school is to enjoy myself by making lasting friendships and following the lead of my interests.

Write at least one draft of your purpose statement below:

____

____

____

____

____

____

____

____

____

____

____

power process

DISCOVER WHAT YOU WANT

Imagine a person who walks up to a counter at the airport to buy a plane ticket for his next vacation. "Just give me a ticket," he says to the reservation agent. "Anywhere will do."

The agent stares back at him in disbelief. "I'm sorry, sir," he replies. "I'll need some more details. Just minor things—such as the name of your destination city and your arrival and departure dates."

"Oh, I'm not fussy," says the would-be vacationer. "I just want to get away. You choose for me."

Compare this with another traveler who walks up to the counter and says, "I'd like a ticket to Ixtapa, Mexico, departing on Saturday, March 23, and returning Sunday, April 7. Please give me a window seat, first class, with vegetarian meals."

Now, ask yourself which traveler is more likely to end up with a vacation that he'll enjoy.

The same principle applies in any area of life. Knowing where we want to go increases the probability that we will arrive at our destination. Discovering what we want makes it more likely that we'll attain it. Once our goals are defined precisely, our brains reorient our thinking and behavior to align with those goals—and we're well on the way there.

There's power in precision

The example about the traveler with no destination seems far-fetched. Before you dismiss it, do an informal experiment: Ask three other students what they want to get out of their education. Be prepared for hemming and hawing, vague generalities, and maybe even a helping of pie-in-the-sky à la mode.

That's amazing, considering the stakes involved. Our hypothetical vacationer is about to invest a couple of weeks of his time and hundreds of dollars—all with no destination in mind. Students routinely invest years of their lives and thousands of dollars with an equally hazy idea of their destination in life.

Suppose that you ask someone what she wants from her education and you get this answer: "I plan to get a degree in journalism with double minors in earth science and Portuguese so that I can work as a reporter covering the environment in Brazil." Chances are you've found a master student. The precision of a person's vision offers a clue to mastery.

Put it in writing

For maximum precision, write down what you want. Goals that reside strictly in your head can remain fuzzy. Writing them down brings them into sharper focus.

As you write about what you want, expand your imagination to many different time frames. Define what you want to be, do, and have next week, next month, and next year. Write about what you want five years from now—and five minutes from now.

It's important to approach this process with a sense of adventure and play. As you write, be willing to put any option on the table. List any goal—including those that might look outrageous in writing.

You might want to travel to India, start a consulting business, or open a library in every disadvantaged neighborhood. Write those goals down.

You might want to own a ranch in a beautiful valley, become a painter, or visit all of the hot springs in the world. Write those down, too.

Perhaps you want to restore the integrity of the ozone layer or eliminate racism through international law. Or perhaps you simply want to be more physically fit, be funnier, or be more loving. Whatever you want, write it down.

One way to determine what you want in detail is to prompt yourself with questions. For starters, ask the "four W's":

- *What* do I want?
- *Who* do I want to be with in the future?
- *Where* do I want to be in the future?
- *When* can I make my desired future occur?

Stay open to possibility

While asking these questions, people sometimes stop themselves with a single line of thought: "Who am I kidding anyway? There's no way I'll ever be able to get what I really want. My goals are just too impractical."

Statements like these can sink us back into the status quo and stop us from painting a bold vision of the future. These are thoughts that erase dreams from the drawing board.

When you follow the path of getting what you truly want, you can enjoy yourself even if the path is uphill.

If this happens to you, remember that many goals—from the invention of the airplane to the lunar landing, to the development of the computer chip—appeared ridiculous or unworkable when they were first proposed. These remarkable ideas came to life because their creators kept lifting their eyes to the horizon and holding fast to a sense of possibility.

When determining what you want, you can also think big. Write down any goal that comes to mind—even those that seem impossible to fulfill. You might discover ways to satisfy even the boldest, most "impractical" desires. And even if you don't achieve *all* your goals, you can achieve *many* of them, including those that radically affect the quality of your life.

Later, if you want, you can let go of some goals. But first live with them for a while. Goals that sound outlandish right now might seem more realistic in a few weeks, months, or years. Time often brings a more balanced perspective, along with an expanded sense of possibility.

Imagine that time and money are no problem

One way to keep worries about practicality from cramping your creativity is to play with the several scenarios.

To begin, imagine that you've just won a lottery with a jackpot of $5 million. You now have all the money needed to sustain yourself for a lifetime. You have a steady stream of income extending decades into the future—enough to support any career you want. Once you've created this mental picture, describe what you want to be, do, and have during the rest of your life.

Or pretend that a philanthropist will pay you $500,000 per year to do whatever project you think will benefit your community most. What would you do?

Another scenario is to imagine that a philanthropist will provide funds for you and 30 people you supervise to do something of value for the entire planet. You have a budget of $1 billion and 30 years to accomplish your project. Again, what would you do?

Expand your goals by asking *How?*

Once you've opened up your imagination and gained some clarity about *what* you want, you can add depth to your dreams by asking *How?* This question helps you to develop action plans—specific steps that will lead to achieving your goals.

When asking *How?* avoid answers that lead to prescriptions—the idea that there is only *one* way to accomplish any goal. In reality, you can create several detailed action plans for getting anything you want. Most goals can be reached through multiple pathways.

For example, you might determine that you want to earn $100,000 per year while working from your home as a freelance consultant. To meet that income goal, you could choose from several strategies. One is to charge $50 per hour and work 40 hours per week for 50 weeks per year. Another is to charge $100 per hour and work only 20 hours per week for the same number of weeks per year. You could also consider working more hours during the winter months so that you could take summers off and still earn $100,000 yearly. These are just a few examples.

Discover the benefits

Discovering what you want greatly enhances your odds of succeeding in higher education. Many students quit school simply because they are unsure of their goals. With well-defined objectives in mind, you can constantly look for connections between what you want and what you study. The more connections you discover, the more likely you'll stay in school—and the more likely you'll benefit from higher education.

Having a clear idea of your goals makes many decisions easier. Knowing what you want from your education helps you choose the school you'll attend, the courses you'll take, the major you'll declare, and the next career you'll pursue.

Discovering what you want also enhances your study skills. An example is memorizing. A skydiver will not become bored learning how to pack her parachute. Her reward for learning the skill is too important. Likewise, when information helps you get something you want, it becomes easier to remember.

You can have more energy when your daily activities lead to what you want. If you're bogged down in quadratic equations, stand back for a minute. Think about how that math course ties in with your goal of becoming an electrical engineer, how your philosophy course relates to your aim of becoming a minister, or how your English course can help you become a better teacher.

Succeeding in higher education takes effort. When you follow the path of getting what you truly want, you can enjoy yourself even if the path is uphill. You can expend great energy and still feel fresh and eager to learn. When you take on courses that you care about and prepare for a career that you look forward to, you can play full out. You can work even to the point of exhaustion at times, and do it happily.

That's one purpose of discovering what you want. Your vision is not meant to be followed blindly—it's meant to pull you forward.

Move from discovery to action

Discovering what you want can be heady fun. And it can quickly become an interesting but irrelevant exercise unless you take action to get what you want. Most discoveries come bundled with hints to *do* something—perhaps to change a habit, contact someone, travel, get educated, or acquire a new skill. Dreams that are not followed with action tend to die on paper. On the other hand, dreams that lead to new behaviors can lead to new results in your life.

To move into action, use this book. It's filled with places to state what you want to accomplish and how you intend to go about it. Every Journal Entry and critical thinking exercise exists for this purpose. Fill up those pages. Take action and watch your dreams evolve from fuzzy ideals into working principles.

Your action plans can include strategies and techniques, including the hundreds of suggestions presented in these pages. However, remember that strategies and techniques are not guarantees. They're just means to an end—moving you into action. Your clarity about what you want and your commitment to get it can be far more powerful than any plan or technique.

With your dreams and new behaviors, you might find that events fall into place almost magically. Start telling people about what you want, and you'll eventually find some who are willing to help. They might offer an idea or two or suggest a person to call or an organization to contact. They might even offer their time or money. The sooner you discover what you want, the sooner you can create the conditions that transform your life.[10]

1 Discovering Yourself

MASTER STUDENT MAP

why this chapter matters . . .

Visible measures of success—such as top grades and résumés filled with accomplishments—start with the willingness to discover who you are and what you want.

how you can use this chapter . . .

Experience the power of telling the truth about your current skills.

Discover your preferred learning styles and develop new ones.

Define what you want from your education and your career.

As you read, ask yourself what if . . .

I could discover my interests, skills, and passions—and build a successful education and career on them?

what is included . . .

FROM THE DESK OF . . .

I was a business major in college. Most of the classes I took involved doing group projects. I think at the time it is hard to realize how valuable those experiences are. I rarely work on my own on the job. In class, you are in groups with people who have very different working habits than you, and it can get frustrating. However, the same exact thing happens on the job. You have to change your style at times to accommodate that of others.

—KATE USDIN, FINANCIAL SERVICES ANALYST

First Step: Truth is a key to mastery

The First Step technique is simple: Tell the truth about who you are and what you want. End of discussion. Now proceed to Chapter Two.

Well, it's not *quite* that simple.

The First Step is one of the most valuable tools in this book. It magnifies the power of all the other techniques. It is a key to becoming a master student.

Unfortunately, a First Step is easier to explain than it is to use. Telling the truth sounds like pie-in-the-sky moralizing, but there is nothing pie-in-the-sky or moralizing about a First Step. It is a practical, down-to-earth way to change our behavior. No technique in this book has been field-tested more often or more successfully, or under tougher circumstances.

Success starts with telling the truth about what *is* working—and what *isn't*—in our lives right now. When we acknowledge our strengths, we gain an accurate picture of what we can accomplish. When we admit that we have a problem, we free up energy to find a solution. Ignoring the truth, on the other hand, can lead to problems that stick around for decades.

The principle of telling the truth is applied universally by people who want to turn their lives around. For members of Alcoholics Anonymous, the First Step is acknowledging that they are powerless over alcohol. For people who join Weight Watchers, the First Step is admitting how much they weigh.

It's not easy to tell the truth about ourselves. And for some of us, it's even harder to recognize our strengths. Maybe we don't want to brag. Maybe we're attached to poor self-images. The reasons don't matter. The point is that using the First Step technique means telling the truth about our positive qualities, too.

Many of us approach a frank evaluation of ourselves about as enthusiastically as we'd anticipate an audit by the IRS. If we could instead see self-evaluations as opportunities to solve problems and take charge of our lives, we might welcome them. Believe it or not, we can begin working with our list of weaknesses by celebrating them.

Consider the most accomplished, "together" people you know. If they were candid with you, they would probably share their mistakes and regrets. Successful people are willing to look at their flaws.

It might seem natural to judge our own shortcomings and feel bad about them. Some people believe that such feelings are necessary in order to bring about change.

journal entry 3

Discovery/Intention Statement

Take five minutes to skim the Discovery Wheel exercise starting on page 28. Find one statement that describes a skill you already possess—a personal strength that will promote your success in school, in your career, or both. Write that statement here:

Reading

Reading the Discovery Wheel might also prompt some thoughts about new skills that you'd like to develop. Describe one of those skills by completing the following sentence:

I discovered that . . .

Now, skim the appropriate chapter in this book for at least three articles that could help you develop this skill. For example, if you want to take more effective notes, turn to Chapter Five. List the names of your chosen articles here and schedule a time to read them in more detail.

I intend to . . .

Others think that a healthy dose of shame can turn negatives into positives.

There is an alternative. We can gain skill without feeling rotten about the past. By taking a First Step, we can change the way things *are* without having to criticize the way things *have been.* We can learn to see shame or blame as excess baggage and just set them aside.

It might also help to remember that weaknesses are often strengths taken to an extreme. The student who carefully revises her writing can make significant improvements in a term paper. If she revises too much and hands in the paper late, though, her grade might suffer. Any success strategy carried too far can backfire.

Whether written or verbal, First Steps are more powerful when they are specific. For example, if you want to improve your note-taking skills, you might write, "I am an awful note taker." It would be more effective to write, "I can't read 80 percent of the notes I took in Introduction to Psychology last week, and I have no idea what was important in that class." Be just as specific about what you plan to achieve. You might declare, "I want to take legible notes that help me predict what questions will be on the final exam."

Completing the exercises in this chapter can help you tap resources you never knew you had. For example, do the Discovery Wheel to get a big-picture view of your personal effectiveness. And use the Learning Styles Inventory, along with the articles about multiple intelligences and the VAK system, to tell the truth about how you perceive and process information.

They're all First Steps. It's just that simple. The truth has power. ☒

TAKING THE FIRST STEP

The purpose of this exercise is to give you a chance to discover and acknowledge your own strengths, as well as areas for improvement. For many students, this is the most difficult exercise in the book. To make the exercise worthwhile, do it with courage.

Some people suggest that looking at areas for improvement means focusing on personal weaknesses. They view it as a negative approach that runs counter to positive thinking. Well, perhaps. Positive thinking is a great technique. So is telling the truth, especially when we see the whole picture—the negative aspects as well as the positive ones.

If you admit that you can't add or subtract and that's the truth, then you have taken a strong, positive First Step toward learning basic math. On the other hand, if you say that you are a terrible math student and that's not the truth, then you are programming yourself to accept unnecessary failure.

The point is to tell the truth. This exercise is similar to the Discovery Statements that appear in every chapter. The difference is that, in this case, for reasons of confidentiality, you won't write down your discoveries in the book.

Be brave. If you approach this exercise with courage, you are likely to disclose some things about yourself that you wouldn't want others to read. You might even write down some truths that could get you into trouble. Do this exercise on separate sheets of paper; then hide or destroy them. Protect your privacy.

To make this exercise work, follow these suggestions.

Be specific. It is not effective to write "I can improve my communication skills." Of course you can. Instead, write down precisely what you can *do* to improve your communication skills, for example, "I can spend more time really listening while the other person is talking, instead of thinking about what I'm going to say next."

Look beyond the classroom. What goes on outside school often has the greatest impact on your ability to be an effective student.

Complete this exercise online.

Student Website

Be courageous. This exercise is a waste of time if it is done half-heartedly. Be willing to take risks. You might open a door that reveals a part of yourself that you didn't want to admit was there. The power of this technique is that once you know what is there, you can do something about it.

Part 1

Time yourself, and for 10 minutes write as fast as you can, completing each of the following sentences at least 10 times with anything that comes to mind. If you get stuck, don't stop. Just write something—even if it seems crazy.

I never succeed when I . . .
I'm not very good at . . .
Something I'd like to change about myself is . . .

Part 2

When you have completed the first part of the exercise, review what you have written, crossing off things that don't make any sense. The sentences that remain suggest possible goals for becoming a master student.

Part 3

Here's the tough part. Time yourself, and for 10 minutes write as fast as you can, completing the following sentences with anything that comes to mind. As in Part 1, complete each sentence at least 10 times. Just keep writing, even if it sounds silly.

I always succeed when I . . .
I am very good at . . .
Something I like about myself is . . .

Part 4

Review what you have written and circle the things that you can fully celebrate. This is a good list to keep for those times when you question your own value and worth.

THE DISCOVERY WHEEL

The Discovery Wheel is another opportunity to tell the truth about the kind of student you are and the kind of student you want to become. It will also preview the topics that are covered throughout this text and help you begin to think about the transferable skills you will be able to master at school and at work.

This is not a test. There are no trick questions, and the answers will have meaning only for yourself.

Here are two suggestions to make this exercise more effective. First, think of it as the beginning of an opportunity to change. There is another Discovery Wheel in the last chapter of this book. You will have a chance to measure your progress, so be honest about where you are now. Second, lighten up. A little laughter can make self-evaluations a lot more effective.

Here's how the Discovery Wheel works. By the end of this exercise, you will have filled in a circle similar to the one on page 29. The Discovery Wheel circle is a picture of how you see yourself. The closer the shading comes to the outer edge of the circle, the higher the evaluation of a specific skill. In the example, the student has rated her reading skills low and her note-taking skills high.

The terms *high* and *low* are not meant to reflect a negative judgment. The Discovery Wheel is not a permanent picture of who you are. It is a picture of how you view your strengths and weaknesses as a student today. To begin this exercise, read the following statements and award yourself points for each one, using the point system described below. Then add up your point total for each section and shade the Discovery Wheel on page 31 to the appropriate level.

5 points
This statement is always or almost always true of me.

4 points
This statement is often true of me.

3 points
This statement is true of me about half the time.

2 points
This statement is seldom true of me.

1 point
This statement is never or almost never true of me.

1. 4 I enjoy learning.
2. 1 I understand and apply the concept of multiple intelligences.
3. 2 I connect my courses to my purpose for being in school and the benefits I intend to get from my education.
4. 1 I regularly assess my personal strengths and areas for improvement.
5. 2 I am satisfied with how I am progressing toward achieving my goals.
6. 3 I use my knowledge of learning styles to support my success in school and at work.
7. 4 I am willing to consider any idea that can help me succeed in school—even if I initially disagree with that idea.
8. 1 I monitor my habits and change them in ways that support my success.

18 Total score (1) ***Self-Discovery***

1. ______ I relate school to what I plan to do for the rest of my life.
2. ______ I plan my career with a detailed knowledge of my skills.
3. ______ I relate my career plan to my interests, attitudes, and core values.
4. ______ I can effectively use the library and the Internet to research possible careers.
5. ______ I use the career planning services offered by my school.
6. ______ I am planning a career that contributes something worthwhile to the world.
7. ______ I have a written career plan and I update it regularly.
8. ______ I use internships, extracurricular activities, information interviews, and on-the-job experiences to test and refine my career plan.

______ Total score (2) ***Career Planning***

1. ______ I set long-term goals and periodically review them.
2. ______ I set mid-term and short-term goals to support my long-term goals.
3. ______ I write a plan for each day and each week.
4. ______ I assign priorities to what I choose to do each day.
5. ______ I plan regular recreation time.

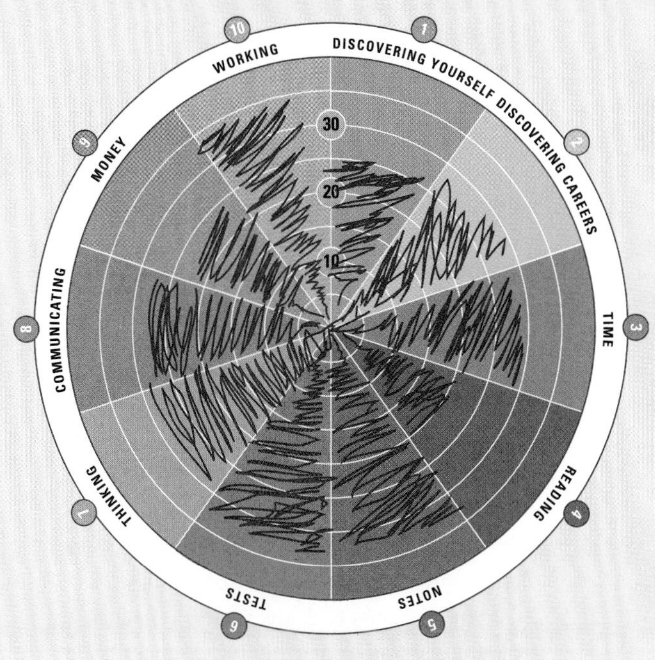

6. ______ I adjust my study time to meet the demands of individual courses.
7. ______ I have adequate time each day to accomplish what I plan.
8. ______ I effectively plan projects and manage time in work settings.

______ Total score (3) ***Time***

1. ______ I preview and review reading materials.
2. ______ When reading, I ask myself questions about the material.
3. ______ I underline or highlight important passages when reading.
4. ______ When I read textbooks or reports, I am alert and awake.
5. ______ I relate what I read to my life.
6. ______ I select a reading strategy to fit the type of material I'm reading.
7. ______ I take effective notes when I read.
8. ______ When I don't understand what I'm reading, I note my questions and find answers.

______ Total score (4) ***Reading***

1. ______ When I am in class, I focus my attention.
2. ______ I take notes in class and during meetings.
3. ______ I am aware of various methods for taking notes and choose those that work best for me.
4. ______ I distinguish major ideas from examples and other supporting material.
5. ______ I copy down material that the presenter writes on the board or overhead projector.
6. ______ I can put important concepts into my own words.
7. ______ My notes are valuable for review.
8. ______ I review notes within 24 hours.

______ Total score (5) ***Notes***

1. ______ I use techniques to enhance my memory.
2. ______ I manage my time during exams and am able to complete them.
3. ______ I am able to successfully predict test questions.
4. ______ I adapt my test-taking strategy to the kind of test I'm taking.
5. ______ I create value from any type of evaluation, including performance reviews.
6. ______ I start reviewing for tests at the beginning of the term and continue reviewing throughout the term.
7. ______ I manage stress and maintain my health even when I feel under pressure.
8. ______ My sense of personal worth is independent of my test scores.

______ Total score (6) ***Tests***

1. ______ I have flashes of insight and often think of solutions to problems at unusual times.
2. ______ I use brainstorming to generate solutions to a variety of problems.
3. ______ When I get stuck on a creative project, I use specific methods to get unstuck.
4. ______ I see problems and tough decisions as opportunities for learning and personal growth.
5. ______ I am open to different points of view and diverse cultural perspectives.
6. ______ I can support my points of view with sound logic and evidence.

7. ______ I use critical thinking to resolve ethical dilemmas.
8. ______ As I share my viewpoints with others, I am open to their feedback.

______ Total score (7) ***Thinking***

1. ______ I am candid with others about who I am, what I feel, and what I want.
2. ______ Other people tell me that I am a good listener.
3. ______ I can communicate my upset and resolve conflict without blaming others.
4. ______ I work effectively as a member of a project team.
5. ______ I am learning ways to thrive with diversity—attitudes and behaviors that will support my career success.
6. ______ I can effectively plan, research, draft, and revise a large writing assignment.
7. ______ I learn effectively from materials and activities that are posted online.
8. ______ I prepare and deliver effective speeches and presentations.

______ Total score (8) ***Communicating***

1. ______ I am in control of my personal finances.
2. ______ I can access a variety of resources to finance my education.
3. ______ I am confident that I will have enough money to complete my education.
4. ______ I take on debts carefully and repay them on time.
5. ______ I have long-range financial goals and a plan to meet them.
6. ______ I make regular deposits to a savings account.
7. ______ I pay off the balance on credit card accounts each month.
8. ______ I can have fun without spending money.

______ Total score (9) ***Money***

1. ______ In work settings, I look for models of success and cultivate mentors.
2. ______ My work creates value for my employer.
3. ______ I see working as a way to pursue my interests, expand my skills, and develop mastery.
4. ______ I support other people in their career planning and job hunting—and am willing to accept their support.
5. ______ I can function effectively in corporate cultures and cope positively with office politics.
6. ______ I create résumés and cover letters that distinguish me from other job applicants.
7. ______ I can accurately predict and prepare responses to questions asked by job interviewers.
8. ______ I see learning as a lifelong process that includes experiences inside and outside the classroom.

______ Total score (10) ***Working***

Filling in your Discovery Wheel

Using the total score from each category, shade in each section of the Discovery Wheel. Use different colors, if you want. For example, you could use green to denote areas you want to work on. When you have finished, complete the Journal Entry on page 32.

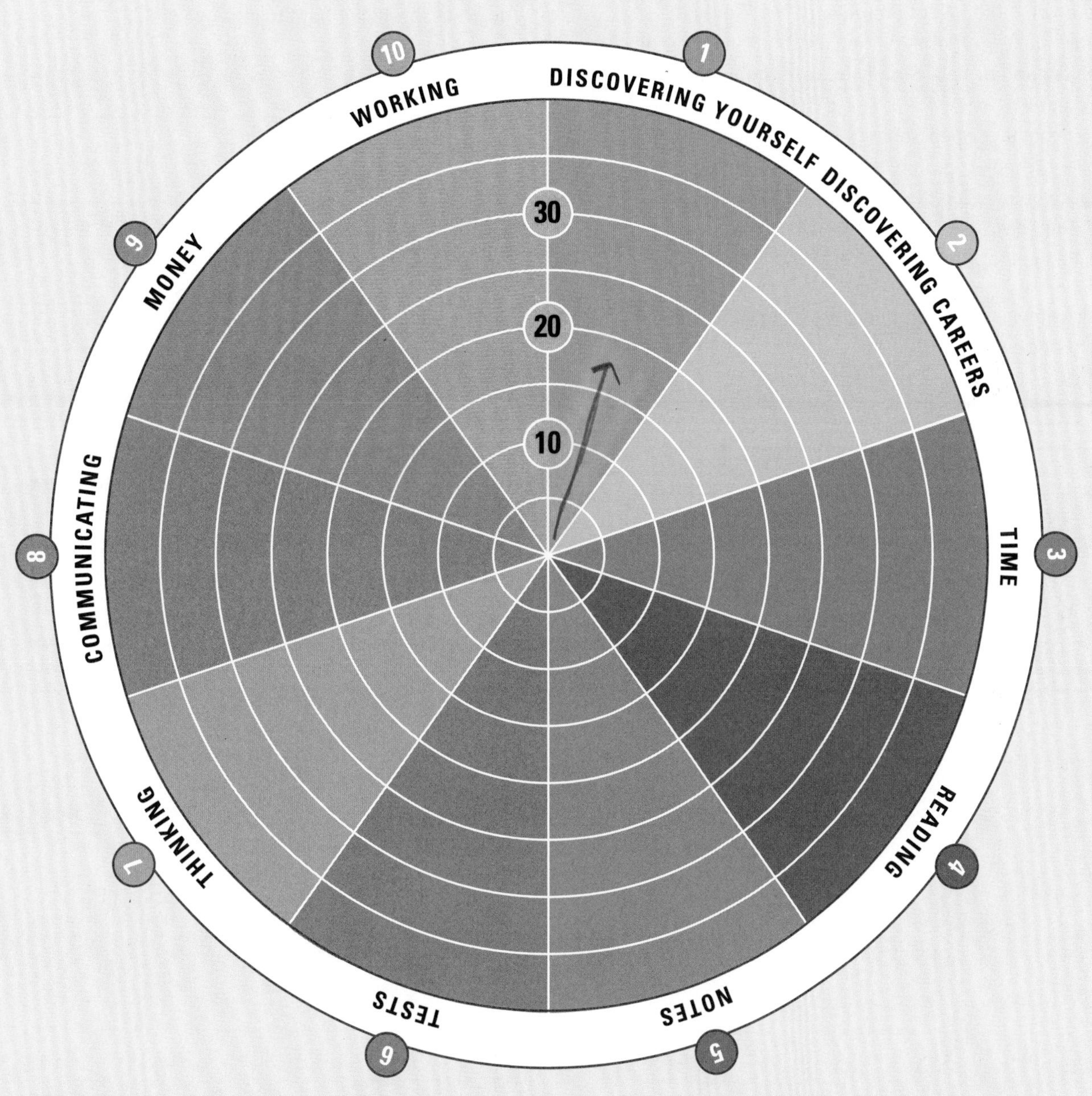
1
DISCOVERING YOURSELF DISCOVERING CAREERS
2
TIME
3
READING
4
NOTES
5
TESTS
6
THINKING
7
COMMUNICATING
8
MONEY
9
WORKING
10
30
20
10

journal entry 4

Discovery/Intention Statement

Now that you have completed your Discovery Wheel, spend a few minutes with it. Get a sense of its weight, shape, and balance. Can you imagine running your hands around it? If you could lift it, would it feel light or heavy? How would it sound if it rolled down a hill? Would it roll very far? Would it wobble? Make your observations without judging the wheel as good or bad. Simply be with the picture you have created.

After you have spent a few minutes studying your Discovery Wheel, complete the following sentences in the space below. Don't worry if you can't think of something to write. Just put down whatever comes to mind. Remember, this is not a test.

This wheel is an accurate picture of my ability as a student because . . .

My self-evaluation surprises me because . . .

The two areas in which I am strongest are . . .

The areas in which I want to improve are . . .

I want to concentrate on improving these areas because . . .

Now, select one of your discoveries and describe how you intend to benefit from it. Complete the statement below.

To gain some practical value from this discovery, I will . . .

Learning by seeing, hearing, and moving: The VAK system

You can approach the topic of learning styles with a simple and powerful system—one that focuses on just three ways of perceiving through your senses:

- Seeing, or *visual* learning
- Hearing, or *auditory* learning
- Movement, or *kinesthetic* learning

To recall this system, remember the letters *VAK*, which stand for **v**isual, **a**uditory, and **k**inesthetic. The theory is that each of us prefers to learn through one of these sense channels. And we can enrich our learning with activities that draw on the other channels.

To reflect on your VAK preferences, answer the following questions. Each question has three possible answers. Circle the answer that best describes how you would respond in the stated situation. This is not a formal inventory—just a way to prompt some self-discovery.

When you have problems spelling a word, you prefer to:

1. *Look it up in the dictionary.*
2. *Say the word out loud several times before you write it down.*
3. *Write out the word with several different spellings and choose one.*

You enjoy courses the most when you get to:

1. *View slides, overhead transparencies, videos, and readings with plenty of charts, tables, and illustrations.*
2. *Ask questions, engage in small-group discussions, and listen to guest speakers.*
3. *Take field trips, participate in lab sessions, or apply the course content while working as a volunteer or intern.*

When giving someone directions on how to drive to a destination, you prefer to:

1. *Pull out a piece of paper and sketch a map.*
2. *Give verbal instructions.*
3. *Say, "I'm driving to a place near there, so just follow me."*

You've made a commitment to learn to play the guitar. The first thing you do is:

1. *Go to a library or music store and find an instruction book with plenty of diagrams and chord charts.*
2. *Pull out your favorite CDs, listen closely to the guitar solos, and see if you can sing along with them.*
3. *Buy or borrow a guitar, pluck the strings, and ask someone to show you how to play a few chords.*

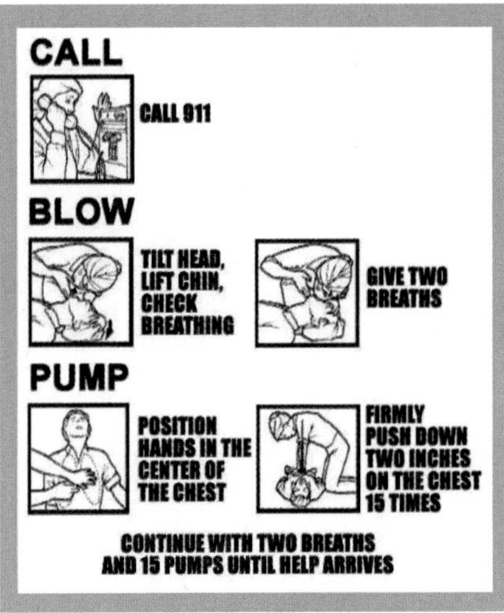

Visual learning

You've saved up enough money to lease a car. When choosing from among several new models, the most important factor in your decision is:

1. *The car's appearance.*
2. *The information you get by talking to people who own the cars you're considering.*
3. *The overall impression you get by taking each car on a test drive.*

You've just bought a new computer system—monitor, central processing unit, keyboard, CD burner, cable modem, and external speakers. When setting up the system, the first thing you do is:

1. *Skim through the printed instructions that come with the equipment.*
2. *Call up someone with a similar system and ask her for directions.*
3. *Assemble the components as best as you can, see if everything works, and consult the instructions only as a last resort.*

You get a scholarship to study abroad next semester, which starts in just three months. You will travel to a country where French is the most widely spoken language. To learn as much French as you can before you depart, you:

1. *Buy a video-based language course that's recorded on a DVD.*
2. *Set up tutoring sessions with a friend who's fluent in French.*
3. *Sign up for a short immersion course in an environment in which you speak only French, starting with the first class.*

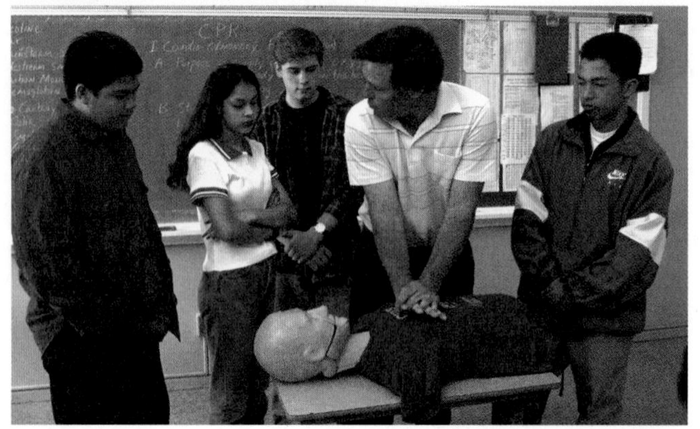

Auditory learning

Now take a few minutes to reflect on the meaning of your responses. All of the answers numbered "1" are examples of visual learning. The "2's" refer to auditory learning, and the "3's" illustrate kinesthetic learning. Finding a consistent pattern in your answers indicates that you prefer learning through one sense channel more than the others. Or you might find that your preferences are fairly balanced.

Listed below are suggestions for learning through each sense channel. Experiment with these examples and create more techniques of your own. Use them to build on your current preferences and develop new options for learning.

To enhance *visual* learning:

- Preview reading assignments by looking for elements that are highlighted visually—bold headlines, charts, graphs, illustrations, and photographs.
- When taking notes in class, leave plenty of room to add your own charts, diagrams, tables, and other visuals later.
- Whenever an instructor writes information on a blackboard or overhead projector, copy it exactly in your notes.
- Transfer your handwritten notes to your computer. Use word processing software that allows you to format your notes in lists, add headings in different fonts, and create visuals in color.
- Before you begin an exam, quickly sketch a diagram on scratch paper. Use this diagram to summarize the key formulas or facts you want to remember.

To enhance *auditory* learning:

- Reinforce memory of your notes and readings by talking about them. When studying, stop often to recite key points and examples in your own words.
- After doing several verbal summaries, record your favorite version or write it out.
- Read difficult passages in your textbooks slowly and out loud.
- Join study groups and create short presentations about course topics.

To enhance *kinesthetic* learning:

- Look for ways to translate course content into three-dimensional models that you can build. While studying biology, for example, create a model of a human cell using different colors of clay.
- Supplement lectures with trips to museums, field observations, lab sessions, tutorials, and other hands-on activities.
- Recite key concepts from your courses while you walk or exercise.
- Intentionally set up situations in which you can learn by trial and error.

One variation of the VAK system has been called VARK.[1] The *R* describes a preference for learning by reading and writing. People with this preference might benefit from translating charts and diagrams into statements, taking notes in lists, and converting those lists into possible items on a multiple-choice test.

The topic of learning styles is relatively new. Approach the VAK system and other models of learning styles not as proven theories but as paths of self-discovery and intention. Knowing that you have certain preferences will not automatically change your school experiences. However, using these ideas to experiment with new learning strategies can make a lasting difference in the quality of your education.

Kinesthetic learning

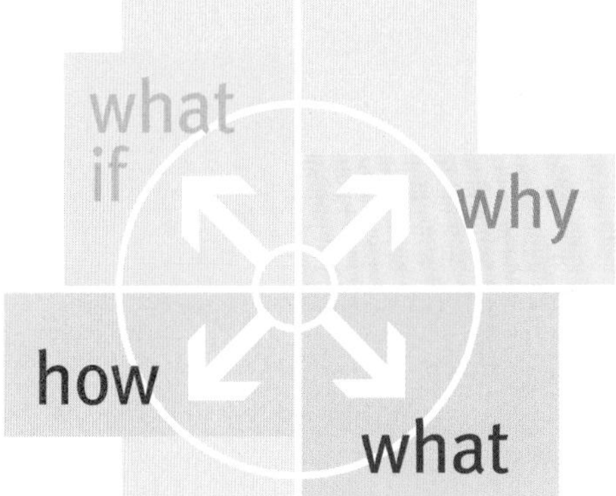

Discovering how you learn

When we learn, two things initially happen. First, we notice new information. We *perceive* and take in what's before us. Second, we make sense of the information. We *process* it in a way that helps us understand what's going on and makes the information our own. *Learning styles* is a term that takes into account differences in how people prefer to perceive and process information.

Knowing your preferred learning style helps you understand why some courses appeal to you while others seem dull or boring. Figuring out when to use your preferences—and when it might be helpful to include another style of learning—can help you create value from any class and function successfully as a student in many different settings.

Perceiving information

The ways that people perceive information typically range from a preference for concrete experience (CE) to a preference for abstract conceptualization (AC):

- People who favor perceiving by concrete experience like to absorb information through their five senses. They learn by getting directly involved in new experiences. When solving problems, they rely on their intuition as much as their intellect. These people typically function well in unstructured learning classes that allow them to take the initiative.
- People who favor perceiving by *abstract conceptualization* take in information best when they can think about it as a subject separate from themselves. They analyze, intellectualize, and create theories. Often these people take a scientific approach to problem solving and excel in traditional classrooms.

Processing information

The ways that people process information typically range from a preference for active experimentation (AE) to a preference for reflective observation (RO):

- People who favor processing information by *active experimentation* prefer to jump in and start doing things immediately. They do not mind taking risks as they attempt to make sense of things because this helps them learn. They are results-oriented and look for practical ways to apply what they have learned.
- People who favor processing information by *reflective observation* prefer to stand back, watch what is going on, and think about it. Often they consider several points of view as they attempt to make sense of things and can generate many ideas about how something happens. They value patience, good judgment, and a thorough approach to understanding information.

According to David Kolb, a psychologist who developed the theory of experiential learning, learners have natural preferences for how they perceive and process information.[2] Yet they benefit most fully if they allow themselves to participate in all four points of the continuums described above. Successful learners:

1. involve themselves fully, openly, and without bias in new experiences (CE);
2. observe and reflect on these experiences from many points of view (RO);
3. integrate these observations into logically sound theories (AC) that include predictions about the consequences of new behaviors; and
4. use these theories to make decisions, solve problems, and take effective action (AE).

This view of learning is quite flexible. You can start learning at any one of the four points listed above and cycle through the rest. In any case, the power of your learning derives from testing theories in your daily life—and in changing those theories based on the feedback you get from concrete experiences.

You can use Kolb's ideas to increase your skills at learning anything. First, start by understanding your natural preferences. Then balance them with activities that you consciously choose to support your learning.

Taking your Learning Style Inventory

To help you become more aware of what you currently do to support your learning, David Kolb has developed the Learning Style Inventory (LSI), which is included on the next several pages. Completing this inventory will help you discover more about how you learn.

Step 1 Keep in mind that this is not a test. There are no right or wrong answers. Your goal is to develop a profile of your learning. Take the inventory quickly. There's no need to agonize over your responses. Recalling a recent situation in which you learned something new at school, at work, or in your life might make it easier for you to focus and answer the questions.

Step 2 Remove the sheet of paper following page LSI-2. When you're ready to write on the inventory, press firmly so that your answers will show up on the page underneath the questions.

Step 3 Note that the LSI consists of 12 sentences, each with four different endings. You will read each sentence, then write a "4" next to the ending that best describes the way you currently learn. Then you will continue ranking the other endings with a "3," "2," or "1." This is a forced choice inventory, so you must rank each ending; no items can be left out. *Look at the example provided at the top of page LSI-1 before you begin.*

When you understand the example, you're ready to respond to the 12 sentences of the LSI:

- After you answer item #1, check to be sure that you wrote one "1," one "2," one "3," and one "4."
- Also check to make sure that your markings are showing through onto the scoring page (LSI-3).
- After you have responded to the 12 items, go to page LSI-3, which has instructions for computing your results.

A note about learning styles

This chapter introduces several approaches to learning styles: the Learning Style Inventory, multiple intelligences, and the VAK system. That's a lot of information to absorb. Remember that each approach presents an option, not the final word on learning styles. Above all, look for ideas from any of these methods that you can put to immediate use, both inside and outside the classroom. When you write Intention Statements, keep these questions in mind: How can I use this idea to be more successful in school and at work? What will I do differently as a result of reading about learning styles? If I develop new learning styles, what skill will I have that I don't have now?

Learning Style Inventory

Fill in the following blanks like this example:

A. When I learn: 2 I am happy. 3 I am fast. 4 I am logical. 1 I am careful.

Remember: **4** = Most like you **3** = Second most like you **2** = Third most like you **1** = Least like you

Remove the sheet of paper following this page. Press firmly while writing.

1. When I learn:	1 I like to deal with my feelings.	3 I like to think about ideas.	2 I like to be doing things.	4 I like to watch and listen.
2. I learn best when:	2 I listen and watch carefully.	3 I rely on logical thinking.	1 I trust my hunches and feelings.	4 I work hard to get things done.
3. When I am learning:	3 I tend to reason things out.	4 I am responsible about things.	1 I am quiet and reserved.	2 I have strong feelings and reactions.
4. I learn by:	1 feeling.	4 doing.	3 watching.	2 thinking.
5. When I learn:	1 I am open to new experiences.	2 I look at all sides of issues.	3 I like to analyze things, break them down into their parts.	4 I like to try things out.
6. When I am learning:	2 I am an observing person.	3 I am an active person.	1 I am an intuitive person.	4 I am a logical person.
7. I learn best from:	4 observation.	1 personal relationships.	2 rational theories.	3 a chance to try out and practice.
8. When I learn:	4 I like to see results from my work.	1 I like ideas and theories.	2 I take my time before acting.	3 I feel personally involved in things.
9. I learn best when:	3 I rely on my observations.	1 I rely on my feelings.	4 I can try things out for myself.	2 I rely on my ideas.
10. When I am learning:	1 I am a reserved person.	2 I am an accepting person.	4 I am a responsible person.	3 I am a rational person.
11. When I learn:	4 I get involved.	3 I like to observe.	1 I evaluate things.	2 I like to be active.
12. I learn best when:	2 I analyze ideas.	1 I am receptive and open-minded.	3 I am careful.	4 I am practical.

Interpreting your Learning Style Graph

NOTE: Before you read this page, score your inventory by following the directions on page LSI-3. Then complete the Learning Style Graph on page LSI-5. The following information appears on this page so that you can more easily compare your completed graph to the samples below. You will make this comparison *after* you remove page LSI-3.

Four modes of learning

When we're learning well, we tend to search out the answers to four key questions: *Why? What? How?* and *What if?* Each of these questions represents a different *mode of learning.* The modes of learning are patterns of behavior—unique combinations of concrete experience, reflective observation, abstract conceptualization, and active experimentation. Read the descriptions below to get a better idea of how you approach learning.

Mode 1: Why? Some of us question why we are learning things. We seek a purpose for information and a personal connection with the content. We want to know a rationale for what we're learning.

Mode 2: What? Some of us crave information. When learning something, we want to know critical facts. We seek a theory or model to explain what's happening and follow up to see what experts have to say on the topic. We break a subject down into its key components or steps and master each one.

Mode 3: How? Some of us hunger for an opportunity to try out what we're studying. We ask ourselves: Does this idea make sense? Will it work, and, if so, *how* does it work? How can I make use of this information? We want to apply and test theories and models.

Mode 4: What if? Some of us get excited about going beyond classroom assignments. We aim to adapt what we're learning to another course or to a situation at work or at home. By applying our knowledge, we want to make a difference in some area that we care about. We ask ourselves: What if we tried...? or What if we combined...?

Your preferred learning mode

When you examine your completed Learning Style Graph on page LSI-5, you will notice that your learning style profile (the "kite" that you drew) might be located primarily in one part of the graph. This will give you an idea of your preferred mode of learning, that is, the kind of behaviors that feel most comfortable and familiar to you when you are learning something.

Note: Remember that, in this exercise, the term preferred learning mode refers to the way you've typically approached learning in the past. It does not describe the way you have to learn in the future. No matter what aspects of learning you've tended to prefer, you can develop the ability to use all four modes. Doing so offers many potential benefits. In summary, exploring all of the learning modes provides more opportunities for you to achieve your goals.

Using the descriptions below and the sample graphs, identify your preferred learning mode.

Mode 1: Why? If the majority of your learning style profile is in the upper right-hand corner of the Learning Style Graph, you probably prefer Mode 1 learning. You like to consider a situation from many different points of view and determine why it is important to learn a new idea or technique.

Mode 2: What? If your learning style profile is mostly in the lower right-hand corner of the Learning Style Graph, you probably prefer Mode 2 learning. You are interested in knowing what ideas or techniques are important.

Mode 3: How? If most of your learning style profile is in the lower left-hand corner of the Learning Style Graph, you probably prefer Mode 3 learning. You get involved with new knowledge by testing it out.

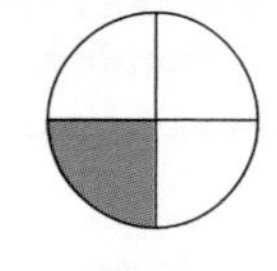

Mode 4: What if? If most of your learning style profile is in the upper left-hand corner of the Learning Style Graph, you probably prefer Mode 4 learning. You like to take what you have practiced and find other uses for it. You seek ways to apply this newly gained skill or information at your workplace or in your personal relationships.

Combinations. Some learning style profiles combine all four modes. The profile to the right reflects a learner who is focused primarily on gathering information—lots of information! People with this profile tend to ask for additional facts from an instructor.

The profile to the right applies to learners who focus more on understanding what they learn and less on gathering lots of information. People with this profile prefer smaller chunks of data with plenty of time to process it.

The profile to the right indicates a learner whose preferences are fairly well balanced. People with this profile can be highly adaptable and tend to excel no matter what the instructor does in the classroom.

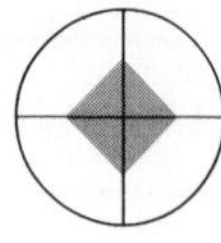

Learning Style Graph

3 Remove the piece of paper that follows this page and then transfer your totals from Step 2 on page LSI-3 to the lines on the Learning Style Graph below. On the brown (F) line, find the number that corresponds to your "**Brown F**" total from page LSI-3. Then write an X on this number. Do the same for your "**Teal W**," "**Purple T**," and "**Orange D**" totals.

4 Now, pressing firmly, draw four straight lines to connect the four X's and shade in the area to form a "kite." This is your learning style profile. Each X that you placed on these lines indicates your preference for a different aspect of learning:

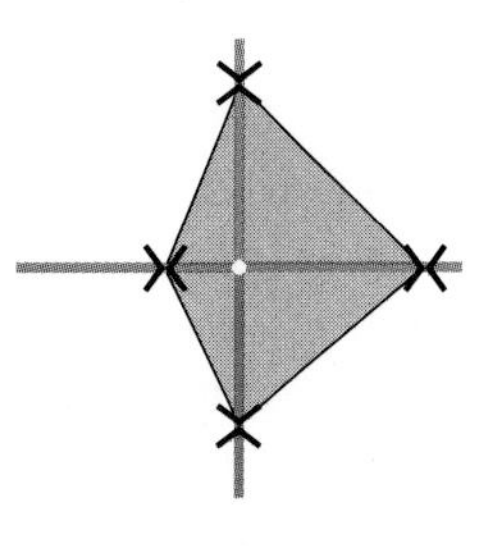

Concrete experience ("Feeling"). The number where you put your X on this line indicates your preference for learning things that have personal meaning. The higher your score on this line, the more you like to learn things that you feel are important and relevant to yourself.

Reflective observation ("Watching"). Your number on this line indicates how important it is for you to reflect on the things you are learning. If your score is high on this line, you probably find it important to watch others as they learn about an assignment and then report on it to the class. You probably like to plan things out and take the time to make sure that you fully understand a topic.

Abstract conceptualization ("Thinking"). Your number on this line indicates your preference for learning ideas, facts, and figures. If your score is high on this line, you probably like to absorb many concepts and gather lots of information on a new topic.

Active experimentation ("Doing"). Your number on this line indicates your preference for applying ideas, using trial and error, and practicing what you learn. If your score is high on this line, you probably enjoy hands-on activities that allow you to test out ideas to see what works.

5 Read page LSI-2 to understand further your preferences for learning.

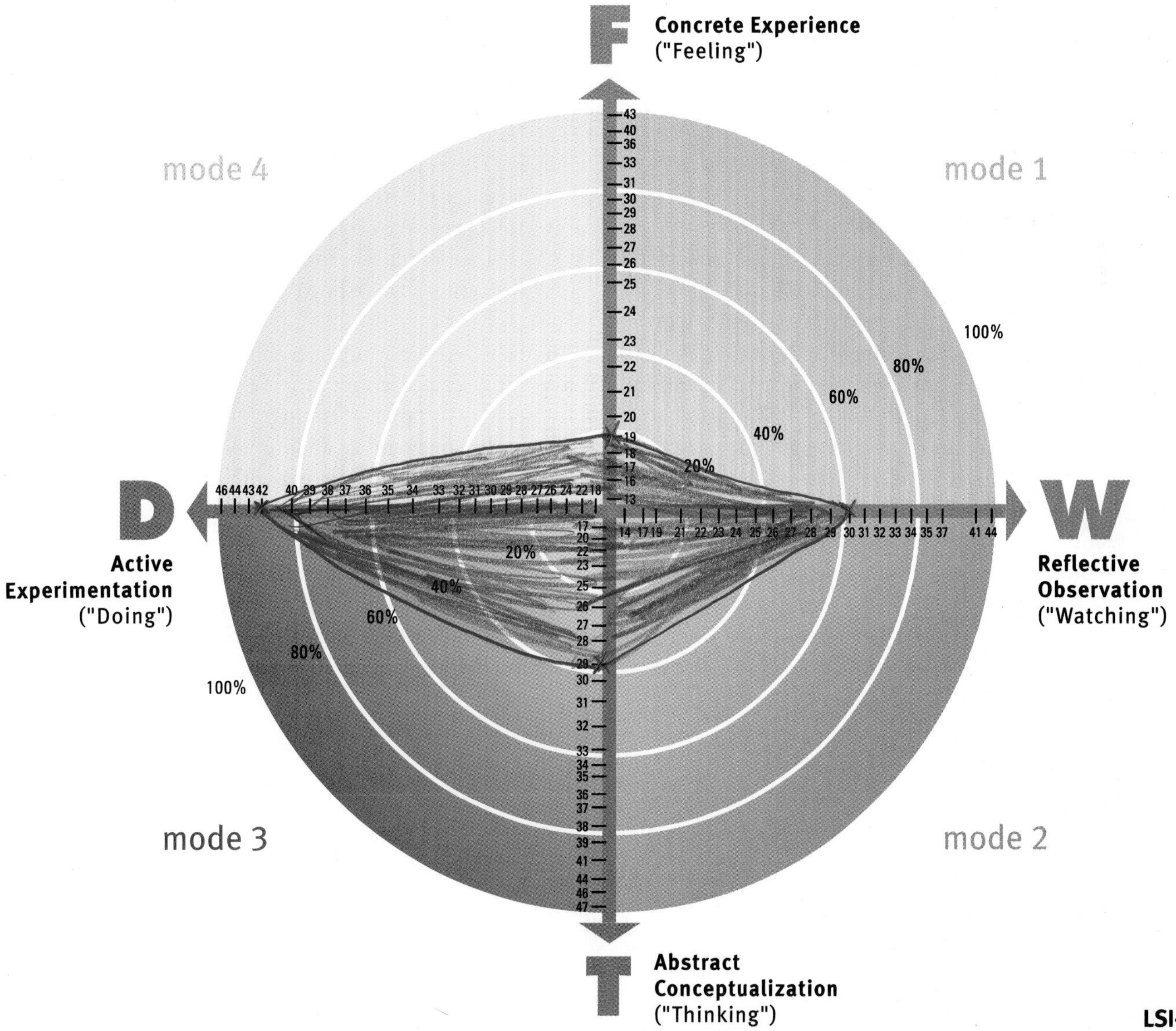

F **Concrete Experience** ("Feeling")

43 40 36 33 31 30 29 28 27 26 25 24 23 22 21 20 19 18 17 16 13

mode 4

mode 1

100% 80% 60% 40% 20%

D 46 44 43 42 40 39 38 37 36 35 34 33 32 31 30 29 28 27 26 24 22 18

Active Experimentation ("Doing")

W 14 17 19 21 22 23 24 25 26 27 28 29 30 31 32 33 34 35 37 41 44

Reflective Observation ("Watching")

20% 40% 60% 80% 100%

17 20 22 23 25 26 27 28 29 30 31 32 33 34 35 36 37 38 39 41 44 46 47

mode 3

mode 2

T **Abstract Conceptualization** ("Thinking")

Cycle of learning

One way to understand the four modes of learning is to see how they relate to actual examples of learning.

Example 1 Learning about immigration

You're required to take an elective in history, and you decide to take a course on the history of immigration in the United States. Your great-grandparents came to this country as immigrants, and immigration is still taking place today. You conclude that this topic is interesting—in part, because of your family background (Mode 1: *Why?*).

Soon you're in class, and you learn that from the early years of the country's history, many Americans have had misconceptions and fears about immigration that persist to the present day (Mode 2: *What?*).

You find yourself re-evaluating your own beliefs and assumptions. You wonder whether new immigrants in your city are experiencing some of the same stereotyping that was commonplace in earlier times. You decide to become more active in a community organization that deals firsthand with the impact of immigration policies (Mode 3: *How?*).

You also start to consider what it would be like to become an attorney and devote your career to creating a system that treats all immigrants with fairness and respect. You realize that you want to make a positive difference in the lives of people who are coming to live in the United States today (Mode 4: *What if?*).

Example 2 Learning about gas prices

Each time that you stop to fill up your car's gas tank, you feel confused and a little angry. In addition to dealing with the overall increase in gas prices, you wonder why prices at the pump seem to change weekly or even daily. One of your friends explains the situation as a "rip-off by the big oil companies and local dealers." Before you discuss this with her again, you want to get informed about the issue (Mode 1: *Why?*).

Using the keywords *cost of gas,* you search the Internet for facts. You discover that a number of factors drive gas prices—crude oil supplies, refining costs, taxes, weather, seasonal demand, and more. During your next stop at the neighborhood gas station, you also ask the owner about how much station owners mark up gas. She tells you that state law prohibits her from adding more than five cents to the cost of each gallon (Mode 2: *What?*).

Next, you think about how to use the information you've gained. Besides telling your friend about the complex causes of gas prices, you look for ways to change your experience at the pump. Your Internet search revealed a site that tracks local gas stations and ranks them daily by price. You plan to visit this site weekly so that you can make competitive gas purchases (Mode 3: *How?*).

In addition, you realize that you can apply your research in a new context—your next car purchase. Your new intention is to buy a model that safely burns ethanol. This fuel is cheaper than gas and emits less of the carbon dioxide that's linked to global warming (Mode 4: *What if?*).

Example 3 Learning about career planning

Your parents are frequently asking you about your career plans. You've just enrolled for your first semester of classes, and you think it's too early to think about careers. Yet you choose to brainstorm some career options anyway. If nothing else, the exercise might be fun, and you'll have some answers for your parents when they call again (Mode 1: *Why?*).

During the next meeting of your psychology class, your instructor mentions the career planning center on campus. You visit the center's Website and discover its list of services. While you're online, you also register for one of the center's workshops about writing a career plan (Mode 2: *What?*).

In this workshop, you learn about the role that internships, service learning, and extracurricular activities play in career planning. All of these are ways to test an early career choice and discover whether it appeals to you. You enjoy being with children, so you choose to volunteer at a campus-based day care center (Mode 3: *How?*).

Your experience at the day care center leads to a work-study assignment there. During your next semester, you choose to declare a major in early childhood education (Mode 4: *What if?*). ☒

Name ______________________________ Date ____/____/____

Note: After completing your Learning Style Inventory (page LSI-1) and filling in the Learning Style Graph (page LSI-5), be sure to read the sections titled "Interpreting Your Learning Style Graph" (page LSI-2) and "Cycle of Learning" (page LSI-6). Then complete the following Journal Entry.

journal entry 5

Discovery/Intention Statement

To make this concept of the learning cycle more useful, start applying it right away. You can begin with the content of this book. For example, as you read the Master Student Profiles, ask questions based on each mode of learning: *Why* is this person considered a master student? *What* attitudes or behaviors helped to create her mastery? *How* can I develop those qualities? *What if* I could use her example to create significant new results in my own life? (Or, *What if* I ignore the lessons to be learned from this Master Student Profile and experience significant costs as a result?) Also see the Master Student Map at the beginning of each chapter for sample answers to *Why? What? How?* and *What if?* questions.

Regarding my preferences for learning, I discovered that...

____

Given my preferences for learning, I intend to...

____

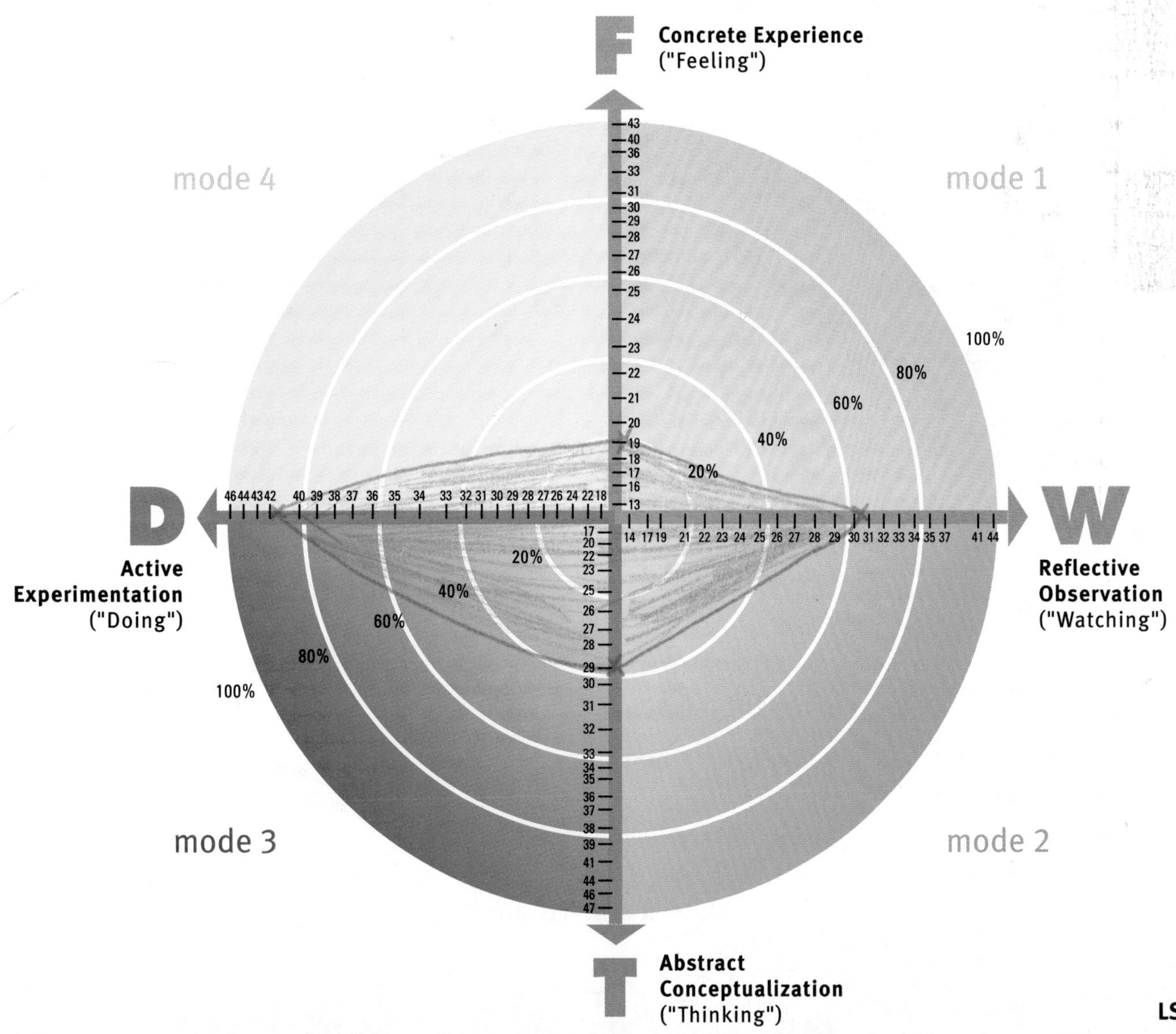

Balancing your preferences

The chart below identifies some of the natural talents as well as challenges for people who have a strong preference for any one mode of learning. For example, if most of your "kite" is in Mode 2 of the Learning Style Graph, then look at the lower right-hand corner of the following chart to see if this is an accurate description of yourself.

After reviewing the description of your preferred learning mode, read all of the sections that start with the words "People with other preferred modes." These sections explain what actions you can take to become a more balanced learner.

Concrete Experience

Active Experimentation

Reflective Observation

Abstract Conceptualization

mode 1

Strengths:
Imaginative ability
Understanding people
Recognizing problems
Brainstorming

Too much of this mode can lead to:
Feeling paralyzed by alternatives
Inability to make decisions

Too little of this mode can lead to:
Lack of ideas
Not recognizing problems and opportunities

People with other preferred modes can develop Mode 1 by:
- Being aware of other people's feelings
- Being sensitive to values
- Listening with an open mind
- Gathering information
- Imagining the implications of ambiguous situations

mode 2

Strengths:
Planning
Creating models
Defining problems
Developing theories

Too much of this mode can lead to:
Vague ideals ("castles in the air")
Lack of practical application

Too little of this mode can lead to:
Inability to learn from mistakes
No sound basis for work
No systematic approach

People with other preferred modes can develop Mode 2 by:
- Organizing information
- Building conceptual models
- Testing theories and ideas
- Designing experiments
- Analyzing quantitative data

mode 3

Strengths:
Problem solving
Decision making
Deductive reasoning
Defining problems

Too much of this mode can lead to:
Solving the wrong problem
Hasty decision making

Too little of this mode can lead to:
Lack of focus
Reluctance to consider alternatives
Scattered thoughts

People with other preferred modes can develop Mode 3 by:
- Creating new ways of thinking and doing
- Experimenting with fresh ideas
- Choosing the best solution
- Setting goals
- Making decisions

mode 4

Strengths:
Getting things done
Leadership
Risk taking

Too much of this mode can lead to:
Trivial improvements
Meaningless activity

Too little of this mode can lead to:
Work not completed on time
Impractical plans
Lack of motivation to achieve goals

People with other preferred modes can develop Mode 4 by:
- Making a commitment to objectives
- Seeking new opportunities
- Influencing and leading others
- Being personally involved
- Dealing with people

Scoring your Inventory

Now that you have taken the Learning Style Inventory, it's time to fill out the Learning Style Graph (page LSI-5) and interpret your results. To do this, please follow the next five steps.

1 First, add up all of the numbers you gave to the items marked with brown **F** letters. Then write down that total to the right in the blank next to "**Brown F**." Next, add up all of the numbers for "**Teal W**," "**Purple T**," and "**Orange D**," and also write down those totals in the blanks to the right.

2 Add the four totals to arrive at a GRAND TOTAL and write down that figure in the blank to the right. (*Note:* The grand total should equal 120. If you have a different amount, go back and re-add the colored letters; it was probably just an addition error.) Now remove this page and continue with Step 3 on page LSI-5.

scorecard

Brown F total ____

Teal W total ____

Purple T total ____

Orange D total ____

GRAND TOTAL ____

F	T	D	W
W	T	F	D
T	D	W	F
F	D	W	T
F	W	T	D
W	D	F	T
W	F	T	D
D	T	W	F
W	F	D	T
W	F	D	T
F	W	T	D
T	F	W	D

Remove this page after you have completed Steps 1 and 2 on page LSI-3. Then continue with Step 3 on page LSI-5.

Once you have completed Step 3, discard this page so that you can more easily compare your completed Learning Style Graph with the examples on page LSI-2.

Using your learning style profile to succeed

what if
why
how
what

To get the most value from knowing your learning style profile, look for ways to apply this knowledge in school and at work. Remember that, in this exercise, the term *preferred learning mode* refers to the way you've typically approached learning in the past. It does not describe the way you have to learn in the future.

No matter what aspects of learning you've tended to prefer, you can develop the ability to use all four modes. Doing so offers many potential benefits. For example, you can excel in different types of courses, seize more opportunities for learning outside the classroom, and expand your options for declaring a major and choosing a career. In addition, you can more fully understand people who learn differently from you. This helps to prevent conflict and make your working relationships more effective.

Exploring all of the learning modes provides more opportunities for you to achieve your goals. Consider the suggestions that follow.

When learning styles conflict, you have options

When they experience difficulty in school, some students say: "The classroom is not conducive to the way I learn." Or "This teacher creates tests that are too hard for me." Or "In class, we never have time for questions." Or "The instructor doesn't teach to my learning style." Such statements can become mental crutches that prevent you from taking responsibility for your education. To stay in charge of your learning, adopt attitudes such as the following:

I will discover the value in learning this information.

I will find out more details and facts about this information.

I will discover how I can experiment with this information.

I will discover new ways to use this information in my life.

Tolerate discomfort. Discomfort is a natural part of the learning process. If you do tasks that fail to energize you, simply notice your struggle or lack of interest. Remember that you are balancing your learning preferences. Resist the temptation to skip a mode of learning or move too quickly through it. By tolerating discomfort and using all of the modes, you gain more strategies for success.

Match activities to your learning style profile. Examine your learning style profile when choosing your major and planning your career. Focus on courses and jobs with assignments that match your preferred modes of learning.

Ask for what you want. You might find that the way an instructor teaches is not the way you prefer to learn, and that teachers don't always promote all four modes of learning. Once you know your learning preferences, you can respond to this fact in a positive way.

- *If you have a strong preference for Mode 1,* you are likely to spend time observing others and planning out your course of action. You probably also enjoy working with other students. To succeed at learning, ask questions that help you understand *why* it is important for you to learn about a specific topic.
- *If you have a strong preference for Mode 2,* you are skilled at comprehending theories and concepts. You are likely to enjoy lectures. Chances are that you also enjoy solitary time more than working in groups.
- *If you have a strong preference for Mode 3,* you probably excel at working with your hands and at laboratory stations. In addition, you probably enjoy working alone or with a small group. To learn effectively, ask questions that help you understand *how* things work. Allow time to practice and experiment with what you learn. You can conduct experiments, create presentations, tabulate findings, or even write a rap that summarizes key concepts.

- *If you have a strong preference for Mode 4,* you are skilled at teaching others what you've learned and helping them see the importance of these concepts. You like to apply facts and theories. You probably enjoy making plans, completing projects, and having new and challenging experiences. You also prefer working with others and are likely to have many friends. Ask questions that help you apply what you've just learned in several areas of your life. Also find ways to demonstrate your understanding.

Associate with students who have different learning style profiles. If your instructor asks your class to form groups to complete an assignment, avoid joining a group in which everyone shares your preferred modes of learning. Get together with people who both complement and challenge you. This is one way you can develop skills in all four learning modes and become a more well-rounded student. Apply the same strategy when joining project teams in the workplace.

Collaborate with coworkers who have different learning style profiles. If you're skilled at project planning, find someone who excels at doing. Also seek people who can draw insights from the team's experience and report the project's results. Combine the strengths that come from different learning styles.

Respond to relationship styles. People also show different ways of relating to coworkers. Authors Barry Reece and Rhonda Brandt suggest that you prepare for several kinds of *relationship styles* in the workplace.[3]

People with an **emotive style** use vigorous gestures, talk rapidly, and behave spontaneously. These people are often described as "extroverted," and "upbeat." They like to be informal and will probably call you by your first name.

In contrast, people with a **director** style may come across as formal, even detached. Their gestures and tone of voice project determination, power, and a desire to control outcomes.

Other people operate with a **reflective** style. These people often value order. At meetings, they prefer a precise agenda distributed in advance. They focus on details and take their time in making decisions. When reflecting on a problem, they may appear to be lost in thought.

You may also meet people with a **supportive** style. They excel at listening and like to function as your equal. They are warm, friendly, and naturally persuasive.

When you meet people with different relationship styles, be flexible in your responses:

Note: This chapter introduces several approaches to learning styles: the Learning Style Inventory, multiple intelligences, and the VAK system. That's a lot of information to absorb. Remember that each approach presents an option, not the final word on learning styles.

Above all, look for ideas from any of these methods that you can put to immediate use. Write Intention Statements with these questions in mind: How can I use this idea to *be* more successful? What will I *do* differently as a result of reading about styles? If I develop new styles, what benefits will I *have* that I don't have now?

Relationship style	Ways to respond
Emotive	• Allow some time for socializing as well as taking care of business. • Focus on main points rather than details. • Allow conversations to be fast-paced and cover a wide range of topics.
Director	• Begin and end meetings on time. • Get down to business right away, keeping written and oral presentations brief and to the point. • Make eye contact and express yourself with confidence. • When presenting a proposal, anticipate possible questions and objections—and be prepared to answer them.
Reflective	• Organize ideas carefully. • Offer plenty of details about your proposal, in both written and verbal form. • Allow for slow-paced, systematic conversations and time to cover all major topics.
Supportive	• Find areas of common interest and identify mutual acquaintances. • Listen carefully to find out how this person feels about a project and what the person wants to gain from it. • Focus on building a "win-win" relationship.

People often think that being smart means the same thing as having a high IQ, and that having a high IQ automatically leads to success. However, psychologists are finding that IQ scores do not always foretell which students will do well in academic settings—or after they graduate.[4]

Claim your *multiple intelligences*

Howard Gardner of Harvard University believes that no single measure of intelligence can tell us how smart we are. Instead, Gardner identifies many types of intelligence, as described below.[5]

People using **verbal/linguistic intelligence** are adept at language skills and learn best by speaking, writing, reading, and listening. They are likely to enjoy activities such as telling stories and doing crossword puzzles.

Those using **mathematical/logical intelligence** are good with numbers, logic, problem solving, patterns, relationships, and categories. They are generally precise and methodical, and are likely to enjoy science.

When people learn visually and by organizing things spatially, they display **visual/spatial intelligence.** They think in images and pictures, and understand best by seeing the subject. They enjoy charts, graphs, maps, mazes, tables, illustrations, art, models, puzzles, and costumes.

People using **bodily/kinesthetic intelligence** prefer physical activity. They enjoy activities such as building things, woodworking, dancing, skiing, sewing, and crafts. They generally are coordinated and athletic, and would rather participate in games than just watch.

Those using **musical/rhythmic intelligence** enjoy musical expression through songs, rhythms, and musical instruments. They are responsive to various kinds of sounds; remember melodies easily; and might enjoy drumming, humming, and whistling. People using **intrapersonal intelligence** are exceptionally aware of their own feelings and values. They are generally reserved, self-motivated, and intuitive.

Evidence of **interpersonal intelligence** is seen in outgoing people. They do well with cooperative learning and are sensitive to the feelings, intentions, and motivations of others. They often make good leaders.

Those using **naturalist intelligence** love the outdoors and recognize details in plants, animals, rocks, clouds, and other natural formations. These people excel in observing fine distinctions among similar items.

Each of us has all of these intelligences to some degree. And each of us can learn to enhance them. Experiment with learning in ways that draw on a variety of intelligences—including those that might be less familiar. When we acknowledge all of our intelligences, we can constantly explore new ways of being smart.

Gardner's theory complements the discussion of different learning styles in this chapter. The main point is that there are many ways to gain knowledge and acquire new behaviors. You can use Gardner's concepts to explore a range of options for achieving success in school, work, and relationships.

The following chart summarizes the multiple intelligences discussed in this article and suggests ways to apply them. This is not an exhaustive list or a formal inventory, so take what you find merely as points of departure. You can invent strategies of your own to cultivate different intelligences.

Type of intelligence	Possible characteristics	Possible learning strategies	Possible careers
Verbal/linguistic	• You enjoy writing letters, stories, and papers. • You prefer to write directions rather than draw maps. • You take excellent notes from textbooks and lectures. • You enjoy reading, telling stories, and listening to them.	• Highlight, underline, and write other notes in your textbooks. • Recite new ideas in your own words. • Rewrite and edit your class notes. • Talk to other people often about what you're studying.	Librarian, lawyer, editor, journalist, English teacher, radio or television announcer
Mathematical/logical	• You enjoy solving puzzles. • You prefer math or science class over English class. • You want to know how and why things work. • You make careful step-by-step plans.	• Analyze tasks into a sequence of steps. • Group concepts into categories and look for underlying patterns. • Convert text into tables, charts, and graphs. • Look for ways to quantify ideas–to express them in numerical terms.	Accountant, auditor, tax preparer, mathematician, computer programmer, actuary, economist, math or science teacher
Visual/spatial	• You draw pictures to give an example or clarify an explanation. • You understand maps and illustrations more readily than text. • You assemble thing from illustrated instructions. • You especially enjoy books that have a lot of illustrations.	• When taking notes, create concept maps, mind maps, and other visuals (see Chapter Five). • Code your notes by using different colors to highlight main topics, major points, and key details. • When your attention wanders, focus it by sketching or drawing. • Before you try a new task, visualize yourself doing it well.	Architect, commercial artist, fine artist, graphic designer, photographer, interior decorator, engineer, cartographer
Bodily/kinesthetic	• You enjoy physical exercise. • You tend not to sit still for long periods of time. • You enjoy working with your hands. • You use a lot of gestures when talking.	• Be active in ways that support concentration; for example, pace as you recite, read while standing up, and create flash cards. • Carry materials with you and practice studying in several different locations. • Create hands-on activities related to key concepts; for example, create a game based on course content. • Notice the sensations involved with learning something well.	Physical education teacher, athlete, athletic coach, physical therapist, chiropractor, massage therapist, yoga teacher, dancer, choreographer, actor

Type of intelligence	Possible characteristics	Possible learning strategies	Possible careers
Musical/rhythmic	• You often sing in the car or shower. • You easily tap your foot to the beat of a song. • You play a musical instrument. • You feel most engaged and productive when music is playing.	• During a study break, play music or dance to restore energy. • Put on background music that enhances your concentration while studying. • Relate key concepts to songs you know. • Write your own songs based on course content.	Professional musician, music teacher, music therapist, choral director, musical instrument sales representative, musical instrument maker, piano tuner
Intrapersonal	• You enjoy writing in a journal and being alone with your thoughts. • You think a lot about what you want in the future. • You prefer to work on individual projects over group projects. • You take time to think things through before talking or taking action.	• Connect course content to your personal values and goals. • Study a topic alone before attending a study group. • Connect readings and lectures to a strong feeling or significant past experience. • Keep a journal that relates your course work to events in your daily life.	Minister, priest, rabbi, professor of philosophy or religion, counseling psychologist, creator of a home-based or small business
Interpersonal	• You enjoy group work over working alone. • You have plenty of friends and regularly spend time with them. • You prefer talking and listening over reading or writing. • You thrive in positions of leadership.	• Form and conduct study groups early in the term. • Create flash cards and use them to quiz study partners. • Volunteer to give a speech or lead group presentations on course topics. • Teach the topic you're studying to someone else.	Manager, school administrator, salesperson, teacher, counseling psychologist, arbitrator, police officer, nurse, travel agent, public relations specialist, creator of a mid-size to large business
Naturalist	• As a child, you enjoyed collecting insects, leaves, or other natural objects. • You enjoy being outdoors. • You find that important insights occur during times you spend in nature. • You read books and magazines on nature-related topics.	• During study breaks, take walks outside. • Post pictures of outdoor scenes where you study and play recordings of outdoor sounds while you read. • Invite classmates to discuss course work while taking a hike or going on a camping trip. • Focus on careers that hold the potential for working outdoors.	Environmental activist, park ranger, recreation supervisor, historian, museum curator, biologist, criminologist, mechanic, woodworker, construction worker, construction contractor or estimator

In 1482, Leonardo da Vinci wrote a letter to a wealthy baron, applying for work. In excerpted form, he wrote,

"I can contrive various and endless means of offense and defense. . . . I have all sorts of extremely light and strong bridges adapted to be most easily carried. . . . I have methods for destroying every turret or fortress. . . . I will make covered chariots, safe and unassailable. . . . In case of need I will make big guns, mortars, and light ordnance of fine and useful forms out of the common type." And then he added, almost as an afterthought, "In times of peace I believe I can give perfect satisfaction and to the equal of any other in architecture . . . can carry out sculpture . . . and also I can do in painting whatever may be done."

The Mona Lisa, for example.

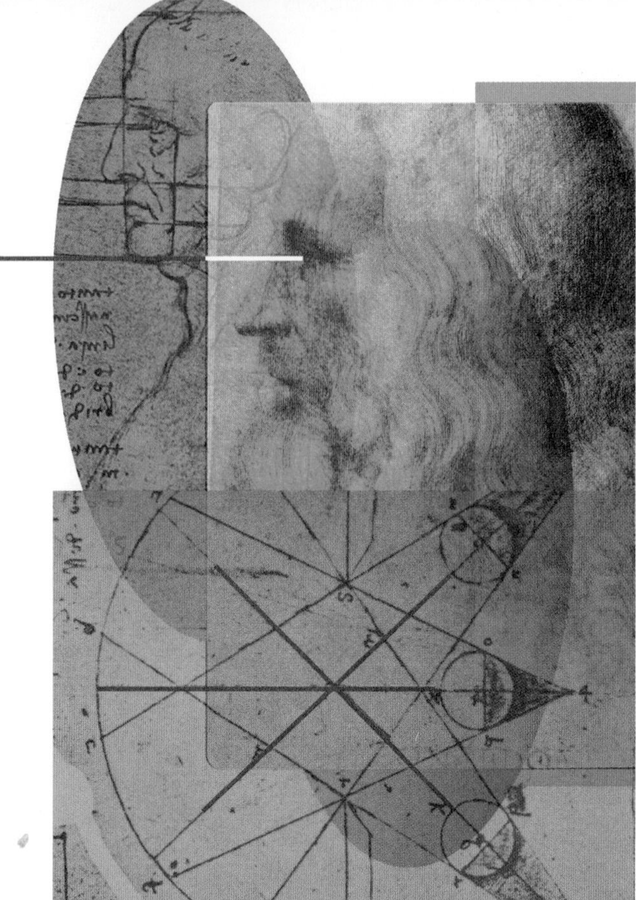

The meaning of mastery

This book is about something that cannot be taught. It's about mastery.

A master is a person who has attained a level of skill that goes beyond technique. For a master, methods and procedures are automatic responses to the needs of the task. Work is effortless; struggle evaporates. The master carpenter is so familiar with her tools, they are part of her. To a master chef, utensils are old friends. Because these masters don't have to think about the details of the process, they bring more of themselves to their work.

Mastery can lead to flashy results—an incredible painting, for example, or a gem of a short story. In basketball, mastery might result in an unbelievable shot at the buzzer. For a musician, it might be the performance of a lifetime, the moment when everything comes together. For the entrepreneur, it might be a business plan that attracts investors or a product that corners the market.

Often the result of mastery is a sense of profound satisfaction, well-being, and timelessness. Work seems self-propelled. The master is *in* control by being *out* of control. He lets go and allows the creative process to take over. That's why after a spectacular performance, it is often said of an athlete or a performer, "He was playing out of his mind." Likewise, the master student is one who "learns out of her mind." And the master employee is one who creates value for her organization in ways that defy analysis.

Psychologist Mihaly Csikszentmihalyi describes such people as being in a state of "flow."[6] In the flow state, a person no longer depends on rules, formulas, or instructions to guide her actions. Her range of behaviors is so vast and so well-tested by experience that she can respond instantly and intuitively.

Of course, these statements make no sense. Mastery, in fact, doesn't make sense. It cannot be captured with words. Mastery cannot be taught, only learned and experienced.

Any description of mastery merely points in a direction. Look in that direction, and you'll see endless diversity. People who demonstrate mastery are old and young, male and female. They exist in every period of history. They are students, business people, educators, inventors, and artists. They work and learn in every kind of setting. They come from every culture, race, and ethnic group.

Also remember to look to yourself. No one can teach us mastery; we are born with this capacity. We are natural learners by design. We are born to love and to work—to care deeply about people and contribute to the world. In the classroom and in the workplace, we can discover that every day.

Following are some aspects of mastery.

Inquisitive. The person who discovers mastery is curious about everything. By posing questions she can generate interest in the most mundane, humdrum situations. When she is bored during a biology lecture, she thinks to herself, "I always get bored when I listen to this instructor. Why is that? Maybe it's because he reminds me of my boring Uncle Ralph, who always tells those endless fishing stories. He even looks like Uncle Ralph. Amazing! Boredom is certainly interesting." Then she asks herself, "What can I do to get value out of this lecture, even though it seems boring?" And she finds an answer.

Able to focus attention. Watch a 2-year-old at play. Pay attention to his eyes. The wide-eyed look reveals an energy and a capacity for amazement that keep his attention absolutely focused in the here and now. With mastery comes focused attention that has a childlike quality. The world, to a child, is always new. Because the person who discovers mastery can focus attention, to him the world is also new.

Willing to change. As we discover mastery, the unknown does not frighten us. In fact, we welcome it—even the unknown in ourselves. We all have pictures of who we think we are, and these pictures can be useful. They also can prevent learning and growth. In discovering mastery, we remain open to changes in our environment and in ourselves.

Able to organize and sort. Mastery enables us to take a large body of information and sift through it to discover relationships. We can play with information, organizing data by size, color, function, timeliness, and hundreds of other categories.

Competent. Skills are key to mastery. When we learn mathematical formulas, we study them until they become second nature. We practice until we know them cold, then put in a few extra minutes. We also are able to apply what we learn to new and different situations.

Joyful. More often than not, the person who discovers mastery is seen with a smile on his face—sometimes a smile at nothing in particular other than amazement at the world and his experience of it.

Able to suspend judgment. In the state of mastery, we have opinions and positions, and we are able to let go of them when appropriate. We can quiet our internal dialogue and listen to an opposing viewpoint. We don't let judgment get in the way of learning. Rather than approaching discussions with a "Prove it to me and then I'll believe it" attitude, we ask, "What if this is true?" and explore the possibilities.

Energetic. Notice the student or employee with a spring in his step, the one who is enthusiastic and involved. When he reads, he often sits on the very edge of his chair, and he plays with the same intensity. He has discovered mastery.

Well. Health is important to mastery, though not necessarily in the sense of being free of illness. Rather, mastery means valuing your body and treating it with respect. You tend to your emotional and spiritual health, as well as your physical health.

Self-aware. With mastery comes the willingness to evaluate ourselves and our behavior. We regularly tell the truth about our strengths and those aspects of ourselves that could be improved.

Responsible. There is a difference between responsibility and blame. As a person discovers mastery, she is willing to take responsibility for everything in her life—even for events that most people would blame on others.

For example, if a master student is served cold eggs in the cafeteria, she chooses to take responsibility for getting cold eggs. This is not the same as blaming herself for cold eggs. Rather, she looks for ways to change the situation. She could choose to eat breakfast earlier, or she might tell someone in the kitchen that the eggs are cold and request a change. The cold eggs might continue. Even then, the master student takes responsibility and gives herself the power to choose her response to the situation.

Willing to take risks. The master student or master employee often takes on projects with no guarantee of success. He participates in dialogues at the risk of looking foolish. He tackles difficult subjects in term papers. He promises results and then delivers. He welcomes the risk of a new challenge.

Willing to participate. Don't look for the master student or employee on the sidelines. She's in the game. She is a player who can be counted on. She is willing to make a commitment and to follow through on it.

A generalist. Master students and master employees are interested in everything around them. They have a broad base of knowledge in many fields and can apply their specialties.

Willing to accept paradox. The word *paradox* comes from two Greek words, *para* (beyond) and *doxen* (opinion). A paradox is something that is beyond opinion or, more accurately, something that might seem contradictory or absurd yet might actually have meaning.

For example, mastery means that we are committed to managing money and reaching our financial goals. At the same time, we can be totally detached from money, knowing that our real worth is independent of how much money we have. We recognize the limitations of the mind and feel at home with paradox. We can accept ambiguity.

Courageous. In a state of mastery, we admit fear and fully experience it. For example, we will approach a tough exam or job interview as an opportunity to explore feelings of anxiety and tension related to the pressure to perform. We do not deny fear; we embrace it.

Self-directed. Rewards or punishments provided by others do not motivate the master student or master employee. Her motivation to learn comes from within.

Spontaneous. Mastery means entering the here and now. We are able to respond to the moment in fresh, surprising, and unplanned ways.

Relaxed about grades. Grades make the master student neither depressed nor euphoric. She recognizes that grades are important, and grades are not the only reason she studies. She does not measure her worth as a human being by the grades she receives.

Intuitive. Mastery taps into sources of knowledge that cannot be explained by logic. We learn to trust our feelings, and we open up to insights that come from beyond the rational mind.

Creative. Where others see dull details and trivia, the master student or master employee sees opportunities to create and innovate. She can gather pieces of knowledge from a wide range of subjects and put them together in new ways. Mastery brings creativity in every aspect of her life.

Willing to be uncomfortable. In the state of mastery, we do not place comfort first. When discomfort is necessary to reach a goal, we are willing to experience it. We can endure personal hardships and can look at unpleasant things with detachment.

Accepting. The master student or master employee accepts herself, the people around her, and the challenges that life offers.

Willing to laugh. Mastery brings the ability to laugh at any moment, and our sense of humor includes the ability to laugh at ourselves.

Going to school or launching a new career is a big investment. The stakes are high. It's OK to be serious about all this, but you don't have to go to school or work on the deferred-fun program. In the state of mastery, we celebrate learning, and one of the best ways to do that is to have a laugh now and then.

Hungry. Human beings begin life with a natural appetite for knowledge and skills. In some people it soon gets dulled. The master student has tapped that hunger, and it gives her a desire to learn for the sake of learning.

Willing to work. Once inspired, the master student or master employee is willing to follow through with sweat. He knows that genius and creativity are the result of persistence and work. When in high gear, he works with the intensity of a child at play.

Caring. In discovering mastery, we uncover a passion for ideas. We also care about people and appreciate learning from others. We flourish in a community that values win-win outcomes, cooperation, and love.

Discover mastery in you. Mastery exists in all of us. By design, human beings are learning machines. We have an innate ability to learn, to love, and to do work that leaves a legacy.

For anyone who wants to gain skills through education and develop them in the workplace, it is important to understand the difference between learning and being taught. Human beings can resist being taught anything. Carl Rogers goes so far as to say that anything that can be taught to a human being is either inconsequential or just plain harmful. What matters, Rogers asserts, is *learning*. And everyone has the ability to learn.[7] Unfortunately, people also learn to hide that ability. As they experience the pain that sometimes accompanies learning, they shut down.

Some children "learn" that they are slow learners. If they learn it well enough, their behavior comes to match that label.

As people grow older, they sometimes accumulate a growing list of ideas to defend, a catalog of familiar experiences that discourages them from learning anything new.

Still, the capacity for mastery survives. To tap that resource, you don't need to acquire anything. You already have everything you need. Every day you can rediscover mastery within you. ☒

Motivation

In large part, this chapter is about your motivation to succeed in school. And a First Step in creating motivation is getting some definitions straight.

The terms *self-discipline, willpower,* and *motivation* are often used to describe something missing in ourselves. Time after time we invoke these words to explain another person's success—or our own shortcomings: "If I were more motivated, I'd get more involved in school." "Of course she got an A. She has self-discipline." "If I had more willpower, I'd lose weight." It seems that certain people are born with lots of motivation, while others miss out on it.

An alternative is to stop assuming that motivation is mysterious, determined at birth, or hard to come by. Perhaps what we call *motivation* is something that you already possess—the ability to do a task even when you don't feel like it. This is a habit that you can develop with practice. The following suggestions offer ways to do that.

Promise it. Motivation can come simply from being clear about your goals and acting on them. Say that you want to start a study group. You can commit yourself to inviting people and setting a time and place to meet. Promise your classmates that you'll do this, and ask them to hold you accountable. Self-discipline, willpower, motivation—none of these mysterious characteristics needs to get in your way. Just make a promise and keep your word.

Befriend your discomfort. Sometimes keeping your word means doing a task you'd rather put off. The mere thought of doing laundry, reading a chapter in a statistics book, or proofreading a term paper can lead to discomfort. In the face of such discomfort, we can procrastinate. Or we can use this barrier as a means to get the job done.

Begin by investigating the discomfort. Notice the thoughts running through your head and speak them out loud: "I'd rather walk on a bed of coals than do this." "This is the last thing I want to do right now."

Also observe what's happening with your body. For example, are you breathing faster or slower than usual? Is your breathing shallow or deep? Are your shoulders tight? Do you feel any tension in your stomach?

Once you're in contact with your mind and body, stay with the discomfort a few minutes longer. Don't judge it as good or bad. Accepting the thoughts and body sensations robs them of power. They might still be there, but in time they can stop being a barrier for you.

Discomfort can be a gift—an opportunity to do valuable work on yourself. On the other side of discomfort lies mastery.

Change your mind—and your body. You can also get past discomfort by planting new thoughts in your mind or changing your physical stance. For example, instead of slumping in a chair, sit up straight or stand up. You can also get physically active by taking a short walk. Notice what happens to your discomfort.

Work with thoughts, also. Replace "I can't stand this" with "I'll feel great when this is done" or "Doing this will help me get something I want."

Sweeten the task. Sometimes it's just one aspect of a task that holds us back. We can stop procrastinating merely by changing that aspect. If distaste for our physical environment keeps us from studying, we can change that environment. Reading about social psychology might seem like a yawner when we're alone in a dark corner of the house. Moving to a cheery, well-lit library can sweeten the task.

Talk about how bad it is. One way to get past negative attitudes is to take them to an extreme. When faced with an unpleasant task, launch into a no-holds-barred gripe session. Pull out all the stops: "There's no way I can start my income taxes now. This is terrible beyond words, an absolute disaster. This is a catastrophe of global proportions!" Griping taken this far can restore perspective. It shows how self-talk can turn inconveniences into crises.

Turn up the pressure. Sometimes motivation is a luxury. Pretend that the due date for your project has been moved up one month, one week, or one day.

Raising the stress level slightly can spur you into action. Then the issue of motivation seems beside the point, and meeting the due date moves to the forefront.

Turn down the pressure. The mere thought of starting a huge task can induce anxiety. To get past this feeling, turn down the pressure by taking "baby steps." Divide a large project into small tasks. In 30 minutes or less, you could preview a book, create a rough outline for a paper, or solve two or three math problems. Careful planning can help you discover many such steps to make a big job doable.

Ask for support. Other people can become your allies in overcoming procrastination. For example, form a support group and declare what you intend to accomplish before each meeting. Then ask members to hold you accountable. If you want to begin exercising regularly, ask another person to walk with you three times weekly. People in support groups ranging from Alcoholics Anonymous to Weight Watchers know the power of this strategy.

Adopt a model. One strategy for succeeding at any task is to hang around the masters. Find someone you consider successful and spend time with her. Observe this person and use her as a model for your own behavior. You can "try on" this person's actions and attitudes. Look for tools that feel right for you. This person can become a mentor for you.

Compare the payoffs to the costs. Behaviors such as cramming for exams or neglecting exercise have payoffs. Cramming might give us more time that's free of commitments. Neglecting exercise can give us more time to sleep.

One way to let go of such unwanted behaviors is first to celebrate them—even embrace them. We can openly acknowledge the payoffs.

Celebration can be especially powerful when we follow it up with the next step—determining the costs. For example, skipping a reading assignment can give you time to go to the movies. However, you might be unprepared for class and have twice as much to read the following week.

Maybe there is another way to get the payoff (going to the movies) without paying the cost (skipping the reading assignment).With some thoughtful weekly planning, you might choose to give up a few hours of television and end up with enough time to read the assignment *and* go to the movies.

Comparing the costs and benefits of any behavior can fuel our motivation. We can choose new behaviors because they align with what we want most.

Do it later. At times, it's effective to save a task for later. For example, writing a résumé can wait until you've taken the time to analyze your job skills and map out your career goals. This is not a lack of motivation—it's planning.

When you do choose to do a task later, turn this decision into a promise. Estimate how long the task will take and schedule a specific date and time for it on your calendar.

Heed the message. Sometimes lack of motivation carries a message that's worth heeding. An example is the student who majors in accounting but seizes every chance to be with children. His chronic reluctance to read accounting textbooks might not be a problem. Instead, it might reveal his desire to major in elementary education. His original career choice might have come from the belief that "real men don't teach kindergarten." In such cases, an apparent lack of motivation signals a deeper wisdom trying to get through. ☒

Ways to change a habit

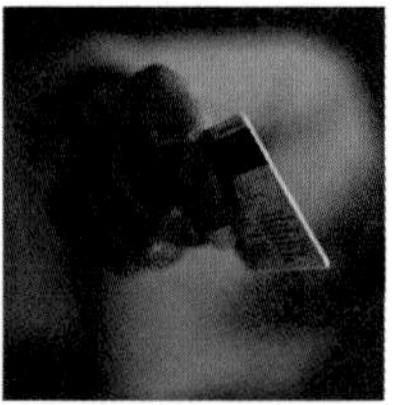

Imagine for a moment that many of our most troublesome problems and even our most basic traits are just habits.

That expanding waistline that someone blames on his spouse's cooking—maybe that's just a habit called overeating.

That fit of rage that a student blames on a teacher—maybe that's just the student's habit of closing the door to new ideas.

Procrastination, stress, and money shortages might just be names that we give to collections of habits—scores of simple, small, repeated behaviors that combine to create a huge result.

When you confront a behavior that undermines your goals or creates a circumstance that you don't want, consider a new attitude: It's just a habit. And it can be changed.

Thinking about ourselves as creatures of habit actually gives us power. Then we are not faced with the monumental task of changing our very nature. Rather, we can take on the doable job of changing our habits. One change in behavior that seems insignificant at first can have positive effects that ripple throughout your life. One way of thinking about success is to focus on habits.

Habit changing is a skill in its own right, and it can help you acquire many other skills. Get started now with the following suggestions.

Tell the truth

Telling the truth about any habit—from chewing our fingernails to cheating on tests—frees us. Without taking this step, efforts to change habits might be as ineffective as rearranging deck chairs on the *Titanic.* Telling the truth allows us to see what's actually sinking the ship.

When we admit what's really going on in our lives, our defenses are down. We're open to accepting help from others. The support we need to change the habit has an opportunity to make an impact.

Choose and commit to a new behavior

It often helps to choose a new habit to replace an old one. First, make a commitment to practice the new habit. Tell key people in your life about your decision to change. Set up a plan for when and how. Answer questions such as these: When will I apply the new habit? Where will I be? Who will be with me? What will I be seeing, hearing, touching, saying, or doing? Exactly how will I think, speak, or act differently?

Take the student who always snacks when he studies. Each time he sits down to read, he positions a bag of potato chips within easy reach. For him, opening a book is a cue to start chewing. Snacking is especially easy, given the place he chooses to study: the kitchen. He decides to change this habit by studying at a desk in his bedroom instead of at the kitchen table. And every time he feels the urge to bite into a potato chip, he drinks from a glass of water instead.

Richard Malott, a psychologist who specializes in helping people overcome procrastination, lists three key steps in committing to a new behavior. First, *specify* your goal in numerical terms whenever possible. For example, commit to reading 30 pages per day, Monday through Friday. Second, *observe* your behavior and record the results—in this case, the number of pages that you actually read every day. Finally, set up a small *consequence* for failing to keep your commitment. For instance, pay a friend one quarter for each day that you read fewer than 30 pages.[8]

Affirm your intention

You can pave the way for a new behavior by clearing a mental path for it. Before you apply the new behavior, rehearse it in your mind. Mentally picture what actions you will take and in what order.

Say that you plan to improve your handwriting when taking notes. Imagine yourself in class with a blank notebook poised before you. See yourself taking up a finely crafted pen. Notice how comfortable it feels in your hand. See yourself writing clearly and legibly. You can even picture how you will make individual letters: the *e*'s, *i*'s, and *r*'s. Then, when class is over, see yourself reviewing your notes and taking pleasure in how easy they are to read.

Start with a small change

You can sometimes rearrange a whole pattern of behaviors by changing one small habit. If you have a habit of always being late for class, and if you want to change that habit, then be on time for one class. As soon as you change the old pattern by getting ready and going on time to one class, you'll likely find yourself arriving at all of your classes on time. You might even start arriving everywhere else on time.

The joy of this process is watching one small change of habit ripple through your whole life.

Get feedback and support

This is a crucial step and a point at which many plans for change break down. It's easy to practice your new behavior with great enthusiasm for a few days. After the initial rush of excitement, however, things can get a little tougher. We begin to find excuses for slipping back into old habits: "One more cigarette won't hurt." "I can get back to my diet tomorrow." "It's been a tough day. I deserve this beer."

One way to get feedback is to bring other people into the picture. Ask others to remind you that you are changing your habit. If you want to stop an old behavior, such as cramming for tests, then it often works to tell everyone you know that you intend to stop. When you want to start a new behavior, though, consider telling only a few people—those who truly support your efforts. Starting new habits might call for the more focused, long-lasting support that close friends or family members can give. Support from others can be as simple as a quick phone call: "Hi. Have you started that outline for your research paper yet?" Or it can be as formal as a support group that meets once a week to review everyone's goals and action plans.

You are probably the most effective source for your own support and feedback. You know yourself better than anyone else does and can design a system to monitor your behavior. Create your own charts to track your behavior or write about your progress in your journal. Figure out a way to monitor your progress.

Practice, practice, practice—without self-judgment

Psychologists such as B. F. Skinner define learning as a stable change in behavior that results from practice.[9] This idea is key to changing habits. Act on your intention. If you fail or forget, let go of any self-judgment. Just keep practicing the new habit and allow whatever time it takes to make a change.

Accept the feelings of discomfort that might come with a new habit. Keep practicing the new behavior, even if it feels unnatural. Trust the process. You will grow into the new behavior. However, if this new habit doesn't work, simply note what happened (without guilt or blame), select a new behavior, and begin this cycle of steps again.

Making mistakes as you practice doesn't mean that you've failed. Even when you don't get the results you want from a new behavior, you learn something valuable in the process. Once you understand ways to change one habit, you understand ways to change almost any habit. ☒

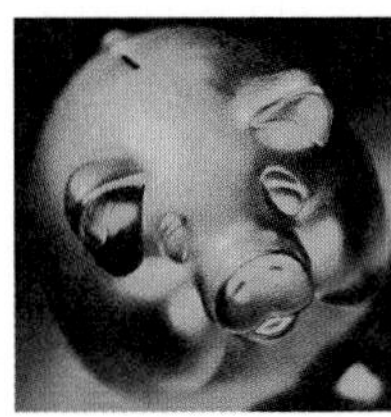

DEMONSTRATING MASTERY

Review the article "Discovering mastery" in this chapter. Then skim the profiles on the last page of each chapter throughout this book. Finally, choose one of the people profiled and describe in the space below how this person demonstrates mastery.

Master Student Profiles

In each chapter of this text there is an example of a person who embodies several qualities of a master student. As you read about these people and others like them, ask yourself: "How can I apply this?" Look for the timeless qualities in the people you read about. Many of the strategies used by master students from another time or place are tools that you can use today.

The master students in this book were chosen because they demonstrate unusual and effective ways to learn. You can read more about them in the Master Student Hall of Fame on the Website.

Remember that these are just a few examples of master students. Also reflect on other master students you've read about or know personally. As you meet new people, look for those who excel at learning. The master student is not a vague or remote ideal. Rather, master students move freely among us.

In fact, there's one living inside your skin.

Student Website

power process

IDEAS ARE TOOLS

There are many ideas in this book. When you first encounter them, don't believe any of them. Instead, think of them as tools.

For example, you use a hammer for a purpose—to drive a nail. When you use a new hammer, you might notice its shape, its weight, and its balance. You don't try to figure out whether the hammer is "right." You just use it. If it works, you use it again. If it doesn't work, you get a different hammer.

This is not the attitude most people adopt when they encounter new ideas. The first thing most people do with new ideas is to measure them against old ones. If a new idea conflicts with an old one, the new one is likely to be rejected.

People have plenty of room in their lives for different kinds of hammers, but they tend to limit their capacity for different kinds of ideas. A new idea, at some level, is a threat to their very being—unlike a new hammer, which is simply a new hammer.

Most of us have a built-in desire to be right. Our ideas, we often think, represent ourselves. And when we identify with our ideas, they assume new importance in our lives. We put them on our mantels. We hang them on our walls. We wear them on our T-shirts and display them on our bumpers. We join associations of people who share our most beloved ideas. We make up rituals about them, compose songs about them, and write stories about them. We declare ourselves dedicated to these ideas.

Some ideas are worth dying for. But please note: This book does not contain any of those ideas. The ideas on these pages are strictly "hammers."

Imagine someone defending a hammer. Picture this person holding up a hammer and declaring, "I hold this hammer to be self-evident. Give me this hammer or give me death. Those other hammers are flawed. There are only two kinds of people in this world: people who believe in this hammer and people who don't."

That ridiculous picture makes a point. This book is not a manifesto. It's a toolbox, and tools are meant to be used. This viewpoint is much like one advocated by psychologist and philosopher William James. His approach to philosophy, which he called pragmatism, emphasized the usefulness of ideas as a criterion of truth.[10] James liked to talk about the "cash value" of an idea—whether it leads to new actions and new results.

If you read about a tool in this book that doesn't sound "right" or one that sounds a little goofy, remember that the ideas here are for using, not necessarily for believing. Suspend your judgment. Test the idea for yourself.

If it works, use it. If it doesn't, don't.

Ask: What if it's true?

When presented with a new idea, some of us take pride in being critical thinkers. We look for problems. We probe for weaknesses. We continue to doubt the idea until there's clear proof. Our main question seems to be "What's wrong with this idea?"

This approach can be useful when it is vital to expose flaws in ideas or reasoning. On the other hand, when we constantly look for what's wrong with new ideas, we might not recognize their value. A different and potentially more powerful approach is to ask yourself: "What if that idea is true?" This opens up all sorts of new possibilities and variations. Rather than looking for what's wrong, we can look for what's potentially valuable. Faced with a new idea, we can stay in the inquiry, look deeper, and go further.

Keep looking for answers

The light bulb, the airplane, the computer chip, the notion of the unconscious—these and many other tools became possible when their inventors practiced the art of continually looking for additional answers.

Another way to expand your toolbox is to keep looking for answers. Much of your education will be about finding answers to questions. Every subject you study—from algebra to history to philosophy—poses a unique set of questions. Some of the most interesting questions are those that admit many answers: How can we create a just society? How can we transmit our values to the next generation? What are the purposes of higher education? How can we prevent an environmental crisis?

Other questions are more personal: What career shall I choose? Shall I get married? Where shall I live and how shall I spend my leisure time? What shall I have, do, and be during my time on earth?

Perhaps you already have answers to these questions. Answers are wonderful, especially when they relate to our most persistent and deeply felt questions. Answers can also get in the way. Once we're convinced that we have the "right" answer, it's easy to stop looking for more answers. We then stop learning. Our range of possible actions becomes limited.

Instead of latching on to one answer, we can look for more. Instead of being content with the first or easiest options that come to mind, we can keep searching. Even when we're convinced that we've finally handled a problem, we can brainstorm until we find five more solutions.

When we keep looking for answers, we uncover fresh possibilities for thinking, feeling, and behaving. Like children learning to walk, we experience the joy of discovery.

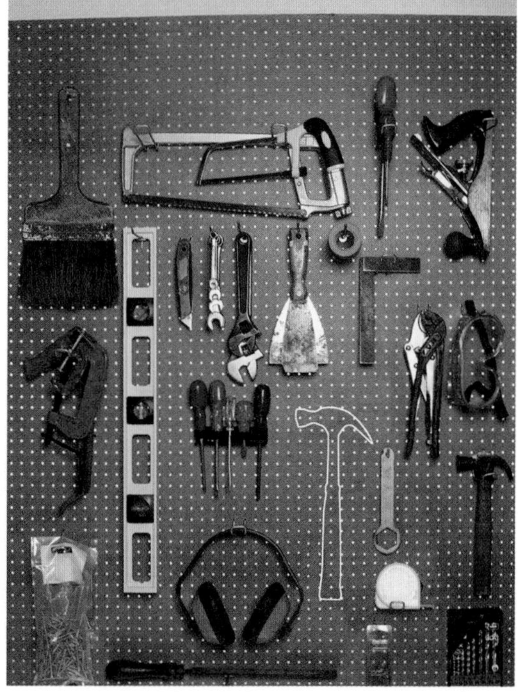

This book is not a manifesto. It's a toolbox, and tools are meant to be used.

A caution

A word of caution: Any tool—whether it's a hammer, a computer program, or a study technique—is designed to do a specific job. A master mechanic carries a variety of tools because no single tool works for all jobs. If you throw a tool away because it doesn't work in one situation, you won't be able to pull it out later when it's just what you need. So if an idea doesn't work for you and you are satisfied that you gave it a fair chance, don't throw it away. File it away instead. The idea might come in handy sooner than you think.

And remember, this book is not about figuring out the "right" way. Even the "ideas are tools" approach is not "right."

It's a hammer . . . (or maybe a saw).

career application

Shortly after graduating with an A.A. degree in Business Administration, Sylvia Lopez was thrilled to land a job as a staff accountant at a market research firm. After one week, she wanted to quit. She didn't think she would ever learn to deal with her coworkers. Their personalities just seemed too different.

For example, there was the account coordinator, Ed Washington. He spent hours a day on the phone calling prospective customers who responded to the corporate Website. Since Ed's office door was always open and he had a loud voice, people inevitably overheard his calls. It seemed to Sylvia that he spent a lot of time socializing with clients—asking about their hobbies and family lives. Even though Ed was regarded as a skilled salesperson, Sylvia wondered when he actually got any work done.

Sylvia also felt uncomfortable with Linda Martinez, the firm's accounting analyst and her direct supervisor. Linda kept her office door closed most of the time. In contrast to Ed, Linda hardly ever stopped to chat informally. Instead of taking lunch breaks, she typically packed a bag lunch and ate it while checking e-mail or updating the company databases. Linda had a reputation as a top-notch employee. Yet the only time people saw her was at scheduled staff meetings. Linda led those meetings and distributed a detailed agenda in advance. And while Ed was on a first-name basis with everyone in the office, Linda made it clear that she wished to be addressed as "Ms. Martinez."

After worrying for several days about how to deal with the differences among her coworkers, Sylvia scheduled times to meet with Ed and Linda individually about her concerns. Before each meeting, she carefully prepared her opening remarks, writing them out beforehand. For Ed, her notes included this comment: "Since I'm new on the job and feel pressed for time, I'd like to get your help in making the most efficient use of our meeting time." And for Linda she wrote: "I'd like to make sure my performance is up to par. Is there any way I can get regular feedback from you about how I'm doing?" ☒

Reflecting on this scenario

1. List two useful skills that Sylvia demonstrates in this scenario.

____

____

____

2. List another skill that would be useful to Sylvia in this situation. Explain why you chose this skill.

____

____

____

3. List two strategies from this chapter that would be useful to Sylvia in this situation. Briefly describe how she could apply each one.

____

____

____

Name ______________________________________ Date _____/_____/_____

quiz

1. Explain three ways that you can apply your knowledge of your learning styles.

2. Define the term *mastery* as it is used in this chapter.

3. The First Step technique refers only to telling the truth about your areas for improvement. True or False? Explain your answer.

4. The four modes of learning are associated with certain questions. List the appropriate question for each mode.

5. According to the text, motivation is mysterious and hard to develop. True or False? Explain your answer.

6. According to the text, thinking of ourselves as creatures of habit can actually empower us. True or False? Explain your answer.

7. Take the following statement and rewrite it as a more effective First Step: "I am terrible at managing money."

8. According to the Power Process: "Ideas are tools," if you want the ideas in this book to work, you must believe in them. True or False? Explain your answer.

9. Briefly describe the difference between active experimentation and reflective observation as ways of processing information.

10. List two strategies that you can use to enhance kinesthetic learning.

learning styles application

Even though you have preferred ways to learn new ideas or skills, you can benefit from using several learning styles. The questions below will "cycle" you through four styles, or modes, of learning as explained earlier in this chapter. (See "Learning styles: Discovering how you learn.") Each question will help you explore a different mode.

Remember that you do not have to start with *Why?* of Mode 1. Any of the four questions can serve as your point of entry into the cycle of learning.

Look for a similar Learning Styles Application at the end of every chapter in this book. Also notice that the first page of each chapter includes a preview based on the four questions that represent the four modes of learning: *Why? What? How?* and *What if?*

why *Think about why the subject of transitions matters to you. Describe a major transition that you have experienced in the past. Examples might include changing schools, moving to a new city, starting a job, or going to college. In a sentence or two, describe what you did to cope with this change in your life.*

what *Review this chapter and the Introduction, looking for ideas that could help you make a major transition in your life. List two or three suggestions, stating each one in a short sentence.*

how *In a short paragraph, explain how you can use one suggestion from this book to master a future transition that you will experience in education. Examples include declaring a major, changing majors, or transferring to a new school.*

what if *Review this chapter and the Introduction, looking for ideas that could help you make the transition from being in school to working in your next career. List two or three suggestions, stating each one in a short sentence.*

master student profile

JERRY YANG

(1968–) Founder and CEO of Yahoo!

In 1994, David Filo and Jerry Yang were in typical start-up mode—working 20 hours a day, sleeping in the office, juiced on the idea that people were discovering their concept and plugging in. There was only one difference between them and most new entrepreneurs: They weren't making any money. We're not talking about an absence of profitability. We're talking about an absence of revenue. There were no sales. None. And, the fact is, the Yahoo! founders didn't care. Filo and Yang were working like maniacs for the sheer joy of it.

Their mission? Bringing order to the terrible, tangled World Wide Web. Back then—in the pre-history of the Internet—plenty of interesting Websites existed. But the forum wasn't organized; there was no system that enabled people to find the sites they wanted in an easy, orderly way . . .

. . . By 1995, the service had become so popular, the partners were able to raise $1 million in venture capital to expand the business. There was no trail to follow, however; back then, Internet commerce was still in its infancy. But the partners knew they had a tiger by the tail. "What we did took 20 hours a day," says Yang, 29. "But we were one of the first to [try to organize the Web], and we did it better than anyone."

Yang, born in Taiwan and raised in San Jose, California, was named Chief Executive Officer of Yahoo! on

June 18, 2007. Yang reflected on his vision and the future of the company on Yahoo's! blog, Yodel Anecdotal ™:

The title of Chief Yahoo takes on new meaning today. I have the great honor of stepping into the role of Yahoo!'s Chief Executive Officer. Yahoo! has an incredibly bright future and I make this move with deep conviction and enthusiasm. I've partnered closely with our executive teams for 12 years to steer our strategy and direction and today I'm ready for this challenge.

What is [my] vision? A Yahoo! that executes with speed, clarity and discipline. A Yahoo! that increases its focus on differentiating its products and investing in creativity and innovation. A Yahoo! that better monetizes its audience. A Yahoo! whose great talent is galvanized to address its challenges. And a Yahoo! that is better focused on what's important to its users, customers, and employees.

. . . We have incredible assets. This company has massive potential, drive, determination and skills, and we won't be satisfied until the external perception of Yahoo! accurately reflects that reality.

I have absolute conviction about Yahoo!'s potential for long-term success as an Internet leader. Yahoo! is a company that started with a vision and a dream and, make no mistake, that dream is very much alive. I'm committed to doing whatever it takes to transform Yahoo! into an even greater success in the future.

The time for me is right. The time is now. The Internet is still young, the opportunities ahead are tremendous, and I'm ready to rally our nearly 12,000 Yahoos around the world to help seize them.

For more biographical information about Jerry Yang, visit the Master Student Hall of Fame on the *From Master Student to Master Employee* Website.

2 Discovering Careers

MASTER STUDENT MAP

why this chapter matters . . .

By learning about the job market and discovering your skills, you can plan to channel your passions into a successful career.

how you can use this chapter . . .

Expand your career options.
Find your place in the world of work through concrete experiences— informational interviews, internships, and more.
Choose a career that aligns with your interests, skills, and values.
Create a career plan.

As you read, ask yourself what if . . .

I could create the career of my dreams—starting today?

what is included . . .

FROM THE DESK OF . . .

While the courses were important, and many apply to "technical" skills that I use every day (i.e., data analysis), the personal/social aspects of my college career were perhaps more important. It's through those aspects that I learned about time management, prioritization, project management, and people management skills.

—ANDY FISHER, EXECUTIVE MARKETING MANAGER

Choosing who you want to be

When people ask about your choice of career, they often pose this question: What do you want to be?

One response is to name a job. "I want to be a computer technician." "I want to be a recording engineer." "I want to be a chef." These answers really suggest what we want to *do.*

Another response is to describe a certain income level or lifestyle. "I want to be rich, with all the free time in the world." "I want to sell all my belongings, move to Hawaii, and live on the beach." These statements are actually about what we'd like to *have.*

Yet another option is to describe what you want your life to stand for—the kind of person you want to become. You could talk about being trustworthy, fun-loving, compassionate, creative, honest, productive, and accountable. These are just a few examples of the core values you can bring to any job or lifestyle that you choose.

Career planning does not begin with grinding out résumés, churning out cover letters, poring over want ads, saving for an MBA, or completing a 100-question vocation interest assessment. Any of those steps can become important or even essential—later. And they can be useless until you take time to exercise your imagination and consider what you want most of all. Career planning starts with dreaming about who you want to *be.*

Dreaming makes sense in a hard-nosed, practical way. Consider people who change careers in midlife. Many of these people have been in the work force for several decades. They've raised families, received promotions, acquired possessions. They've spent a lifetime being "practical." These people are looking for more than just another job. They want a career that pays the bills *and* excites their passions.

There's no need to wait 10, 20, or 30 years to discover your passions. You can start now by reading and completing the exercises in this chapter.

Bring up the subject of career planning and someone might say, "Well, just remember that even if you hate your job, you can always do what you want in your free time." Consider that *all* your time is free time. You give your time freely to your employers or clients, and you do this for your own purposes. All of us are "self-employed," even if we work full-time for someone else.

Through the ideas and activities included in this chapter, you can translate your dreams for the future into plans to develop specific skills. These are the core elements of any career. Skills are the essence of what you "sell" to any employer. Start thinking about them now. Once you discover the skills that you want to use, your career choices can fall into place like magic.[1]

journal entry 6

Discovery/Intention Statement

Recall a time when you felt powerful, competent, and fulfilled. Examples might include writing a paper when the words flowed effortlessly, skillfully leading a bar mitzvah service, or working in a restaurant and creating a new dish that won rave reviews. Mentally re-create this experience and the feelings that came with it.

Now, reflect on this experience. Briefly describe the skills that you were using at that moment, the values you were demonstrating, or both.

I discovered that I . . .

____

____

Next, review what you just wrote for an intention that can guide your overall career plan. For example, you might write, "I intend, no matter what job I have, to be an effective leader." Or "I intend to create a career that gives free expression to my creativity."

I intend to . . .

____

____

Now scan this chapter for ideas that can help you act on your intention. List at least four ideas here, along with the page numbers where you can read more about them.

Strategy	*Page number*

Our society offers a limitless array of careers. You no longer have to confine yourself to a handful of traditional categories, such as business, education, government, or manufacturing.

You've got a world of choices

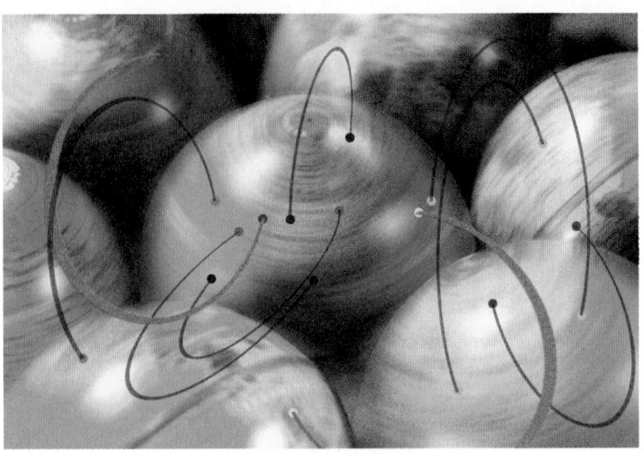

People are constantly creating new products and services to meet emerging demands. The number of job titles is expanding so rapidly that we can barely track them. And some of them lead to careers outside the 9-to-5 office setting.

For instance, there are people who work as *ritual consultants*, helping people to plan weddings, anniversaries, graduations, and other ceremonies.

Space planners help individuals and organizations to arrange furniture and equipment efficiently.

Auto brokers visit dealers, shop around, and buy a car for you.

Professional organizers walk into your home or office and coach you on managing time and paperwork.

Pet psychologists help you raise a happy and healthy animal.

Life coaches assist you in setting and achieving goals related to your career or anything else. Some coaches specialize in working with executives, a form of self-employment that can lead to a six-figure annual income.

Court reporters can use their skills for lucrative gigs outside the courtroom, including real-time captioning for television shows and Webcasts.

If you're a self-employed graphic designer, an *artists' representative* can help you find well-paying work. And if you're in the mood for climbing a mountain or two, an *adventure tour guide* will lead the way.

The global marketplace creates even more options for you. Through Internet connections and communication satellites that bounce phone calls around the planet, you can exchange messages with almost anyone, anywhere. Your customers or clients could be located in Colorado or China, Pennsylvania or Panama. You can track packages worldwide in real time and stay on top of investment opportunities as they emerge. Your skills in thinking globally could help you create a new product or service for a new market—and perhaps a career that does not even exist today.

In addition to choosing the *content* of your career, you have many options for integrating work into the context of your life. You can work full-time. You can work part-time. You can commute to a cubicle in a major corporation. Or you can work at home and take the one-minute commute from your bedroom to your desk. You can join a thriving business—or create one of your own.

If the idea of self-employment seems far-fetched, consider that as a student you already *are* self-employed. You are setting your own goals, structuring your time, making your own financial decisions, and monitoring your performance. These are all transferable skills that you can use to become your own boss.

Reading this chapter and completing its exercises and Journal Entries will help you start gathering information on possible careers. Just remember that there is no reason to limit your choices too soon. You've got the world to choose from.[2] ⊠

The world of work—an overview

Perhaps the most comprehensive guide to the work world is the O*NET Online system. O*NET stands for Occupational Information Network, and it includes a series of Websites posted by the U.S. Department of Labor.

O*NET classifies American workers into 22 categories of occupations outside the military. Those categories are listed below, along with a few examples of the many careers included in each category. Go online to **http://online.onetcenter.org/find/** for more information. Also check out O*NET's companion Websites for career planning at **http://online.onetcenter.org/**.

Architecture and engineering

Aerospace engineers
Architects, including landscape and naval architects
Biomedical engineers
Chemical engineers
Civil drafters
Computer hardware engineers
Mechanical engineers

Arts, design, entertainment, sports, and media

Advertising copywriters
Art directors
Athletes
Commercial and industrial designers
Commercial artists
Painters and sculptors
Writers and editors

Building and grounds cleaning and maintenance

Managers of housekeepers and janitorial workers
Managers of landscaping, lawn service, and groundskeeping workers

Business and financial operations

Accountants
Agents for artists, performers, and athletes
Auditors
Budget and financial analysts
Claims adjusters and examiners
Loan officers and counselors
Meeting and convention planners

Community and social services

Clergy
Health educators
Mental health counselors
Probation officers
Social workers
Substance abuse counselors
Therapists

Computer and mathematical

Actuaries
Computer programmers
Computer security specialists
Computer systems analysts
Operations research analysts
Software engineers
Statisticians

Construction and extraction

Construction and building inspectors
Hazardous materials removal workers
Managers of construction trades and extraction workers

Education, training, and library

Adult education and remedial education instructors
Archivists
Curators
GED teachers and instructors
Librarians
Museum conservators
Teachers

Farming, fishing, and forestry

Agricultural inspectors
Managers of agricultural crop and horticultural workers
Managers of animal care workers

Food preparation and serving-related

Chefs and head cooks
Cooks, institution and cafeteria
Managers of food preparation and serving workers

Health care practitioners and technical
Anesthesiologists
Chiropractors
Dental hygienists
Medical assistants
Physical therapists
Physicians
Surgeons

Health care support
Dental assistants
Medical transcriptionists
Occupational therapist assistants

Installation, maintenance, and repair
Aircraft mechanics
Automotive master mechanics
Avionics technicians
Electrical and electronics repairers
Industrial machinery mechanics
Millwrights
Mobile heavy equipment mechanics

Legal
Administrative law judges
Arbitrators, mediators, and conciliators
Court reporters
Judges and magistrates
Lawyers
Paralegals and legal assistants
Title examiners, abstractors, and searchers

Life, physical, and social science
Agricultural technicians
Biophysicists
Chemists
Epidemiologists
Food science technicians
Market research analysts
Urban and regional planners

Management
Advertising and promotions managers
Chief executives
Computer and information systems managers
Construction managers
Engineering managers
Financial managers
Sales managers

Office and administrative support
Executive secretaries
Legal secretaries
Medical secretaries

Personal care and service
Fitness trainers and aerobics instructors
Flight attendants
Gaming supervisors

Production
Aircraft structure and systems assemblers
Dental laboratory technicians
Managers of production and operating workers

Protective service
Criminal investigators, detectives, and special agents
Firefighters
Fire inspectors
Immigrations and customs inspectors
Police officers
Sheriffs
Transit and railroad police

Sales and related
Advertising sales agents
Insurance sales agents
Models
Real estate brokers
Sales representatives

Transportation and material moving
Air traffic controllers
Ambulance drivers and attendants
Aviation inspectors
Commercial pilots
Flight engineers
Ship pilots
Transportation vehicle, equipment, and systems inspectors

It all starts with *skills*

When meeting with an academic advisor, some students say, "I've just been taking general education courses," "I just have a liberal arts major," or "I haven't got any marketable skills."

Think again.

Few words are as widely misunderstood as *skill.* Defining it carefully can have an immediate and positive impact on your career planning.

Two kinds of skills

One dictionary defines *skill* as "the ability to do something well, usually gained by training or experience."

Some skills—such as the ability to repair fiber-optic cables or do brain surgery—are acquired through formal schooling, on-the-job training, or both. These abilities are called *work-content skills.* People with such skills have mastered a specialized body of knowledge needed to do a specific kind of work.

However, we develop another category of skills through experiences both inside and outside the classroom. We may never receive formal training to develop these abilities. Yet they are key to success in the workplace. These are *transferable skills.* Transferable skills are the kind of abilities that help people thrive in any job—no matter what work-content skills they have. Perhaps you've heard someone described this way: "She's really smart and knows what she's doing, but she's got lousy people skills." People skills—such as *listening* and *negotiating*—are prime examples of transferable skills.

Succeeding in many situations

Transferable skills are often invisible to us. The problem begins when we assume that a given skill can be used in only one context, such as being in school or working at a particular job. Thinking in this way places an artificial limit on our possibilities.

As an alternative, think about the things you routinely do to succeed in school. Analyze your activities to isolate specific skills. Then brainstorm a list of jobs where you can use the same skills.

Consider the task of writing a research paper. This calls for skills such as the following:

- *Planning*—setting goals for completing your outline, first draft, second draft, and final draft.
- *Managing time* to meet your writing goals.
- *Interviewing* people who know a lot about the topic of your paper.
- *Researching* on the Internet and in the campus library to discover key facts and ideas to include in your paper.
- *Writing* to present those facts and ideas in an original way.
- *Editing* your drafts for clarity and correctness.

Now consider the kinds of jobs that draw on these skills. For example, you could transfer your skill at writing papers to a possible career in journalism, technical writing, or advertising copywriting. You could use your editing skills to work in the field of publishing as a magazine or book editor. Interviewing and research skills could help you enter the field of market research. And the abilities to plan, manage time, and meet deadlines will help you succeed in all the jobs mentioned so far.

Use the same kind of analysis to think about transferring skills from one job to another. Say that you work part-time as an administrative assistant at a computer dealer that sells a variety of hardware and software. You take phone calls from potential customers, help current customers solve problems using their computers, and attend meetings where your coworkers plan ways to market new products. You are developing skills at *selling, serving customers,* and *working on teams* that could help you land a job as a sales representative for a computer manufacturer or software developer.

The basic idea is to take a cue from the word *transferable.* Almost any skill you use to succeed in one situation can *transfer* to success in another situation.

The concept of transferable skills creates a powerful link between higher education and the work world. While taking any course, list the specific skills you are developing and how you can transfer them to the work world. Almost everything you do in school can be applied to your career—if you consistently pursue this line of thought.

Ask four questions

To experiment further with this concept of transferable skills, ask and answer four questions derived from the Master Student Map.

Why *identify my transferable skills?* Getting past the "I-don't-have-any-skills" syndrome means that you can approach job hunting with more confidence. As you uncover these hidden assets, your list of qualifications will grow as if by magic. You won't be padding your résumé. You'll simply be using action words to tell the full truth about what you can do.

Identifying your transferable skills takes a little time. And the payoffs are numerous. A complete and accurate list of transferable skills can help you land jobs that involve more responsibility, more variety, more freedom to structure your time, and more money.

Transferable skills also help you thrive in the midst of constant change. Technology will continue to upgrade. Ongoing discoveries in many fields could render current knowledge obsolete. Jobs that exist today may disappear in a few years, to be replaced by entirely new ones. Your keys to prospering in this environment are transferable skills—those that you can carry from one career to another.

What *are my transferable skills?* Discover your transferable skills by reflecting on key experiences. Recall a time when you performed at the peak of your ability, overcame obstacles, won an award, gained a high grade, or met a significant goal. List the skills you used to create those successes.

In each case, remember that the word *skill* applies to something that you *do*. In your list of transferable skills, start each item with an action verb such as *budget* or *coach* or *consult*. Or use a closely related part of speech—*budgeting* or *coaching*.

For a more complete picture of your transferable skills, describe the object of your action. For instance, if one of the skills on your list is *organizing*, this action verb could refer to organizing ideas, organizing people, or organizing objects in a room. Specify the kind of organizing that you like to do.

How *do I perform these skills?* You can bring your transferable skills into even sharper focus by adding adverbs—words that describe *how* you take action. You might say that you edit *accurately* or learn *quickly*. These words can point out personal traits that employers treasure.

In summary, you can use a three-column chart to list your transferable skills. For example:

Verb	Object	Adverb
Organizing	Records	Effectively
Serving	Customers	Courteously
Coordinating	Special events	Efficiently
Meeting	Goals	Reliably

Add a specific example of each skill to your list, and you're well on the way to an engaging résumé and a winning job interview.

As you list your transferable skills, focus on the skills that you enjoy using the most. Then look for careers and jobs that directly involve those skills.

What if *I could expand my transferable skills?* In addition to thinking about the skills you already have, consider the skills you'd like to acquire. Describe them in detail and list experiences that can help you develop them. Possibilities include extracurricular activities, group memberships, internships, volunteer positions, work-study assignments, and other part-time jobs. As you read this book, pay attention to articles that highlight the transferable skills you can build in the classroom and in your current job. Let your list of transferable skills grow and develop as you do.

What employers want

Transferable skills top the list of personal qualities that are most valued by employers. According to the Job Outlook 2007 survey conducted by the National Association of Colleges and Employers, the top 10 skills that employers seek are[3]:

- Communication skills (verbal and written)
- Honesty and integrity
- Interpersonal skills
- Motivation and initiative
- Strong work ethic
- Teamwork skills
- Computer skills
- Analytical skills
- Flexibility and adaptability
- Attention to detail

100 transferable skills

There are literally hundreds of transferable skills. The following list offers 100 examples. Use this list as a tool to jog your thinking when you take an inventory of *your* transferable skills.

For more information on transferable skills, see the reports produced by the Secretary's Commission on Achieving Necessary Skills (SCANS). These are available online at **http://wdr.doleta.gov/SCANS/**.

While you're on the computer, also check out Skills Search, part of the Occupational Information Network (O*NET Online) at **http://online.onetcenter.org/skills/#group4.** There, you'll find tools for discovering your skills and matching them to specific occupations.

Self-discovery skills

Assessing your current knowledge and skills
Choosing and applying learning strategies
Selecting strategies to acquire new knowledge and skills
Showing flexibility by adopting new attitudes and behaviors

For more information on self-discovery skills, see Chapter One.

Career planning skills

Discovering career-related values and interests
Discovering content and transferable skills
Discovering options for possible careers
Setting goals
Updating career goals to reflect new insights and work experience

For more information about career planning skills, keep reading this chapter.

Time-management skills

Choosing materials and facilities needed to meet goals
Choosing technology and applying it to goal-related tasks
Delivering projects and outcomes on schedule
Designing other processes, procedures, or systems to meet goals
Managing multiple projects at the same time
Monitoring progress toward goals
Persisting in order to meet goals
Planning projects for teams
Planning special events
Scheduling due dates for project outcomes
Scheduling time for goal-related tasks
Working independently to meet goals

For more information about time-management skills, see Chapter Three.

Reading skills

Reading for detail
Reading for key ideas and major themes
Reading to discover strategies for solving problems or meeting goals
Reading to follow instructions
Reading to synthesize ideas and information from several sources

For more information about reading skills, see Chapter Four.

Note-taking skills

Creating pictures, graphs, and other visuals to summarize and clarify information
Gathering data through field research or working with primary sources
Organizing information and ideas in digital and paper-based forms
Researching by finding information online or in the library
Taking notes on material presented verbally, in print, or online

For more information about note-taking skills, see Chapter Five.

Test-taking and related skills

Applying scientific findings and methods to solve problems
Assessing personal performance at school or at work
Managing stress
Using mathematics to do basic computations and solve problems

Using test results and other assessments to improve performance
Working cooperatively in study groups and project teams

For more information about skills related to test taking, see Chapter Six.

Thinking skills

Choosing and implementing solutions
Choosing appropriate strategies for making decisions
Choosing ethical behaviors
Diagnosing the sources of problems
Evaluating material presented verbally, in print, or online
Evaluating products, services, or programs
Generating possible solutions to problems
Interpreting information needed for problem solving or decision making
Stating problems accurately
Thinking to create new ideas, products, or services
Thinking to evaluate ideas, products, or services
Weighing the benefits and costs of potential solutions

For more information about thinking skills, see Chapter Seven.

Communication skills

Assigning and delegating tasks
Coaching
Consulting
Counseling
Demonstrating empathy
Editing publications
Entertaining people
Giving people feedback about the quality of their performance
Interpreting and responding to nonverbal messages
Interviewing people for assessment purposes (such as performance reviews)
Interviewing people for hiring purposes
Leading meetings
Leading project teams
Listening fully (without judgment or distraction)
Managing relationships with vendors or suppliers
Meeting the public
Negotiating settlements
Preventing conflicts (defusing a tense situation)
Researching by conducting focus groups
Researching by conducting interviews
Resolving conflicts
Responding to complaints
Responding to requests
Selling products, programs, or services
Serving clients and customers
Speaking to clearly explain ideas, information, or procedures
Speaking to diverse audiences
Speaking to persuade people to adopt policies or take action
Supervising people while they perform assigned tasks
Teaching
Training
Tutoring
Working with difficult people
Working with the press
Writing instructional materials
Writing sales, marketing, or promotional materials
Writing to persuade
Writing to summarize or explain

For more information about communication skills, see Chapter Eight.

Money skills

Decreasing expenses
Estimating costs
Monitoring income and expenses
Preparing budgets
Raising funds

For more information about money skills, see Chapter Nine.

Skills for adapting to work environments

Answering job interview questions
Finding and working with a mentor
Finding potential employers or clients
Networking with contacts to discover job openings
Understanding the culture of an organization and working within it
Using a computer for common tasks (managing money, maintaining records, sending and receiving messages, creating documents, and posting information online)
Working well with people from a variety of backgrounds

For more information about workplace adaptation skills, see Chapter Ten.

INVENTORY YOUR SKILLS

This exercise is about discovering the full range of your skills. Before you begin, gather at least 100 3 × 5 cards and a pen or pencil. Allow about one hour for this exploration. Warning: The results may be personally empowering!

Step 1

Think back over your activities during the past month. See if you can remember every activity during which you demonstrated *any* skill. The idea behind this exercise is to list as many such activities as possible.

Write down these many activities, listing each one on a *separate* 3 × 5 card. Some of your cards might read "cooked meals," "tuned up my car," or "weeded a garden."

Spend 10 minutes on this step.

Step 2

Now spend another 10 minutes reflecting on your school activities. Focus especially on those that involved some extra effort on your part. Examples might include:

- Class presentations or speeches
- Independent study, theses, or capstone projects
- Teaching or research assistantships
- Tutoring or mentoring assignments
- Work on a student newspaper, radio station, or Website
- Student government activities

Again, describe any such activities in a word or short phrase. List each one on a 3 × 5 card.

Step 3

Your next step is to spend another 10 minutes reviewing work experiences, both paid and unpaid. Start by listing as many major job activities as you can recall. Remember to include internships and volunteer work.

Step 4

This step is for any skill-developing activities that haven't occurred to you so far. Keep brainstorming and filling up cards!

Have you planned special trips or vacations? Write those down.

Have you published anything—a recipe, letter to the editor, newsletter article, family history, blog, or Website? List those also.

Also create cards for:

- Hobbies
- Special licenses or credentials
- Continuing education credits
- Workshops, conferences, seminars, and training experiences
- Membership in Girl Scouts, Boy Scouts, or related groups
- Activities for your church, synagogue, mosque, meditation community, or other spiritual group

Step 5

For the next few minutes, take a well-deserved break. Then quickly scan all the cards you just created. Then take another 10 minutes to list any specialized knowledge or procedures needed to complete those activities.

For example, tutoring a French class requires a working knowledge of that language. Tuning up a car requires knowing how to adjust a car's timing and replace spark plugs. You could list several such skills for any one activity.

These are your *content skills*. Write each one on a separate card and label it "Content."

Step 6

Go over your activity cards one more time. Look for examples of *transferable skills*. For instance, giving a speech or working as a salesperson in a computer store requires the ability to persuade people. That's a transferable skill. Tuning up a car means that you can attend to details and troubleshoot. Tutoring in French requires teaching, listening, and speaking skills.

Write each of your transferable skills on a separate card and label each card "Transferable."

Step 7

Congratulations—you now have a detailed picture of your content and transferable skills. The work you've just done will pay off every time that you revise your résumé, prepare for job interviews, and complete other career-planning and job-hunting tasks.

USE INFORMAL WAYS TO DISCOVER YOURSELF

During career planning, take time to explore your interests in an informal and playful way. The results can be revealing and useful.

Answer the following questions by writing the first ideas that come to mind. Use additional paper as needed or create a computer file for your writing. Have fun and stay open to new insights.

Imagine that you're at a party and you're having a fascinating conversation with someone you just met. What does this person do for a living? What is your conversation about?

What do you enjoy doing most with your unscheduled time? List any hobby or other activity that you do not currently define as "work."

Think about the kinds of books, newspaper and magazine articles, and television shows that are most likely to capture your attention. What subjects or situations do they involve?

If you bookmark Websites in your Internet browser, review that list. What interests does it reveal?

What kinds of problems do you most enjoy solving—those that involve ideas, people, or products? Give an example.

Finally, reread your answers to the above questions. List three to five interests that are critical to your choice of career.

Ways to learn about careers

To discover the full range of jobs that exist in our society, you can turn to many sources. These include friends, family members, teachers, classmates, coworkers—and anyone else who's ever held a job. Also check out the following sources of career information. They can lead you to more.

Publications. Visit the career planning and job-hunting sections in bookstores and libraries. Look for books, magazines, videos, and other nonprint materials related to career planning. Libraries may subscribe to trade journals and industry newsletters.

Career counseling. Your school may offer career counseling as well as links to similar services in the off-campus community. Private consultants and companies offer career counseling for a fee. Ask around to find someone who's seen a career counselor and get some recommendations.

Before you pay for career counseling, find out exactly what kind of help you'll get and how much it will cost. Read contracts carefully before you sign. Talk directly to a career counselor rather than a salesperson, and see if you can get permission to contact some of the counselor's former clients.

Group sessions led by career counselors are valuable because you get to hear about the problems that other people are facing and work together to create solutions.

The Internet. Through your own searching and suggestions from others, you can find useful Websites devoted to job hunting and career planning. One place to start is JobHuntersBible.com, which includes links to sites screened by Richard Bolles, author of *What Color Is Your Parachute?* It's online at **http://www.jobhuntersbible.com.** Bolles organizes this site around five ways that the Internet can be used in career planning and job hunting:

- To search for job openings posted online
- To post your résumé online
- To get career counseling, assess your skills, and find job-hunting tips
- To research potential careers and places that you might like to work
- To make contacts with people who can provide information or help you get a job interview

Also visit the Occupational Information Network (O*NET) site posted by the U.S. Department of Labor at **http://online.onetcenter.org.** Here you'll find information on hundreds of jobs that you can search by using keywords or browsing a complete list. You'll also find Skills Search, an online tool that helps you list your skills and then matches the list with potential jobs.

Another site that may interest you is CareerOneStop at **http://www.careeronestop.org.** It includes America's Job Bank (where you can search job openings and post your résumé), America's Career InfoNet (information on wages and employment trends), and America's Service

Locator (a way to find career-planning and job-hunting services in your local area).

The Riley Guide at **http://www.rileyguide.com/** is one of the most comprehensive guides to careers and job hunting on the Internet. It's been around since 1994 and includes hundreds of pages. Besides career information, you'll find suggestions for using the Internet to full advantage while career planning and job hunting.

Job-Hunt at **http://www.job-hunt.org/** shows up on several lists of top sites for finding work. Included are over 6,000 links to career-planning and job-hunting resources in all 50 states.

Also look at CollegeGrad.com at **http://www.collegegrad.com/.** This site specializes in information about entry-level jobs and internships.

Of course, your searching may turn up hundreds of other sites. Evaluate them carefully.

Organizations. Professional associations exist for people in almost any career—from the American Institute of Certified Public Accountants to the American Association of Zookeepers. One function of these associations is to publicize career options and job openings of interest to their members. Search the Internet with the keywords *professional associations* and follow the links that interest you. Consider joining organizations that interest you. Many offer student rates.

Government agencies at all levels—from local employment agencies to the U.S. Department of Labor—can assist you with learning about the world of work. Search the government listings in your local Yellow Pages under *employment* and *job placement.*

Trade unions, chambers of commerce, and branches of the armed forces are additional sources of information.

Working people. Remember that career publications and job-hunting guides may not reflect the constantly evolving careers generated by our economy. Also, several job titles can apply to a core set of skills. For instance, people with journalism skills who work in corporate settings might be called *information officers, publicists,* and *public relations specialists.*

One powerful way to sort through all this information is to seek out people working in the careers that interest you. Working people can update you on the latest terminology and trends in their field.

Elected representatives. One duty of your congressional representatives, senators, city council members, and school board members is to help create a thriving work force. Contact these people for career-planning and job-hunting services in your community.[4]

critical thinking exercise 8

DIG OUT THE "LIFE STORY" OF A PRODUCT

All the goods and services in our society result from work done by people. Pondering this fact may give you new possibilities for career planning.

For example, pick up any object near the place where you sit or stand right now—perhaps a computer, notebook, pen, pencil, CD, DVD, or piece of clothing. If possible, choose something that holds a special interest for you.

Next, reflect for a moment on the path that this product took from its creator into your hands. See if you can list the job title of every person who helped to plan, produce, distribute, and sell this item. If you're not sure, just brainstorm answers. After doing this exercise, you can do some research to confirm your answers.

Create your list of job titles in the space below.

____

____

____

____

Finally, scan this list for any jobs that interest you. To find out more about them, use the resources listed in the article "Ways to learn about careers."

As you do this exercise, think creatively and keep your options open. You might think of titles for jobs that don't exist yet. Instead of tossing out these ideas, consider them as starting points in creating an entirely new career for yourself.[5]

When you clearly define both your career goal and path to reaching that goal, you can plan your education effectively.

Create your career

After leaving higher education and before retiring, you may spend at least 100,000 hours working. That might be more time than you'll spend at anything else that matters to you, including your family, friends, and hobbies. From this perspective, the stakes of your career choice are enormous.

Career planning is an adventure that involves continuous exploration. There are dozens of effective ways to plan your career. You can begin your career-planning adventure now by remembering the following ideas.

Acknowledge what you already know

Realize that you've already made many decisions about your career. This is true for young people who say, "I don't have any idea what I want to be when I grow up." It's also true for midlife career changers.

Consider the student who can't decide if he wants to be a cost accountant or a tax accountant and then jumps to the conclusion that he is totally lost when it comes to career planning. He's already narrowed his list of career choices to a number of jobs in the same field—jobs that draw on the same core skills.

This might be true for you as well. Go to any comprehensive directory of careers, such as the Find Occupations Website at **http://online.onetcenter.org/find/**, where you can browse occupations that are categorized by "Job Family." Notice how many of these careers do *not* interest you. This reveals that you've already made many choices about what to be when you "grow up."

See your career as your creation

Many people approach career planning as if they were panning for gold. They keep sifting through the dirt, clearing the dust, and throwing out the rocks. They are hoping to strike it rich and discover the perfect career.

Other people believe that they'll wake up one morning, see the heavens part, and suddenly know what they're supposed to do. Many of them are still waiting for that magical day to dawn.

We can approach career planning in a different way. Instead of seeing a career as something we discover, we can see it as something we choose. We don't find the right career. We create it.

Viewing your career as your creation helps you relax. Instead of anguishing over finding the right career, you can stay open to possibilities. You can choose one career today, knowing that you can choose again later.

Suppose that you've narrowed your list of possible careers to five, and you still can't decide. Then just choose one. Any one. You might have several careers during your lifetime. You might be able to do any one of these careers next. The important thing is to choose.

One caution is in order. Choosing your career is not something to do in an information vacuum. Rather, choose after you've done a lot of research. That includes research into yourself—your skills and interests—and a thorough knowledge of what careers are available.

In your career plan, also leave room for the unexpected. A chance encounter during a vacation or an idle conversation in a coffee shop might trigger life-changing insights or lead you to people you want to work with for the rest of your life.

Plan by naming names

One key to making your career plan real and to ensuring that you can act on it is naming. When you create your career plan, see that you include specific names whenever they're called for:

- *Name your job.* Take the skills you enjoy using and find out which jobs use them. What are those jobs called? List them. Note that the same job might have different names.

- *Name your company—the agency or organization you want to work for.* If you want to be self-employed or start your own business, name the product or service you'd sell. Also list some possible names for your business. If you plan to work for others, name the organizations or agencies that are high on your list.
- *Name your contacts.* Take the list of organizations you just compiled. What people in these organizations are responsible for hiring? List those people and contact them directly. If you choose self-employment, list the names of possible customers or clients. All of these people are job contacts.

  Expand your list of contacts by brainstorming with your family and friends. Come up with a list of names—anyone who can help you with career planning and job hunting.

  Consider everyone you meet a potential member of your job network, and be prepared to talk about what you do. Develop a "pitch"—a short statement of your career goal that you can easily share with your contacts. For example: "After I graduate, I plan to work in the travel business. I'm looking for an internship in a travel agency for next summer. Do you know of any agencies that take interns?"
- *Name your location.* Ask if your career choices are consistent with your preferences about where to live and work. For example, someone who wants to make a living as a studio musician might consider living in a large city such as New York or Toronto. This contrasts with the freelance graphic artist who conducts his business mainly by phone, fax, and e-mail. He might be able to live anywhere and still pursue his career.

Remember your purpose

While digging deep into the details of career planning, take some time to back up to the big picture. Listing skills, researching jobs, writing résumés—all of this is necessary and useful. At the same time, attending to these tasks can obscure our broadest goals. To get perspective, we can go back to the basics—a life purpose.

Your deepest desire might be to see that hungry children are fed, to make sure that beautiful music keeps getting heard, or to help alcoholics become sober. When such a large purpose is clear, smaller decisions about what to do are often easier.

Test your career choice—and be willing to change

Read books about careers and search for career-planning Websites. Ask career counselors about skills assessments that can help you discover more about your skills and identify jobs that call for those skills. Take career-planning courses and workshops sponsored by your school. Visit the career-planning office on campus.

Once you have a possible career choice in mind, run some informal tests to see if it will work for you. For example:

- Contact people who are actually doing the job you're researching and ask them what it's like.
- Choose an internship or volunteer position in a field that interests you.
- Get a part-time or summer job in your career field.

The people you meet through these experiences are possible sources of recommendations, referrals, and employment in the future.[6]

critical thinking exercise 9

CREATE A SUPPORT TEAM

To fuel your energy for career planning, create your own support team.

Begin by listing the names of at least five people with whom you can share your frustrations and successes in career planning and job hunting. These can be friends, family members, coworkers, or classmates. Include each person's name, telephone number, and e-mail address. Begin your list in the space below.

From this list, recruit people to be on your support team. Tell each team member your goals and intended actions. Ask them to help in holding you accountable to your plan. Keep touching base with each member of your team and support them in return.

Keep adding to your support team. Post the most current list of members in a conspicuous place. Then use it.[7]

critical thinking exercise 10

BRAINSTORM CAREER OPTIONS

It's time to take some First Steps toward your career plan. Nothing too heavy or serious is required. Just be willing to dream and dwell in possibilities for a few minutes. In fact, be prepared to create some exciting and even outrageous ideas.

Remember that you can eventually refine these ideas and turn them into a practical plan for action. That step is important. And it will come later in this chapter.

Schedule an hour to do this exercise. If you can set aside even more time, you may get more interesting results. Feel free to take a break between steps or spread the exercise over several sessions. Use additional paper as needed to write your responses to each step.

Step 1: Imagine a wonderful life

In the space below, write a paragraph that describes an ideal day for you. Mentally remove your current limitations and let your imagination run free. What would you be doing right now if you had enough money to live on for the rest of your life and nothing scheduled on your calendar?

Describe one day from this perspective. Write in the present tense. Include some details about where you live, what you own, what you're doing, and the important people in your life. Above all, give yourself permission to create a compelling vision, and don't worry for now about how "practical" it is.

Step 2: Create a personal definition of success

Now reflect for a moment on how you define success. Many of the advertisements you see every day offer visions of what success means—fat bank accounts, big homes, luxury cars, great clothes, good looks, and friends who look like fashion models. However, these visions may have nothing to do with *your* definition of success. Complete the following sentence:

To me, success means . . .

Step 3: Look "back" on a successful career

Next, take a mental trip at least 10 years into the future. (If you can, extend that timeline even more, to 20 or 30 years from today.) After completing this amount of time in the work world, you are talking to a newspaper reporter who is writing a feature story about people who have successful careers.

Write a paragraph describing what you will tell this reporter about the highlights of your career. Include any awards, recognitions, major accomplishments, or special events that marked this period of your life.

Step 4: Describe your career in more detail

Fill in some more details about the career you just described. More specifically, describe two or three of your primary job activities, and write in the present tense.

Do you interact primarily with ideas and information, people, or pieces of technology? And what are the main results or outcomes of your work? Explain.

Also describe the conditions in which you work. Do you work primarily alone or with other people? Do you work at home or away from home? What does your office look like?

What do you value most about your work? Salary and benefits? Leadership roles? Opportunities for advancement? Tangible results? Working on teams? Working independently? Social contribution? These are just a few examples. List your core career values below.

Step 5: List the careers that interest you most

Congratulations for completing all the creative thinking you've been asked to do. There's just one more step to this exercise.

Find a long list of possible jobs or careers. (One source is the Occupational Information Network, published by the U.S. Department of Labor and available online at **http://online.onetcenter.org/find/**. A reference librarian can help you find other sources.

Spend five minutes scanning the list. Keeping in mind all the values and preferences you described in steps 1 to 4 of this exercise, list the five jobs or careers from the list that interest you most right now.[8]

Sample formats for **career plans**

Following are excerpts from career plans in several different formats. You can review these samples for useful ideas. Your career plan can combine any of these formats—and others that you create.[9]

Sample #1: Timeline

Note: The following timeline could also include dates for events related to family life, recreation, and other areas of life. Also notice that this person's timeline includes a date years into the future. His plan is to take part in projects that will go well beyond his death.

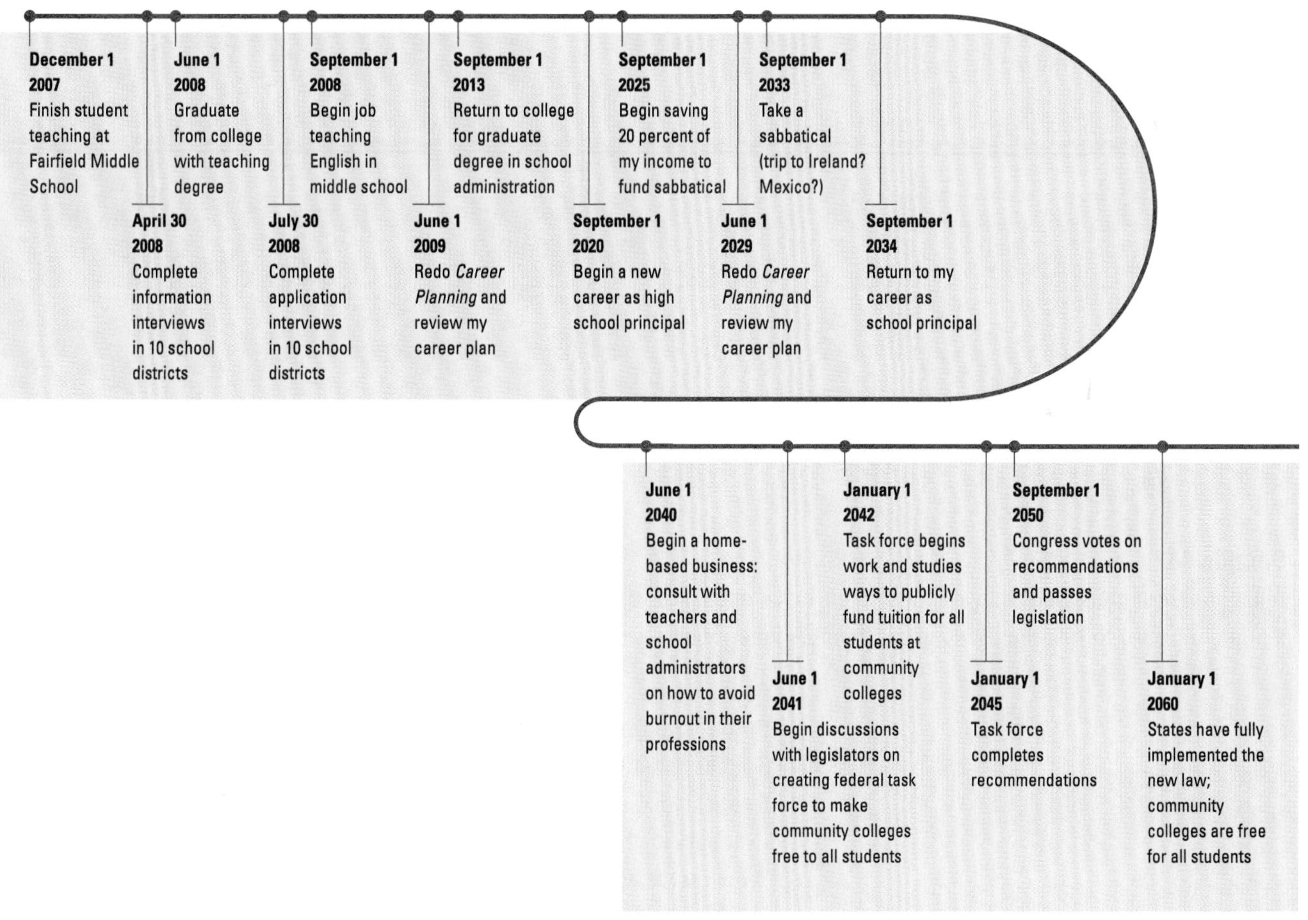

Sample #2

A mind map that links personal values to desired skills that could be used in several careers.

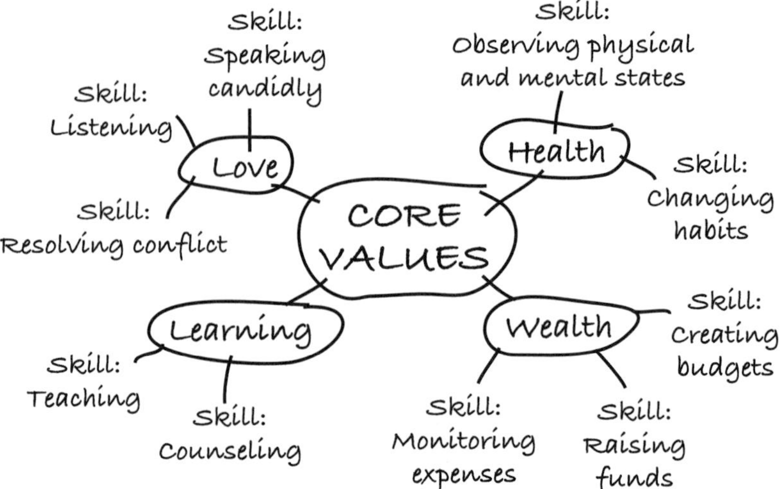

Sample #3

A pie chart summarizing the amounts of time devoted to career-related activities.

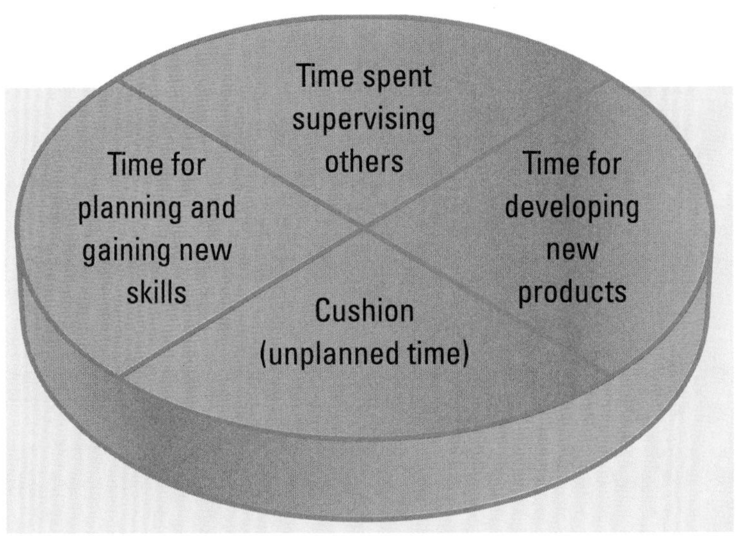

Sample #4

A list of career goals sorted by priority. In this case, each goal is assigned a number from 1 to 100. Higher numbers denote higher priority.

- Consult college career services department on law school options (100)
- Prepare rigorously for LSAT and do well (100)
- Get into top-10 law school (95)
- Get position as editor on *Law Review* (90)
- Graduate in top of class at law school (85)
- Work for state district attorney's office (80)
- Use my position and influence to gain political and judicial contacts (75)
- Found private law firm focused on protection of workers' rights (70)
- Win major lawsuits in defense of individual liberties in the workplace (60)
- Leave law practice to travel to developing countries in aid of poor for two years (60)
- Found international agency in protection of human rights (50)
- Win Nobel Prize (30)

CHOOSE YOUR CAREER—NOW

This exercise offers you to the opportunity to make a trial career choice. Now.

Remember that this is a *trial* choice. You can choose again later based on new insights into yourself and the job market. You may change your mind several times during your stay in higher education based on what you learn from courses, internships, work-study assignments, information interviews, part-time jobs, and other work experiences. These experiences are ways to test your career choices. With each choice, you'll come closer to a career that provides you with rewarding work on a daily basis.

In addition to choosing a career, make your choice come alive. Determine the very next actions that you will take to make your choice a reality. This can be just a rough draft of your career plan, which you can revise many times. The point is to start getting your ideas in visible form, and to do it now.

The format of your career plan is up to you. You could include many details, such as the next job title you'd like to have, the courses required for your major, and other training that you want to complete. You could list companies to research and people that could hire you. You could also include target dates to complete each of these tasks. Another option is to represent your plan visually through flow charts, timelines, mind maps, drawings, paintings, sculpture, computer animation, songs, or any other medium that inspires you. No matter what format you choose, get started now and do what works.

Come back to this exercise once each semester and do it again. Include your latest discoveries and intentions. Make your career plan a living document that grows and changes as you do.

To get started, just complete the following sentences. Use the space here and continue on additional paper or other materials.

The career I choose for now is . . .

____

____

____

The next steps that will lead me to this career are . . .

1. ______________________________

____

____

____

2. ______________________________

____

____

____

3. ______________________________

____

____

____

4. ______________________________

____

____

____

5. ______________________________

____

____

____

Gearing up for a global economy

One generation ago, only low-skilled factory workers worried about automation—being laid off and replaced by machines. Today, even skilled employees might fear losing their jobs to computer-driven robots, or to workers across the globe who will do the same job for a fraction of the wages.

You are entering a global economy. Your toughest competitors for a new job might be people from India or China with technical skills and a blazing fast Internet connection.

So far, only a small percentage of American jobs have been outsourced or off-shored to workers in other countries. But that percentage could grow.

The biggest reason is technology. Much of what workers produce now ends up in digital form. Books, music, movies, television shows, radio programs, technical publications, drawings and designs, slide presentations, X-rays—all can be created on a computer, saved to a CD or DVD, and sent instantly across the world.

This means that employers can hire from a global work force. Project teams in the future might include people from several nations who connect via e-mail, cell phones, teleconferencing, and digital devices that have yet to be invented.

You can thrive in this global economy. It will take foresight and a willingness to learn, along with the following strategies.

Complete your education. According to *Tough Choices or Tough Times: The Report of the New Commission on the Skills of the American Workforce*, the United States will remain an economic powerhouse only if its citizens are educated to do creative work—research, development, design, marketing, sales, and management. Careers in these areas are the least likely to be outsourced.[10]

The authors of *Tough Choices* note that people with computer skills and strong backgrounds in mathematics and science will have key tools to succeed in the new global economy. Yet they will also need to work with abstract ideas, think creatively, learn quickly, write well, develop new products, and work on culturally diverse project teams. These skills are all potential benefits of higher education.

Create a long-term career plan. When planning your career, look beyond your next job. Think in terms of a career *path*. Discover opportunities for advancement and innovation over the long term.

If you're a computer programmer, think about what you could do beyond writing code—perhaps by becoming a systems analyst or software engineer. If you're a musician, find out how you can use the Internet to promote your band, book gigs, and distribute recordings. And if you're a stockbroker, plan to offer more than advice about buying and selling. Help your clients plan their retirement and fund their children's college education as well.

No matter what your plan, consider gaining sales and marketing skills. Every organization depends on people who can bring in new customers and clients. If you can attract new sources of revenue, you'll be harder to replace.

Develop two key sets of skills. In *The New Division of Labor: How Computers Are Creating the Next Job Market*, Frank Levy and Richard J. Murnane describe two sets of skills that will not be taken over by robots or computers.[11]

First is *expert thinking*. This is the ability to handle problems that cannot be solved simply by applying rules. The doctor who successfully treats a person with a rare set of symptoms offers an example of expert thinking. So does the mechanic who repairs a car engine defect that the computer diagnostics missed.

Second is *complex communication*—the ability to find information, explain it to other people, and persuade them how to use it. An example is the engineer who convinces his colleagues that his design for a DVD player will outstrip the competition and reduce production costs. Complex communication is essential to education, sales, marketing, and management.

Even in a high-tech world, there will always be a need for the human touch. Learn to lead meetings, guide project teams, mentor people, nurture new talent, and create long-term business relationships. Then you'll offer employers something that they cannot get from a software package or contract worker. ⊠

Explore vocational assessments

Vocational assessments can be a helpful resource for self-discovery and career planning. These assessments might also be called vocational aptitude tests, skill inventories, or interest assessments. They can provide useful information about personality, comfort with technology, and work preferences.

Your school's career planning, counseling, or job placement center may offer one or more of these assessments. Ask if there is a cost and if anyone will review the results with you.

The following are some better-known vocational assessments. Bear in mind that they are not tests. There are no right or wrong answers to the questions they ask. And what you do with the results is always a personal choice. No assessment can dictate your career direction. The choice is always yours.

California Psychological Inventory. The California Psychological Inventory provides a view of your professional and personal style by measuring a range of individual differences: interpersonal skills, social skills, values, achievement-seeking needs, and stylistic modes. The inventory also measures managerial potential and creative temperament.

Career Ability Placement Survey (CAPS). CAPS provides you with information about your abilities. It helps you understand your potential and your strengths and weaknesses, and gives you a prediction of success in various types of occupations.

Career Thoughts Inventory. This vocational assessment can help you uncover negative thoughts that may impede effective, successful career planning. The inventory provides suggestions about how to change negative thoughts to positive ones required for good career choices.

Hall Occupational Orientation Inventory (HOOI). This values inventory is designed to help you rank personal factors that are important aspects of choosing your career. The HOOI gives you information about your interests, abilities, needs, and values.

Myers-Briggs Type Indicator® (MBTI) Instrument. The MBTI provides insight about yourself and how someone like you fits into the world of work, working with others of similar and different profiles. Results provide personal awareness and help you identify careers and work environments where you are most likely to thrive and feel fulfilled.

Personal Career Development Profile (PCDP). The PCDP shows you how your personality relates to your career plans and potential job performance. The profile provides you with insights into your choices and preferences, emphasizing your personal strengths, including an analysis of your approach to problem solving and stress management.

The Self-Directed Search (SDS). The SDS asks you to answer a questionnaire about your interests and abilities. Upon completion, you receive a computerized report that provides you with a personality summary code. The report then lists occupations and fields of study that correlate with your personality code. You can begin career exploration with a list of occupations at your fingertips.

Strong Interest Inventory. This inventory helps you identify your interests and matches them with possible occupations. It measures interests rather than abilities and compares your likes and dislikes to those of people who are satisfied in specific careers.

System for Interactive Guidance and Information (SIGI). Using this tool, you can explore your values, interests, and skills in a way that guides choices of college major and career. SIGI is computer-based and self-directed.

Vocational Preference Inventory (VPI). This inventory is a brief personality test based on the theory that occupations can be based on personality traits. It is especially useful to people who've had ambiguous results on other vocational assessments.[12]

Testing your career plan—jump into the job market

Do information interviews. Talk to people who actually do the kind of work that you'd like to do. Schedule an informational interview to ask them about their work. With their permission, go to their job sites. Spend time with them during a workday. Hang around. Ask questions.

To get the most out of an informational interview, first research the career field you've chosen and the particular business or organization you're going to visit. For example, before you interview a mutual funds manager, be sure you know what a mutual fund is. Also find some basic information about the manager's company, such as its general investment policies and recent financial history.

When scheduling an informational interview, make it clear that your purpose is not job hunting but career research. If you set up an informational interview and then use the occasion to ask for a job, you send mixed messages and risk making a negative impression.

Before your interview, prepare a list of questions, such as:

- How did you enter this line of work?
- What are your major tasks and responsibilities?
- What kinds of problems and decisions do you regularly face?
- What do you like most—and least—about your job?
- What changes are occurring in this field?
- What are the salary ranges and opportunities for employment and promotion?
- How can I effectively prepare to work in this field?

While informational interviews are often one-time events, they can also involve multiple visits to several people at the same work site. You might even spend several days or weeks following people on the job. Such extended experience is sometimes referred to as job-shadowing or an externship.

Volunteer. Volunteering offers another path to work experience that you can list on your résumé. To gain the most from this experience, research and choose volunteer positions as carefully as you would a full-time, salaried job. Identify organizations that are doing the kind of work that excites you. Contact them and ask for the person who supervises volunteers. Then schedule a face-to-face meeting to find out more.

Work. To find out more about working, go to work. Beyond gaining experience, you'll get insights that can change your life. A short-term job assignment can help you define your current skills, develop new ones, refine your career plan, develop contacts, and even lead to doing work that you love.

Cooperative (co-op) education programs offer one option. These programs combine specific classroom assignments with carefully supervised work experience. In addition to getting academic credit, most co-op students get paid and function as productive employees.

Other options include freelancing and temping. Rather than becoming an employee, a freelancer works for organizations on specific projects. Rates of payment, due dates, and other details are specified by contract. Freelancers typically work off site at their own office. A temporary worker (temp) also works on a contract basis but reports to an organization's work site.

Share the process with others. Consider forming a career-planning group. Working in groups allows you to give and receive career coaching. Group members can brainstorm options for each other's careers, research the work world, share information of mutual interest, trade contacts, and pair up for informational interviews. This is one way to raise your energy level for career planning.

Taking part in a group can open you up to your dream career. Others can point out ideas and information you've overlooked. They may alert you to opportunities you never considered or skills you were not aware you had. Working with such a group gives you a firm foundation for networking—building relationships that can lead directly to a job offer. For more ideas on networking, see Chapter Ten.[13] ☒

Gaining experience as an intern

One way to start your career path is an internship. Internships blend classroom learning with on-the-job experience and let you put your transferable skills into action. As an intern, you work in a job that relates directly to your career interests. Internships often offer academic credit. Some involve paid positions, while other internships are volunteer opportunities. Interns usually prepare for their assignments by completing courses in a specific field.

Note that internships may be called by other names. You might talk to people who use the terms *co-op experience, practicum, externship, field experience,* and *internship* synonymously.

Develop job skills now. Through an internship, you develop skills specific to your field—as well as transferable skills that you can apply to other jobs in the same field (or even a different field). For instance, you might perform administrative duties that give you professional experience in fielding phone calls, writing correspondence, and serving customers.

Internships are also ways to learn about organizational culture, hone your skills at coping with office politics, and add contacts to your job-hunting network. These are key aspects of the work world that you experience by getting outside the classroom.

Find internships. To find an internship, make an appointment with someone at the career-planning and job placement office on your campus. There you can connect with employers in your area who are looking for interns. You will likely submit a résumé and cover letter explaining your career interests. This is valuable in itself as experience in applying for jobs.

You can also locate organizations that interest you and contact them directly about internships. Even companies that do not have formal internship programs may accept applications.

Other suggestions to keep in mind:

- *Start early.* Think two or three terms ahead. During a fall semester, for example, start searching for internships for the spring or summer.
- *Network.* Talk to your friends, parents, family, neighbors, and instructors to discover if they know about internships for you. Mention your career interests and ask for suggestions.
- *Surf the Internet.* Use Internet search engines to find employment or internship listings. Research organizations that interest you and contact them via e-mail.
- *Use the library.* Ask a reference librarian to help you find internship guides. Some look like college catalogs, listing popular positions with key contacts, due dates for applications, and information about getting paid.

Cultivate contacts. If the internship offers an experience aligned with your career goals and skills, your role as an intern may help lead to permanent job offers following graduation. Keep in touch with the people you meet through internships. They may be working at another company when you graduate and offer help to get your foot in the door.

Reflect on your internship. After you have completed your internship, review your experience. Write Discovery Statements about what worked well and what you would like to improve. Referring to the transferable skills on page 63, list the skills that you used and additional skills you want to gain.

Internships offer a great way to test a career choice—even if you find out that you don't like a particular field or job. Discovering what you do *not* want in a career can be just as valuable as gaining any type of work experience. You can benefit from ruling out an inappropriate career choice early on—especially if it involves a major with a lot of required courses.

Even if you find that the workplace setting or tasks involved in your internship did not meet your expectations, you can create a list of criteria that you want your next work experience to include. Be sure to incorporate the skills and experiences from any internship on your résumé—no matter what career field or job you eventually choose.

Service learning: Career planning as contribution

As part of a service-learning project for a sociology course, students volunteer at a community center for older adults. For another service-learning project, history students interview people in veteran's hospitals about their war experiences. These students plan to share their interview results with a psychiatrist on the hospital staff.

Meanwhile, business students provide free tax-preparation help at a center for low-income people. Students in graphic arts classes create free promotional materials for charities. Other students staff a food cooperative and community credit union.

These examples of actual projects from the National Service-Learning Clearinghouse demonstrate the working premise of service learning—that volunteer work and other forms of contributing can become a vehicle for higher education. Students who do service learning also gain experiences that can guide their career choices and help them develop job skills.

Service learning generally includes three elements: meaningful community service, a formal academic curriculum, and time for students to reflect on what they learn from service. That reflection can include speeches, journal writing, and research papers.

When you design a service-learning project, consider these suggestions:

- Work with a community agency that has experience with students. Make sure that the agency has liability insurance to cover volunteers.
- Handle logistics. Integrating service learning into your schedule can call for detailed planning. If your volunteer work takes place off-campus, arrange for transportation and allow for travel time.
- Reflect on your service-learning project with a tool you've used throughout this book—the Discovery and Intention Journal Entry system explained in the Introduction. Write Discovery Statements about what you want to gain from service learning and how you feel about what you're doing. Follow up with Intention Statements about what you'll do differently for your next volunteer experience.
- Include ways to evaluate your project. From your Intention Statements, create action goals and outcome goals. *Action goals* state what you plan to do and how many people you intend to serve; for instance, "We plan to provide 100 hours of literacy tutoring to 10 people in the community." *Outcome goals* describe the actual impact that your project will have: "At the end of our project, 60 percent of the people we tutor will be able to write a résumé and fill out a job application." Build numbers into your goals whenever possible. That makes it easier to evaluate the success of your project.
- Create a way to build long-term impact into your project. One potential pitfall of service learning is that the programs are often short-lived. After students pack up and return to campus, programs can die. To avoid this outcome, make sure that other students or community members are willing to step in and take over for you when the semester ends.
- Celebrate mistakes. Even if your project fails to meet its goals, have a party. State—in writing—the obstacles you encountered and ways to overcome them. The solutions you offer will be worth gold to the people who follow in your footsteps. Sharing the lessons learned from your mistakes is an act of service in itself.
- Connect service learning to career planning. List the skills you used in your project. Underline those that you enjoyed using the most. Ask the people you worked with about how those skills can be used in the job market. Also get contact information for your coworkers so that they can become part of your job-hunting network. With some planning and people skills, you might turn your career into a source of full-time contribution to your community. ☒

Setting and achieving GOALS

Many of us have vague, idealized notions of what we want out of life. These notions float among the clouds in our heads. They are wonderful, fuzzy, safe thoughts such as "I want to be a good person," "I want to be financially secure," or "I want to be happy."

The essence of planning is goal setting. If you want to master career planning, then get some practical experience at writing goals and creating ways to meet them.

If you really want to meet a goal, translate it into specific, concrete behaviors. Find out what that goal looks like. Listen to what it sounds like. Pick it up and feel how heavy that goal is. Inspect the switches, valves, joints, cogs, and fastenings of the goal. Make your goal as real as a chain saw. There is nothing vague or fuzzy about chain saws. You can see them, feel them, and hear them. They have a clear function. Goals can be every bit as real and useful. And the ability to set and achieve goals enhances several transferable skills—allocating time and monitoring and correcting your performance.

Writing down your goals exponentially increases your chances of meeting them. Writing exposes undefined terms, unrealistic time frames, and other symptoms of fuzzy thinking. If you've been completing Intention Statements as explained in the Introduction to this book, then you've already had experience writing goals. Goals and Intention Statements both address changes you want to make in your behavior, your values, your circumstances—or all of these. To keep track of your goals, write each one on a separate 3 × 5 card or key them all into a word processing file on your computer.

There are many useful methods for setting goals. Following is one of them. In this method, the key words to remember are *specific, time, areas*, and *reflect*. Combine the first letter of each word and you get the acronym *STAR*. Use this acronym to remember the suggestions that follow.

Write specific goals. Suppose that one of your goals is to become a better student by studying harder. You're headed in a powerful direction; now go for the specifics. Translate that goal into a concrete action, such as "I will study two hours for every hour I'm in class." Specific goals make clear what actions are needed or what results are expected. Consider these examples:

Vague goal	Specific goal
Get a good education.	Graduate with B.S. degree in engineering, with honors, by 2009.
Enhance my spiritual life.	Meditate for 15 minutes daily.
Improve my appearance.	Lose six pounds during the next six months.

When stated specifically, a goal might look different to you. If you examine it closely, a goal you once thought you wanted might not be something you want after all. Or you might discover that you want to choose a new path to achieve a goal that you are sure you want.

Write goals in several time frames. To get a comprehensive vision of your future, write down:

- *Long-term goals.* Long-term goals represent major targets in your life. These goals can take 5 to 20 years to achieve. In some cases, they will take a lifetime.
- *Mid-term goals.* Mid-term goals are objectives you can accomplish in one to five years. They include goals such as completing a course of education, paying off a car loan, or achieving a specific career level. These goals usually support your long-term goals.
- *Short-term goals.* Short-term goals are the ones you can accomplish in a year or less. These goals are specific achievements, such as completing a particular course or group of courses, hiking down the Appalachian Trail, or organizing a family reunion.

Write goals in several areas of life. People who set goals in only one area of life—such as their career—can find that their personal growth becomes one-sided. To avoid this outcome, set goals in a variety of categories. Consider what you want to experience in your:

- education
- career
- financial life
- family life
- social life
- spiritual life
- level of health

Add goals in other areas as they occur to you.

Reflect on your goals. Each week, take a few minutes to think about your goals. You can perform the following spot checks:

- *Check in with your feelings.* Think about how the process of setting your goals felt. Consider the satisfaction you'll gain in attaining your objectives. If you don't feel a significant emotional connection with a written goal, consider letting it go or filing it away to review later.
- *Check for alignment.* Look for connections between your goals. Do your short-term goals align with your mid-term goals? Will your mid-term goals help you achieve your long-term goals?
- *Check for obstacles.* All kinds of things can come between you and your goals, such as constraints on time and money. Anticipate obstacles and start looking now for workable solutions.
- *Check for immediate steps.* Here's a way to link goal setting to time management. Decide on a list of small, achievable steps you can take right away to accomplish each of your short-term goals. Write these small steps down on a daily to-do list. If you want to accomplish some of them by a certain date, enter them in a calendar that you consult daily. Then, over the coming weeks, review your to-do list and calendar. Take note of your progress and celebrate your successes.

GET REAL WITH YOUR GOALS

One way to make goals effective is to examine them up close. That's what this exercise is about. Using a process of brainstorming and evaluation, you can break a long-term goal into smaller segments until you have taken it completely apart. When you analyze a goal to this level of detail, you're well on the way to meeting it.

For this exercise, you will use a pen, extra paper, and a watch with a second hand. (A digital watch with a built-in stopwatch is even better.) Timing is an important part of the brainstorming process, so follow the stated time limits. This entire exercise takes about an hour. Use it to set and meet any goal related to your education, career, or personal life.

Part one: Long-term goals

Brainstorm. Begin with an eight-minute brainstorm. For eight minutes write down everything you think you want in your life. Write as fast as you can and write whatever comes into your head. Leave no thought out. Don't worry about accuracy. The object of a brainstorm is to generate as many ideas as possible. Use a separate sheet of paper for this part of the exercise.

Evaluate. After you have finished brainstorming, spend the next six minutes looking over your list. Analyze what you wrote. Read the list out loud. If something is missing, add it. Look for common themes or relationships between goals. Then select three long-term goals that are important to you—goals that will take many years to achieve. Write these goals below in the space provided.

____

____

____

Before you continue, take a minute to reflect on the process you've used so far. What criteria did you use to select your top three goals?

Part two: Mid-term goals

Brainstorm. Read out loud the three long-term goals you selected in Part One. Choose one of them. Then brainstorm a list of goals you might achieve in the next one to five years that would lead to the accomplishment of that one long-term goal. These are mid-term goals. Spend eight minutes on this brainstorm.

Evaluate. Analyze your brainstorm of mid-term goals. Then select three that you determine to be important in meeting the long-term goal you picked. Allow yourself six minutes for this part of the exercise. Write your selections below in the space provided.

____

____

____

Again, pause for reflection before going on to the next part of this exercise. Why do you see these three goals as more important than the other mid-term goals you generated? Write about your reasons for selecting these three goals.

Part three: Short-term goals

Brainstorm. Review your list of mid-term goals and select one. In another eight-minute brainstorm, generate a list of short-term goals—those you can accomplish in a year or less that will lead to the attainment of that mid-term goal. Write down everything that comes to mind. Do not evaluate or judge these ideas yet. For now, the more ideas you write down, the better.

Evaluate. Analyze your list of short-term goals. The most effective brainstorms are conducted by suspending judgment, so you might find some bizarre ideas on your list. That's fine. Now is the time to cross them out. Next evaluate your remaining short-term goals and select three that you are willing and able to accomplish. Allow yourself six minutes for this part of the exercise, then write your selections below.

____

____

____

The more you practice, the more effective you can be at choosing goals that have meaning for you. You can repeat this exercise, employing the other long-term goals you generated or creating new ones.

Do this exercise online.

Student Website

Choosing your major

One decision that troubles many students in higher education is the choice of an academic major. Here is an opportunity to apply your skills at critical thinking, decision making, and problem solving. The following four suggestions can guide you through this process.

1 Discover options

Follow the fun. Perhaps you look forward to attending one of your classes and even like completing the assignments. This is a clue to your choice of major.

See if you can find lasting patterns in the subjects and extracurricular activities that you've enjoyed over the years. Look for a major that allows you to continue and expand on these experiences.

Also sit down with a stack of 3 × 5 cards and brainstorm answers to the following questions:

- What do you enjoy doing most with your unscheduled time?
- Imagine that you're at a party and having a fascinating conversation. What is this conversation about?
- What Websites do you frequently visit or have bookmarked in a Web browser?
- What kind of problems do you enjoy solving—those that involve people? Products? Ideas?
- What interests are revealed by your choices of reading material, television shows, and other entertainment?
- What would an ideal day look like for you? Describe where you'd live, who would be with you, and what you'd do throughout the day. Do any of these visions suggest a possible major?

Questions like these are not frivolous. They can uncover a "fun factor" that energizes you to finish the work of completing a major.

Consider ability. In choosing a major, ability counts as much as interest. Einstein enjoyed playing the violin, but his love of music didn't override his choice of a career in science. In addition to considering what you enjoy, think about times and places when you excelled. List the courses that you "aced," the work assignments that you mastered, and the hobbies that led to rewards or recognition. Let your choice of a major reflect a discovery of your passions *and* potentials.

Use formal techniques for self-discovery. Writing is a path to the kind of self-knowledge involved in choosing your major. Start with the exercises and Journal Entries in this book. Review what you've written, looking for statements about your interests and abilities.

Also consider questionnaires and inventories that are designed to correlate your interests with specific majors. Examples include the Strong Interest Inventory and the Self-Directed Search. Your academic advisor or someone at your school's job placement office can give you more details about these and related inventories. For some fun, take several of them and meet with an advisor to interpret the results.

Remember that there is no questionnaire, inventory, test, or formula for choosing a major or career. Likewise, there is no expert who can make these choices for you. Inventories can help you gain self-knowledge, and other people can offer valuable perspectives. However, what you *do* with all this input is entirely up to you.

Link to long-term goals. Your choice of a major can fall into place once you determine what you want in life. Before you choose a major, back up to a bigger picture. List your core values, such as contributing to society, achieving financial security and professional recognition, enjoying good health, or making time for fun. Also write down specific goals that you want to accomplish in 5 years, 10 years, or even 50 years from today.

Many students find that the prospect of getting what they want in life justifies all of the time, money, and day-to-day effort invested in going to school. Having a major gives you a powerful incentive for attending classes, taking part in discussions, reading textbooks, writing papers, and completing other assignments. When you see a clear connection between finishing school and creating the life of your dreams, the daily tasks of higher education become charged with meaning.

Studies indicate that the biggest factor associated with completing a degree in higher education is commitment to personal goals.[14] A choice of major reflects those goals.

Ask other people. Key people in your life might have valuable suggestions about your choice of major. Ask for their ideas and listen with an open mind. At the same time, distance yourself from any pressure to choose a major or career that fails to interest you. If you make a choice based solely on the expectations of other people, you could end up with a major you don't enjoy.

Gather information. Check your school's catalog or Website for a list of available majors. Here is a gold mine of information. Take a quick glance and highlight all the majors that interest you. Then talk to students who have declared them.

Also read descriptions of courses required for these majors. Chat with instructors who teach courses in these areas and ask for copies of their class syllabi. Go to the bookstore and browse required texts.

Based on all this information, write a list of prospective majors. Discuss them with an academic advisor and someone at your school's career-planning center.

Invent a major. When choosing a major, you might not need to limit yourself to those listed in your course catalog. Many schools now have flexible programs that allow for independent study. Through such programs, you might be able to combine two existing majors or invent an entirely new one of your own.

Consider a complementary minor. You can add flexibility to your academic program by choosing a minor to complement or contrast with your major. The student who wants to be a minister could opt for a minor in English; all of those courses in composition can help in writing sermons. Or the student with a major in psychology might choose a minor in business administration, with the idea of managing a counseling service some day. An effective choice of a minor can expand your skills and career options.

Think critically about the link between your major and your career. Your career goals might have a significant impact on your choice of major. For an overview of career planning and an immediate chance to put ideas down on paper, see Chapter Ten: Working.

On the other hand, you might be able to pursue a rewarding career by choosing among *several* different majors. Even students planning to apply for law school or medical school have flexibility in their choice of majors. In addition, many people are employed in jobs with little relationship to their major. And you might choose a career in the future that is unrelated to any currently available major.

2 Make a trial choice

At many schools, declaring a major offers some benefits. For example, you might get priority when registering for certain classes and qualify for special scholarships or grants.

Don't delay such benefits. Even if you feel undecided, you probably have a good idea about what your major will be.

To verify this, do a simple experiment. Pretend that you have to choose a major today. Based on the options you've already discovered, write down the first three ideas that come to mind. Review the list for a few minutes and then just choose one.

Hold onto your list, however. It reflects your current intuition or "gut feelings," and it may come in handy during the next step. This step might confirm your trial choice of major—or return you to one of the majors that you originally listed.

3 Test your trial choice

When you've made a trial choice of major, take on the role of a scientist. Treat your choice as a hypothesis and then design a series of experiments to test it. For example:

- Schedule office meetings with instructors who teach courses in the major. Ask about required course work and career options in the field.

- Discuss your trial choice with an academic advisor or career counselor.
- Enroll in a course related to your possible major. Remember that introductory courses might not give you a realistic picture of the workloads involved in advanced courses. Also, you might not be able to register for certain courses until you've actually declared a related major.
- Find a volunteer experience, internship, part-time job, or service-learning experience related to the major.
- Interview students who have declared the same major. Ask them in detail about their experiences and suggestions for success.
- Interview someone who works in a field related to the major.
- Think about whether you can complete your major given the amount of time and money that you plan to invest in higher education.
- Consider whether declaring this major would require a transfer to another program or even another school.

If these factors confirm your choice of major, celebrate that fact. If they result in choosing a new major, celebrate that outcome as well.

Also remember that higher education represents a safe place to test your choice of major—and to change your mind. As you sort through your options, help is always available from administrators, instructors, advisors, and peers.

4 Choose again

Keep your choice of a major in perspective. There is probably no single "correct" choice. Your unique collection of skills is likely to provide the basis for majoring in several fields.

Odds are that you'll change your major at least once—and that you'll change careers several times during your life. One benefit of higher education is mobility. This means gaining general skills and knowledge that can help you move into a new major or career field at any time.

Viewing a major as a one-time choice that determines your entire future can raise your stress levels. Instead, look at choosing a major as the start of a continuing path that involves discovery, choice, and passionate action. ⊠

critical thinking exercise 13

MAKE A TRIAL CHOICE OF MAJOR

Read the list of majors available from your school's catalog or Website. Make a copy of this list or print it out so that you can write on it.

Next, take your list and cross out all the majors that you already know are not right for you. You will probably eliminate well over half the list.

Now scan the remaining majors. Next to the ones that definitely interest you, write "yes." Next to majors that you're willing to consider but are unsure about, write "maybe."

Review the choices you just made. See if you can narrow your list down to three majors. List those here.

____

____

____

Finally, mark an asterisk next to the major that interests you most right now. This is your trial choice of major.

journal entry 7

Discovery/Intention Statement

Reflect for a moment on your experience with Critical Thinking Exercise #13: "Make a trial choice of major." If you had already chosen a major, did it confirm that choice? Did you uncover any new or surprising possibilities for declaring a major?

I discovered that I . . .

____

____

____

____

____

Now, list the major that is your top choice for right now. Also list publications you will find and people you will consult to gather more information about this major.

I intend to . . .

____

____

____

____

____

____

____

____

____

Plan to repeat this Journal Entry and the preceding Critical Thinking Exercise several times. You may find yourself researching several majors and changing your mind. That's fine. The aim is to start thinking about your major now.

power process

LOVE YOUR PROBLEMS (AND EXPERIENCE YOUR BARRIERS)

We all have problems and barriers that block our progress or prevent us from moving into new areas. Often, the way we respond to our problems puts boundaries on our experiences. We place limitations on what we allow ourselves to be, do, and have.

Our problems might include fear of speaking in front of a group, anxiety about math problems, or reluctance to sound ridiculous when learning a foreign language. We might have a barrier about looking silly when doing something new at work. Some of us even have anxiety about being successful.

Problems often work like barriers. When we bump up against one of our problems, we usually turn away and start walking along a different path. And all of a sudden—bump!—we've struck another barrier. And we turn away again. As we continue to bump into problems and turn away from them, our lives stay inside the same old boundaries. Inside these boundaries, we are unlikely to have new adventures. We are unlikely to improve or to make much progress.

The word *problem* is a wonderful word coming from the ancient Greek word *proballein,* which means "to throw forward." In other words, problems are there to provide an opportunity for us to gain new skills. If we respond to problems by loving them instead of resisting them, we can expand the boundaries in which we live our lives. The willingness to recognize that a problem exists is a transferable skill. When approached with acceptance, and even love, the problem can "throw" us forward.

Three ways to handle a barrier

It's natural to have barriers, but sometimes they limit our experience so much that we get bored, angry, or frustrated with life. When this happens, consider the following three ways of dealing with a barrier. One way is to pretend it doesn't exist. Avoid it, deny it, lie about it. It's like turning your head the other way, putting on a fake grin, and saying, "See, there's really no problem at all. Everything is fine. Oh, that problem. That's not a problem—it's not really there."

In addition to making us look foolish, this approach leaves the barrier intact, and we keep bumping into it. We deny the barrier and might not even be aware that we're bumping into it. For example, a student who has a barrier about math might subconsciously avoid enriching experiences that include math.

A second approach is to fight the barrier, to struggle against it. This usually makes the barrier grow. It increases the barrier's magnitude. A person who is obsessed with weight might constantly worry about being fat. She might struggle with it every day, trying diet after diet. And the more she struggles, the bigger the problem gets.

The third alternative is to love the barrier. Accept it. Totally experience it. Tell the truth about it. Describe it in detail. When you do this, the barrier loses its power. You can literally love it to death.

The word *love* might sound like an overstatement. In this Power Process, the word means to accept your problems, to allow and permit them. When we fight a problem, it grows bigger. The more we struggle against it, the stronger it seems to become. When we accept the fact that we have a problem, we are more likely to find effective ways to deal with it.

Suppose one of your barriers is fear of speaking in front of a group. You can use any of these three approaches.

First, you can get up in front of the group and pretend that you're not afraid. You can fake a smile, not admitting to yourself or the group that you have any concerns about speaking—even though your legs have turned to rubber bands and your mind to jelly. The problem is that everyone in the room, including you, will know you're scared when your hands start shaking, your voice cracks, and you forget what you were going to say.

The second way to approach this barrier is to fight it. You can tell yourself, "I'm not going to be scared," and then try to keep your knees from knocking. Generally, this doesn't work. In fact, your knee-knocking might get worse.

The third approach is to go to the front of the room, look out into the audience, and say to yourself, "I am scared. I notice that my knees are shaking and my mouth feels dry, and I'm having a rush of thoughts about what might happen if I say the wrong thing. Yup, I'm scared, and that's OK. As a matter of fact, it's just part of me, so I accept it and I'm not going to try to fight it. I'm going to make this presentation even though I'm scared." You might not actually eliminate the fear; however, your barrier about the fear—which is what inhibits you—might disappear. And you might discover that if you examine the fear, love it, accept it, and totally experience it, the fear itself also disappears.

When we accept the fact that we have a problem, we are more likely to find effective ways to deal with it.

Applying this process

Applying this process is easier if you remember three ideas. First, loving a problem is not necessarily the same as enjoying it. Love in this sense means total and unconditional acceptance.

This can work even with problems as thorny as physical pain. When we totally experience pain, it often diminishes and sometimes it disappears. This strategy can work with emotions and even with physical pain. Make it your aim to love the pain, that is, to fully accept the pain and know all the details about it. Most pain has a wavelike quality. It rises, reaches a peak of intensity, and then subsides for a while. See if you can watch the waves as they come and go.

Second, unconditional acceptance is not the same as unconditional surrender. Accepting a problem does not mean escaping from it or giving up on finding a solution. Rather, this process involves freeing ourselves from the grip of the problem by diving *into* the problem headfirst and getting to know it in detail.

Third, love and laughter are allies. It's hard to resist a problem while you are laughing at it. Sure, that incident when you noticed the spinach in your teeth only *after* you got home from a first date was a bummer. But with the passage of time, you can admit that it was kind of funny. You don't have to wait weeks to gain that perspective. As long as you're going to laugh anyway, why wait? The sooner you can see the humor in your problems, the sooner you can face them.

When people first hear about loving their problems, they sometimes think it means being resigned to problems. Actually, loving a problem does not need to stop us from solving it. In fact, fully accepting and admitting the problem usually helps us take effective action—which can free us of the problem once and for all. ☒

career application

Tiana Kabiri earned her B.A. in computer science and found a job in her field within a month after she graduated.

She now works as a systems programmer for a large bank with seven local branches. Tiana was the first person in her family to gain a college degree. Her friends and relatives are thrilled with her accomplishments.

While in school, Tiana took part in several workshops on career planning. However, she never did many of the suggested exercises and largely downplayed the concept of career planning. Defining her interests, thinking about the skills she most wanted to develop, and researching employment trends just seemed like too much work.

Besides, according to the National Association of Colleges and Employers, starting salary offers for graduates with a bachelor's degree in computer programming averaged $45,558 a year in 2003. When Tiana heard this, she figured that was all the information she needed to choose her career.

One day at work, Tiana received an e-mail from a friend who was still in school—a student majoring in computer science and actively engaged in career planning. The message included these quotations from the Website published by the U.S. Department of Labor:

> *Employment of programmers is expected to grow more slowly than the average for all occupations through the year 2014. Sophisticated computer software now has the capability to write basic code, eliminating the need for many programmers to do this routine work. The consolidation and centralization of systems and applications, developments in packaged software, advances in programming languages and tools, and the growing ability of users to design, write, and implement more of their own programs mean that more of the programming functions can be transferred from programmers to other types of information workers, such as computer software engineers.*[15]

Tiana read this and felt a wave of panic. As an entry-level programmer, she was now worried about her long-term job security. She was happy with her salary, and her job seemed secure for the near future. But she worried that her skills would eventually become obsolete or that her job would be outsourced and eliminated.

Reflecting on this scenario

1. Imagine that you are a career counselor and that Tiana has scheduled an appointment with you. You have one hour to give her a crash course on career planning. What are two or three of the major points you would make?

___

___

___

2. Do an Internet search on the term *computer and mathematical occupations.* Based on the kinds of jobs you find, what computer skills could you recommend that Tiana develop to enhance her long-term job security?

___

___

___

3. Looking beyond Tiana's skills in programming, list five transferable skills that you would recommend Tiana to develop that will help her in the future.

___

___

___

quiz

Name ______________________________ Date ____/____/____

1. Aside from posting your résumé on the Internet, name two useful ways to use the Web as a tool for career planning.

2. The text suggests that you add specifics to your career plan by "naming names." List three examples of these specifics.

3. Rewrite the following intention into an effective goal statement: "I want to be wealthy."

4. Explain how service learning can contribute to your career plan.

5. The best way to get useful information from a vocational assessment is to take one and make it a blueprint for choosing your career. True or False? Explain your answer.

6. List three questions that you could ask during an information interview.

7. Briefly describe a strategy that you can use to prosper in a global economy.

8. Briefly explain the difference between career planning as a process of *discovery* and career planning as a process of *choice*.

9. Explain the difference between work-content skills and transferable skills.

10. List three examples of work-content skills and three examples of transferable skills.

learning styles application

The questions below will "cycle" you through four styles, or modes, of learning as explained in the article "Learning styles: Discovering how you learn" in Chapter One. Each question will help you explore a different mode. You can answer the questions in any order.

what if *Imagine that you will do no career planning. After reading this chapter, do you see any advantages to this approach? How about any disadvantages? Summarize your thoughts in the space below.*

why *Supposed that another student in one of your classes says, "Career planning is irrelevant to me. Besides being in school, I work full-time and have a family. I don't have time to plan a career." In a brief paragraph, sum up your response to this statement.*

how *Name a job you would like to have in the next 3 to 10 years. Then, list the five most important skills you will need to have in order to do that job.*

what *Do a very brief career plan by naming the job titles you would like to hold in 3 years, 5 years, and 10 years from today.*

master student profile

LISA PRICE

(1962–) Author of *Success Never Smelled So Sweet: How I Followed My Nose and Found My Passion*

Today I am a successful businesswoman. But when I was twenty-eight years old, I filed for personal bankruptcy. I had spent a number of years chasing dreams, living over my head and hoping that I would be able to pay for it later. Well. . . I did pay—just not the way I had hoped. I reached a point where my credit-card balances were sky high. And I would later learn that with penalties and interest, I was also about $33,000 in debt to the Internal Revenue Service. I wasn't even thirty and I had already screwed up my life. . . .

. . .Over the next ten years, I focused on turning my life around—and did. . . . In my early thirties, I had taken one hundred dollars and created a business out of my love of good scents and lifelong hobby of creating fragrances. I started selling perfumes at flea markets as a way of supplementing my income, always reinvesting the profit back into my business. As it turns out, people liked my products and my venture began to blossom. My hobby-turned-business grew slowly, without bank loans or credit cards—my finances were too bad to qualify for either. . . . In time, my company, Carol's Daughter: Beauty by Nature, transformed itself into a successful boutique in the Fort Greene neighborhood of Brooklyn and online business. . . .

. . .How did I get myself into such a tough situation—and, more importantly, how did I dig myself out? Like many people I overextended myself by trying to keep up with others. . . . But when we're open to it, life's difficulties can teach us lessons. . . . I stopped trying to keep up with the Joneses and began to pay attention to myself—my inner Self. I learned to listen to the internal voice that spoke to me without fail, each and every day, whether or not I paid attention.

. . .As this was happening I learned to trust my gifts and talents. In my case I literally followed my nose out of my difficulties and into a life I could never have imagined.

. . .As I run my company, teach classes, and speak to people, many tell me they long to do work that they love. Most tell me that financial fear keeps them stuck where they are. Not too long ago I felt trapped in a dead-end job like the seekers I describe. I want more women and men to experience the feeling of exhilaration and sense of satisfaction that living your passion brings.

For more biographical information about Lisa Price, visit the Master Student Hall of fame on the *From Master Student to Master Employee* Website.

3 Time

MASTER STUDENT MAP

why this chapter matters . . .

Your personal productivity is a major predictor of your success in school and in the work world.

how you can use this chapter . . .

Know exactly what you want to accomplish today, this month, and this year.
Eliminate stress due to poor planning and procrastination.
Gain the ability to focus your attention whenever you choose.

As you read, ask yourself what if . . .

I could have more than enough time to accomplish whatever I choose?

what is included . . .

FROM THE DESK OF . . .

Time management is the key to keeping my commitments of career and personal life separate but focused. I have to understand what each part of my life requires of me and how much time I can dedicate to this event. Once that is calculated and prioritized, I try to maximize my free time while reducing time spent on lower-level goals. This increases my choices on how to spend this time, which reduces stress and confusion.

—JONATHAN WOLF, LIBRARY INFORMATION ASSISTANT

You've got the time

The words *time management* can call forth images of restriction and control. You might visualize a prune-faced Scrooge hunched over your shoulder, stopwatch in hand, telling you what to do every minute. Bad news.

Good news: You do have enough time for the things you want to do. All it takes is thinking about the possibilities and making conscious choices.

Time is an equal opportunity resource. All of us, regardless of gender, race, creed, or national origin, have exactly the same number of hours in a week. No matter how famous we are, no matter how rich or poor, we get 168 hours to spend each week—no more, no less.

Time is also an unusual commodity. It cannot be saved. You can't stockpile time like wood for the stove or food for the winter. It can't be seen, felt, touched, tasted, or smelled. You can't sense time directly. Even scientists and philosophers find it hard to describe. Because time is so elusive, it is easy to ignore. That doesn't bother time at all. Time is perfectly content to remain hidden until you are nearly out of it. And when you are out of it, you are out of it.

Time is a nonrenewable resource. If you're out of wood, you can chop some more. If you're out of money, you can earn a little extra. If you're out of love, there is still hope. If you're out of health, it can often be restored. But when you're out of time, that's it. When this minute is gone, it's gone.

Time seems to pass at varying speeds. Sometimes it crawls and sometimes it's faster than a speeding bullet. There are moments when you are so absorbed in what you're doing that hours disappear like magic.

Approach time as if you are in control. Sometimes it seems that your friends control your time, that your boss controls your time, that your teachers or your parents or your kids or somebody else controls your time. Maybe that is not true. When you say you don't have enough time, you might really be saying that you are not spending the time you *do* have in the way that you want.

Everything written about managing yourself in relation to time boils down to two topics. One is knowing exactly *what* you want, which is the art of planning. The other is knowing *how* to get what you want, which is the essence of time management. Mastering both of these transferable skills can help you develop all the other skills presented in the upcoming chapters of this book.

Spend your most valuable resource in the way you choose. Start by observing how you use time. The next Critical Thinking Exercise gives you this opportunity.

journal entry 8

Discovery/Intention Statement

Think back to a time during the past year when you rushed to finish a project or when you did not find time for an activity that was important to you. List one thing you might have done to create this outcome.

I discovered that I . . .

____

____

____

Take a few minutes to skim this chapter. Find three to five articles that might help you avoid such outcomes in the future and list them below.

Title *Page number*

____

____

____

____

____

If you don't have time to read these articles in depth right now, schedule a time to do so.

I intend to . . .

____

____

____

____

____

THE TIME MONITOR/TIME PLAN PROCESS

The purpose of this exercise is to transform time into a knowable and predictable resource. You can do this by repeating a two-phase cycle of monitoring and planning. This exercise takes place over two weeks. During the first week, you can monitor your activities to get a detailed picture of how you spend your time. Then you can plan the second week thoughtfully. Monitor your time during the second week, compare it to your plan, and discover what changes you want to make in the following week's plan.

Monitor your time in 15-minute intervals, 24 hours a day, for seven days. Record how much time you spend sleeping, eating, studying, attending lectures, traveling to and from class, working, watching television, listening to music, taking care of the kids, running errands—everything.

If this sounds crazy, hang on for a minute. This exercise is not about keeping track of the rest of your life in 15-minute intervals. It is an opportunity to become conscious of how you spend your time, your life. Use the Time Monitor/Time Plan process only for as long as it is helpful to do so.

When you know how your time is spent, you can find ways to adjust and manage it so that you spend your life doing the things that are most important to you. Monitoring your time is a critical First Step toward putting you in control of your life.

Some students choose to keep track of their time on 3×5 cards, calendars, campus planners, or software designed for this purpose. You might even develop your own form for monitoring your time.

1. Get to know the Time Monitor/Time Plan. Look at the Time Monitor/Time Plan on page 97. Note that each day has two columns, one labeled "monitor" and the other labeled "plan." During the first week, use only the "monitor" column. After that, use both columns simultaneously to continue the monitor-plan process.

To become familiar with the form, look at the example on page 97. When you begin an activity, write it down next to the time you begin and put a line just above that spot. Round off to the nearest 15 minutes. If, for example, you begin eating at 8:06, enter your starting time as 8:00. Over time, it will probably even out. In any case, you will be close enough to realize the benefits of this exercise. (Note that you can use the blank spaces in the "monitor" and "plan" columns to cover most of the day.)

Do this exercise online.

On Monday, the student in this example got up at 6:45 a.m., showered, and got dressed. He finished this activity and began breakfast at 7:15. He put this new activity in at the time he began and drew a line just above it. He ate from 7:15 to 7:45. It took him 15 minutes to walk to class (7:45 to 8:00), and he attended classes from 8:00 to 11:00.

Keep your Time Monitor/Time Plan with you every minute you are awake for one week. Take a few moments every two or three hours to record what you've done. Or enter a note each time you change activities.

Here's an eye opener for many students. If you think you already have a good idea of how you manage time, predict how many hours you will spend in a week on each category of activity listed in the form on page 98. (Four categories are already provided; you can add more at any time.) Do this before your first week of monitoring. Write your predictions in the margin to the left of each category. After monitoring your time for one week, see how accurate your predictions were.

2. Remember to use your Time Monitor/Time Plan. It might be easy to forget to fill out your Time Monitor/Time Plan. One way to remember is to create a visual reminder for yourself. You can use this technique for any activity you want to remember.

Relax for a moment, close your eyes, and imagine that you see your Time Monitor/Time Plan. Imagine that it has arms and legs and is as big as a person. Picture the form sitting at your desk at home, in your car, in one of your classrooms, or in your favorite chair. Visualize it sitting wherever you're likely to sit. When you sit down, the Time Monitor/Time Plan will get squashed.

You can make this image more effective by adding sound effects. The Time Monitor/Time Plan might scream, "Get off me!" Or since time can be related to money, you might associate the Time Monitor/Time Plan with the sound of an old-fashioned cash register. Imagine that every time you sit down, a cash register rings.

MONDAY 9 / 12		
	Monitor	**Plan**
	Get up	
	Shower	
7:00		7:00
7:15	Breakfast	
7:30		
7:45	Walk to	
8:00	class	8:00
8:15		
8:30	Econ 1	
8:45		
9:00		9:00
9:15		
9:30		
9:45		
10:00	Bio 1	10:00
10:15		
10:30		
10:45		
11:00		11:00
11:15	Study	
11:30		
11:45		
12:00		12:00
12:15	Lunch	
12:30		
12:45		
1:00		1:00
1:15	Eng. Lit	
1:30		
1:45		
2:00		2:00
2:15	Coffeehouse	
2:30		
2:45		
3:00		3:00
3:15		
3:30		
3:45		
4:00		4:00
4:15	Study	
4:30		
4:45		
5:00		5:00
5:15	Dinner	
5:30		
5:45		
6:00		6:00
6:15		
6:30	Babysit	
6:45		
7:00		7:00

TUESDAY 9 / 13		
	Monitor	**Plan**
	Sleep	
7:00		7:00
7:15		
7:30		
7:45	Shower	
8:00	Dress	8:00
8:15	Eat	
8:30		
8:45		
9:00	Art	9:00
9:15	Apprec.	
9:30	Project	
9:45		
10:00		10:00
10:15		
10:30		
10:45		
11:00	Data	11:00
11:15	process	
11:30		
11:45		
12:00		12:00
12:15		
12:30		
12:45		
1:00		1:00
1:15	Lunch	
1:30		
1:45		
2:00	Work	2:00
2:15	on book	
2:30	report	
2:45		
3:00	Art	3:00
3:15	Apprec.	
3:30		
3:45		
4:00		4:00
4:15		
4:30		
4:45		
5:00	Dinner	5:00
5:15		
5:30		
5:45		
6:00	Letter to	6:00
6:15	Uncle Jim	
6:30		
6:45		
7:00		7:00

3. Evaluate the Time Monitor/Time Plan. After you've monitored your time for one week, group your activities together by categories. The form on page 98 lists the categories "sleep," "class," "study," and "meals." Think of other categories you could add. "Grooming" might include showering, putting on makeup, brushing teeth, and getting dressed. "Travel" can include walking, driving, taking the bus, and riding your bike. Other categories might be "exercise," "entertainment," "work," "television," "domestic," and "children."

Write in the categories that work for you, and then add up how much time you spent in each of your categories. Put the totals in the "monitored" column. Make sure that the grand total of all categories is 168 hours.

Now take a minute and let these numbers sink in. Compare your totals to your predictions and notice your reactions. You might be surprised. You might feel disappointed or even angry about where your time goes. Use those feelings as motivation to plan your time differently. Go to the "planned" column and decide how much time you want to spend on various daily activities. As you do so, allow yourself to have fun. Approach planning in the spirit of adventure. Think of yourself as an artist who's creating a new life.

In several months you might want to take another detailed look at how you spend your life. You can expand the two-phase cycle of monitoring and planning to include a third phase: evaluating. Combine this with planning your time, following the suggestions in this chapter. You can use a continuous cycle: monitor, evaluate, plan; monitor, evaluate, plan. When you make it a habit, this cycle can help you get the full benefits of time management for the rest of your life. Then time management becomes more than a technique. It's transformed into a habit, a constant awareness of how you spend your lifetime.

WEEK OF ___ / ___ / ___ /		
Category	Monitored	Planned
Sleep		
Class		
Study		
Meals		

MONDAY ___ / ___ / ___ /

Monitor	Plan
7:00	7:00
7:15	
7:30	
7:45	
8:00	8:00
8:15	
8:30	
8:45	
9:00	9:00
9:15	
9:30	
9:45	
10:00	10:00
10:15	
10:30	
10:45	
11:00	11:00
11:15	
11:30	
11:45	
12:00	12:00
12:15	
12:30	
12:45	
1:00	1:00
1:15	
1:30	
1:45	
2:00	2:00
2:15	
2:30	
2:45	
3:00	3:00
3:15	
3:30	
3:45	
4:00	4:00
4:15	
4:30	
4:45	
5:00	5:00
5:15	
5:30	
5:45	
6:00	6:00
6:15	
6:30	
6:45	
7:00	7:00
7:15	
7:30	
7:45	
8:00	8:00
8:15	
8:30	
8:45	
9:00	9:00
9:15	
9:30	
9:45	
10:00	10:00
10:15	
10:30	
10:45	
11:00	11:00
11:15	
11:30	
11:45	
12:00	12:00

TUESDAY ___ / ___ / ___ /

Monitor	Plan
7:00	7:00
7:15	
7:30	
7:45	
8:00	8:00
8:15	
8:30	
8:45	
9:00	9:00
9:15	
9:30	
9:45	
10:00	10:00
10:15	
10:30	
10:45	
11:00	11:00
11:15	
11:30	
11:45	
12:00	12:00
12:15	
12:30	
12:45	
1:00	1:00
1:15	
1:30	
1:45	
2:00	2:00
2:15	
2:30	
2:45	
3:00	3:00
3:15	
3:30	
3:45	
4:00	4:00
4:15	
4:30	
4:45	
5:00	5:00
5:15	
5:30	
5:45	
6:00	6:00
6:15	
6:30	
6:45	
7:00	7:00
7:15	
7:30	
7:45	
8:00	8:00
8:15	
8:30	
8:45	
9:00	9:00
9:15	
9:30	
9:45	
10:00	10:00
10:15	
10:30	
10:45	
11:00	11:00
11:15	
11:30	
11:45	
12:00	12:00

WEDNESDAY ___ / ___ / ___ /

Monitor	Plan
7:00	7:00
7:15	
7:30	
7:45	
8:00	8:00
8:15	
8:30	
8:45	
9:00	9:00
9:15	
9:30	
9:45	
10:00	10:00
10:15	
10:30	
10:45	
11:00	11:00
11:15	
11:30	
11:45	
12:00	12:00
12:15	
12:30	
12:45	
1:00	1:00
1:15	
1:30	
1:45	
2:00	2:00
2:15	
2:30	
2:45	
3:00	3:00
3:15	
3:30	
3:45	
4:00	4:00
4:15	
4:30	
4:45	
5:00	5:00
5:15	
5:30	
5:45	
6:00	6:00
6:15	
6:30	
6:45	
7:00	7:00
7:15	
7:30	
7:45	
8:00	8:00
8:15	
8:30	
8:45	
9:00	9:00
9:15	
9:30	
9:45	
10:00	10:00
10:15	
10:30	
10:45	
11:00	11:00
11:15	
11:30	
11:45	
12:00	12:00

THURSDAY___ / ___ / ___ /	
Monitor	**Plan**
7:00	7:00
7:15	
7:30	
7:45	
8:00	8:00
8:15	
8:30	
8:45	
9:00	9:00
9:15	
9:30	
9:45	
10:00	10:00
10:15	
10:30	
10:45	
11:00	11:00
11:15	
11:30	
11:45	
12:00	12:00
12:15	
12:30	
12:45	
1:00	1:00
1:15	
1:30	
1:45	
2:00	2:00
2:15	
2:30	
2:45	
3:00	3:00
3:15	
3:30	
3:45	
4:00	4:00
4:15	
4:30	
4:45	
5:00	5:00
5:15	
5:30	
5:45	
6:00	6:00
6:15	
6:30	
6:45	
7:00	7:00
7:15	
7:30	
7:45	
8:00	8:00
8:15	
8:30	
8:45	
9:00	9:00
9:15	
9:30	
9:45	
10:00	10:00
10:15	
10:30	
10:45	
11:00	11:00
11:15	
11:30	
11:45	
12:00	12:00

FRIDAY ___ / ___ / ___ /	
Monitor	**Plan**
7:00	7:00
7:15	
7:30	
7:45	
8:00	8:00
8:15	
8:30	
8:45	
9:00	9:00
9:15	
9:30	
9:45	
10:00	10:00
10:15	
10:30	
10:45	
11:00	11:00
11:15	
11:30	
11:45	
12:00	12:00
12:15	
12:30	
12:45	
1:00	1:00
1:15	
1:30	
1:45	
2:00	2:00
2:15	
2:30	
2:45	
3:00	3:00
3:15	
3:30	
3:45	
4:00	4:00
4:15	
4:30	
4:45	
5:00	5:00
5:15	
5:30	
5:45	
6:00	6:00
6:15	
6:30	
6:45	
7:00	7:00
7:15	
7:30	
7:45	
8:00	8:00
8:15	
8:30	
8:45	
9:00	9:00
9:15	
9:30	
9:45	
10:00	10:00
10:15	
10:30	
10:45	
11:00	11:00
11:15	
11:30	
11:45	
12:00	12:00

SATURDAY ___ / ___ / ___ /	
Monitor	**Plan**

SUNDAY ___ / ___ / ___ /	
Monitor	**Plan**

Discovery Statement

After one week of monitoring my time, I discovered that . . .

I want to spend more time on . . .

I want to spend less time on . . .

I was surprised that I spent so much time on . . .

I was surprised that I spent so little time on . . .

I had strong feelings about my use of time when (describe the feeling and the situation) . . .

The ABC daily to-do list

One of the most effective ways to stay on track and actually get things done is to use a daily to-do list. While the Time Monitor/Time Plan gives you a general picture of the week, your daily to-do list itemizes specific tasks you want to complete within the next 24 hours.

One advantage of keeping a daily to-do list is that you don't have to remember what to do next. It's on the list.

A typical day in the life of a student is full of separate, often unrelated tasks—reading, attending lectures, reviewing notes, working at a job, writing papers, researching special projects, running errands. It's easy to forget an important task on a busy day. When that task is written down, you don't have to rely on your memory.

The following steps present one method for to-do lists. Experiment with these steps, modify them as you see fit, and invent new techniques that work for you.

Step 1 **Brainstorm tasks.** To get started, list all of the tasks you want to get done tomorrow. Each task will become an item on a to-do list. Don't worry about putting the entries in order or scheduling them yet. Just list everything you want to accomplish on a sheet of paper, in a planning calendar, or in a special notebook. You can also use 3×5 cards, writing one task on each card. Cards work well because you can slip them into your pocket or rearrange them, and you never have to copy to-do items from one list to another.

Step 2 **Estimate time.** For each task you wrote down in step 1, estimate how long it will take you to complete it. This can be tricky. If you allow too little time, you end up feeling rushed. If you allow too much time, you become less productive. For now, give it your best guess. Your estimates will improve with practice. Now pull out your calendar or Time Monitor/Time Plan. You've probably scheduled some hours for activities such as classes or work. This leaves the unscheduled hours for tackling your to-do lists.

Add up the time needed to complete all your to-do items. Also add up the number of unscheduled hours in your day. Then compare the two totals. The power of this step is that you can spot overload in advance. If you have eight hours' worth of to-do items but only four unscheduled hours, that's a potential problem. To solve it, proceed to step 3.

Step 3 **Rate each task by priority.** To prevent overscheduling, decide which to-do items are the most important given the time you have available. One suggestion for doing this comes from the book *Take Control of Your Time and Life* by Alan Lakein: Simply label each task A, B, or C.[1] The A's on your list are those things that are the most critical. These are assignments that are coming due or jobs that need to be done immediately. Also included are activities that lead directly to your short-term goals.

The B's on your list are important, but less so than the A's. B's might someday become A's. For the present, these tasks are not as urgent as A's. They can be postponed, if necessary, for another day.

The C's do not require immediate attention. C priorities include activities such as "shop for a new blender" and "research genealogy on the Internet." C's are often small, easy jobs with no set timeline. These, too, can be postponed.

Once you've labeled the items on your to-do list, schedule time for all of the A's. The B's and C's can be done randomly during the day when you are in between tasks and are not yet ready to start the next A.

Step 4 **Cross off tasks.** Keep your to-do list with you at all times, crossing off activities when you finish them and adding new ones when you think of them. If you're using 3 × 5 cards, you can toss away or recycle the cards with completed items. Crossing off tasks and releasing cards can be fun—a visible reward for your diligence. This step fosters a sense of accomplishment.

When using the ABC priority method, you might experience an ailment common to students: C fever. This is the uncontrollable urge to drop that A task and begin crossing C's off your to-do list. If your history paper is due tomorrow, you might feel compelled to vacuum the rug, call your third cousin in Tulsa, and go to the store for shoelaces. The reason C fever is so common is that A tasks are usually more difficult or time-consuming to achieve, with a higher risk of failure.

If you notice symptoms of C fever, ask yourself: "Does this job really need to be done now?" "Do I really need to alphabetize my CD collection, or might I better use this time to study for tomorrow's data processing exam?" Use your to-do list to keep yourself on task, working on your A's. Don't panic or berate yourself when you realize that in the last six hours, you have completed 11 C's and not a single A. Calmly return to the A's.

Step 5 **Evaluate.** At the end of the day, evaluate your performance. Look for A priorities you didn't complete. Look for items that repeatedly turn up as B's or C's on your list and never seem to get done. Consider changing these to A's or dropping them altogether. Similarly, you might consider changing an A that didn't get done to a B or C priority. When you're done evaluating, start on tomorrow's to-do list. Be willing to admit mistakes. You might at first rank some items as A's only to realize later that they are actually C's. Some of the C's that lurk at the bottom of your list day after day might really be A's. When you keep a daily to-do list, you can adjust these priorities *before* they become problems.

The ABC system is not the only way to rank items on your to-do list. Some people prefer the "80-20" system. This is based on the idea that 80 percent of the value of any to-do list comes from only 20 percent of the tasks on that list. So on a to-do list of 10 items, find the two that will contribute most to your life, and complete those tasks without fail.

Another option is to rank items as "yes," "no," or "maybe." Do all of the tasks marked "yes." Ignore those marked "no." And put all of the "maybe's" on the shelf for later. You can come back to the "maybe's" at a future point and rank them as "yes" or "no."

Or you can develop your own style for to-do lists. You might find that grouping items by categories such as "errands" or "reading assignments" works best.

Keep in mind the power of planning a whole week or even two weeks in advance. Planning in this way can make it easier to put activities in context and see how your daily goals relate to your long-term goals. Weekly planning can also free you from feeling that you have to polish off your whole to-do list in one day. Instead, you can spread tasks out over the whole week.

In any case, make starting your own to-do list an A priority.

critical thinking exercise 15

CHOOSE STRATEGIES TO MANAGE TIME AND TASKS

Read the article "The ABC daily to-do list." Then choose one technique to apply—preferably within the next 24 hours. In the space below, summarize that technique in one sentence:

____

____

After using the technique for at least one week and observing the results, use the space below to describe how well it worked for you:

____

____

If the technique worked well, consider making it a habit. If it did *not* work well, list a way to modify the strategy so that it becomes a better fit for you:

____

____

Stop procrastination NOW

Consider a bold idea: One way to begin to stop procrastinating is to choose to stop procrastinating. Giving up procrastination is actually a simple choice, and people just try to make it complicated.

Test this idea for yourself. Think of something that you've been putting off. Choose a small, specific task—one that you can complete in five minutes or less. Then do it today.

Tomorrow, choose another task and do it. Repeat this strategy each day for one week. Notice what happens to your habit of procrastination.

If the above suggestion just doesn't work for you, then experiment with any strategy from the list below.

Discover the costs. Find out if procrastination keeps you from getting what you want. Clearly seeing the costs of procrastination can help you kick the habit.

Discover your procrastination style. Psychologist Linda Sapadin identifies different styles of procrastination.[2] For example, *dreamers* have big goals that they seldom translate into specific plans. *Worriers* focus on the "worst case" scenario and are likely to talk more about problems than about solutions. *Defiers* resist new tasks or promise to do them and then don't follow through. *Overdoers* create extra work for themselves by refusing to delegate tasks and neglecting to set priorities. And *perfectionists* put off tasks for fear of making a mistake.

Trick yourself into getting started. If you have a 50-page chapter to read, then grab the book and say to yourself, "I'm not really going to read this chapter right now. I'm just going to flip through the pages and scan the headings for 10 minutes." Tricks like these can get you started on a task you've been dreading.

Let feelings follow action. If you put off exercising until you feel energetic, you might wait for months. Instead, get moving now. Then watch your feelings change. After five minutes of brisk walking, you might be in the mood for a 20-minute run.

Choose to work under pressure. Sometimes people thrive under pressure. As one writer put it, "I don't do my *best* work under deadline. I do my *only* work under deadline." Used selectively, this strategy might also work for you.

Think ahead. Use the monthly calendar on page 116 or the long-term planner on page 118 to list due dates for assignments in all your courses. Using these tools, you can anticipate heavy demands on your time and take action to prevent last-minute crunches.

Give up "some day." Procrastination rests on this vague notion: *I'll do it some day.* Other people reinforce this notion by telling you that your life will *really* start when you . . . . (Fill in the blank with phrases like *graduate from college, get married, have kids, get promoted,* or *retire.*) Using this logic, you could wait your whole life to start living. Avoid this fate. Take action today.

Create goals that draw you forward. A goal that grabs you by the heart strings is an inspiration to act now. If you're procrastinating, then set some goals that excite you. Then you might wake up one day and discover that procrastination is part of your past. ⊠

The seven-day antiprocrastination plan

Listed here are seven strategies you can use to reduce or eliminate many sources of procrastination. The suggestions are tied to the days of the week to help you remember them. Use this list to remind yourself that each day of your life presents an opportunity to stop the cycle of procrastination.

MONDAY **Make it meaningful.** What is important about the task you've been putting off? List all the benefits of completing it. Look at it in relation to your short-, mid-, or long-term goals. Be specific about the rewards for getting it done, including how you will feel when the task is completed. To remember this strategy, keep in mind that it starts with the letter *M*, like the word *Monday.*

TUESDAY **Take it apart.** Break big jobs into a series of small ones you can do in 15 minutes or less. If a long reading assignment intimidates you, divide it into two-page or three-page sections. Make a list of the sections and cross them off as you complete them so you can see your progress. Even the biggest projects can be broken down into a series of small tasks. This strategy starts with the letter *T*, so mentally tie it to *Tuesday.*

WEDNESDAY **Write an intention statement.** For example, if you can't get started on a term paper, you might write, "I intend to write a list of at least 10 possible topics by 9 p.m. I will reward myself with an hour of guilt-free recreational reading." Write your intention on a 3 × 5 card and carry it with you, or post it in your study area where you can see it often. In your memory, file the first word in this strategy—*write*—with *Wednesday.*

THURSDAY **Tell everyone.** Publicly announce your intention to get a task done. Tell a friend that you intend to learn 10 irregular French verbs by Saturday. Tell your spouse, roommate, parents, and children. Include anyone who will ask whether you've completed the assignment or who will suggest ways to get it done. Make the world your support group. Associate *tell* with *Thursday.*

FRIDAY **Find a reward.** Construct rewards to yourself carefully. Be willing to withhold them if you do not complete the task. Don't pick a movie as a reward for studying biology if you plan to go to the movie anyway. And when you legitimately reap your reward, notice how it feels. Remember that *Friday* is a fine day to *find* a reward. (Of course, you can find a reward on any day of the week. Rhyming *Friday* with *fine* day is just a memory trick.)

SATURDAY **Settle it now.** Do it now. The minute you notice yourself procrastinating, plunge into the task. Imagine yourself at a cold mountain lake, poised to dive. Gradual immersion would be slow torture. It's often less painful to leap. Then be sure to savor the feeling of having the task behind you. Link *settle* with *Saturday.*

SUNDAY **Say no.** When you keep pushing a task into a low-priority category, re-examine your purpose for doing it at all. If you realize that you really don't intend to do something, quit telling yourself that you will. That's procrastinating. Just say no. Then you're not procrastinating. You don't have to carry around the baggage of an undone task. *Sunday*—the last day of this seven-day plan—is a great day to finally let go and just *say* no.

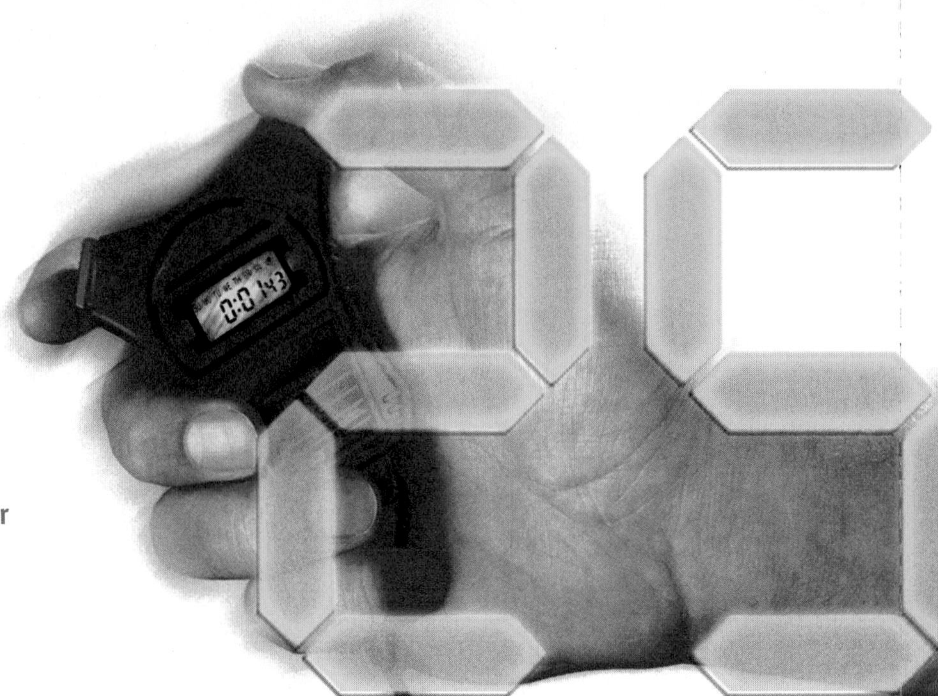

ways to get the **most** out of **now**

The following techniques are listed in four categories:

- **When to study**
- **Where to study**
- **Ways to handle the rest of the world**
- **Things to ask yourself if you get stuck**

While the first three categories are about getting the most from study time, the last category is about using time effectively in any context—at work, home, or school.

Don't feel pressured to use all of the techniques listed below or to tackle them in order. As you read, note the suggestions you think will be helpful. Pick one technique to use now. When it becomes a habit, come back to this article and select another one. Repeat this cycle and enjoy the results as they unfold in your life.

When to study

1 **Study difficult (or "boring") subjects first.** If your chemistry problems put you to sleep, get to them first, while you are fresh. We tend to give top priority to what we enjoy studying, yet the courses we find most difficult often require the most creative energy. Save your favorite subjects for later. If you find yourself avoiding a particular subject, get up an hour earlier to study it before breakfast. With that chore out of the way, the rest of the day can be a breeze.

Continually being late with course assignments indicates a trouble area. Further action is required. Clarify your intentions about the course by writing down your feelings in a journal, talking with an instructor, or asking for help from a friend or counselor. Consistently avoiding study tasks can also be a signal to re-examine your major or course program.

2 **Be aware of your best time of day.** Many people learn best in daylight hours. If this is true for you, schedule study time for your most difficult subjects before nightfall.

Unless you grew up on a farm, the idea of being conscious at 4 a.m. might seem ridiculous. Yet many successful business people begin the day at 5 a.m. or earlier. Athletes and yogis use this time, too. Some writers complete their best work before 9 a.m.

For others, the same benefits are experienced by staying up late. They flourish after midnight. If you aren't convinced, then experiment. When you're in a time crunch, get up early or stay up late. You might even see a sunrise.

3 **Use waiting time.** Five minutes waiting for a subway, 20 minutes waiting for the dentist, 10 minutes in between classes—waiting time adds up fast. Have short study tasks ready to do during these periods. For example, you can carry 3 × 5 cards with facts, formulas, or definitions and pull them out anywhere.

A tape recorder can help you use commuting time to your advantage. Make tape cassettes of yourself reading your notes. Then play these tapes in a car stereo as you drive, or listen through your headphones as you ride on the bus or subway.

4 **Study two hours for every hour in class.** Students in higher education are regularly advised to allow two hours of study time for every hour spent in class. If you are taking 15 credit hours, then plan to spend 30 hours a week studying. The benefits of following this advice will be apparent at exam time.

This guideline is just that—a guideline, not an absolute rule. Consider what's best for you. If you do the Time Monitor/Time Plan exercise in this chapter, note how many hours you actually spend studying for each hour of class. Then ask how your schedule is working. You might want to allow more study time for some subjects.

Keep in mind that the "two hours for one" rule doesn't distinguish between focused time and unfocused time. In one four-hour block of study time, it's possible to use up two of those hours with phone calls, breaks, daydreaming, and doodling. With study time, quality counts as much as quantity.

Avoid marathon study sessions. When possible, study in shorter sessions. Three three-hour sessions are usually more productive than one nine-hour session. If you must study in a large block of time, work on several subjects and avoid studying similar topics one after the other.

Where to study

5 **Use a regular study area.** Your body and your mind know where you are. Using the same place to study, day after day, helps train your responses. When you arrive at that particular place, you can focus your attention more quickly.

Study where you'll be alert. In bed, your body gets a signal. For most students, that signal is more likely to be "Time to sleep!" than "Time to study!" Just as you train your body to be alert at your desk, you also train it to slow down near your bed. For that reason, don't study where you sleep.

Easy chairs and sofas are also dangerous places to study. Learning requires energy. Give your body a message that energy is needed. Put yourself in a situation that supports this message.

Some schools offer empty classrooms as places to study. Many students report finding themselves studying effectively in a classroom setting.

6 **Use a library.** Libraries are designed for learning. The lighting is perfect. The noise level is low. A wealth of material is available. Entering a library is a signal to focus the mind and get to work. Many students can get more done in a shorter time frame at the library than anywhere else. Experiment for yourself.

Ways to handle the rest of the world

7 **Pay attention to your attention.** Breaks in concentration are often caused by internal interruptions. Your own thoughts jump in to divert you from your studies. When this happens, notice these thoughts and let them go. Perhaps the thought of getting something else done is distracting you. One option is to handle that other task now and study later. Or you can write yourself a note about it, or schedule a specific time to do it.

8 **Agree with living mates about study time.** This includes roommates, spouses, and children. Make the rules clear, and be sure to follow them yourself. Explicit agreements—even written contracts—work well. One student always wears a colorful hat when he wants to study. When his wife and children see the hat, they respect his wish to be left alone.

9 **Get off the phone.** The telephone is the ultimate interrupter. People who wouldn't think of distracting you might call at the worst times because they can't see that you are studying. You don't have to be a telephone victim. If a simple "I can't talk, I'm studying" doesn't work, use dead silence. It's a conversation killer. Or short-circuit the whole problem: Unplug the phone. Other solutions include getting an answering machine and studying at the library.

10 **Learn to say no.** This is a timesaver and a valuable life skill for everyone. Some people feel it is rude to refuse a request. But saying no can be done effectively and courteously. Others want you to succeed as a student. When you tell them that you can't do what they ask because you are busy educating yourself, most people will understand.

11 **Hang a "do not disturb" sign on your door.** Many hotels will give you a free sign, for the advertising. Or you can create a sign yourself. They work. Using signs can relieve you of making a decision about cutting off each interruption—a timesaver in itself.

12 **Get ready the night before.** Completing a few simple tasks just before you go to bed can help you get in gear the next day. If you need to make some phone calls first thing in the morning, look up those numbers, write them on 3 × 5 cards, and set them near the phone. If you need to drive to a new location, make a note of the address and put it next to your car keys. If you plan to spend the next afternoon writing a paper, get your materials together: dictionary, notes, outline, paper, and pencil (or computer disks and portable computer). Pack your lunch or put gas in the car. Organize the baby's diaper bag and your briefcase or backpack.

13 **Call ahead.** We often think of talking on the telephone as a prime time-waster. Used wisely, the telephone can actually help manage time. Before you go shopping, call the store to see if it carries the items you're looking for. If you're driving, call for directions to your destination. A few seconds on the phone can save hours in wasted trips and wrong turns.

14 **Avoid noise distractions.** To promote concentration, avoid studying in front of the television and turn off the radio. Many students insist that they study better with background noise, and this might be true. Some students report good results with carefully selected and controlled music. For many others, silence is the best form of music to study by.

At times noise levels might be out of your control. A neighbor or roommate might decide to find out how far he can turn up his boom box before the walls crumble. Meanwhile, your ability to concentrate on the principles of sociology goes down the drain. To avoid this scenario, schedule study sessions during periods when your living environment is usually quiet. If you live in a residence hall, ask if study rooms are available. Or go somewhere else where it's quiet, such as the library. Some students have even found refuge in quiet cafés, self-service laundries, and places of worship.

15 **Manage interruptions.** Notice how others misuse your time. Be aware of repeat offenders. Ask yourself if there are certain friends or relatives who consistently interrupt your study time.

If avoiding the interrupter is impractical, send a clear message. Sometimes others don't realize that they are breaking your concentration. You can give them a gentle yet firm reminder: "What you're saying is important. Can we schedule a time to talk about it when I can give you my full attention?" If this doesn't work, there are other ways to make your message more effective. For more ideas, see Chapter Eight: Communicating.

See if you can "firewall" yourself for selected study periods each week. Find a place where you can count on being alone and working without interruption.

Sometimes interruptions still happen. Create a system for dealing with them. One option is to take an index card and write a quick note about what you're doing the moment an interruption occurs. As soon as possible, return to the card and pick up the task where you left off.

Keep on going?

Some people keep on going, even when they get stuck or fail again and again. To such people belongs the world. Consider the hapless politician who compiled this record:

- Failed in business, 1831
- Defeated for legislature, 1832
- Second failure in business, 1833
- Suffered nervous breakdown, 1836
- Defeated for Speaker of the House, 1838
- Defeated for elector, 1840
- Defeated for Congress, 1843
- Defeated for Senate, 1855
- Defeated for vice president, 1856
- Defeated for Senate, 1858
- Elected president, 1860

Who was the fool who kept on going in spite of so many failures?

Answer: The fool was Abraham Lincoln.

Things to ask yourself if you get stuck

16 **Ask: "What's my MIT?"** Your first thought of the day might be *I've got a million things to do!* Take a moment to think more deeply. Pretend that you have time to accomplish only one major task in the next few hours. What would it be? Even if you have dozens of items on your to-do list, one of them will probably rise to the top for now. This is your most important task (MIT). Do it first. Get it out of the way before you check your e-mail, run errands, or complete other easier and lower-priority tasks.

Not surprisingly, your MIT might also be your *toughest* task for the day. At home, it might be making time for exercise. At work, it might be returning a call from an angry customer. No matter what the MIT, tackling it first can deliver sweet feelings of relief that linger for hours.

You can get a head start on your MIT by choosing it in advance. On a Friday afternoon at work, for example, choose your MIT for Monday. Write it down on a 3 × 5 card and attach it to your computer keyboard, your phone, your bathroom mirror, or another place where you're sure to see it.

Sometimes you can discover your MIT by asking another question: "What is *one* task I can accomplish toward achieving a goal?" This is a helpful technique to use when faced with a big, imposing job. Pick out one small accomplishment, preferably one you can complete in about five minutes; then do it. The satisfaction of getting one thing done can spur you on to get one more thing done. Meanwhile, the job gets smaller.

One benefit of using the MIT technique is avoiding "rush hour." In time-management terms, this does not refer to sitting in a traffic jam. Instead, it means racing to finish a task during the final minutes of your workday. Choosing and completing your MIT early makes it easier to leave work on time with the feeling that you actually accomplished something, with time to spare.

17 **Ask: "Am I being too hard on myself?"** If you are feeling frustrated with a reading assignment, if your attention wanders repeatedly, or if you've fallen behind on math problems that are due tomorrow, take a minute to listen to the messages you are giving yourself. Are you scolding yourself too harshly? Lighten up. Allow yourself to feel a little foolish and then get on with the task at hand. Don't add to the problem by berating yourself.

Worrying about the future is another way people beat themselves up: "How will I ever get all this done?" "What if every paper I'm assigned turns out to be this hard?" "If I can't do the simple calculations now, how will I ever pass the final?" Instead of promoting learning, such questions fuel anxiety.

Labeling and generalizing weaknesses are other ways people are hard on themselves. Being objective and specific will help eliminate this form of self-punishment and will likely generate new possibilities. An alternative to saying "I'm terrible in algebra" is to say "I don't understand factoring equations." This rewording suggests a plan to improve.

You can also take pressure off yourself by building some flexibility into your weekly schedule. Unexpected things will happen, so allow for them. Leave some holes in your schedule. Schedule fixed blocks of time first, such as class and work hours. Then build in blocks of unplanned time. In your calendar, mark these hours as "flextime" or "open time." Use this time for emergencies, errands, spontaneous activities, or catching up with people.

Remember travel time. If you're a commuter student, allow time to navigate between school and home. And if you work, allow for the time it takes to get there.

Also make room for fun. Fun is important. Brains that are constantly stimulated by new ideas and new challenges need time off to digest them. Take time to browse aimlessly through the library, stroll with no destination, ride a bike, or do other things you enjoy. It's important to "waste" time once in a while.

18 **Ask: "Is this a piano?"** Carpenters who construct rough frames for buildings have a saying they use when they bend a nail or accidentally hack a chunk out of a two-by-four: "Well, this ain't no piano." It means that perfection is not necessary. Ask yourself if what you are doing needs to be perfect. Perhaps you don't have to apply the same standards of grammar to lecture notes that you would apply to a term paper. If you can complete a job 95 percent perfectly in two hours and 100 percent perfectly in four hours, ask yourself whether the additional 5 percent improvement is worth doubling the amount of time you spend.

Sometimes it *is* a piano. A tiny miscalculation can ruin an entire lab experiment. A misstep in solving a complex math problem can negate hours of work. Computers are notorious for turning little errors into nightmares. Accept lower standards only when appropriate.

A related suggestion is to weed out low-priority tasks. The to-do list for a large project can include dozens of items, not all of which are equally important. Some can be done later, while others can be skipped altogether, if time is short.

Apply this idea when you study. In a long reading assignment, look for pages you can skim or skip. When it's appropriate, read chapter summaries or article abstracts. As you review your notes, look for material that might not be covered on a test and decide whether you want to study it.

19 **Ask: "Would I pay myself for what I'm doing right now?"** If you were employed as a student, would you be earning your wages? Ask yourself this question when you notice that you've taken your third snack break in 30 minutes. Most students are, in fact, employed as students. They are investing in their own productivity and paying a big price for the privilege of being a student. Sometimes they don't realize that doing a mediocre job now might result in fewer opportunities for the future.

20 **Ask: "Can I do just one more thing?"** Ask yourself this question at the end of a long day. Almost always you will have enough energy to do just one more short task. The overall increase in your productivity might surprise you.

21 **Ask: "Am I making time for things that are important but not urgent?"** If we spend most of our time putting out fires, we can feel drained and frustrated. According to Stephen R. Covey, this happens when we forget to take time for things that are not urgent but are truly important.[3] Examples include exercising regularly, reading, praying or meditating, spending quality time alone or with family members and friends, traveling, and cooking nutritious meals. Each of these can contribute directly to a long-term goal or life mission. Yet when schedules get tight, we often forgo these things, waiting for that elusive day when we'll "finally have more time."

That day won't come until we choose to make time for what's truly important. Knowing this, we can use some of the suggestions in this chapter to free up more time.

22 **Ask: "Can I delegate this?"** Instead of slogging through complicated tasks alone, you can draw on the talents and energy of other people. Busy executives know the value of delegating tasks to coworkers. Without delegation, many projects would flounder or die.

You can apply the same principle. Instead of doing all the housework or cooking by yourself, for example, you can assign some of the tasks to family members or roommates. Rather than making a trip to the library to look up a simple fact, you can call and ask a library assistant to research it for you. Instead of driving across town to deliver a package, you can hire a delivery service to do so. All of these tactics can free up extra hours for studying.

It's not practical to delegate certain study tasks, such as writing term papers or completing reading assignments. However, you can still draw on the ideas of others in completing such tasks. For instance, form a writing group to edit and critique papers, brainstorm topics or titles, and develop lists of sources.

If you're absent from a class, find a classmate to summarize the lecture, discussion, and any upcoming assignments. Presidents depend on briefings. You can use this technique, too.

23 **Ask: "How did I just waste time?"** Notice when time passes and you haven't accomplished what you had planned to do. Take a minute to review your actions and note the specific ways you wasted time. We tend to operate by habit, wasting time in the same ways over and over again. When you are aware of things you do that drain your time, you are more likely to catch yourself in the act next time. Observing one small quirk might save you hours. But keep this in mind: Asking you to notice how you waste time is not intended to make you feel guilty. The point is to increase your skill by getting specific information about how you use time.

24 **Ask: "Could I find the time if I really wanted to?"** The way people speak often rules out the option of finding more time. An alternative is to speak about time with more possibility.

The next time you're tempted to say, "I just don't have time," pause for a minute. Question the truth of this statement. Could you find four more hours this week for studying? Suppose that someone offered to pay you $10,000 to find those four hours. Suppose, too, that you will get paid only if you don't lose sleep, call in sick for work, or sacrifice anything important to you. Could you find the time if vast sums of money were involved?

Remember that when it comes to school, vast sums of money *are* involved.

25 **Ask: "Am I willing to promise it?"** This might be the most powerful time-management idea of all. If you want to find time for a task, promise yourself—and others—that you'll get it done.

To make this technique work, do more than say that you'll try or that you'll give it your best shot. Take an oath, as you would in court. Give it your word.

One way to accomplish big things in life is to make big promises. There's little reward in promising what's safe or predictable. No athlete promises to place seventh in the Olympic Games. Chances are that if we're not making big promises, we're not stretching ourselves.

The point of making a promise is not to chain ourselves to a rigid schedule or to impossible expectations. We can also promise to reach goals without unbearable stress. We can keep schedules flexible and carry out our plans with ease, joy, and satisfaction.

At times we can go too far. Some promises are truly beyond us, and we might break them. However, failing to keep a promise is just that—failing to keep a promise. A broken promise is not the end of the world.

Promises can work magic. When our word is on the line, it's possible to discover reserves of time and energy we didn't know existed. Promises can push us to exceed our expectations. ⊠

Remember cultural differences

There are as many different styles for managing time as there are people. These styles vary across cultures.

In the United States and England, for example, business meetings typically start on time. That's also true in Scandinavian countries such as Norway and Sweden. However, travelers to Panama might find that meetings start about a half-hour late. And people who complain about late meetings while doing business in Mexico might be considered rude.

When you study or work with people of different races and ethnic backgrounds, look for differences in their approach to time. A behavior that you might view as rude or careless—such as showing up late for appointments—could simply result from seeing the world in a different way.

More information is available online. *Student Website*

Organizing time and tasks at work

To succeed at getting organized, think in terms of two broad strategies. First, get the big picture—what you intend to accomplish this month, this quarter, this year, and beyond. Another name for this is *macro-organizing.* (*Macro* is a prefix that means "large" or "inclusive.")

Second, set priorities for your day-to-day, hour-to-hour tasks. This process of working with shorter time intervals can be called *micro-organizing.* (*Micro* means "small.")

Macro-organizing

Get real with project due dates. The more complicated the project, the more you can benefit from getting organized. This is especially true with projects that extend well into the future.

Start by scheduling a long-term goal—the due date for the final product. Next, set interim due dates—what you'll produce at key points leading up to that final date. These interim dates function as mid-term goals. In turn, each mid-term goal can lead you to more immediate, short-term goals.

For example, say that you're a computer technician and your team plans to complete a major hardware and software upgrade for your company in one year (long-term goal). As a team, set goals for finishing major parts of this project, such as due dates for installing new computers in individual departments (mid-term goals). You could also set up meetings with each department head over the next month to update them on your plans (short-term goals).

You may end up juggling several major projects at once. To plan effectively, enter all the relevant due dates in a weekly or monthly calendar so that you can see several of them at a glance.

Think beyond the next project. As you schedule projects, take some time to lift your eyes to the horizon. Step back for a few minutes and consider your longer-range goals—what you want to accomplish at your job and in your career in the next six months, the next year, and the next five years.

Ask whether the activities you've scheduled actually contribute to those goals. If they do, great. If not, determine whether you can delete some items from your daily calendar and to-do list to free up more hours for meeting longer-term goals.

Monitor work time and tasks. Another way to get a big picture of your work life is to look for broad patterns in how you currently spend your work time. Use the Time Monitor/Time Plan explained earlier in this chapter to do this analysis. Find out which tasks burn up most of your hours on the job.

With this data in hand, you can make immediate choices to minimize downtime and boost your productivity. Start by looking for low-value activities to eliminate. Also note your peak periods of energy during the workday. Schedule your most challenging tasks for these times.

Micro-organizing

Schedule fixed blocks of time first. Start with recurring meetings, for instance. These time periods are usually determined in advance and occur at regular times each week or month. Be realistic about how much time you need for such events. Then schedule other tasks around them.

Set realistic goals. Don't set yourself up for failure by telling yourself you can do a four-hour job in two hours.

There are only 40 to 50 hours in a typical full-time workweek. If you schedule 65 hours, you've lost before you begin.

This is where your Time Monitor/Time Plan can really help. Monitor your time often to obtain a realistic idea of how long it takes to complete typical tasks. This will help you in scheduling future projects.

Set clear starting and stopping times. Tasks often expand to fill the time we allot for them. "It always takes me two hours just to deal with my e-mails each day" might become a self-fulfilling prophecy.

As an alternative, schedule a certain amount of time for reading and responding to e-mail. Set a timer and stick to it. People often find that they can gradually decrease such time by forcing themselves to work a little more efficiently. This can usually be done without sacrificing the quality of your work.

Feeling rushed or sacrificing quality is not the goal here. The point is to push ourselves a little and discover what our time requirements really are.

Calculate the cost of attending meetings. Meetings can eat up hours each week. If you're in a management or supervisory position, in fact, meetings can make up most of your job. The problem is that some meetings take place without a clear agenda. Or the discussion wanders off in irrelevant directions, agreements are not clarified, and the people who attend fail to take follow-up action.

To get a concrete sense of such problems, calculate what it costs you to attend meetings. On your Time Monitor/ Time Plan, add up the number of hours you spend in meetings each week. Then multiply this number by your hourly wage. The result is how much it costs you to attend those meetings. (If you receive a salary instead of an hourly wage, estimate the total number of hours you will work this year. Then take your gross annual salary and divide it by this total. This will give you an hourly "wage.")

Knowing how many dollars it costs to attend meetings can motivate you to use that time wisely. Write an Intention Statement about how you plan to get the most value out of upcoming meetings. See if you can stop attending meetings that consistently fail to produce any value.

Involve others when appropriate. Sometimes the activities we schedule depend on gaining information, assistance, or direct participation from supervisors or other coworkers. If we neglect to inform them of our plans or forget to ask for their cooperation at the outset—surprise! Our schedules can crash.

Statements such as these often follow the breakdown: "I just assumed you were free for a working lunch at 11:30 a.m. on Tuesday." Or "I'm working overtime this month and hoped that you'd lead the weekly staff meetings for a while."

When you schedule a task that depends on another person's involvement, let that person know—the sooner, the better.

Avoid the perils of multi-tasking. Our effectiveness often decreases when we try to do several things at once, such as talking on a cell phone while driving. When you get busy at work, you might feel tempted to multi-task. Yet studies indicate that multi-tasking reduces metabolic activity in the brain, lowers one's ability to complete tasks efficiently, and increases the number of errors made in following a procedure.[4] To avoid these problems, plan your workday as a succession of tasks, then do each task with full attention. Use the ABC priority system to weed out tasks of lower importance. This can give you more time to focus on the A's.

Clean your desk. For starters, purge your cubicle and files of everything you don't need. Start tossing junk mail the moment that it arrives. Next, start a "to read" file for documents that you can review at any time. Pack this folder for your next plane trip or bus ride. Finally, avoid the habit of writing reminder notes on random scraps of paper. Store all your to-do items in a unified system, such as a stack of 3 × 5 cards or a single file on your computer. Having an uncluttered desk makes it easier for you to find things, which saves time.

Beyond time management

Staying focused on what matters

Sometimes people who pride themselves on efficiency are merely keeping busy. In their rush to check items off a to-do list, they might be fussing over activities that create little value in the first place. An effective planner is productive and relaxed at the same time. That's the purpose of the following suggestions.

Discover your style. Remember that there are many styles of planning. Instead of writing a conventional to-do list, for instance, plot your day on a mind map. (Mind maps are explained in Chapter Five: Notes.)

Focus on values. As a way to define your values, write your own obituary. Describe the ways you want to be remembered. List the contributions you intend to make during your lifetime and the kind of person you wish to become. Then, as you plan the upcoming week, make time for activities that relate directly to your obituary.

Do less. Planning is as much about dropping worthless activities as about adding new ones. See if you can reduce or eliminate activities that contribute little to your values.

Forget about time. Take time away from time. Schedule downtime—a space in your day where you ignore to-do lists, appointments, and accomplishments. This is a period when you're accountable to no one else and have nothing to accomplish.

Forget time management—just get things done. David Allen, author of *Getting Things Done: The Art of Stress-Free Productivity*, offers a unique approach to personal productivity.[5] Following are Allen's main suggestions.

Collect. To begin, gather every unfinished project, incomplete task, misplaced object—or anything else that's nagging you—and dump it into a bucket or collection area.

Process. Now go to each of your buckets, one at a time. Take whatever item is at the top of the pile and ask: "Do I truly want to or need to do something about this?" If the answer is no, then calmly dispose of the item. If the answer is yes, then choose immediately how to respond. If you can complete action on this item in two minutes or less, then do so now. If you're dealing with an item that will take more than two minutes for you to do, then write a reminder to do it later. Repeat this procedure until you empty your buckets.

Organize. Now group your reminders into appropriate categories. The categories are ultimately up to you, but Allen's recommendations include:

- A calendar for listing actions to be completed on a specific date or at a specific time.
- A list of current projects.
- A next action list. Instead of ranking these items by priority, simply group them by the context or physical location where you will do them—for example, *at phone* or *at computer*.

Review. Every week, review your reminders and ask yourself: What are all my current projects? And what is the *very next physical action* (such as a phone call or errand) that I can take to move each project forward?

Do. Every day, review your calendar and lists. Based on this information and on your intuition, make moment-to-moment choices about how to spend your time. ✕

MASTER MONTHLY CALENDAR

This exercise will give you an opportunity to step back from the details of your daily schedule and get a bigger picture of your life. The more difficult it is for you to plan beyond the current day or week, the greater the benefit of this exercise.

Your basic tool is a one-month calendar. Use it to block out specific times for upcoming events, such as study group meetings, due dates for assignments, review periods before tests, and other time-sensitive tasks.

To get started, you might want to copy the blank monthly calendar on page 116 onto both sides of a sheet of paper. Or make several copies of this page and tape them together so that you can see several months at a glance.

Also be creative. Experiment with a variety of uses for your monthly calendar. For instance, you can note day-to-day changes in your health or moods, list the places you visit while you are on vacation, or circle each day that you practice a new habit. For examples of filled-in monthly calendars, see below.

Name ______________ Month ______________

MONDAY	TUESDAY	WEDNESDAY	THURSDAY	FRIDAY	SATURDAY	SUNDAY

Gearing up:

Using a long-term planner

Planning a day, a week, or a month ahead is a powerful practice. Using a long-term planner—one that displays an entire quarter, semester, or year at a glance—can yield even more benefits.

With a long-term planner, you can eliminate a lot of unpleasant surprises. Long-term planning allows you to avoid scheduling conflicts—the kind that obligate you to be in two places at the same time three weeks from now. You can also anticipate busy periods, such as finals week, and start preparing for them now. Good-bye, all-night cram sessions. Hello, serenity.

Find a long-term planner, or make your own. Many office supply stores carry academic planners in paper form that cover an entire school year. Computer software for time management offers the same feature. You can also be creative and make your own long-term planner. A big roll of newsprint pinned to a bulletin board or taped to a wall will do nicely.

Enter scheduled dates that extend into the future. Use your long-term planner to list commitments that extend beyond the current month. Enter test dates, lab sessions, days that classes will be canceled, and other events that will take place over this term and next term.

Create a master assignment list. Find the syllabus for each course you're currently taking. Then, in your long-term planner, enter the due dates for all of the assignments in all of your courses. This can be a powerful reality check.

The purpose of this technique is to not to make you feel overwhelmed with all the things you have to do. Rather, its aim is to help you take a First Step toward recognizing the demands on your time. Armed with the truth about how you use your time, you can make more accurate plans.

Include nonacademic events. In addition to tracking academic commitments, you can use your long-term planner to mark significant events in your life outside school. Include birthdays, doctor's appointments, concert dates, credit card payment due dates, and car maintenance schedules.

Use your long-term planner to divide and conquer. Big assignments such as term papers or major presentations pose a special risk. When you have three months to do a project, you might say to yourself, "That looks like a lot of work, but I've got plenty of time. No problem." Two months, three weeks, and six days from now, it could suddenly be a problem.

For some people, academic life is a series of last-minute crises punctuated by periods of exhaustion. You can avoid that fate. The trick is to set due dates *before* the final due date.

When planning to write a term paper, for instance, enter the final due date in your long-term planner. Then set individual due dates for each milestone in the writing process—creating an outline, completing your research, finishing a first draft, editing the draft, and preparing the final copy. By meeting these interim due dates, you make steady progress on the assignment throughout the term. That sure beats trying to crank out all those pages at the last minute.

Week of	Monday	Tuesday	Wednesday	Thursday	Friday	Saturday	Sunday
9 / 5							
9 / 12		English quiz					
9 / 19			English paper due		Speech #1		
9 / 26	Chemistry test					Skiing at the lake	
10 / 3		English quiz			Speech #2		
10 / 10				Geography project due			
10 / 17				--- No classes ---			

Name ___________________________

LONG-TERM PLANNER ___ /___ /___ to ___ /___ /___

Week of	Monday	Tuesday	Wednesday	Thursday	Friday	Saturday	Sunday
___ /___							
___ /___							
___ /___							
___ /___							
___ /___							
___ /___							
___ /___							
___ /___							
___ /___							
___ /___							
___ /___							
___ /___							
___ /___							
___ /___							
___ /___							
___ /___							
___ /___							
___ /___							
___ /___							
___ /___							
___ /___							
___ /___							
___ /___							
___ /___							
___ /___							
___ /___							
___ /___							
___ /___							
___ /___							
___ /___							

Name ______________________________

LONG-TERM PLANNER ___ /___ /___ to ___ /___ /___

Week of	Monday	Tuesday	Wednesday	Thursday	Friday	Saturday	Sunday
___ /___							
___ /___							
___ /___							
___ /___							
___ /___							
___ /___							
___ /___							
___ /___							
___ /___							
___ /___							
___ /___							
___ /___							
___ /___							
___ /___							
___ /___							
___ /___							
___ /___							
___ /___							
___ /___							
___ /___							
___ /___							
___ /___							
___ /___							
___ /___							
___ /___							
___ /___							
___ /___							
___ /___							
___ /___							
___ /___							

power process

BE HERE NOW

Being right here, right now, is such a simple idea. It seems obvious. Where else can you be but where you are? When else can you be there but when you are there?

The answer is that you can be somewhere else at any time—in your head. It's common for our thoughts to distract us from where we've chosen to be. When we let this happen, we lose the benefits of focusing our attention on what's important to us in the present moment.

To "be here now" means to do what you're doing when you're doing it and to be where you are when you're there. Students consistently report that focusing attention on the here and now is one of the most powerful tools in this book.

Leaving the here and now

We all have a voice in our head that hardly ever shuts up. If you don't believe it, conduct this experiment: Close your eyes for 10 seconds and pay attention to what is going on in your head. Please do this right now.

Notice something? Perhaps your voice was saying, "Forget it. I'm in a hurry." Another might have said, "I wonder when 10 seconds is up." Another could have been saying, "What little voice? I don't hear any little voice." That's the voice.

This voice can take you anywhere at any time—especially when you are studying. When the voice takes you away, you might appear to be studying, but your brain is at the beach.

All of us have experienced this voice, as well as the absence of it. When our inner voices are silent, time no longer seems to exist. We forget worries, aches, pains, reasons, excuses, and justifications. We fully experience the here and now. Life is magic.

There are many benefits of such a state of consciousness. It is easier to discover the world around us when we are not chattering away to ourselves about how we think it ought to be, has been, or will be. Letting go of inner voices and pictures—being totally in the moment—is a powerful tool. Do not expect to be rid of daydreams entirely. That is neither possible nor desirable. Inner voices serve a purpose. They enable us to analyze, predict, classify, and understand events out there in the "real" world.

Your stream of consciousness serves a purpose. When you are working on a term paper, your inner voice might suggest ideas. When you are listening to your sociology instructor, your inner voice can alert you to possible test questions. When you're about to jump out of an airplane, it can remind you to take a parachute. The trick is to consciously choose when to be with your inner voice and when to let it go.

Returning to the here and now

A powerful step toward returning to the here and now is to notice when we leave it. Our mind has a mind of its own, and it seems to fight back when we try to control it too much. If you doubt this, for the next 10 seconds do not, under any circumstances, think of a pink elephant. Please begin not thinking about one now.

Persistent image, isn't it? Most ideas are this insistent when we try to deny them or force them out of our consciousness. For example, during class you might notice yourself thinking about a test you took the previous day, or a party planned for the weekend, or the DVD player you'd like to have.

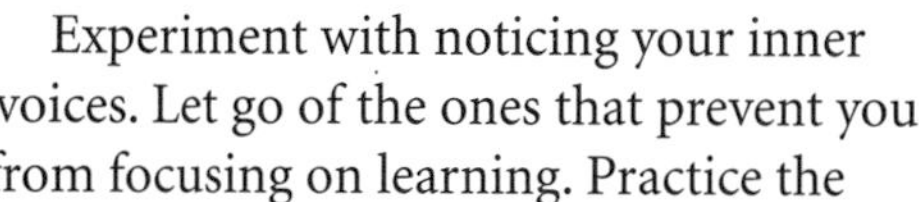

Instead of trying to force a stray thought out of your head—a futile enterprise—simply notice it. Accept it. Tell yourself, "There's that thought again." Then gently return your attention to the task at hand. That thought, or another, will come back. Your mind will drift. Simply notice again where your thoughts take you and gently bring yourself back to the here and now.

Another way to return to the here and now is to notice your physical sensations. Notice the way the room looks or smells. Notice the temperature and how the chair feels. Once you've regained control of your attention by becoming aware of your physical surroundings, you can more easily take the next step and bring your full attention back to your present task.

We can often immediately improve our effectiveness—and our enjoyment—by fully entering into each of our activities, doing one thing at a time.

For example, take something as simple as peeling and eating an orange. Carefully notice the color, shape, and texture of the orange. Hold it close to your nose and savor the pungent, sweet smell. Then slowly peel the orange and see if you can hear every subtle sound that results. Next take one piece of the orange and place it in your mouth. Notice the feel of the fruit on your tongue. Chew the piece slowly, letting the delicious juice bathe your taste buds. Take note of each individual sensation of pleasure that ripples through your body as you sample this delicious treat.

"Be here now" can turn the act of eating an orange into a rich experience. Imagine what can happen when you bring this quality of attention to almost everything that you do.

Choose when to be here now

Remember that no suggestion is absolute—including the suggestion to do one thing at a time with full, focused attention. Sometimes choosing to do two or more things at once is useful, even necessary. For example, you might study while doing laundry. You might ask your children to quiz you with flash cards while you fix dinner.

The key to this Power Process is to *choose*. When you choose, you overcome distractions and stay in charge of your attention.

Experiment with noticing your inner voices. Let go of the ones that prevent you from focusing on learning. Practice the process. Be here now, moment by moment.

The here and now in your future

You also can use this Power Process to keep yourself pointed toward your goals. In fact, one of the best ways to get what you want in the future is to realize that you do not have a future. The only time you have is right now.

The problem with this idea is that some students might think: "No future, huh? Terrific! Party time!" Being in the here and now, however, is not the same as living for today and forgetting about tomorrow.

Nor is the "be here now" idea a call to abandon goals. Goals are merely tools we create to direct our actions right now. They are useful only in the present. Goals, like our ideas of the past and future, are creations of our minds. The only time they are real is in the here and now.

The power of this idea lies in a simple but frequently overlooked fact: The only time to do anything is now. You can think about doing something next Wednesday. You can write about doing something next Wednesday. You can daydream, discuss, ruminate, speculate, and fantasize about what you will do next Wednesday. But you can't do anything on Wednesday until it is Wednesday.

Sometimes students think of goals as things that exist in the misty future. And it's easy to postpone action on things in the misty future, especially when everyone else is going to a not-so-misty party.

However, the word *goal* comes from the Anglo-Saxon *gaelan*, which means "to hinder or impede," as in the case of a boundary. That's what a goal does. It restricts, in a positive way, our activity in the here and now. It channels our energy into actions that are more likely to get us what we really want. That's what goals are for. And they are useful only when they are directing action in the here and now.

The idea behind this Power Process is simple. When you plan for the future, plan for the future. When you listen to a lecture, listen to a lecture. When you read this book, read this book. And when you choose to daydream, daydream. Do what you're doing when you're doing it.

Be where you are when you're there. Be here now . . . and now . . . and now.

career application

Steve Carlson is a technical writer for DCS, a company that makes products for multimedia teleconferencing: digital video cameras, large-screen televisions, and software. He joined DCS two years ago, after graduating with a B.A. in Technical Communications. This is his first full-time, professional job.

Steve works in a five-person Documentation Department. The department creates sales brochures, user manuals, and other documents about DCS products. Working with his manager, Louise Chao, Steve helps decide which documents are needed for each DCS product. He then writes documents, edits documents written by others, and works closely with a graphic designer who oversees document production.

On a Friday afternoon, Louise knocks on the door of Steve's office. She wants Steve to handle a rush project—a new product brochure to be researched, written, designed, and printed in two weeks. Louise is on the way to another meeting and only has five minutes to talk.

Steve's schedule is already full of projects. For the last month, he has been working Saturdays to stay on top of his workload. As Louise describes the project, Steve listens without comment. When Louise is finished, Steve points to a large wallboard in his office.

This wallboard is a chart that shows all of Steve's active projects. Included is a visual timeline for each project that shows due dates for researching, outlining, drafting, and revising each document. Steve has negotiated these dates with the product development teams. Each timeline is color-coded—red for urgent projects, green for other active projects, and yellow for planned projects that are not yet active. Steve uses the wallboard to plan his day-to-day tasks and visually represent his workload.

"I estimate that it would take me at least three full days to research and write the document you're talking about," Steve says. "In addition, meetings with my designer would take up another two days. So doing the brochure means that I'd need to free up at least one week of my time."

Steve then points to the projects shown in red on his wallboard. "Louise, I know this new product brochure is important to you," he says. "Can we schedule a time to choose which of these urgent projects I could delay for a week to meet your request?"

Reflecting on this scenario

1. Recall the four modes of learning explained in Chapter One: *Why? What? How?* and *What if?* In this example, what was Steve's primary learning mode? Explain your reason for choosing this mode.

___

___

2. List two transferable skills that Steve demonstrates in this scenario. (For information on skills, see "It all starts with skills" on page 61.)

___

___

3. List two more skills that would be useful to Steve in this situation. Explain why you chose those two.

___

___

4. List two strategies from this chapter that would be useful to Steve in this situation. Briefly describe how he could apply each one.

___

___

Name ______________________________ Date _____/_____/_____

quiz

1. Name three ways you can control interruptions when you are trying to concentrate.

2. It is effective to leave holes in your schedule to allow for the unexpected. True or False? Explain your answer.

3. Suppose that after you choose where to focus your attention, your mind wanders. The Power Process: "Be here now" suggests that one of the most effective ways to bring your focus back to the here and now is to:
   (a) Slap your cheek and shout "Attention" as loudly as you can.
   (b) Notice that your thoughts have wandered and gently bring them back.
   (c) Sleep.
   (d) Concentrate as hard as you can to force distracting thoughts out of your head.
   (e) Ignore physical sensations.

4. What are at least 5 of the 25 ways to get the most out of now?

5. In time-management terms, what is meant by "This ain't no piano"?

6. Define "C fever" as it applies to the ABC priority method.

7. Describe at least three strategies for overcoming procrastination.

8. Summarize the difference between macro-organizing and micro-organizing as explained in this chapter.

9. Define the term *MIT* and suggest one way to choose your MIT for the day.

10. Summarize the main steps in David Allen's system for getting things done.

learning styles application

The questions below will "cycle" you through four styles, or modes, of learning as explained in the article "Learning styles: Discovering how you learn" in Chapter One. Each question will help you explore a different mode. You can answer the questions in any order.

what if *Describe how you can free up four additional hours each week for the upcoming month. (That's a total of 16 extra hours over the next four weeks.) Choose from the techniques presented in this chapter or any that you create yourself.*

why *Suppose that you could use the techniques in this chapter to free up four additional hours each week to do whatever you please. Describe the things you would do with this extra time and why these activities matter to you.*

how *Describe exactly how you will use the technique you have chosen.*

what *Choose a technique from this chapter that you can use to free up four additional hours in the next week. Summarize that technique here.*

master student profile

BARBARA JORDAN

(1936–1996) The first African American to become a state senator in Texas and the first African American to enter Congress since the Reconstruction.

So I was at Boston University in this new and strange and different world, and it occurred to me that if I was going to succeed at this strange new adventure, I would have to read longer and more thoroughly than my colleagues at law school had to read. I felt that in order to compensate for what I had missed in earlier years, I would have to work harder, and study longer, than anybody else. . . . I did my reading not in the law library, but in a library at my graduate dorm, upstairs where it was very quiet, because apparently nobody else studied there. So I would go there at night after dinner. I would load my books under my arm and go to the library, and I would read until the wee hours of the morning and then go to bed. . . .

I was always delighted when I would get called upon to recite in class. But the professors did not call on the "ladies" very much. There were certain favored people who always got called on, and then on some rare occasions a professor would come in and would announce: "We're going to have Ladies Day today." And he would call on the ladies. We were just tolerated. We weren't considered really top drawer when it came to the study of law.

At some time in the spring, Bill Gibson, who was dating my new roommate, Norma Walker, organized a black study group, as we blacks had to form our own. This was because

we were not invited into any of the other study groups. There were six or seven in our group—Bill, and Issie, and I think Maynard Jackson—and we would just gather and talk it out and hear ourselves do that. One thing I learned was that you had to talk out the issues, the facts, the cases, the decisions, the process. You couldn't just read the cases and study alone in your library as I had been doing; and you couldn't get it all in the classroom. But once you had talked it out in the study group, it flowed more easily and made a lot more sense. . . .

Finally I felt I was really learning things, really going to school. I felt that I was getting educated, whatever that was. I became familiar with the process of thinking. I learned to think things out and reach conclusions and defend what I had said.

In the past I had got along by spouting off. Whether you talked about debates or oratory, you dealt with speechifying. But I could no longer orate and let that pass for reasoning because there was not any demand for an orator in Boston University Law School. You had to think and read and understand and reason. I had learned at twenty-one that you couldn't just say a thing is so because it might not be so, and somebody brighter, smarter, and more thoughtful would come out and tell you it wasn't so. Then, if you still thought it was, you had to prove it. Well, that was a new thing for me. I cannot, I really cannot describe what that did to my insides and to my head. I thought: I'm being educated finally.

For more biographical information about Barbara Jordan, visit the Master Student Hall of Fame on the *From Master Student to Master Employee* Website.

4 Reading

MASTER STUDENT MAP

why this chapter matters ...

Success in the workplace and in higher education requires extensive reading.

how you can use this chapter ...

Analyze what effective readers do and experiment with new techniques.
Increase your vocabulary and adjust your reading speed for different types of material.
Comprehend difficult content with more ease.

As you read, ask yourself what if ...

I could finish my reading with time to spare, easily recall the key points, and put the ideas I read about into action?

what is included ...

FROM THE DESK OF . . .

With three children and having not been to school in 10 years, it has been a real challenge for me. I require that my children spend a certain amount of time each evening studying as well as doing chores. I cook several meals on the weekend for the week. The time they spend studying, I study with them. I find that it encourages them to study when they see me do it with them. It helps me because when I don't study, my 14-year-old will peek in my room and say, "Ahhhhh, do you have all A's? Don't you think it's a good time to be studying?" When hear your own words come back to you, what can you say?

—KIMANI JONES, PARENT AND STUDENT

Muscle Reading

Picture yourself sitting at a desk, a book in your hands. Your eyes are open, and it looks as if you're reading. Suddenly your head jerks up. You blink. You realize your eyes have been scanning the page for 10 minutes, and you can't remember a single thing you have read.

Or picture this: You've had a hard day. You were up at 6 a.m. to get the kids ready for school. A coworker called in sick, and you missed your lunch trying to do his job as well as your own. You picked up the kids, then had to shop for dinner. Dinner was late, of course, and the kids were grumpy.

Finally, you get to your books at 8 p.m. You begin a reading assignment on something called "the equity method of accounting for common stock investments." "I am preparing for the future," you tell yourself, as you plod through two paragraphs and begin the third. Suddenly, everything in the room looks different. Your head is resting on your elbow, which is resting on the equity method of accounting. The clock reads 11:00 p.m. Say good-bye to three hours.

Sometimes the only difference between a sleeping pill and a textbook is that the textbook doesn't have a warning on the label about operating heavy machinery.

Muscle Reading is a technique you can use to avoid mental minivacations and reduce the number of unscheduled naps during study time, even after a hard day.

The ability to find information, locate main ideas, and identify relevant details are all transferable skills that can be further developed and practiced through Muscle Reading. Once you learn this technique, you can actually spend less time on your reading and get more out of it.

Keep in mind that this chapter applies to all kinds of reading beyond textbooks. Use Muscle Reading to get what you want from work-related reading materials as well: reports, brochures, trade journals, meeting minutes, e-mails, and Web pages.

This is not to say that Muscle Reading will make your education or job a breeze. Muscle Reading might even look like more work at first. Effective reading is an active, energy-consuming, sit-on-the-edge-of-your-seat business. That's why this strategy is called Muscle Reading.

journal entry 10

Discovery/Intention Statement

Recall a time when you encountered problems with reading, such as words you didn't understand or paragraphs you paused to reread more than once. Sum up the experience and how you felt about it by completing the following statement.

I discovered that I . . .

____

Now list three to five specific reading skills you want to gain from this chapter.

I intend to . . .

____

How Muscle Reading works

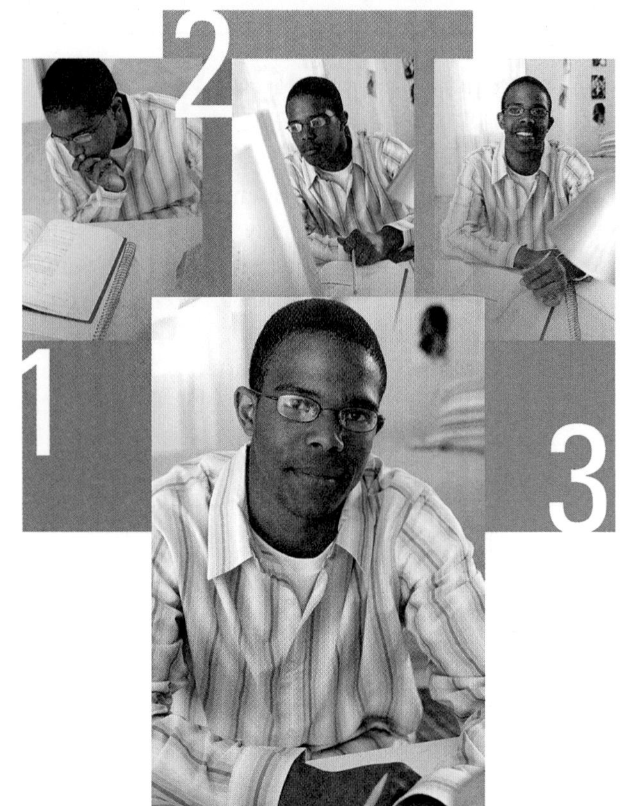

Muscle Reading is a three-phase technique you can use to extract the ideas and information you want.

Phase one includes steps to take *before* you read.
Phase two includes steps to take *while* you read.
Phase three includes steps to take *after* you read.

Each phase has three steps.

PHASE ONE:
Before you read
Step 1: **Preview**
Step 2: **Outline**
Step 3: **Question**

PHASE TWO:
While you read
Step 4: **Read**
Step 5: **Underline**
Step 6: **Answer**

PHASE THREE:
After you read
Step 7: **Recite**
Step 8: **Review**
Step 9: **Review again**

A nine-step reading strategy might seem cumbersome and unnecessary for a two-page reading assignment. It is. Use the steps appropriately. Choose which ones to apply as you read.

To assist your recall of Muscle Reading strategies, memorize three short sentences:

Pry Out Questions.
Root Up Answers.
Recite, Review, and Review again.

These three sentences correspond to the three phases of the Muscle Reading technique. Each sentence is an acrostic. The first letter of each word stands for one of the nine steps listed here.

Take a moment to invent images for each of those sentences.

For *phase one*, visualize or feel yourself prying out questions from a text. These are questions you want answered based on a brief survey of the assignment. Make a mental picture of yourself scanning the material, spotting a question, and reaching into the text to pry it out. Hear yourself saying, "I've got it. Here's my question."

Then for *phase two*, get your muscles involved. Feel the tips of your fingers digging into the text as you root up the answers to your questions.

Finally, you enter *phase three*. Hear your voice reciting what you have learned. Listen to yourself making a speech or singing a song about the material as you review it.

To jog your memory, write the first letters of the Muscle Reading acrostic in a margin or at the top of your notes. Then check off the steps you intend to follow. Or write the Muscle Reading steps on 3×5 cards and then use them for bookmarks.

Muscle Reading could take a little time to learn. At first you might feel it's slowing you down. That's natural when you're gaining a new skill. Mastery comes with time and practice.

Step 1 **Preview** Before you start reading, preview the entire assignment. Previewing sets the stage for incoming information by warming up a space in your mental storage area. It is also a way to get yourself started when an assignment looks too big to handle. Previewing is an easy way to step into the material.

If you are starting a new book, look over the table of contents and flip through the text page by page. If you're going to read one chapter, flip through the pages of that chapter. Even if your assignment is merely a few pages in a book, you can benefit from a brief preview.

Keep the preview short. If the entire reading assignment will take less than an hour, your preview might take five minutes.

Keep an eye out for summary statements. If the assignment is long or complex, read the summary first. Many textbooks have summaries in the introduction or at the end of each chapter.

Read all chapter headings and subheadings. Like the headlines in a newspaper, these are usually printed in large, bold type. Often headings are brief summaries in themselves.

When previewing, seek out familiar concepts, facts, or ideas. These items can help increase comprehension by linking new information to previously learned material. Look for ideas that spark your imagination or curiosity. Inspect drawings, diagrams, charts, tables, graphs, and photographs. Imagine what kinds of questions will show up on a test.

Step 2 **Outline** With complex material, take time to understand the structure of what you are about to read.

If your textbook provides chapter outlines, spend some time studying them. When an outline is not provided, sketch a brief one in the margin of your book or at the beginning of your notes on a separate sheet of paper. Later, as you read and take notes, you can add to your outline.

Headings in the text can serve as major and minor entries in your outline. For example, the heading for this article is "Phase one: Before you read," and the subheadings list the three steps in this phase. When you outline, feel free to rewrite headings so that they are more meaningful to you.

The amount of time you spend on this step will vary. For some assignments, a 10-second mental outline is all you might need. For other assignments (fiction and poetry, for example), you can skip this step altogether.

Step 3 **Question** Before you begin a careful reading, determine what you want from an assignment. Then write down a list of questions, including any that resulted from your preview of the materials.

Another useful technique is to turn chapter headings and subheadings into questions. For example, if a heading is "Transference and suggestion," you can ask yourself, "What are *transference* and *suggestion*? How does *transference* relate to *suggestion*?" Make up a quiz as if you were teaching this subject to your classmates.

If there are no headings, look for key sentences and turn these into questions. These sentences usually show up at the beginnings or ends of paragraphs and sections.

Have fun with this technique. Make the questions playful or creative. You don't need to answer every question that you ask. The purpose of making up questions is to get your brain involved in the assignment. Take your unanswered questions to class, where they can be springboards for class discussion.

Demand your money's worth from your textbook. If you do not understand a concept, write specific questions about it. The more detailed your questions, the more powerful this technique becomes.

Step 4 **Reflect** At last! You have previewed the assignment, organized it in your mind, and formulated questions. Now you are ready to begin reading.

Before you dive into the first paragraph, take a few moments to reflect on what you already know about this subject. Do this even if you think you know nothing. This technique prepares your brain to accept the information that follows.

As you read, be conscious of where you are and what you are doing. Use the Power Process: "Be here now" in Chapter Three. When you notice your attention wandering, gently bring it back to the present moment.

One way to stay focused is to avoid marathon reading sessions. Schedule breaks and set a reasonable goal for the entire session. Then reward yourself with an enjoyable activity for five or 10 minutes every hour or two.

For difficult reading, set more limited goals. Read for a half-hour and then take a break. Most students find that shorter periods of reading distributed throughout the day and week can be more effective than long sessions. You can use the following four techniques to stay focused as you read.

First, visualize the material. Form mental pictures of the concepts as they are presented. If you read that a voucher system can help control cash disbursements, picture a voucher handing out dollar bills. Using visual imagery in this way can help deepen your understanding of the text while allowing information to be transferred into your long-term memory.

Second, read the material out loud, especially if it is complicated. Some of us remember better and understand more quickly when we hear an idea.

Third, get a "feel" for the subject. For example, let's say you are reading about a microorganism, a paramecium, in your biology text. Imagine what it would feel like to run your finger around the long, cigar-shaped body of the organism. Imagine feeling the large fold of its gullet on one side and the tickle of the hairy little cilia as they wiggle in your hand.

Fourth, remember that a goal of your reading is to answer the questions you listed during phase one. After you've identified the key questions, predict how the author will answer them. Then read to find out if your predictions were accurate.

A final note: It's easy to fool yourself about reading. Just having an open book in your hand and moving your eyes across a page doesn't mean you are reading effectively. Reading textbooks takes energy, even if you do it sitting down.

If you do an informal study of chief executive officers, you'll find some who wear out the front of their chairs first. Approach your reading assignment like a company president. Sit up. Keep your spine straight. Use the edge of your chair. And avoid reading in bed—except for fun.

Step 5 **Underline** Deface your books. Use them up. Have fun writing in them. Indulge yourself as you never could with your grade-school books.

The purpose of making marks in a text is to call out important concepts or information that you will need to review later. Underlining can save lots of time when you are studying for tests.

Underlining offers a secondary benefit. When you read with a pen or pencil in your hand, you involve your kinesthetic senses of touch and motion. Being physical with your books can help build strong neural pathways in your memory.

Avoid underlining too soon. Wait until you complete a chapter or section to make sure you know the key points. Then mark up the text. Sometimes, underlining after you read each paragraph works best.

Underline sparingly, usually less than 10 percent of the text. If you mark up too much on a page, you defeat the purpose—to flag the most important material for review.

In addition to underlining, you can mark up a text in the following ways:

- Place an asterisk (*) or an exclamation point (!) in the margin next to an especially important sentence or term.

Five smart ways to highlight a text

Underlining a text with a pen can make underlined sections—the important parts—harder to read. As an alternative, many students use colored highlighters to flag key words and sentences.

Highlighting can be a powerful tool. It also presents a danger—the ever-present temptation to highlight too much text. Excessive highlighting leads to wasted time during reviews and can also spoil the appearance of your books. Get the most out of all that money you pay for books. Highlight in an efficient way that leaves texts readable for years to come.

Read carefully first. Read an entire chapter or section at least once before you begin highlighting. Don't be in a hurry to mark up your book. Get to know the text first. Make two or three passes through difficult sections before you highlight.

Make choices up front about what to highlight. Perhaps you can accomplish your purposes by highlighting only certain chapters or sections of a text. When you highlight, remember to look for passages that directly answer the questions you posed during step 3 of Muscle Reading. Within these passages, highlight individual words, phrases, or sentences rather than whole paragraphs. The important thing is to choose an overall strategy before you put highlighter to paper.

Recite first. You might want to apply step 7 of Muscle Reading before you highlight. Talking about what you read—to yourself or with other people—can help you grasp the essence of a text. Recite first, then go back and highlight. You'll probably highlight more selectively.

Underline, then highlight. Underline key passages lightly in pencil. Then close your text and come back to it later. Assess your underlining. Perhaps you can highlight less than you underlined and still capture the key points.

Use highlighting to monitor your comprehension. Critical thinking plays a role in underlining and highlighting. When highlighting, you're making moment-by-moment decisions about what you want to remember from a text. You're also making inferences about what material might be included on a test.

Take your critical thinking a step further by using highlighting to check your comprehension. Stop reading periodically and look back over the sentences you've highlighted. See if you are making accurate distinctions between main points and supporting material. Highlighting too much—more than 10 percent of the text—can be a sign that you're not making this distinction and that you don't fully understand what you're reading. See the article "When reading is tough" later in this chapter for suggestions that can help.

- Circle key terms and words to look up later in a dictionary.
- Write short definitions of key terms in the margin.
- Write a "Q" in the margin to highlight possible test questions, passages you don't understand, and questions to ask in class.
- Write personal comments in the margin—points of agreement or disagreement with the author.
- Write mini-indexes in the margin, that is, the numbers of other pages in the book where the same topic is discussed.
- Write summaries by listing the main points or key events covered in a chapter.
- Rewrite chapter titles, headings, and subheadings so that they're more meaningful to you.
- Draw diagrams, pictures, tables, or maps that translate text into visual terms.
- Number each step in a list or series of related points.

Step 6

Answer As you read, seek out the answers to your questions and write them down. Fill in your outline. Jot down new questions and note when you don't find the answers you are looking for. Use these notes to ask questions in class, or see your instructor personally.

When you read, create an image of yourself as a person in search of the answers. You are a detective, watching for every clue, sitting erect in your straight-back chair, demanding that your textbook give you what you want—the answers.

Step 7

Recite When you recite, you practice an important aspect of metacognition—synthesis, or combining individual ideas and facts into a meaningful whole.

One way to get yourself to recite is to look at each underlined point. Note what you marked, then put the book down and start talking out loud. Explain as much as you can about that particular point.

You can recite with your classmates. Form a group and practice teaching each other what you have read. One of the best ways to learn anything is to teach it to someone else.

Talking about your reading reinforces a valuable skill—the ability to summarize. To practice this skill, pick one chapter (or one section of one chapter) from any of your textbooks. State the main topic covered in this chapter. Then state the main points that the author makes about this topic.

For example, the main topic up to this point in this chapter is Muscle Reading. The main point about this topic is that Muscle Reading includes three phases—steps to take before you read, while you read, and after you read. For a more detailed summary, you could name each of the nine steps.

Step 8

Review Plan to do your first complete review within 24 hours of reading the material. Sound the trumpets! This point is critical: A review within 24 hours moves information from your short-term memory to your long-term memory.

Review within one day. If you read it on Wednesday, review it on Thursday. During this review, look over your notes and clear up anything you don't understand. Recite some of the main points again.

This review can be short. You might spend as little as 15 minutes reviewing a difficult two-hour reading assignment. Investing that time now can save you hours later when studying for exams.

Step 9

Review again The final step in Muscle Reading is the weekly or monthly review. This step can be very short—perhaps only four or five minutes per assignment. Simply go over your notes. Read the highlighted parts of your text. Recite one or two of the more complicated points.

You can accomplish these short reviews anytime, anywhere, if you are prepared. Three-by-five cards are a handy review tool. Write ideas, formulas, concepts, and facts on cards and carry them with you. These short review periods can be effortless and fun.

Sometimes longer review periods are appropriate. For example, if you found an assignment difficult, consider rereading it. Start over, as if you had never seen the material before. Sometimes a second reading will provide you with surprising insights.

Muscle Reading—a leaner approach

Keep in mind that Muscle Reading is an overall approach, not a rigid, step-by-step procedure. Here's a shorter variation that students have found helpful. Practice it with any chapter in this book.

- ***Preview and question.*** Flip through the pages, looking at anything that catches your eye—headings, subheadings, illustrations, photographs. Turn the title of each article into a question. For example, "How Muscle Reading works" can become "How does Muscle Reading work?" List your questions on a separate sheet of paper, or write each question on a 3×5 card.
- ***Read to answer your questions.*** Read each article, then go back over the text and underline or highlight answers to the appropriate questions on your list.
- ***Recite and review.*** When you're done with the chapter, close the book. Recite by reading each question—and answering it—out loud. Review the chapter by looking up the answers to your questions. (It's easy—they're already highlighted.) Review again by quizzing yourself one more time with your list of questions.

Muscle Reading at work

Researchers from the University of California at Berkeley estimated that the world produces between two and three exabytes of information each year.[1] To put this figure in perspective, consider that one exabyte equals 250 megabytes for each individual on earth. The complete works of Shakespeare would take up only five megabytes of space on your computer's hard drive.

Much of your personal megabytes can come in the form of work-related reading: technical manuals, sales manuals, policies and procedures, memos, e-mail, Websites, newsletters, invoices, application forms, meeting minutes, brochures, annual reports, job descriptions, and more.

The techniques of Muscle Reading can help you plow through all that material and extract what you want to know. Keep the following suggestions in mind.

Start with a purpose. At work, your purpose for reading is probably to produce a specific outcome—to gain a skill or gather information needed to complete a task. Fix that purpose in mind before you read in depth about a topic.

This is where step 3 of Muscle Reading—asking questions—comes in handy. See if you can express your purpose as one or more questions.

Suppose that your purpose for reading is to gather information for a PowerPoint presentation. Visualize a headline for each slide in your presentation. Then turn each headline into a question. A headline that reads "The elements of extraordinary marketing" then becomes "What are the elements of extraordinary marketing?" As you read, look for specific answers.

Extract value with nonlinear reading. Consider how you first learned to read as a child. You opened up a book, fixed your eyes on the first word, and worked straight through until the end of the sentence or page. As you got older, you approached longer and longer documents with essentially the same strategy—start at the beginning and plow through word-by-word until you reach the last period of the last paragraph.

Instead, read with the alertness of someone who's in a crowd of people and searching for someone she knows. Her eyes scan the environment at high speed until—presto!—they land on the familiar face.

When reading, your brain can operate with that kind of efficiency. Rather than looking for people, however, you're scanning to land on the paragraphs that contain exactly what you want to know.

The key is to make several passes through the material. Remember that you don't have to "get it all" the first time or even read sections in order.

Make your first pass a quick scan—step 1 of Muscle Reading. Then go for a second pass, reading the first sentence of each paragraph or the first and last paragraphs of each section. If you want more detail, then make additional passes, slowing down and picking up a little more detail each time.

During each pass through a document, you can skip entire sections or take them out of order. This is the nonlinear technique. You might even want to start at the end of a chapter or article to see if there's a summary or review section placed there. This section might be all that you need.

One immediate benefit of this approach is saving time. If the content that you really want is on page 23, you don't have to invest an hour reading through the preceding 22 pages. Instead, your preview might unearth that valuable passage within a minute or two.

Besides saving time, this approach mirrors the way that your mind works. Your brain is a nonlinear organ. It can make instant connections between ideas and arrange them in any order. Your brain doesn't care *where* ideas are located. It's just looking for the good stuff.

Of course, you can always choose to read in a linear way—from the beginning straight through to the end—if that creates the most value for you. Just make it a conscious choice rather than an unconscious habit.

Hint: Many business documents include an executive summary near the beginning. Look for such a section. Everything you want to know might be there, all neatly presented on a single page.

Print online documents to read later. Research indicates that people can read faster on paper than on the computer screen.[2] Be kind to your eyes. Print out long attachments and e-mails before reading them.

Create a "to read" folder. Much of the paper that crosses your field of attention at work will probably consist of basic background material—items that are important but not urgent. Place these documents in a folder, label it "to read," and pull it out the next time you have a few minutes to spare. Or tuck the folder in a carry-on bag and plow through it during your next plane trip.

To make this technique work, be selective. Before putting something in your folder, spend a minute or two previewing it. If it offers little or no value, recycle it immediately. Avoid overstuffing your "to read" folder. Save this file for documents that are likely to contain hidden gems.

Beware of blog overload. Weblogs (or blogs)—Websites that function as online journals—offer both promise and peril. Because a blog takes on the personality of its author, the site can make for fascinating reading. Blogs from people who share your career interests can also help you stay current in your field and make new contacts.

However, blog reading can also become addictive—an activity that devours precious hours at work and at home. To get the most value from blogs while maintaining your productivity:

- Create a schedule. Rather than checking blogs for updates at random points throughout the workday, set specific times for visiting these sites.
- Set limits. If you're an avid blog reader, monitor how much time you spend reading them each week. The results might surprise you. Tell the truth in a Discovery Statement. Then follow up with an Intention Statement about setting limits to your blog consumption. Consider setting a timer before you go online to visit your favorite sites. Or ask a coworker to hold you accountable to your time limits.
- Use an RSS reader to monitor blogs. (RSS stands for "rich site summary" or "really simple syndication.") RSS readers are online tools that create summaries of frequently updated Websites. Examples include NetNewsWire, My Yahoo!, and Google Reader. For each article posted on a Website, an RSS reader displays a headline and short summary. You can add several sets of summaries, or feeds, to your RSS reader. This allows you to scan the contents of several Websites in a single window on your computer.
- Limit the number of blogs you read. If you add a new feed to your RSS reader, see if you can delete an old one.

From time to time, choose a blog to leave unread for a month. If the end of the month arrives and you discover that you haven't miss the content, take that blog off your reading list.

Strike up a conversation. The novelist Henry Miller once observed that "We do not talk—we bludgeon one another with facts and theories gleaned from cursory readings of newspapers, magazines, and digests."[3]

You can reverse this trend. Read a lot and then talk to coworkers about what you're reading. This kind of conversation helps you remember what you read. And as you respond to the questions that other people ask, your understanding of the material will deepen.

Starting a stimulating conversation at work is also one way to promote more creative workplaces. An idea from the next business book that you read could be the catalyst for a new product, a new service, or a new company. ✖

Building your vocabulary

A large vocabulary makes reading more enjoyable and increases the range of materials you can read. In addition, building your vocabulary gives you more options for self-expression when speaking or writing. When you can choose from a larger pool of words, you increase the precision and power of your thinking. One strategy for success in the workplace is quickly mastering the specialized vocabulary that people in your career field use. Building vocabulary also helps to develop the transferable skills related to reading, strengthening your ability to infer or locate the meaning of unknown terms.

Keep a dictionary handy

One potent ally in building your vocabulary is a dictionary. Print dictionaries come in many shapes and sizes and media: pocket dictionary, desk dictionary, and unabridged (the heftiest and most complete).

Don't forget digital dictionaries. You can buy dictionary software to use on your computer. Also search for dictionary sites on the World Wide Web. To find them, go to your favorite search site and use the keywords *dictionary* or *reference.*

Put your dictionaries to active use. When you find an unfamiliar word, write it down on an index card. Copy the sentence in which it occurred below the word. You can look up each word immediately or accumulate a stack of these cards and look them up later. Write definitions on the back of the cards.

Consider using a computer to create a specialized glossary for each of your courses. As you complete assigned readings and review your class notes, underline key terms. Use a word processing program to catalog these words and their definitions into an electronic file. Revise definitions and add new terms as the course proceeds. Then print your glossaries to study for tests.

Look for context clues

You can often deduce the meaning of an unfamiliar word simply by paying attention to context—the surrounding words or images. Later you can confirm your trial definition of the word by consulting a dictionary.

Context clues include:

- *Definitions.* A key word may be defined right in the text. Look for phrases such as *the definition is* or *in other words.*
- *Examples.* Authors often provide examples to clarify a word meaning. If the word is not explicitly defined, then study the examples. They're often preceded by the phrases *for example, for instance,* or *such as.*
- *Lists.* When a word is listed in a series, pay attention to the other items in the series. They may, in effect, define the unfamiliar word.
- *Comparisons.* You may find a new word surrounded by synonyms—words with a similar meaning. Look for synonyms after words such as *like* and *as.*
- *Contrasts.* A writer may juxtapose a word with its antonym—a word or phrase with the opposite meaning. Look for phrases such as *on the contrary* and *on the other hand.*

Distinguish between word parts

Words consist of discrete elements that can be combined in limitless ways.

Roots are "home base," a word's core meaning. A single word can have more than one root. *Bibliophile*, for example, has two roots: *biblio* ("book") and *phile* ("love"). A *bibliophile* is a book lover.

Prefixes come at the beginning of a word and often modify the meaning of the word root. In English, a common prefix is the single letter *a*, which often means "not." Added to *typical*, for example, this prefix results in the word *atypical*, which means "not typical."

Suffixes come at the end of a word. Like prefixes, they can alter or expand the meaning of the root. For instance, the suffix *ant* means "one who." Thus, an *assistant* is "one who assists."

See an unabridged dictionary for more word parts. The time you spend is an investment in your word power.

Learn strategies for further enhancing your vocabulary with a dictionary on the *From Master Student to Master Employee* Website.

Reading *fast*

One way to read faster is to read faster. This might sound like double talk, but it is a serious suggestion. The fact is, you can probably read faster—without any loss in comprehension—simply by making a conscious effort to do so. Your comprehension might even improve.

Experiment with the "just do it" method right now. Read the rest of this article as fast as you can. After you finish, come back and reread the same paragraphs at your usual rate. Note how much you remember from your first sprint through the text. You might be surprised to find out how well you comprehend material even at dramatically increased speeds. Build on that success by experimenting with the following guidelines.

Get your body ready. Gear up for reading faster. Get off the couch. Sit up straight at a desk or table, on the edge of your chair, with your feet flat on the floor. If you're feeling adventurous, read standing up.

Set a time limit. When you read, use a clock or a digital watch with a built-in stopwatch to time yourself. You are not aiming to set speed records, so be realistic. For example, set a goal to read two or three sections of a chapter in an hour, using all of the Muscle Reading steps. If that works, set a goal of 50 minutes for reading the same number of sections.

Test your limits. The idea is to give yourself a gentle push, increasing your reading speed without sacrificing comprehension.

Relax. It's not only possible to read fast when you're relaxed, it's easier. Relaxation promotes concentration. And remember, relaxation is not the same as sleep. You can be relaxed *and* alert at the same time.

Move your eyes faster. When we read, our eyes leap across the page in short bursts called *saccades* (pronounced *să - käds*). A saccade is also a sharp jerk on the reins of a horse—a violent pull to stop the animal quickly. Our eyes stop like that, too, in pauses called *fixations.*

Although we experience the illusion of continuously scanning each line, our eyes actually take in groups of words, usually about three at a time. For more than 90 percent of reading time, our eyes are at a dead stop, in those fixations.

One way to decrease saccades is to follow your finger as you read. The faster your finger moves, the faster your eyes move. You can also use a pen, pencil, or 3 × 5 card as a guide.

Your eyes can move faster if they take in more words with each burst—for example, six instead of three. To practice taking in more words between fixations, find a newspaper with narrow columns. Then read down one column at a time and fixate only once per line.

In addition to using the above techniques, simply make a conscious effort to fixate less. You might feel a little uncomfortable at first. That's normal. Just practice often, for short periods of time.

Notice and release ineffective habits. Our eyes make regressions, that is, they back up and reread words. You can reduce regressions by paying attention to them. Use the handy 3 × 5 card to cover words and lines that you have just read. You can then note how often you stop and move the card back to reread the text. Don't be discouraged if you stop often at first. Being aware of it helps you regress less frequently.

Also notice vocalizing. You are more likely to read faster if you don't read out loud or move your lips. You can also increase your speed if you don't subvocalize—that is, if you don't mentally "hear" the words as you read them. To stop doing it, just be aware of it.

Another habit to release is reading letter by letter. When we first learn to read, we do it one letter at a time. By now you have memorized many words by their shape, so you don't have to focus on the letters at all. Read this example: "Rasrhcers at Cbmrigae Uivnretisy funod taht eprxert raeedrs dno't eevn look at the lteters." You get the point. Skilled readers recognize many words and phrases in this way, taking them in at a single glance.

When you first attempt to release these habits, choose simpler reading material. That way, you can pay closer attention to your reading technique. Gradually work your way up to more complex material.

If you're pressed for time, skim. When you're in a hurry, experiment by skimming the assignment instead of reading the whole thing. Read the headings, subheadings, lists, charts, graphs, and summary paragraphs. Summaries are especially important. They are usually found at the beginning or end of a chapter or section.

Stay flexible. Remember that speed isn't everything. Skillful readers vary their reading rate according to their purpose and the nature of the material. An advanced text in analytic geometry usually calls for a different reading rate than the Sunday comics.

You also can use different reading rates on the same material. For example, you might first sprint through an assignment for the key words and ideas, then return to the difficult parts for a slower and more thorough reading.

critical thinking exercise 17

RELAX

Eye strain can be the result of continuous stress. Take a break from your reading and use this exercise to release tension.

1. Sit on a chair or lie down and take a few moments to breathe deeply.
2. Close your eyes, place your palms over your eyes, and visualize a perfect field of black.
3. Continue to be aware of the blackness for two or three minutes while you breathe deeply.
4. Now remove your hands from your eyes and open your eyes slowly.
5. Relax for a minute more, then continue reading.

Explore more resources. You can find many books about speed-reading. Ask a librarian to help you find a few. Using them can be a lot of fun. For more possibilities, including courses and workshops, go to your favorite search engine on the Internet and key in the words *speed reading.*

One word of caution: Courses and workshops range from free to expensive. Before you lay out any money, check the instructor's credentials and talk to people who've taken the course. Also find out whether the instructor offers free "sampler sessions" and whether you can cancel at some point in the course for a full refund.

Finally, remember the first rule of reading fast: Just do it!

Becoming an online learner

If you're returning to school after a long break from classroom settings, you might be surprised at all the online reading you're asked to do—Web-based articles and exercises, e-books, PowerPoint presentations, e-mail messages, chat room sessions, and more.

Of course, it's fine to print out online material. You can treat these printouts like conventional textbooks and apply the steps of Muscle Reading. In addition, consider the following ways to prevent glitches with course content that's delivered online.

Take a First Step about technology. Before you begin your next experience with online learning, practice telling the truth about your current skills in this area.

Check out the technology requirements for your courses. Contact instructors before courses begin. Ask about the specifications your computer will need to meet and the software you'll be expected to use. Your instructors might also assume that students have a certain amount of experience with online learning, so ask about that as well.

If you're planning to use a computer lab on campus, find one with hardware and software that meets course requirements. Whenever possible, choose a single computer for online coursework—one that's available when you need it, complete with the specifications that you want.

Do a trial run with technology. Verify your access to course Websites, including online tutorials, PowerPoint presentations, readings, quizzes, tests, assignments, bulletin boards, and chat rooms. Ask your instructors for Website addresses, e-mail addresses, and passwords. Work out any bugs when you start the course and well before that first reading assignment or paper is due.

Develop a contingency plan. Murphy's Law of Computer Crashes states that technology tends to break down at the moment of greatest inconvenience. Prepare for it:

- Find a "technology buddy" in each of your classes—someone who can contact the instructor if you lose Internet access or experience other computer problems.
- Every day, make backup copies of files created for your courses.
- Keep extra printer supplies—paper and toner or ink cartridges—always on hand. Don't run out of either on the day that a paper is due.

Prevent procrastination. Early in the term, create a detailed schedule for online courses. In your calendar, list a due date for each assignment. Break big assignments into smaller steps and schedule a due date for each step.

Consider scheduling times in your calendar to complete online reading and other coursework. Give these scheduled sessions the same priority as regular classroom meetings. At these times, check for online announcements relating to assignments, tests, and other course events.

Focus your attention. Some students are used to visiting Websites while watching television, listening to loud music, or using instant messaging software. When applied to online reading, these habits can reduce your learning and imperil your grades. To succeed with technology, turn off the television, quit online chat sessions, and turn down the music. Whenever you go online, stay in charge of your attention.

When reading is tough

Sometimes ordinary reading methods are not enough. Many students get bogged down in a murky reading assignment. The solution starts with a First Step: When you are confused, tell the truth about it. Successful readers monitor their understanding of reading material. They do not see confusion as a mistake or a personal shortcoming. Instead, they take it as a cue to change reading strategies and process ideas at a deeper level. If you are ever up to your neck in textbook alligators, you can use the following techniques to drain the swamp.

Read it again. Somehow, students get the idea that reading means opening a book and dutifully slogging the text—line by line, page by page—moving in a straight line from the first word until the last. Actually, this can be an ineffective way to read much of the published material you'll encounter in college.

Feel free to shake up your routine. Make several passes through any reading material. During a preview, for example, just scan the text to look for key words and highlighted material.

Next, skim the entire chapter or article again, spending a little more time and taking in more than you did during your preview. Finally, read in more depth, proceeding word by word through some or all of the text.

Difficult material—such as the technical writing in science texts—is often easier the second time around. Isolate difficult passages and read them again, slowly.

If you read an assignment and are completely lost, do not despair. Sleep on it. When you return to the assignment the next day, see it with fresh eyes.

Look for essential words. If you are stuck on a paragraph, mentally cross out all of the adjectives and adverbs and read the sentence without them. Find the important words. These will usually be verbs and nouns.

Hold a minireview. Pause briefly to summarize—either verbally or in writing—what you've read so far. Stop at the end of a paragraph and recite, in your own words, what you have just read. Jot down some notes or create a short outline or summary.

Read it out loud. Make noise. Read a passage out loud several times, each time using a different inflection and emphasizing a different part of the sentence. Be creative. Imagine that you are the author talking.

Talk to your instructor. Admit when you are stuck and make an appointment with your instructor. Most teachers welcome the opportunity to work individually with students. Be specific about your confusion. Point out the paragraph that you found toughest to understand.

Stand up. Changing positions periodically can combat fatigue. Experiment with standing as you read, especially if you get stuck on a tough passage and decide to read it out loud.

Skip around. Jump to the next section or end of a tough article or chapter. You might have lost the big picture. Simply seeing the next step, the next main point, or summary might be all you need to put the details in context. Retrace the steps in a chain of ideas and look for examples. Absorb facts and ideas in whatever order works for you—which may be different than the author's presentation.

Find a tutor. Many schools provide free tutoring services. If tutoring services are not provided by your school, other students who have completed the course can assist you.

Use another text. Find a similar text in the library. Sometimes a concept is easier to understand if it is expressed another way. Children's books, especially children's encyclopedias, can provide useful overviews of baffling subjects.

Pretend you understand, then explain it. We often understand more than we think we do. Pretend that the material is clear as a bell and explain it to another person, or even to yourself. Write down your explanation. You might be amazed by what you know.

Ask: "What's going on here?" When you feel stuck, stop reading for a moment and diagnose what's happening. At these stop points, mark your place in the margin of the page with a penciled "S" for "Stuck." A pattern to your marks over several pages might indicate a question you want to answer before going further. Or you might discover a reading habit you'd like to change.

Stop reading. When none of the above suggestions work, do not despair. Admit your confusion and then take a break. Catch a movie, go for a walk, study another subject, or sleep on it. The concepts you've already absorbed might come together at a subconscious level as you move on to other activities. Allow some time for that process. When you return to the reading material, see it with fresh eyes.

journal entry 11

Discovery Statement

Now that you've read about Muscle Reading, review your assessment of your reading skills in the Discovery Wheel on page 29. Do you still think your evaluation was accurate? What new insights do you have about the way you read? Are you a more effective reader than you thought you were? Less effective? Record your observations below.

The twenty-first century researcher—using your library

Libraries house treasures. Getting familiar with the resources and services at campus and community libraries will help you succeed. Knowing ways to unearth a library's treasures can enhance your writing, boost your presentation skills, help you plan your career, update your skills, and do lifelong learning.

In addition to housing print and audiovisual publications, libraries give you access to online sources. Remember that much published material is available only in print. The book—a form of information technology that's been with us for hundreds of years—still has something to offer the twenty-first century researcher.

Ask a librarian. Libraries give you access to a resource that goes even beyond the pages of a book or a Website. That resource is a living person—a librarian.

Librarians are trained explorers who can guide your expedition into the information jungle. They chose this line of work because they enjoy helping people. They also understand that some people feel nervous about finding materials. Asking a librarian for help can save you hours.

Librarians have different specialties. Start with a reference librarian. If the library has the material that you want, this person will find it. If not, he will direct you to another source. This might be a business, community agency, or government office.

If you have trouble finding something in your library, don't give up. Perhaps the book you want is on a cart waiting to be reshelved. A librarian can find out.

Take a tour. Libraries—from the smallest one in your hometown to the Smithsonian in Washington, D.C.—consist of just three basic elements:

- *Catalogs*—online databases that list all of the library's accessible sources.
- *Collections*—materials, such as periodicals (magazines and newspapers), books, pamphlets, audiovisual materials, and materials available from other collections via interlibrary loans.
- *Computer resources*—Internet access; connections to campuswide computer networks; and databases stored on CD-ROMs, CDs, DVDs, or online. Through your library, you might have access to databases that are available only by subscription. Ask a librarian for a list of these and how to access them.

Before you start your next research project, take some time to investigate all three elements of your campus or community library. Start with a library orientation session or tour. Step into each room and ask what's available there. Also find out whether the library houses any special collections. You might find one related to your major or another special interest.

Search the catalog. The library catalog is a database that lists all available materials. Some catalogs include listings for several libraries. To find materials, do a key word search—much like using a search engine on the Internet.

The catalog lists materials by subject, author, and title. Each listing includes a Library of Congress or Dewey decimal system number. These call numbers are used to shelve and locate materials. When you find a book by its call number, look at the materials on the shelf around it. There you will find sources of information on the same topic.

Some catalogs let you see if material is on the shelf or checked out. You may even be able to put a hold on materials that are currently in circulation. Ask a librarian if you can do this from a computer at your home or workplace.

Inspect the collection. When inspecting a library's collections, look for materials such as the following:

- *Encyclopedias*—Use leading print encyclopedias like *Encyclopedia Britannica.* Specialized encyclopedias cover many fields and include, for example, *Encyclopedia of Psychology, Encyclopedia of the Biological Sciences, Encyclopedia of Asian History,* and *McGraw-Hill Encyclopedia of Science and Technology.*
- *Biographies*—Read accounts of people's lives in biographical works such as *Who's Who, Dictionary of American Biography,* and *Biography Index: A Cumulative Index to Biographical Material in Books and Magazines.*
- *Critical works*—Read what scholars have to say about works of art and literature in *Oxford Companion* volumes (such as *Oxford Companion to Art* and *Oxford Companion to African American Literature*).
- *Statistics and government documents*—Among many useful sources are *Statistical Abstract of the United States, Handbook of Labor Statistics, Occupational Outlook Handbook,* and U.S. Census publications.
- *Almanacs, atlases, and gazetteers*—For population statistics and boundary changes, see *The World Almanac, Countries of the World,* or *Information Please.*
- *Dictionaries*—Consult *American Heritage Dictionary of the English Language, Oxford English Dictionary,* and specialized dictionaries such as *Dictionary of Literary Terms and Literary Theory* and *Dictionary of the Social Sciences.*
- *Indexes and databases*—Databases contain publication information and an abstract, or sometimes the full text, of an article available for downloading or printing from your computer. Your library houses print and CD-ROM databases and subscribes to some online databases; others are accessible through online library catalogs or Web links.
- *Reference works in specific subject areas*—These references cover a vast range of material. Examples include the *Oxford Companion to Art, Encyclopedia of the Biological Sciences,* and *Concise Oxford Companion to Classical Literature.* Ask a librarian for more information.
- *Periodical articles*—Find articles in periodicals (works issued periodically, such as scholarly journals, popular magazines, and newspapers) by using a periodical index. Use electronic indexes for recent works, print indexes for earlier works—especially for works written before 1980. Check to see which services your library subscribes to and the dates the indexes cover. Indexes might provide abstracts. Some, such as Lexis-Nexis Academic Universe, Infotrac, OCLC FirstSearch, and New York Times Ondisc, provide the full text of articles. You might be able to access such indexes from a computer in your dorm room or apartment.[4]

Access computer resources. Many libraries have access to special databases that are not available on the Internet. A reference librarian can tell you about them.

Also remember that the Web gives you access to the online resources of many libraries. Some useful sites are: Library of Congress (**http://lcweb.loc.gov**), Smithsonian Institution Libraries (**http://www.sil.si.edu/**), New York Public Library (**http://www.nypl.org/**), Internet Public Library (**http://www.ipl.org**), and WWW Virtual Library (**http://www.vlib.org**).

Also ask about e-books (electronic books). These texts are delivered straight to your computer. Like almost everything else at the library, these treasures are free.

Gain information literacy. *Information literacy* is the ability to locate, evaluate, use, and document sources of ideas and facts. Considering the variety of materials available at modern, fully equipped libraries, improving your ability to access information efficiently will help promote your success in school.

Start with the distinction between primary and secondary sources. *Primary sources* are often the researcher's dream. These are firsthand materials such as personal journals, letters, speeches, reports of scientific research, scholarly articles, field observations, archeological digs, and original works of art.

Secondary sources explain and comment on primary sources. Examples are nationally circulated newspapers such as the *Washington Post, New York Times,* and *Los Angeles Times.* Magazines with wide circulation but substantial treatment of current issues—such as the *Atlantic Monthly* and *Scientific American*—are secondary sources. So are general reference works such as the *Encyclopedia Britannica.*

Secondary sources are useful places to start your research by getting an overview of your topic. They might even be all you need for informal research. Other research projects in higher education—major papers, presentations, theses, or manuscripts you want to publish—will call on you to find primary sources.

Once you find the sources you want, inspect each one. With print sources, look at the preface, publication data, table of contents, bibliography, glossary, endnotes, and index. (Nonprint materials, including online documents, often include similar types of information.) Also scan any headings, subheadings, and summaries. If you have time, read a chapter or section. Then evaluate sources according to their:

- *Relevance*—Look for sources that deal directly with your research questions. If you're in doubt about the relevance of a particular source, ask yourself: "Will this material help me achieve the purpose of my research and support my thesis?"
- *Currentness*—Notice the published date of your source material (usually found in the front matter on the copyright page). If your topic is time-sensitive, set some guidelines about how current you want your sources to be.
- *Credibility*—Scan the source for biographical information about the author. Look for education, training, and work experience that qualifies this person to publish on the topic. Also notice any possible sources of bias, such as political affiliations or funding sources that might color the author's point of view.

The process of research is like climbing Mount Everest. You'll make observations, gather facts, trek into unfamiliar intellectual terrain, and ascend from one plateau of insight to another.

Keen researchers see facts and relationships. They focus their attention on the details, then discover unifying patterns. Far from being a mere academic exercise, library research can evolve into a path of continual discovery.

Find what you want on the Internet

Joe Barker, a librarian at the University of California at Berkeley, suggests that you analyze your topic *before* you look for information about it on the Internet. Then you can determine a useful way to find what you want. His suggestions are summarized in the following chart.[5]

If...	***Then...***
Your topic includes distinctive words or phrases (for example, *affirmative action*)	Enclose the words or phrases in quotation marks and use a **search engine** such as Google (**www.google.com**) or Yahoo! (search.yahoo.com).
Your topic does *not* include distinctive words or phrases (for example, *Iraq war*)	Enclose several words or phrases related to the topic in quotation marks and use a **search engine**.
	See if you can find distinctive words or phrases related to your topic. Use a **subject directory** such as Librarians' Index (**www.lii.org**), Infomine (infomine.ucr.edu), About.com (**www.about.com**), Google Directory (directory.google.com), or Yahoo! (**dir.yahoo.com**).
Your topic could be summarized in a broad overview (for example, *alternative energy sources*)	Look for a specialized subject directory related to your topic. Start by searching one of the **subject directories** listed above. Look for results labeled as *directories*, *virtual libraries*, *guides*, or *gateway pages*.
	Also add the words *Web directories* to your search term (for example, *alternative energy sources Web directories*).
Your topic includes various words or phrases that identify the same subject (for example, *MP3 players* or *portable music players*)	Use a search engine such as Google (**www.google.com**) or Yahoo! (**search.yahoo.com**) that allows you to search with words such as *AND* and *OR* (for example, *MP3 players AND portable music players*).
You are confused about the topic or totally new to it.	Look up the topic in an encyclopedia and ask a reference librarian for help.

English as a second language

If you grew up reading and speaking a language other than English, you're probably called a student of English as a Second Language (ESL), or English Language Learner (ELL). Experiment with the following suggestions to learn English with more success.

Build confidence. Many ESL/ELL students feel insecure about using English in social settings, including the classroom. Choosing not to speak, however, can delay your mastery of English and isolate you from other students.

As an alternative, make it your intention to speak up in class. List several questions and plan to ask them. Also schedule a time to meet with your instructors during office hours. These strategies can help you build relationships while developing English skills.

In addition, start a conversation with at least one native speaker of English in each of your classes. For openers, ask about their favorite instructors or for ideas about future courses to take.

English is a complex language. Whenever you extend your vocabulary and range of expression, the likelihood of making mistakes increases. The person who wants to master English yet seldom makes mistakes is probably being too careful. Do not look upon mistakes as a sign of weakness. Mistakes can be your best teachers—if you are willing to learn from them.

Learn by speaking and listening. You probably started your English studies by using textbooks. Writing and reading in English are important. Both can help you add to your English vocabulary and master grammar. To gain greater fluency and improve your pronunciation, also make it your goal to *hear* and *speak* English.

For example, listen to radio talk shows. Imitate the speaker's pronunciation by repeating phrases and sentences that you hear. During conversations, also notice the facial expressions and gestures that accompany certain English words and phrases.

Take advantage of opportunities to read and hear English at the same time. For instance, turn on English subtitles when watching a film on DVD. Also check your library for books on tape or CD. Check out the printed book and follow along as you listen.

Gain skills in note taking and testing. When taking notes, remember that you don't have to capture everything that an instructor says. To a large extent, the art of note taking consists of choosing what *not* to record. Listen for key words, main points, and important examples. Remember that instructors will often repeat these. You'll have more than one chance to pick up on the material. When you're in doubt, ask for repetition or clarification. For additional suggestions, see Chapter Five: Notes.

When in doubt, use expressions you understand. Native speakers of English use many informal expressions that are called *slang*. You are more likely to find slang in spoken conversations than in written English.

Native speakers also use *idioms*—colorful expressions with meanings that are not always obvious. Idioms can often be misunderstood. For instance, a "fork in the road" does not refer to an eating utensil discarded on a street.

Learning how to use slang and idioms is part of gaining fluency in English. However, these elements of the language are tricky. During informal conversations with friends, try out new expressions and ask for feedback about your use of them.

Celebrate your gains. Every time you analyze and correct an error in English, you make a small gain. Celebrate those gains. Taken together over time, they add up to major progress in mastering English as a second language. ⊠

Reading with children underfoot

It is possible to combine effective study time and quality time with children. The following suggestions come mostly from students who are also parents. The specific strategies you use will depend on your schedule and the ages of your children.

Attend to your children first. When you first come home from school, keep your books out of sight. Spend 10 minutes with your children before you settle in to study. Give them hugs and ask about their day. Then explain that you have some work to do. Your children might reward you with 30 minutes of quiet time. A short time of full, focused attention from a parent can be more satisfying than longer periods of partial attention.

Of course, this suggestion won't work with the youngest children. If your children are infants or toddlers, schedule sessions of concentrated study for when they are asleep.

Use "pockets" of time. See if you can arrange study time at school before you come home. If you arrive at school 15 minutes earlier and stay 15 minutes later, you can squeeze in an extra half-hour of study time that day. Also look for opportunities to study between classes.

Before you shuttle children to soccer games or dance classes, throw a book in the car. While your children are warming up for the game or changing clothes, steal another 15 minutes to read.

Plan special activities for your child. Find a regular playmate for your child. Some children can pair off with close friends and safely retreat to their rooms for hours of private play. You can check on them occasionally and still get lots of reading done.

Another option is to take your children to a public playground. While they swing, slide, and dig in the sand, you can dig into your textbooks. Lots of physical activity will tire out your children in constructive ways. If they go to bed a little early, that's extra time for you to read.

After you set up appropriate activities for your children, don't attend to them every second, even if you're nearby as they play. Obviously, you want to break up fights, stop unsafe activity, and handle emergencies. Short of such incidents, you're free to read.

Use television responsibly. Another option is to use television as a baby sitter—when you can control the programming. Rent a videotape for your child to watch as you study. If you're concerned about your child becoming a "couch potato," select educational programs that keep his mind active and engaged.

See if your child can use headphones while watching television. That way, the house stays quiet while you study.

Allow for interruptions. It's possible that you'll be interrupted even if you set up special activities for your child in advance. If so, schedule the kind of studying that can be interrupted. For instance, you could write out or review flash cards with key terms and definitions. Save the tasks that require sustained attention for other times.

Plan study breaks with children. Another option is to spend 10 minutes with your children for every 50 minutes that you study. View this not as an interruption but as a study break.

Or schedule time to be with your children when you've finished studying. Let your children in on the plan: "I'll be done reading at 7:30. That gives us a whole hour to play before you go to bed."

Many children love visible reminders that "their time" is approaching. An oven timer works well for this purpose. Set it for 15 minutes of quiet time. Follow that with five minutes of show-and-tell, storybooks, or another activity with your child. Then set the timer for another 15 minutes of studying, another break, and so on.

Develop a routine. Many young children love routines. They often feel more comfortable and secure when they know what to expect. You can use this to your benefit. One option is to develop a regular time for studying and let your child know this schedule: "I have to do my homework between 4 p.m. and 5 p.m. every day." Then enforce it.

Bargain with children. Reward them for respecting your schedule. In return for quiet time, give your child an extra allowance or a special treat. Children might enjoy gaining "credits" for this purpose. Each time they give you an hour of quiet time for studying, make an entry on a chart, put a star on their bulletin board, or give them a "coupon." After they've accumulated a certain number of entries, stars, or coupons, they can cash them in for a big reward—a movie or a trip to the zoo.

Ask other adults for help. This suggestion for studying with children is a message repeated throughout the book: Enlist other people to help support your success. Getting help can be as simple as asking your spouse, partner, neighbor, or a fellow student to take care of the children while you study. Offer to trade childcare with a neighbor: You will take his kids and yours for two hours on Thursday night if he'll take them for two hours on Saturday morning. Some parents start blockwide babysitting co-ops based on the same idea.

Find community activities and services. Ask if your school provides a day care service. In some cases, these services are available to students at a reduced cost. Community agencies such as the YMCA might offer similar programs.

You can also find special events that appeal to children. Storytelling hour at the library is one example. While your child is being entertained or supervised, you can stay close by. Use the time in this quiet setting to read a chapter or review class notes.

Make it a game. Reading a chemistry textbook with a 3-year-old in the same room is not as preposterous as it sounds. The secret is to involve your child. For instance, use this time to recite. Make funny faces as you say the properties of the transition elements in the periodic table. Talk in a weird voice as you repeat Faraday's laws. Draw pictures and make up an exciting story about the process of titration.

Read out loud to your children, or use them as an audience for a speech. If you invent rhymes, poems, or songs to help you remember formulas or dates, teach them to your children. Be playful. Kids are attracted to energy and enthusiasm.

Whenever possible, involve family members in tasks related to reading. Older children can help you with research tasks—finding books at the library, looking up news articles, even helping with typing.

When you can't read everything, just read something. One objection to reading with children nearby is "I just can't concentrate. There's no way I can get it all done while children are around."

That's OK. Even if you can't absorb an entire chapter while the kids are running past your desk, you can skim the chapter. Or you can just read the introduction and summary. When you can't get it *all* done, just get *something* done.

Caution: If you always read this way, your education might be compromised. Supplement this strategy with others so that you can get all of your reading done. ⊠

Discover more ways to study with children underfoot on the *From Master Student to Master Employee* Website.

REVISIT YOUR GOALS

One powerful way to achieve any goal is to periodically assess your progress in meeting it. This is especially important with long-term goals—those that can take years to achieve.

When you did Critical Thinking Exercise #12: "Get real with your goals" on page 83, you focused on one long-term goal and planned a detailed way to achieve it. This involved setting mid-term and short-term goals that will lead to achieving your long-term goal. Take a minute to review that exercise and revisit the goals you set. Then complete the following steps.

1. Take your long-term goal from Critical Thinking Exercise #12 and rewrite it in the space below. If you can think of a more precise way to state it, feel free to change the wording.

2. Next, check in with yourself. How do you feel about this goal? Does it still excite your interest and enthusiasm? On a scale of 1 to 10, how committed are you to achieving this goal? Write down your level of commitment in the space below.

3. If your level of commitment is 5 or less, you might want to drop the goal and replace it with a new one. To set a new goal, just turn back to Critical Thinking Exercise #12 and do it again. And release any self-judgment about dropping your original long-term goal. Letting go of one goal creates space in your life to set and achieve a new one.

4. If you're committed to the goal you listed in step 1 of this exercise, consider whether you're still on track to achieve it. Have you met any of the short-term goals related to this long-term goal? If so, list your completed goals in the space below.

Before going on to the next step, take a minute to congratulate yourself and celebrate your success.

5. Finally, consider any adjustments you'd like to make to your plan. For example, write additional short-term or mid-term goals that will take you closer to your long-term goal. Or cross out any goals that you no longer deem necessary. Make a copy of your current plan in the space below.

   Long-term goal (to achieve within your lifetime):

   Supporting mid-term goals (to achieve in one to five years):

   Supporting short-term goals (to achieve within the coming year):

power process

NOTICE YOUR PICTURES AND LET THEM GO

One of the brain's primary jobs is to manufacture images. We use mental pictures to make predictions about the world, and we base much of our behavior on those predictions.

When a cook adds chopped onions, mushrooms, and garlic to a spaghetti sauce, he has a picture of how the sauce will taste and measures each ingredient according to that picture. When an artist is creating a painting or sculpture, he has a mental picture of the finished piece. Novelists often have mental images of the characters that they're about to bring to life. Many parents have a picture about what they want their children to become.

These kinds of pictures and many more have a profound influence on us. Our pictures direct our thinking, our conversations, and our actions—all of which help create our immediate circumstances. That's amazing, considering that we often operate with little, if any, conscious knowledge of our pictures.

Just about any time we feel a need, we conjure up a picture of what will satisfy that need. A baby feels hunger pangs and starts to cry. Within seconds, his mother appears and he is satisfied. The baby stores a mental picture of his mother feeding him. He connects that picture with stopping the hunger pangs. Voilà! Now he knows how to solve the hunger problem. The picture goes on file.

According to psychologist William Glasser, the mind functions like a huge photo album.[6] Its pages include pictures of all the ways we've satisfied needs in the past. Whenever we feel dissatisfied, we mentally search the album for a picture of how to make the dissatisfaction go away. With that picture firmly in mind, we act in ways to make the world outside our heads match the pictures inside.

Remember that pictures are not strictly visual images. They can involve any of the senses. When you buy a CD, you have a picture of how it will sound. When you buy a sweater, you have a picture of how it will feel.

A problem with pictures

The pictures we make in our heads are survival mechanisms. Without them, we couldn't get from one end of town to the other. We couldn't feed or clothe ourselves. Without a picture of a socket, we couldn't screw in a light bulb.

Pictures can also get in our way. Take the case of a student who plans to attend a school he hasn't visited. He chose this school for its strong curriculum and good academic standing, but his brain didn't stop there. In his mind, the campus has historic buildings with ivy-covered walls and tree-lined avenues. The professors, he imagines, will be as articulate as Bill Moyers and as entertaining as Oprah Winfrey. His roommate will be his best friend. The cafeteria will be a cozy nook serving delicate quiche and fragrant teas. He will gather there with fellow students for hours of stimulating, intellectual conversation. The library will have every book, while the computer lab will boast the newest technology.

The school turns out to be four gray buildings downtown, next to the bus station. The first class he attends is taught by an overweight, balding professor who is wearing a purple-and-orange bird of paradise tie and has a bad case of the sniffles. The cafeteria is a nondescript hall with machine-dispensed food, and the student's apartment is barely large enough to accommodate his roommate's tuba. This hypothetical student gets depressed. He begins to think about dropping out of school.

The problem with pictures is that they can prevent us from seeing what is really there. That happened to the student in this story. His pictures prevented him from noticing that his school is in the heart of a culturally vital city—close to theaters, museums, government offices, clubs, and all kinds of stores. The professor with the weird tie is not only an expert in his field but is also a superior teacher. The school cafeteria is skimpy because it can't compete with the variety of inexpensive restaurants in the area. There might even be hope for a tuba-playing roommate.

Our pictures direct our thinking, our conversations, and our actions—all of which help create our immediate circumstances.

Anger and disappointment are often the results of our pictures. We set up expectations of events before they occur, which can lead to disappointment. Sometimes we don't even realize that we have these expectations. The next time you discover you are angry, disappointed, or frustrated, look to see which of your pictures aren't being fulfilled.

Take charge of your pictures

Having pictures is unavoidable. Letting these pictures control our lives *is* avoidable. Some techniques for dealing with pictures are so simple and effortless, they might seem silly.

One way to deal with pictures is to be aware of them. Open up your mental photo album and notice how the pictures there influence your thoughts, feelings, and actions. Just becoming aware of your pictures—and how they affect you—can help you take a huge step toward dealing with them effectively.

When you notice that pictures are getting in your way, then, in the most gentle manner possible, let your pictures go. Let them drift away like wisps of smoke picked up by a gentle wind.

Pictures are persistent. They come back over and over. Notice them again and let them go again. At first, a picture might return repeatedly and insistently. Pictures are like independent beings. They want to live. If you can see the picture as a thought independent from you, you will likely find it easier to let it go.

You are more than your pictures. Many images and words will pop into your head in the course of a lifetime. You do not have to identify with these pictures. You can let pictures go without giving up yourself.

If your pictures are interfering with your education, visualize them scurrying around inside your head. See yourself tying them to a brightly colored helium balloon and letting them go. Let them float away again and again.

Sometimes we can let go of old pictures and replace them with new ones. We stored all of those pictures in the first place. We can replace them. Our student's new picture of a great education can include the skimpy cafeteria, the professor with the weird tie, and the roommate with the tuba.

We can take charge of the images that float through our minds. We don't have to be ruled by an album of outdated pictures. We can stay aware of our pictures and keep looking for new ones. And when *those* new pictures no longer serve us, we can also let them go.

career application

Sachin Aggarwal worked as a bank teller during the summers while he was in school. After earning an Associate in Science degree in Marketing, he was promoted and gained a new job title: personal banker. When bank customers want to open a new account or take out a car loan, Sachin is the first person they see.

His career plan is to stay at this job for two years and then transfer his degree to a college where he can earn a four-year degree. While working as a teller, Sachin gained a reputation as a quick study. When the bank installed a new computer system, he completed the online tutorials and stayed on top of the software updates. Within a few weeks, Sachin was training new tellers to use the system.

In addition, he often fielded questions from some of the bank's older employees who described themselves as "computer challenged." Sachin's most recent performance review acknowledged his patience and ability to adapt his explanations to people with various levels of computer experience.

Right now, Sachin's biggest challenge is job-related reading. He never anticipated the number of documents—both printed and online—that would cross his desk after he got promoted. His supervisor has asked him to read technical manuals for each of the bank's services and account plans. He's also taking a customer service course with a 400-page textbook. In addition, he gets about 10 e-mail messages each day, some of them several screens long.

Within the first week after his promotion, Sachin often asked himself, "Why am I being bombarded with all this material? Most of it doesn't seem relevant to my job." Even so, he decided to put these reactions on hold and just dig into his reading stack. He figures the best way to proceed is start with any document at random and read it straight through before starting another one. Eventually, he hopes, he'll see a use for it all.

Reflecting on this scenario

1. Based on his initial response to his reading load, how would you describe Sachin's learning style?

2. Referring to "100 transferable skills" on page 63, list a transferable skill that Sachin demonstrates in this scenario.

3. Identify another skill that would be useful to Sachin in this situation. Explain why you chose this skill.

4. List three strategies from this chapter that would be useful to Sachin.

quiz

Name ______________________________ Date ____/____/____

1. Name the acrostic that can help you remember the steps of Muscle Reading.

2. You must complete all nine steps of Muscle Reading to get the most out of any reading assignment. True or False? Explain your answer.

3. Give three examples of what to look for when previewing a reading assignment.

4. Briefly explain how to use headings in a text to create an outline.

5. In addition to underlining, there are other ways to mark up a text. List three possibilities.

6. To get the most benefit from marking a book, underline at least 10 percent of the text. True or False? Explain your answer.

7. Explain at least three techniques you can use when reading is tough.

8. The Power Process in this chapter includes this sentence: “The next time you discover you are angry, disappointed, or frustrated, look to see which of your pictures aren’t being fulfilled.” Give an example of this from your own experience.

9. Define the “topic-point” method of summarizing and give a brief example based on an article in this book.

10. List at least three techniques for increasing your reading speed.

learning styles application

The questions below will "cycle" you through four styles, or modes, of learning as explained in the article "Learning styles: Discover how you learn" in Chapter One. Each question will help you explore a different mode. You can answer the questions in any order.

what if *Consider how you might adapt or modify Muscle Reading to make it more useful. List any steps that you would add, subtract, or change.*

why *List current reading assignments that you can use to practice Muscle Reading.*

how *Describe how you will apply a suggestion from this chapter to a current reading assignment.*

what *List the three most useful suggestions for reading that you gained from this chapter.*

master student profile

CRAIG KIELBURGER

(1984–) In 1995, at age 12, Craig Kielburger founded Free the Children International, an organization of children helping children who are the victims of poverty and exploitation. He has also served as an ambassador to the Children's Embassy in Sarajevo and was named a Global Leader of Tomorrow at the 1998 World Economic Forum.

I picked up the Toronto Star and put it on the table. But I didn't make it past the front page. Staring back at me was the headline, "BATTLED CHILD LABOUR, BOY, 12, MURDERED." It was a jolt. Twelve, the same age as I was. My eyes fixed on the picture of a boy in a bright-red vest. He had a broad smile, his arm raised straight in the air, a fist clenched. . . .

Riding the bus to school later that morning, I could think of nothing but the article I had read on the front page. What kind of parents would sell their children into slavery at four years of age? And who would ever chain a child to a carpet loom?

Throughout the day I was consumed by Iqbal's story. In my Grade Seven class we had studied the American Civil War, and Abraham Lincoln, and how some of the slaves in the United States had escaped into Canada. But that was history from centuries ago. Surely slavery had been abolished throughout the world by now. If it wasn't, why had I never heard about it?

The school library was no help. After a thorough search I still hadn't found a scrap of information. After school, I decided to make the trek to the public library.

The librarian knew me from my previous visits. Luckily, she had read the same article that morning and was just as intrigued. Together, we searched out more information on

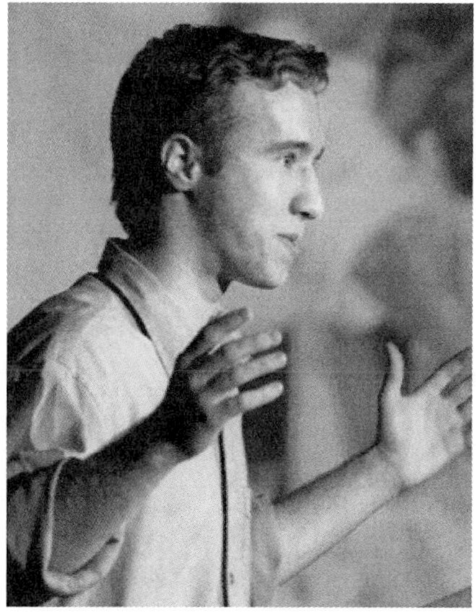

child labour. We found a few newspaper and magazine articles, and made copies.

By the time I returned home, images of child labour had imbedded themselves in my mind: children younger than me forced to make carpets for endless hours in dimly lit rooms; others toiling in underground pits, struggling to get coal to the surface; others maimed or killed by explosions raging through fireworks factories. I was angry at the world for letting these things happen to children. Why was nothing being done to stop such cruelty? . . .

At lunchtime that day, some of us got together and talked about what we could do. I was amazed at how enthusiastic they all were. I told them about the youth fair on Friday.

"Do you think we could put together a display?" I asked. "We haven't got much time."

"Sure. Let's do it."

"We can all meet at my house," I said.

That night, twelve of us got together. It was a very tight deadline, with just two days to prepare. We found an old science fair board, and we covered it with coloured paper, pasting on all the information I had found on child labour in the library, then drawing pictures to illustrate it.

We had determined that our first objective should be to inform people of the plight of child labourers. Armed with such knowledge, they might be willing to help. We decided to draw up a petition to present to the government, and called on the expertise of a couple of human rights groups to refine the wording for us.

But we were still without a name for our group. For more than an hour we struggled to come up with something suitable. We flipped through the newspaper clippings for inspiration. One of them reported on a demonstration in Delhi, India, where 250 children had marched through the streets with placards, chanting, "We want an education," "We want freedom," "Free the children!"

"That's it!" someone shouted. "Free the Children."

5 Notes

MASTER STUDENT MAP

why this chapter matters . . .

Note taking makes you an active learner, enhances memory, and influences how well you do on tests and other evaluations.

how you can use this chapter . . .

Experiment with several formats for note taking.

Create a note-taking format that works especially well for you.

Take effective notes in special situations—while reading, when speakers talk fast, and during meetings.

As you read, ask yourself what if . . .

I could take notes that remain informative and useful for weeks, months, or even years to come?

what is included . . .

FROM THE DESK OF . . .

Note taking is a skill that plays a significant role in my daily responsibilities. I attend every meeting with my supervisor and take notes for his files. As administrative assistant for the managing director, I am also responsible for taking notes at the biweekly companywide meetings and distributing them to the entire staff. Because the employees value my detailed notes, they are willing to slow down or repeat information if it is requested.

—TASHIANA CLARKE, ADMINISTRATIVE ASSISTANT

The note-taking process flows

One way to understand note taking is to realize that taking notes is just one part of the process. Effective note taking consists of three parts: observing, recording, and reviewing. First, you observe an "event"—a statement by an instructor, a lab experiment, a slide show of an artist's works, or a chapter of required reading. Then you record your observations of that event, that is, you "take notes." Finally, you review what you have recorded.

Each part of the process is essential, and each depends on the others. Your observations determine what you record. What you record determines what you review. And the quality of your review can determine how effective your next observations will be. For example, if you review your notes on the Sino-Japanese War of 1894, the next day's lecture on the Boxer Rebellion of 1900 will make more sense.

Legible and speedy handwriting is also useful in taking notes. Knowledge about outlining is handy, too. A nifty pen, a new notebook, and a laptop computer are all great note-taking devices. And they're all worthless—unless you participate as an energetic observer *in* class and regularly review your notes *after* class. If you take those two steps, you can turn even the most disorganized chicken scratches into a powerful tool.

Sometimes note taking looks like a passive affair, especially in large groups. One person at the front of the room does most of the talking. Everyone else is seated and silent, taking notes. The speaker seems to be doing all of the work.

Don't be deceived. Observe more closely, and you'll see some students taking notes in a way that radiates energy. They're awake and alert, poised on the edge of their seats. They're writing, a physical activity that expresses mental engagement. These students listen for levels of ideas and information, make choices about what to record, and compile materials to review.

In higher education, you might spend hundreds of hours taking notes. Making them more effective is a direct investment in your success. Think of your notes as a textbook that *you* create—one that's more current and more in tune with your learning preferences than any textbook you could buy.

journal entry **12**

Discovery/Intention Statement

Think about the possible benefits of improving your skills at note taking. Recall a recent incident in which you had difficulty taking notes. Perhaps you were listening to an instructor who talked fast, or you got confused during a meeting at work and stopped taking notes altogether. Describe the incident in the space below.

____

____

____

____

____

Now preview this chapter to find at least five strategies that you can use right away to help you take better notes. Sum up each of those strategies in a few words and note page numbers where you can find out more about each suggestion.

Strategy	*Page number*

Reflect on your intention to experiment actively with this chapter. Describe a specific situation in which you might apply the strategies you listed above. If possible, choose a situation that will occur within the next 24 hours.

I intend to . . .

____

____

____

____

The note-taking process flows

Sherlock Holmes, a fictional master detective and student of the obvious, could track down a villain by observing the fold of his scarf and the mud on his shoes. In real life, a doctor can save a life by observing a mole—one a patient has always had—that undergoes a rapid change.

An accountant can save a client thousands of dollars by observing the details of a spreadsheet. A student can save hours of study time by observing that she gets twice as much done at a particular time of day.

Keen observers see facts and relationships. They know ways to focus their attention on the details, then tap their creative energy to discover patterns. To sharpen your classroom observation skills, experiment with the following techniques and continue to use those that you find most valuable.

Set the stage

Complete outside assignments. Nothing is more discouraging (or boring) than sitting through a lecture about the relationship of Le Chatelier's principle to the principle of kinetics if you've never heard of Henri Louis Le Chatelier or kinetics. Instructors usually assume that students complete assignments, and they construct their lectures accordingly. The more familiar you are with a subject, the more easily you can absorb important information during class lectures.

Bring the right materials. A good pen does not make you a good observer, but the lack of a pen or a notebook can be distracting enough to take the fine edge off your concentration. Make sure you have a pen, pencil, notebook, and any other materials you will need. Bring your textbook to class, especially if the lectures relate closely to the text.

If you are consistently unprepared for a class, that might be a message about your intentions concerning the course. Find out if it is. The next time you're in a frantic scramble to borrow pen and paper 37 seconds before the class begins, notice the cost. Use the borrowed pen and paper to write a Discovery Statement about your lack of preparation. Consider whether you intend to be successful in the course.

Sit front and center. Students who get as close as possible to the front and center of the classroom often do better on tests for several reasons. The closer you sit to the lecturer, the harder it is to fall asleep. The closer you sit to the front, the fewer interesting, or distracting, classmates are situated between you and the instructor. Material on the board is easier to read from up front. Also, the instructor can see you more easily when you have a question.

Instructors are usually not trained to perform. While some can project their energy to a large audience, some cannot. A professor who sounds boring from the back of the room might sound more interesting up close.

Sitting up front enables you to become a constructive force in the classroom. By returning the positive energy that an engaged teacher gives out, you can reinforce the teacher's enthusiasm and enhance your experience of the class.

In addition, sound waves from the human voice begin to degrade at a distance of eight to 12 feet. If you sit more than 15 feet from the speaker, your ability to hear and take effective notes might be compromised. Get close to the source of the sound. Get close to the energy.

Sitting close to the front is a way to commit yourself to getting what you want out of school. One reason students gravitate to the back of the classroom is that they think the instructor is less likely to call on them. Sitting in back can signal a lack of commitment. When you sit up front, you are declaring your willingness to take a risk and participate.

Conduct a short preclass review. Arrive early, then put your brain in gear by reviewing your notes from the previous class. Scan your reading assignment. Look at the sections you have underlined. Review assigned problems and exercises. Note questions you intend to ask.

Clarify your intentions. Take a 3 × 5 card to class with you. On that card, write a short Intention Statement about what you plan to get from the class. Describe your intended level of participation or the quality of attention you will bring to the subject. Be specific. If you found your previous class notes to be inadequate, write down what you intend to do to make your notes from this class session more useful.

"Be here now" in class

Accept your wandering mind. The techniques in the Power Process: "Be here now" can be especially useful when your head soars into the clouds. Don't fight daydreaming. When you notice your mind wandering during class, look at this as an opportunity to refocus your attention. If thermodynamics is losing out to beach parties, let go of the beach.

Notice your writing. When you discover yourself slipping into a fantasyland, feel the weight of your pen in your hand. Notice how your notes look. Paying attention to the act of writing can bring you back to the here and now.

You also can use writing in a more direct way to clear your mind of distracting thoughts. Pause for a few seconds and write those thoughts down. If you're distracted by thoughts of errands you need to run after class, list them on a 3 × 5 card and stick it in your pocket. Or simply put a symbol, such as an arrow or asterisk, in your notes to mark the places where your mind started to wander. Once your distractions are out of your mind and safely stored on paper, you can gently return your attention to taking notes.

Be with the instructor. In your mind, put yourself right up front with the instructor. Imagine that you and the instructor are the only ones in the room and that the lecture is a personal conversation between the two of you. Pay attention to the instructor's body language and facial expressions. Look the instructor in the eye.

Notice your environment. When you become aware of yourself daydreaming, bring yourself back to class by paying attention to the temperature in the room, the feel of your chair, or the quality of light coming through the window. Run your hand along the surface of your desk. Listen to the chalk on the blackboard or the sound of the teacher's voice. Be in that environment. Once your attention is back in the room, you can focus on what's happening in class.

Postpone debate. When you hear something you disagree with, note your disagreement and let it go. Don't allow your internal dialogue to drown out subsequent material. If your disagreement is persistent and strong, make note of this and then move on. Internal debate can prevent you from absorbing new information. It is OK to absorb information you don't agree with. Just absorb it with the mental tag "My instructor says . . . , and I don't agree with this."

Let go of judgments about lecture styles. Human beings are judgment machines. We evaluate everything, especially other people. If another person's eyebrows are too close together (or too far apart), if she walks a certain way or speaks with an unusual accent, we instantly make up a story about her. We do this so quickly that the process is usually not a conscious one.

Don't let your attitude about an instructor's lecture style, habits, or appearance get in the way of your education. You can decrease the power of your judgments if you pay attention to them and let them go.

You can even let go of judgments about rambling, unorganized lectures. Turn them to your advantage. Take the initiative and organize the material yourself. While taking notes, separate the key points from the examples and supporting evidence. Note the places where you got confused and make a list of questions to ask.

Participate in class activities. Ask questions. Volunteer for demonstrations. Join in class discussions. Be willing to take a risk or look foolish, if that's what it takes for you to learn. Chances are, the question you think is "dumb" is also on the minds of several of your classmates.

Relate the class to your goals. If you have trouble staying awake in a particular class, write at the top of your notes how that class relates to a specific goal. Identify the reward or payoff for reaching that goal.

Think critically about what you hear. This might seem contrary to the previously mentioned technique "Postpone debate." It's not. You might choose not to think critically about the instructor's ideas during the lecture. That's fine. Do it later, as you review and edit your notes. This is a time to list questions or write down your agreements and disagreements.

Watch for clues

Be alert to repetition. When an instructor repeats a phrase or an idea, make a note of it. Repetition is a signal that the instructor thinks the information is important.

Listen for introductory, concluding, and transition words and phrases. These include phrases such as "the following three factors," "in conclusion," "the most important consideration," "in addition to," and "on the other hand." These phrases and others signal relationships, definitions, new subjects, conclusions, cause and effect, and examples. They reveal the structure of the lecture. You can use these phrases to organize your notes.

Watch the board or overhead projector. If an instructor takes the time to write something down, consider the material to be important. Copy all diagrams and drawings, equations, names, places, dates, statistics, and definitions.

Watch the instructor's eyes. If an instructor glances at her notes and then makes a point, it is probably a signal that the information is especially important. Anything she reads from her notes is a potential test question.

Highlight the obvious clues. Instructors will often tell students point-blank that certain information is likely to appear on an exam. Make stars or other special marks in your notes next to this information. Instructors are not trying to hide what's important.

Notice the instructor's interest level. If the instructor is excited about a topic, it is more likely to appear on an exam. Pay attention when she seems more animated than usual. ☒

What do you do when you miss a class?

For most courses, you'll benefit by attending every class session. If you miss a class, catch up as quickly as possible.

Clarify policies on missed classes. On the first day of classes, find out about your instructors' policies on absences. See if you can make up assignments, quizzes, and tests. Also inquire about doing extra-credit assignments.

Contact a classmate. Early in the semester, identify a student in each class who seems responsible and dependable. Exchange e-mail addresses and phone numbers. If you know you won't be in class, contact this student ahead of time. When you notice that your classmate is absent, pick up extra copies of handouts, make assignments lists, and offer copies of your notes.

Contact your instructor. If you miss a class, e-mail, phone, or fax your instructor, or put a note in her mailbox. Ask if she has another section of the same course that you can attend so you won't miss the lecture information. Also ask about getting handouts you might need before the next class meeting.

Consider technology. Free online services such as NoteMesh and **stu.dicio.us** allow students to share notes with each other. These services use wiki software, which allows you to create and edit Web pages using any browser. Before using such tools, however, check with instructors for their policies on note sharing.

Record

The note-taking process flows

The format and structure of your notes are more important than how fast you write or how elegant your handwriting is. The following techniques can improve the effectiveness of your notes.

General techniques for note taking

Use key words. An easy way to sort the extraneous material from the important points is to take notes using key words. Key words or phrases contain the essence of communication. They include

- Concepts, technical terms, names, and numbers.
- Linking words, including words that describe action, relationship, and degree (*most, least, faster,* etc.).

Key words evoke images and associations with other words and ideas. They trigger your memory. That makes them powerful review tools. One key word can initiate the recall of a whole cluster of ideas. A few key words can form a chain from which you can reconstruct an entire lecture.

To see how key words work, take yourself to an imaginary classroom. You are now in the middle of an anatomy lecture. Picture what the room looks like, what it feels like, how it smells. You hear the instructor say:

> *OK, what happens when we look directly over our heads and see a piano falling out of the sky? How do we take that signal and translate it into the action of getting out of the way? The first thing that happens is that a stimulus is generated in the neurons—receptor neurons—of the eye. Light reflected from the piano reaches our eyes. In other words, we see the piano. The receptor neurons in the eye transmit that sensory signal, the sight of the piano, to the body's nervous system. That's all they can do, pass on information. So we've got a sensory signal coming into the nervous system. But the neurons that initiate movement in our legs are effector neurons. The information from the sensory neurons must be transmitted to effector neurons or we will get squashed by the piano. There must be some kind of interconnection between receptor and effector neurons. What happens between the two? What is the connection?*

Key words you might note in this example include *stimulus, generated, receptor neurons, transmit, sensory signals, nervous system, effector neurons,* and *connection.* You can reduce the instructor's 163 words to these 12 key words. With a few transitional words, your notes might look like this:

Stimulus (piano) generated
in receptor neurons (eye)

Sensory signals transmitted
by nervous system to
effector neurons (legs)

What connects receptor to
effector?

Note the last key word of the lecture above: *connection.* This word is part of the instructor's question and leads to the next point in the lecture. Be on the lookout for questions like this. They can help you organize your notes and are often clues for test questions.

Use pictures and diagrams. Make relationships visual. Copy all diagrams from the board and invent your own.

A drawing of a piano falling on someone who is looking up, for example, might be used to demonstrate the relationship of receptor neurons to effector neurons. Label the eyes "receptor" and the feet "effector." This picture implies that the sight of the piano must be translated into a motor response. By connecting the explanation of the process with the unusual picture of the piano falling, you can link the elements of the process together.

Write notes in paragraphs. When it is difficult to follow the organization of a lecture or to put information into outline form, create a series of informal paragraphs. These paragraphs will contain few complete sentences. Reserve complete sentences for precise definitions, direct quotations, and important points that the instructor emphasizes by repetition or other signals—such as the phrase "This is an important point." For other material, apply the suggestions in this article for using key words.

Copy material from the board. Record all formulas, diagrams, and problems that the teacher writes down. Copy dates, numbers, names, places, and other facts. If it's on the board, put it in your notes. You can even use your own signal or code to flag that material. If it appears on the board, it can appear on a test.

Use a three-ring binder. Three-ring binders have several advantages over other kinds of notebooks. First, pages can be removed and spread out when you review. This way, you can get the whole picture of a lecture. Second, the three-ring-binder format allows you to insert handouts right into your notes. Third, you can insert your own out-of-class notes in the correct order. Fourth, you can easily make additions, corrections, and revisions.

Use only one side of a piece of paper. When you use one side of a page, you can review and organize all your notes by spreading them out side by side. Most students find the benefit well worth the cost of the paper. Perhaps you're concerned about the environmental impact of consuming more paper. If so, you can use the blank side of old notes and use recycled paper.

Use 3 × 5 cards. As an alternative to using notebook paper, use 3 × 5 cards to take lecture notes. Copy each new concept onto a separate 3 × 5 card. Later, you can organize these cards in an outline form and use them as pocket flash cards.

Keep your own thoughts separate. For the most part, avoid making editorial comments in your lecture notes. The danger is that when you return to your notes, you might mistake your own idea for that of the instructor. If you want to make a comment—either a question to ask later or a strong disagreement—clearly label it as your own. Pick a symbol or code and use it in every class.

Use an "I'm lost" signal. No matter how attentive and alert you are, you might get lost and confused in a lecture. If it is inappropriate to ask a question, record in your notes that you were lost. Invent your own signal—for example, a circled question mark. When you write down your code for "I'm lost," leave space for the explanation or clarification that you will get later. The space will also be a signal that you missed something. Later, you can speak to your instructor or ask to see a fellow student's notes. As long as you are honest with yourself when you don't understand, you can stay on top of the course.

Label, number, and date all notes. Develop the habit of labeling and dating your notes at the beginning of each class. Number the page, too. Sometimes the sequence of material in a lecture is important. Write your name and phone number in each notebook in case you lose it. Class notes become more and more valuable as a term or semester progresses.

Use standard abbreviations. Be consistent with your abbreviations. If you make up your own abbreviations or symbols, write a key explaining them in your notes. Avoid vague abbreviations. When you use an abbreviation such as *comm.* for *committee*, you run the risk of not being able to remember whether you meant *committee, commission, common, commit, community, communicate*, or *communist.*

One way to abbreviate is to leave out vowels. For example, *talk* becomes *tlk, said* becomes *sd, American* becomes *Amrcn.*

Leave blank space. Notes tightly crammed into every corner of the page are hard to read and difficult to use for review. Give your eyes a break by leaving plenty of space.

Later, when you review, you can use the blank spaces in your notes to clarify points, write questions, or add other material. Instructors often return to material covered earlier in the lecture.

Take notes in different colors. You can use colors as highly visible organizers. For example, you can signal important points with red. Or use one color of ink for notes about the text and another color for lecture notes. Notes that are visually pleasing can be easier to review.

Use graphic signals. The following ideas can be used with any note-taking format:

- Use brackets, parentheses, circles, and squares to group information that belongs together.

- Use stars, arrows, and underlining to indicate important points. Flag the most important points with double stars, double arrows, or double underlines.
- Use arrows and connecting lines to link related groups and to replace words such as *leads to, becomes,* and *produces.*
- Use equal signs and greater-than and less-than signs to indicate compared quantities.
- Use question marks for their obvious purpose. Double question marks can signal tough questions or especially confusing points.

To avoid creating confusion with graphic symbols, use them carefully and consistently. Write a "dictionary" of your symbols in the front of your notebooks, such as the one shown below.

[ ], ( ), ◯, ▭ = info
that belongs together

*, ↘, ═ = important

**, ↘↘, ≡, !!! = extra important

> = greater than < = less than
═ = equal to

⟶ = leads to, becomes
Ex: school → job → money

? = huh ?, lost

?? = big trouble, clear up
immediately

Use recorders effectively. There are persuasive arguments for not using an audio recorder or digital recorder. Here are the main ones.

When you record a lecture, there is a strong temptation to daydream. After all, you can always listen to the lecture again later on. Unfortunately, if you let the recorder do all of the work, you are skipping a valuable part of the learning process. Actively participating in class can turn a lecture into a valuable study session.

There are more potential problems. Listening to recorded lectures can take a lot of time—more time than reviewing written notes. Recorders can't answer the questions you didn't ask in class. Also, recording devices malfunction. In fact, the unscientific Hypothesis of Recording Glitches states that the tendency of recorders to malfunction is directly proportional to the importance of the material. With those warnings in mind, some students use a recorder effectively. For example, you can use recordings as backups to written notes. (Check with your instructor first. Some prefer not to be recorded.) Turn the recorder on, then take notes as if it weren't there. Recordings can be especially useful if an instructor speaks fast.

You can also record yourself after class, reading your written notes. Teaching the class to yourself is a powerful review tool. Instead of recording all of your notes, for example, you might record only the key facts or concepts.

The Cornell method

A note-taking system that has worked for students around the world is the *Cornell method.*[1] Originally developed by Walter Pauk at Cornell University during the 1950s, this approach continues to be taught across the United States and in other countries as well.

The cornerstone of this method is what Pauk calls the *cue column*—a wide margin on the left-hand side of the paper. The cue column is the key to the Cornell method's many benefits. Here's how to use it.

Cue column	Notes
What are the 3 phases of Muscle Reading?	Phase 1: Before you read Phase 2: While you read Phase 3: After you read
What are the steps in phase 1?	1. Preview 2. Outline 3. Question
What are the steps in phase 2?	4. Read 5. Underline 6. Answer
What are the steps in phase 3?	7. Recite 8. Review 9. Review again
What is an acronym for Muscle Reading?	Pry = preview Out = outline Questions = question Root = read Up = underline Answers = answer Recite Review Review again

Summary
Muscle Reading includes 3 phases: before, during, and after reading. Each phase includes 3 steps. Use the acronym to recall all the steps.

Format your paper. On each sheet of your note paper, draw a vertical line, top to bottom, about two inches from the left edge of the paper. This line creates the cue column—the space to the left of the line. You can also find Websites that allow you to print out pages in this format. Just do an Internet search using the keywords *cornell method pdf.*

Take notes, leaving the cue column blank. As you read an assignment or listen to a lecture, take notes on the right-hand side of the paper. Fill up this column with sentences, paragraphs, outlines, charts, or drawings. Do not write in the cue column. You'll use this space later, as you do the next steps.

Condense your notes in the cue column. Think of the notes you took on the right-hand side of the paper as a set of answers. In the cue column, list potential test questions that correspond to your notes. Write one question for each major term or point.

As an alternative to questions, you can list key words from your notes. Yet another option is to pretend that your notes are a series of articles on different topics. In the cue column, write a newspaper-style headline for each "article." In any case, be brief. If you cram the cue column full of words, you defeat its purpose—to reduce the number and length of your notes.

Write a summary. Pauk recommends that you reduce your notes even more by writing a brief summary at the bottom of each page. This step offers you another way to engage actively with the material. It can also make your notes easier to review for tests.

Use the cue column to recite. Cover the right-hand side of your notes with a blank sheet of paper. Leave only the cue column showing. Then look at each item you wrote in the cue column and talk about it. If you wrote questions, answer each question. If you wrote key words, define each word and talk about why it's important. If you wrote headlines in the cue column, explain what each one means and offer supporting details. After reciting, uncover your notes and look for any important points you missed. Repeat this cycle of reciting and checking until you've mastered the material.

Mind mapping

This system, developed by Tony Buzan,[2] can be used in conjunction with the Cornell format. In some circumstances, you might want to use mind maps exclusively.

To understand mind maps, first review the features of traditional note taking. Outlines (explained in the next section) divide major topics into minor topics, which, in turn, are subdivided further. They organize information in a sequential, linear way.

This kind of organization doesn't reflect certain aspects of brain function, a point that has been made in discussions about "left-brain" and "right-brain" activities. People often use the term *right brain* when referring to creative, pattern-making, visual, intuitive brain activity. They use the term *left brain* when talking about orderly, logical, step-by-step characteristics of thought. Writing teacher Gabrielle Rico uses another metaphor. She refers to the left-brain mode as our "sign mind" (concerned with words) and the right-brain mode as our "design mind" (concerned with visuals).[3] A mind map uses both kinds of brain functions. Mind maps can contain lists and sequences and show relationships. They can also provide a picture of a subject. Mind maps are visual patterns that can serve as a framework for recalling information. They work on both verbal and nonverbal levels.

One benefit of mind maps is that they quickly, vividly, and accurately show the relationships between ideas. Also, mind mapping helps you think from general to specific. By choosing a main topic, you focus first on the big picture, then zero in on subordinate details. And by using only key words, you can condense a large subject into a small area on a mind map. You can review more quickly by looking at the key words on a mind map than by reading notes word for word.

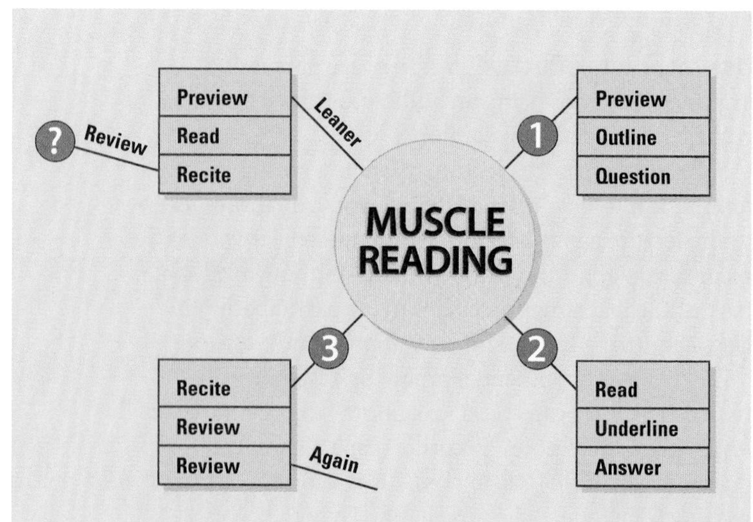

Give yourself plenty of room. Use blank paper that measures at least 11 by 17 inches. If that's not available, turn regular notebook paper on its side so that you can take notes in a horizontal (instead of vertical) format. Another option is to find software that allows you to draw flow charts or diagrams. Then you can generate mind maps on a computer.

Determine the main concept of the lecture. Write that concept in the center of the paper and circle it, underline it, or highlight it with color. You can also write the concept in large letters. Record concepts related to the main concept on lines that radiate outward from the center. An alternative is to circle these concepts.

Use key words only. Whenever possible, reduce each concept to a single word per line or circle in your mind map. Though this might seem awkward at first, it prompts you to summarize and to condense ideas to their essence. That means fewer words for you to write now and fewer to review when it's time to prepare for tests. (Using shorthand symbols and abbreviations can help.) Key words are usually nouns and verbs that communicate the bulk of the speaker's ideas. Choose words that are rich in associations and that can help you re-create the lecture.

Jazz it up. Use color to organize your mind map. If there are three main subjects covered in the lecture, you can record each subject in a different color. Add symbols and other images as well.

Create links. One mind map doesn't have to include all of the ideas in a book or an article. Instead, you can link mind maps. For example, draw a mind map that sums up the five key points in a chapter, and then make a separate, more detailed mind map for each of those key points. Within each mind map, include references to the other mind maps. This helps explain and reinforce the relationships among many ideas. Some students pin several mind maps next to each other on a bulletin board or tape them to a wall. This allows for a dramatic—and effective—look at the big picture.

Outlining

An outline shows the relationship between major points and supporting ideas. One benefit of taking notes in the outline format is that doing so can totally occupy your attention. You are recording ideas and also organizing them. This can be an advantage if the material has been presented in a disorganized way. Perhaps you've had negative experiences with outlining in the past. Teachers might have required you to use complex, rigid outlining formats based exclusively on Roman numerals or on some unfamiliar system. By playing with variations, you can discover the power of outlining to reveal relationships between ideas. Technically, each word, phrase, or sentence that appears in an outline is called a *heading*. These are arranged in different levels:

- In the first or "top" level of headings, note the major topics that are presented in a lecture or reading assignment.
- In the second level of headings, record the key points that relate to each topic in the first-level headings.
- In the third level of headings, record specific facts and details that support or explain each of your second-level headings. Each additional level of subordinate heading supports the ideas in the previous level of heading.

Roman numerals offer one way to illustrate the difference between levels of headings. See the following example.

You can also use other heading styles, as illustrated below:

Distinguish levels with indentations only:

Muscle Reading includes 3 phases
    Phase 1: Before you read
        Preview

Distinguish levels with bullets and dashes:

MUSCLE READING INCLUDES 3 PHASES
- Phase 1: Before you read
  - Preview

Distinguish headings by size:

MUSCLE READING INCLUDES 3 PHASES
Phase 1: Before you read
Preview

Combining formats

Feel free to use different note-taking systems for different subjects and to combine formats. Do what works for you.

For example, combine mind maps along with the Cornell format. You can modify the Cornell format by dividing your note paper in half, reserving one half for mind maps and the other for linear information, such as lists, graphs, and outlines, as well as equations, long explanations, and word-for-word definitions. You can incorporate a mind map into your paragraph-style notes whenever you feel one is appropriate. Minds maps are also useful for summarizing notes taken in the Cornell format.

John Sperry, a teacher at Utah Valley State College, developed a note-taking system that can include all of the formats discussed in this article:

- Fill up a three-ring binder with fresh paper. Open your notebook so that you see two blank pages—one on the left and one on the right. Plan to take notes across this entire two-page spread.
- During class or while reading, write your notes only on the left-hand page. Place a large dash next to each main topic or point. If your instructor skips a step or switches topics unexpectedly, just keep writing.
- Later, use the right-hand page to review and elaborate on the notes that you took earlier. This page is for anything you want. For example, add visuals such as mind maps. Write review questions, headlines, possible test questions, summaries, outlines, mnemonics, or analogies that link new concepts to your current knowledge.
- To keep ideas in sequence, place appropriate numbers on top of the dashes in your notes on the left-hand page. Even if concepts are presented out of order during class, they'll still be numbered correctly in your notes.

journal entry 13

Discovery Statement

Think about the way you have conducted reviews of your notes in the past. Respond to the following statements by checking "Always," "Often," "Sometimes," "Seldom," or "Never" after each.

I review my notes immediately after class.
______ Always ______ Often ______ Sometimes
______ Seldom ______ Never

I conduct weekly reviews of my notes.
______ Always ______ Often ______ Sometimes
______ Seldom ______ Never

I make summary sheets of my notes.
______ Always ______ Often ______ Sometimes
______ Seldom ______ Never

I edit my notes within 24 hours.
______ Always ______ Often ______ Sometimes
______ Seldom ______ Never

Before class, I conduct a brief review of the notes I took in the previous class.
______ Always ______ Often ______ Sometimes
______ Seldom ______ Never

Review

The note-taking process flows

Think of reviewing as an integral part of note taking rather than as an added task. To make new information useful, encode it in a way that connects to your long-term memory. The key is reviewing.

Review within 24 hours. In the last chapter, when you read the suggestion to review what you've read within 24 hours, you were asked to sound the trumpet. Well, if you have one, get it out and sound it again. This might be the most powerful note-taking technique you can use. It might save you hours of review time later in the term.

Many students are surprised that they can remember the content of a lecture in the minutes and hours after class. They are even more surprised by how well they can read the sloppiest of notes. Unfortunately, short-term memory deteriorates quickly. The good news is that if you review your notes soon enough, you can move that information from short-term to long-term memory. And you can do it in just a few minutes—often 10 minutes or less.

The sooner you review your notes, the better, especially if the class was difficult. In fact, you can start reviewing during class. When your instructor pauses to set up the overhead projector or erase the board, scan your notes. Dot the i's, cross the t's, and write out unclear abbreviations. Another way to use this technique is to get to your next class as quickly as you can. Then use the four or five minutes before the lecture begins to review the notes you just took in the previous class. If you do not get to your notes immediately after class, you can still benefit by reviewing later in the day. A review right before you go to sleep can also be valuable.

Think of the day's unreviewed notes as leaky faucets, constantly dripping, losing precious information until you shut them off with a quick review. Remember, it's possible to forget most of the material within 24 hours—unless you review.

Edit notes. During your first review, fix words that are illegible. Write out abbreviated words that might be unclear to you later. Make sure you can read everything. If you can't read something or don't understand something you *can* read, mark it, and make a note to ask your instructor or another student. Check to see that your notes are labeled with the date and class and that the pages are numbered. You can edit with a different colored pen or pencil if you want to distinguish between what you wrote in class and what you filled in later.

Fill in key words in the left-hand column. This task is important if you are to get the full benefit of using the Cornell method. Using the key word principles described earlier in this chapter, go through your notes and write key words or phrases in the left-hand column.

These key words will speed up the review process later. As you read your notes and focus on extracting important concepts, your understanding of the lecture is further reinforced.

Use your key words as cues to recite. With a blank sheet of paper, cover your notes, leaving only the key words in the left-hand margin showing. Take each key word in order and recite as much as you can about the point. Then uncover your notes and look for any important points you missed.

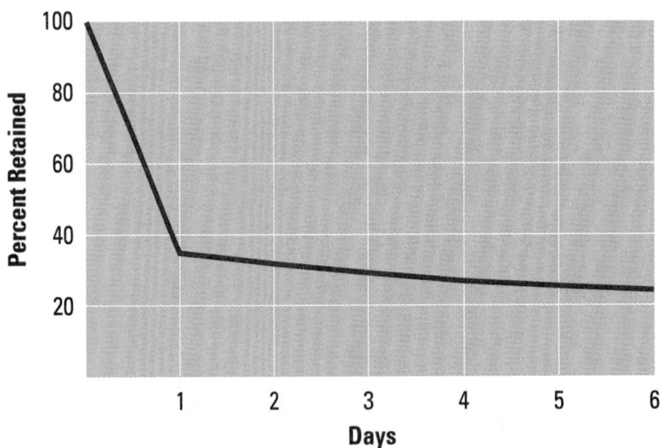

To study the process of memory and forgetting, Hermann Ebbinghaus devised a method for testing memory. The results, shown here in what has come to be known as the Ebbinghaus forgetting curve, demonstrate that forgetting occurs most rapidly shortly after learning and then gradually declines over time.

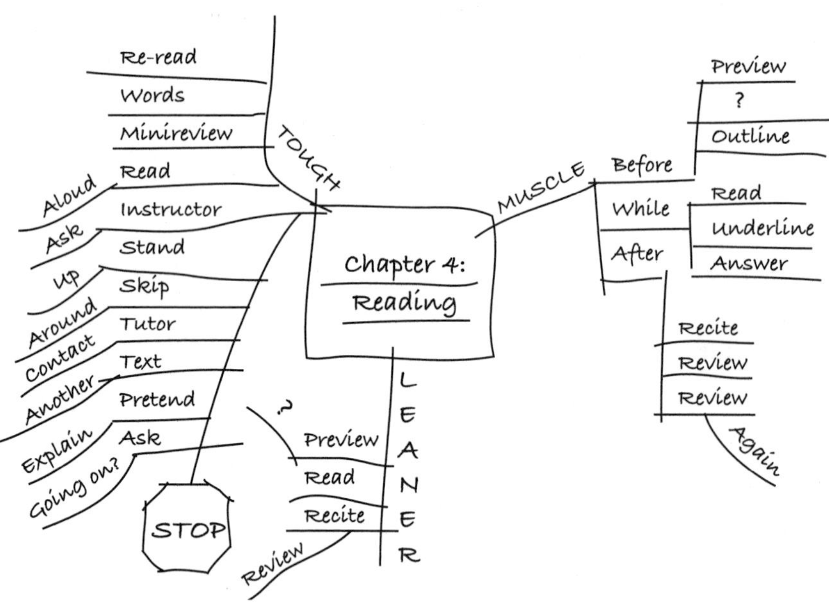

Conduct short weekly review periods. Once a week, review all of your notes again. The review sessions don't need to take a lot of time. Even a 20-minute weekly review period is valuable. Some students find that a weekend review, say, on Sunday afternoon, helps them stay in continuous touch with the material. Scheduling regular review sessions on your calendar helps develop the habit.

As you review, step back to see the larger picture. In addition to reciting or repeating the material to yourself, ask questions about it: "Does this relate to my goals? How does this compare to information I already know, in this field or another? Will I be tested on this material? What will I do with this material? How can I associate it with something that deeply interests me? Am I unclear on any points? If so, what exactly is the question I want to ask?"

Consider typing your notes. Some students type their handwritten notes using a computer. The argument for doing so is threefold. First, typed notes are easier to read. Second, they take up less space. Third, the process of typing them forces you to review the material.

Another alternative is to bypass handwriting altogether and take notes in class on a laptop computer. This solution has drawbacks: laptops are more expensive than PCs, and computer errors can wipe out your notes, leaving you with no handwritten backup.

Experiment with typing notes and see what works for you. For example, type up only key portions of notes, such as summaries or outlines.

Create summaries. Mind mapping is an excellent way to summarize large sections of your course notes or reading assignments. Create one map that shows all the main topics you want to remember. Then create another map about each main topic. After drawing your maps, look at your original notes and fill in anything you missed. This system is fun and quick.

Another option is to create a "cheat sheet." There's only one guideline: Fit all your review notes on a single sheet of paper. Use any note-taking format that you want—mind map, outline, Cornell, or a combination of all of them. The beauty of this technique is that it forces you to pick out main ideas and key details. There's not enough room for anything else!

If you're feeling adventurous, create your cheat sheet on a single index card. Start with the larger sizes (5×7 or 4×6) and then work down to a 3×5 card.

Some instructors might let you use a summary sheet during an exam. But even if you can't, you'll benefit from creating one while you study for the test. Summarizing is a powerful way to review. ☒

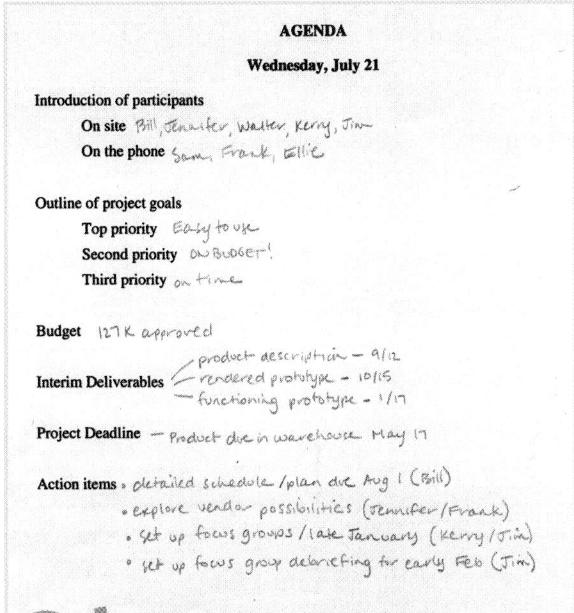

AGENDA

Wednesday, July 21

Introduction of participants

On site Bill, Jennifer, Walter, Kerry, Jim

On the phone Sam, Frank, Ellie

Outline of project goals

Top priority Easy to use

Second priority ON BUDGET!

Third priority on time

Budget 127K approved

Interim Deliverables
- product description – 9/12
- rendered prototype – 10/15
- functioning prototype – 1/17

Project Deadline – Product due in warehouse May 17

Action items
- detailed schedule/plan due Aug 1 (Bill)
- explore vendor possibilities (Jennifer/Frank)
- set up focus groups/late January (Kerry/Jim)
- set up focus group debriefing for early Feb (Jim)

Observe, record, and review at work

In the workplace, notes matter. During meetings, people are hired, fired, and promoted. Problems are tackled. Negotiations are held. Decisions are made. Your job might depend on what you observe during meetings, what you record, and how you respond.

Be prepared. Before meetings, complete background reading on the topics to be discussed, include minutes from relevant meetings in the past. Doing this sets the stage for taking better notes in upcoming meetings. It's easier to make sense of what people say when you already know something about the meeting topics.

Experiment with formats. During meetings, experiment with Cornell format notes, mind mapping, outlining, concept mapping, or some combination of these. Feel free to add boldface headings, charts, tables, graphs, and other visuals that make the main ideas stand out. If you're taking notes to distribute to coworkers, they will appreciate it if you get to the point and keep paragraphs short.

Your employer may have specific guidelines for taking meeting notes. Ask your supervisor about this. Note that in some cases—such as minutes taken during a board of directors meeting—notes may function as legal documents reviewed by the IRS or another independent auditor. Keeping this fact in mind can help you take better notes.

Keep up with speakers. When taking notes during fast-paced meetings and conference calls, use suggestions from the article "When a speaker talks *fast*" in this chapter. Immediately after the call or meeting, review and edit your notes.

Notice your handwriting. Colleagues may read your handwriting often—for example, on expense reports, time sheets, or reviews of a proposal or report. If your penmanship creates communication problems or does not convey a positive image, simply notice this fact. Then pay conscious attention to your handwriting as you take notes.

Remember the "four A's." Consider adding the following topics to your notes on a meeting:

- *Attendance.* Start by observing who shows up. In many organizations, people expect meeting notes to include a list of attendees.
- *Agenda.* One path to more powerful meeting notes is observing the agenda. Think of it as a road map—a way to keep the discussion on track. Skilled planners often put an agenda in writing and distribute it in advance of a meeting. Record this agenda and use it to organize your notes.
- *Agreements.* The purpose of most meetings is to reach an agreement about something—a policy, project, or plan. Record each agreement.
- *Actions.* During meetings, people often commit to take some type of action in the future. Record each follow-up action and who agreed to do it.

Follow-up action is often a make-or-break point for project teams. One mark of exceptional teams is that people make agreements about what they will do—and then keep those agreements.

You can set a powerful example. Ask whether any of the points you included in your notes call for follow-up action on your part—perhaps a phone call to make, a fact to find, or another task to complete. Highlight such items in your notes. Then add them to your calendar or to-do list and follow through.

Get to the bones of your book with concept maps

Concept mapping, pioneered by Joseph Novak and D. Bob Gowin, is a tool to make major ideas in a book leap off the page.[4] In creating a concept map, you reduce an author's message to its essence—its bare bones. Concept maps can also be used to display the organization of lectures and discussions.

The building blocks of knowledge are concepts and links. A *concept* is a name for a group of related things or ideas. *Links* are words or phrases that describe the relationship between concepts. Consider the following paragraph:

> *Muscle Reading consists of three phases. Phase 1 includes tasks to complete before reading. Phase 2 tasks take place during reading. Finally, phase 3 includes tasks to complete after reading.*

In this paragraph, examples of concepts are *Muscle Reading, reading, phases, tasks, phase 1, phase 2,* and *phase 3*. Links include *consists of, includes, before, during,* and *after*.

To create a concept map, list concepts and then arrange them in a meaningful order from general to specific. Then fill in the links between concepts, forming meaningful statements.

Concept mapping promotes critical thinking. It alerts you to missing concepts or faulty links between concepts. In addition, concept mapping mirrors the way that your brain learns—that is, by linking new concepts to concepts that you already know.

To create a concept map, use the following steps:

1. List the key concepts in the text. Aim to express each concept in three words or less. Most concept words are nouns, including terms and proper names. At this point, you can list the concepts in any order. For ease in ranking the concepts later, write each one on a single 3 × 5 card.

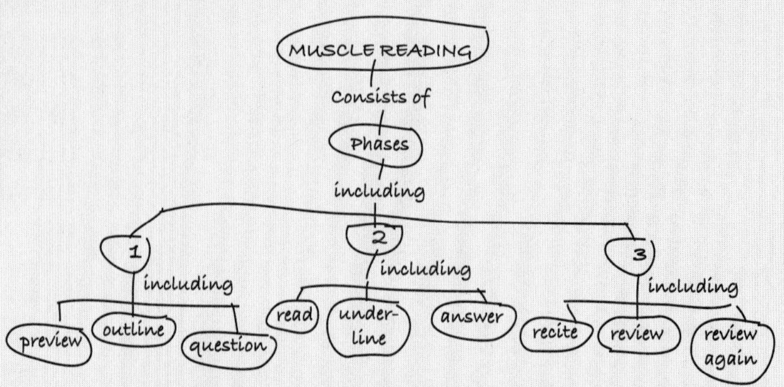

2. Rank the concepts so that they flow from general to specific. On a large sheet of paper, write the main concept at the top of the page. Place the most specific concepts near the bottom. Arrange the rest of the concepts in appropriate positions throughout the middle of the page. Circle each concept.

3. Draw lines that connect the concepts. On these connecting lines, add words that describe the relationship between the concepts. Again, limit yourself to the fewest words needed to make an accurate link—three words or less. Linking words are often verbs, verb phrases, or prepositions.

4. Finally, review your map. Look for any concepts that are repeated in several places on the map. You can avoid these repetitions by adding more links between concepts.

As you gain facility with concept maps, you might wish to create them on a computer. Use any software with drawing capabilities. For example, the software program inspiration, a visual thinking and learning tool, is specifically designed to create concept maps.

Sample concept maps based on selected articles in this book are available on the *From Master Student to Master Employee* Website.

Student Website

journal entry 14

Discovery/Intention Statement

Think back on the last few lectures you have attended. How do you currently observe (listen to) lectures? What specific behaviors do you have as you sit and listen? Briefly describe your responses in the space below.

I discovered that I . . .

____

____

____

Now write an Intention Statement about any changes you want to make in the way you respond to lectures.

I intend to . . .

____

____

____

____

Taking notes while *reading*

Taking notes while reading requires the same skills that apply to class notes: observing, recording, and reviewing. Use these skills to take notes for review and for research.

Review notes. These will look like the notes you take in class. Take review notes when you want more detailed notes than writing in the margin of your text allows. You might want to single out a particularly difficult section of a text and make separate notes. You can't underline or make notes in library books, so these sources will require separate notes, too.

Use a variety of formats. Mind maps and concept maps are useful for review, especially for summaries of overlapping lecture and textbook materials. You can also outline or take notes in paragraph form. Another option is the Cornell method. Use the left-hand column for key words and questions, just as you do in your class notes.

When you read mathematic, scientific, or other technical materials, copy important formulas or equations. Re-create important diagrams and draw your own visual representations of concepts. Also write down data that might appear on an exam.

Research notes. Take research notes when preparing to write a paper or deliver a speech.

One traditional tool for research notes is the mighty 3 × 5 card. Create two kinds of cards: source cards and information cards.

- *Source cards.* These cards identify where you found the information contained in your paper or speech. For example, a source card for a book will show the author, title, date and place of publication, and publisher. Ask your instructor what information to include for each type of source.

  When you write source cards, give each source a code—the initials of the author, a number, or a combination of numbers and letters.

  A key advantage of using source cards is that you create your bibliography as you do the research. When you are done, simply alphabetize the cards by author and—voilà!—instant bibliography.

- *Information cards.* Write the actual research notes on information cards. At the top of each information card, write the code for the source of the information. For printed sources, also include the page numbers your notes are based on. When recording your own ideas, simply note the source as "me."

  Write only *one* piece of information on each information card—a single quotation, fact, or concept. You can then sort the cards in various ways to construct an outline of your paper or speech.

- *Avoid plagiarism.* When people take words or images from a source and present them as their own, they are committing plagiarism. Even when plagiarism is accidental, the consequences can be harsh. For essential information on this topic, see "Avoiding plagiarism" on page 267.

- *Consider a computer.* Another option is to take research notes using a computer. This offers the same flexibility as 3 × 5 cards when it comes to sorting and organizing ideas. However, be especially careful to prevent plagiarism. If you copy text or images from a Website, separate these notes from your own ideas. Use a different font for copied material or enclose it in quotation marks.

Thinking about notes. Whenever you take notes, use your own words as much as possible. When you do so, you are thinking about what you are reading. If you do quote your source word for word, put that material within quotation marks.

Close the book after reading an assignment and quickly jot down a summary of the material. This writing can be loose, without any structure or format. The important thing is to do it right away, while the material is still fresh in your mind. Restating concepts in this way helps you remember them.

Special cases. The style of your notes can vary according to the nature of the material. If you are assigned a short story or poem, read the entire work once without taking any notes. On your first reading, simply enjoy the piece. When you finish, write down your immediate impressions. Then go over the piece and make brief notes on characters, images, symbols, settings, plot, point of view, or other aspects of the work.

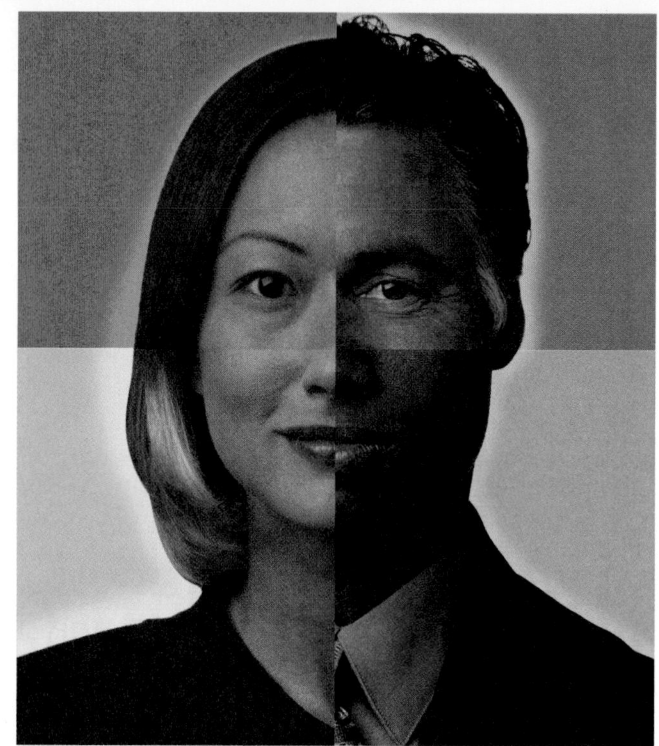

CREATE your *instructor*

Faced with an instructor you don't like, you have choices. One is to label the instructor a "dud" and let it go at that. When you make this choice, you get to endure class and complain to other students. This choice puts you at the mercy of circumstance. It gives your instructor sole responsibility for the quality of your education and the value of your tuition payments.

There is another option. Don't give away your power. Instead, take responsibility for your education.

Usually we think of students as the people who enroll in school. Turn this idea on its head. See if *you* can enroll your instructors as partners in getting what you want from higher education.

Research the instructor. There are formal and informal sources of information about instructors. One is the school catalog. Alumni magazines or newsletters or the school newspaper might run articles on teachers. In some schools, students post informal evaluations of instructors on Websites. Also talk to students who have taken courses from the instructor.

Or introduce yourself to the instructor. Set up a visit during office hours and ask about the course. This can help you get the flavor of a class and clues to the instructor's teaching style.

Show interest in class. Students give teachers moment-by-moment feedback in class. That feedback comes through posture, eye contact, responses to questions, and participation in class discussions. If you find a class boring, re-create the instructor through a massive display of interest. Ask lots of questions. Sit up straight, make eye contact, take detailed notes. Your enthusiasm might enliven your instructor. If not, you are still creating a more enjoyable class for yourself.

Etiquette is a word that refers to socially acceptable behavior. In the classroom, it's simply being courteous, which includes turning off cell phones, portable music players, and other electronic distractions. There's a payoff: When you treat instructors courteously, you're more likely to be treated that way in return.

Release judgments. Maybe your instructor reminds you of someone you don't like—your annoying Aunt Edna, a rude store clerk, or the fifth-grade teacher who kept you after school. Your attitudes are in your own head and beyond the instructor's control.

Likewise, an instructor's beliefs about politics, religion, or feminism are not related to teaching ability. Being aware of such things can help you let go of negative judgments.

Get to know the instructor. Meet with your instructor during office hours. Teachers who seem boring in class can be fascinating in person. Prepare to notice your pictures and let them go.

Open up to diversity. Sometimes students can create their instructors by letting go of pictures about different races and ethnic groups. According to one picture, a Hispanic person cannot teach English literature. According to other pictures, a white teacher cannot have anything valid to say about African music, a teacher in a wheelchair cannot command the attention of 100 people in a lecture hall, and a male instructor cannot speak credibly about feminism. All of those pictures can clash with reality. Releasing them can open up new opportunities for understanding and appreciation.

Separate liking from learning. You don't have to like an instructor to learn from one. See if you can focus on content instead of form. *Form* is the way something is organized or presented. If you are irritated at the sound of an instructor's voice, you're focusing on form. When you put aside your concern about her voice and turn your attention to the points she's making, you're focusing on *content.*

Form your own opinion about each instructor. You might hear conflicting reports about teachers from other students. The same instructor could be described as a riveting speaker or as completely lacking in charisma. See for yourself.

Seek alternatives. You might feel more comfortable with another teacher's style or method of organizing course materials. Consider changing teachers, asking another teacher for help outside class, or attending an additional section taught by a different instructor. You can also learn from other students, courses, tutors, study groups, books, DVDs, and tapes. Be a master student, even when you have teachers you don't like. Your education is your own creation.

Avoid excuses. Instructors know them all. Most teachers can see a snow job coming before the first flake hits the ground. Accept responsibility for your own mistakes, and avoid thinking that you can fool the teacher.

Submit professional work. Prepare papers and projects as if you were submitting them to an employer. Imagine that a promotion and raise will be determined by your work. Instructors often grade hundreds of papers during a term. Your neat, orderly, well-organized paper can lift a teacher's spirits.

Accept criticism. Learn from your teachers' comments about your work. It is a teacher's job to give feedback. Don't take it personally.

Use course evaluations. In many classes you'll have an opportunity to evaluate the instructor. Respond honestly. Write about the aspects of the class that did not work well for you. Offer specific ideas for improvement. Also note what *did* work well.

Take further steps, if appropriate. Sometimes severe conflict develops between students and instructors. In such cases, you might decide to file a complaint or ask for help from an administrator.

Be prepared to document your case in writing. Describe specific actions that created problems. Stick to the facts—events that other class members can verify. Your school might have a set of established grievance procedures to use in these cases. Use them. You are a consumer of education and have a right to fair treatment.

Meeting with your instructor

Meeting with an instructor outside class can save hours of study time and help your grade. To get the most from these meetings:

- Schedule a meeting time during the instructor's office hours.
- If you need to cancel or reschedule, let your instructor know in advance.
- During the meeting, relax. This is not a graded activity.
- Come prepared with a list of questions and any materials you'll need. During the meeting, take notes on the instructor's suggestions.
- Show the instructor your class notes to see if you're capturing essential material.
- Get feedback on outlines that you've created for papers.
- Ask about ways to prepare for upcoming exams.
- If the course is in a subject area that interests you, ask about the possibilities of declaring a major in that area and the possible careers that are associated with that major.
- Avoid questions that might offend your instructor, for example: "I missed class on Monday. Did we do anything important?"
- Ask if your instructor is willing to answer occasional short questions via e-mail or a phone call.
- When the meeting is over, thank your instructor for making time for you.

Instead of trying to resolve a conflict with an instructor in the few minutes before or after class, schedule a time during office hours. During this meeting, state your concerns in a respectful way. Then focus on finding solutions.

When a speaker talks *fast*

Take more time to prepare for class. Familiarity with a subject increases your ability to pick up on key points. If an instructor lectures quickly or is difficult to understand, conduct a thorough preview of the material to be covered.

Be willing to make choices. When an instructor talks fast, focus your attention on key points. Instead of trying to write everything down, choose what you think is important. Occasionally, you will make a wrong choice and neglect an important point. Worse things could happen. Stay with the lecture, write down key words, and revise your notes immediately after class.

Exchange photocopies of notes with classmates. Your fellow students might write down something you missed. At the same time, your notes might help them. Exchanging photocopies can fill in the gaps.

Leave large empty spaces in your notes. Leave plenty of room for filling in information you missed. Use a symbol that signals you've missed something, so you can remember to come back to it.

See the instructor after class. Take your class notes with you and show the instructor what you missed.

Use an audio recorder. Recording a lecture gives you a chance to hear it again whenever you choose. Some audio recorders allow you to vary the speed of the recording. With this feature, you can perform magic and actually slow down the instructor's speech.

Before class, take notes on your reading assignment. You can take detailed notes on the text before class. Leave plenty of blank space. Take these notes with you to class and simply add your lecture notes to them.

Go to the lecture again. Many classes are taught in multiple sections. That gives you the chance to hear a lecture at least twice—once in your regular class and again in another section of the class.

Learn shorthand. Some note-taking systems, known as shorthand, are specifically designed for getting ideas down fast. Books and courses are available to help you learn these systems. You can also devise your own shorthand method by inventing one- or two-letter symbols for common words and phrases.

Ask questions—even if you're totally lost. Many instructors allow a question session. This is the time to ask about the points you missed.

There might be times when you feel so lost that you can't even formulate a question. That's OK. One option is to report this fact to the instructor. She can often guide you to a clear question. Another option is to ask a related question. This might lead you to the question you really wanted to ask.

Ask the instructor to slow down. This is the most obvious solution. If asking the instructor to slow down doesn't work, ask her to repeat what you missed.

journal entry 15

Discovery/Intention Statement

Choose a set of notes that you've taken in class recently. Next to it, place notes that you took during a meeting at work.

Now compare the two sets of notes. Look past their content and consider their format. What visual differences do you see between the notes from work and the notes from class?

I discovered that . . .

____

____

____

____

____

Also think about the *process* of taking notes in these two settings. Did you find it easier or more difficult to take notes at work than in class?

I discovered that . . .

____

____

____

____

____

After comparing these two sets of notes, reflect on what you can do differently in the future to take more effective notes at work.

I intend to . . .

____

____

____

____

____

critical thinking exercise 19

TELEVISION NOTE TAKING

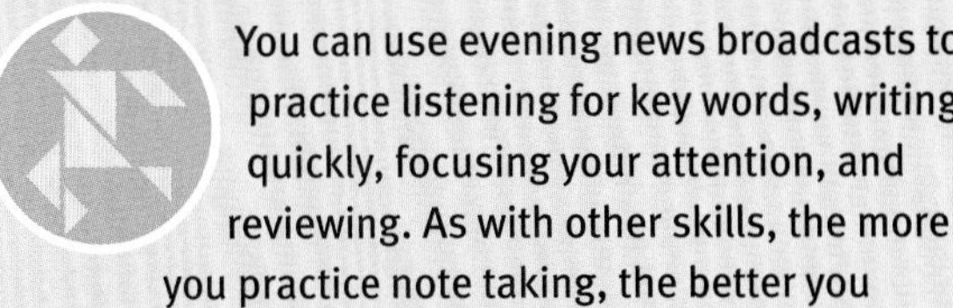

You can use evening news broadcasts to practice listening for key words, writing quickly, focusing your attention, and reviewing. As with other skills, the more you practice note taking, the better you become.

The next time you watch the news, use pen and paper to jot down key words and information. During the commercials, review and revise your notes. At the end of the broadcast, spend five minutes reviewing all of your notes. Create a mind map of a few news stories, then sum up the news of the day for a friend.

This exercise will help you develop an ear for key words. Since you can't ask questions or request that the speaker slow down, you train yourself to stay totally in the moment. If you get behind, relax, leave a space, and return your attention to the broadcast.

Don't be discouraged if you miss a lot the first time around. Do this exercise several times and observe how your mind works.

If you find it too difficult to take notes during a fast-paced television news show, check your local broadcast schedule for a news documentary. These are often slower paced. Another option is to tape a program and then take notes. You can stop the tape at any point to review your notes.

You can also ask a classmate to do the same exercise, and then compare notes the next day.

power process

This is a powerful tool in times of trouble. In a crisis, "I create it all" can lead the way to solutions. "I create it all" means treating experiences, events, and circumstances in your life as if you created them.

I CREATE IT ALL

When your dog tracks fresh tar on the white carpet, when your political science teacher is a crushing bore, when your spouse dents the car, when your test on Latin American literature focuses on an author you've never read—it's time for a Power Process. Tell yourself, "I created it all."

"Baloney!" you shout. "I didn't let the dog in, that teacher really is a bore, I wasn't even in the car, and nobody told me to read Gabriel García Márquez. I didn't create these disasters."

Good points. Obviously, "I create it all" is one of the most unusual and bizarre suggestions in this book. It certainly is not an idea that is easily believed. In fact, believing it can get you into trouble. "I create it all" is strictly a practical idea. Use it when it works. Don't when it doesn't.

Keeping that caution in mind, consider how powerful this Power Process can be. It is really about the difference between two distinct positions in life: being a victim or being responsible for yourself.

A victim of circumstances is controlled by outside forces. We've all felt like victims at one time or another. When tar-footed dogs tromped on the white carpets of our lives, we felt helpless.

In contrast, we can take responsibility. *Responsibility* is the important word. It does not mean "blame." Far from it. Responsibility is "response-ability"—the ability to choose a response.

Practicing resignation

By not taking responsibility, we are acknowledging that the power to determine what happens in our lives is beyond our grasp. When we feel as if we don't have control over our lives, we feel resigned. The opposite of practicing "I create it all" is practicing resignation.

There is a phenomenon called *learned resignation.*[5] An interesting experiment with dogs demonstrates how learned resignation works. A dog is put in a caged pen with a metal floor that can be electrified. When the cage door is left open and the dog is given a mild shock, she runs out of the cage to escape the discomfort. Then the dog is put back into the cage, the door is shut and locked, and a mild shock is given again. The dog runs around, looking for an escape. When she doesn't find one, she just lies down, sits, or stands there, and quits trying to find a way out. She has no control over her circumstances and is learning to be resigned.

Now, here comes the interesting part. After the dog has consistently stopped trying to escape the shock, the door is opened and the dog is led in and out several times. Then the dog is left in the cage, the door is left open, and the shock is administered once again. Amazingly, the dog doesn't even try to escape, even though the open door is right there in front of her. Instead, the dog continues to endure the shock. She has learned to be resigned.

A variety of this phenomenon can occur in human beings as well. When we consistently give control of our lives to other people and to circumstances, we run the risk of learning to give up. We might develop the habit of being resigned, even though there is abundant opportunity all around us.

Applying this process

Many students approach grades from the position of being victims. When the student who sees the world this way gets an F, she reacts something like this:

"Oh, no!" (Slaps forehead)

"Rats!" (Slaps forehead again) (Students who get lots of F's often have flat foreheads.)

"Another F! That teacher couldn't teach her way out of a wet paper bag. She can't teach English for anything. And that textbook—what a bore! How could I read it with a houseful of kids making noise all the time? And then friends came over and wanted to party, and . . . ."

The problem with this viewpoint is that in looking for excuses, the student is robbing herself of the power to get any grade other than an F. She's giving all of her power to a bad teacher, a boring textbook, noisy children, and friends.

There is another way, called *taking responsibility*. You can recognize that you choose your grades by choosing your actions. Then you are the source, rather than the result, of the grades you get. The student who got an F could react like this:

"Another F! Oh, shoot! Well, hmmm. . . . How did I choose this F? What did I do to create it?"

Now, that's power. By asking "How did I contribute to this outcome?" you give yourself a measure of control. You are no longer the victim. This student might continue by saying, "Well, let's see. I didn't review my notes after class. That might have done it." Or "I studied in the same room with my children while they watched TV. Then I went out with my friends the night before the test. Well, that probably helped me fulfill some of the requirements for getting an F."

The point is this: When the F is the result of your kids, your friends, the book, or the teacher, you probably can't do anything about it. However, if you *chose* the F, you can choose a different grade next time. You are in charge.

Choosing our thoughts

There are times when we don't create it all. We do not create earthquakes, floods, avalanches, or monsoons. Yet if we look closely, we discover that we *do* create a larger part of our circumstances than most of us are willing to admit.

For example, we can choose our thoughts. And thoughts can control our perceptions by screening information from our senses. We can never be aware of every single thing in our environment. If we could, we'd go crazy from sensory overload. Instead, our brains filter out most sensory inputs. This filtering colors the way we think about the world.

Choosing our behaviors

Moment by moment we make choices about what we will do and where we will go. The results of these choices are where we are in life. A whole school of psychology called *control theory* is based on this idea, and psychiatrist William Glasser has written extensively about it.[6]

All of those choices help create our current circumstances—even those circumstances that are not "our fault." After a car accident, we tell ourselves, "It just happened. That car came out of nowhere and hit me." We forget that driving five miles per hour slower and paying closer attention might have allowed us to miss the driver who was "to blame."

Some cautions

The presence of blame is a warning that this Power Process is being misused. "I create it all" is not about blaming yourself or others.

Feeling guilty is another warning signal. Guilt actually involves the same dynamic as blame. If you are feeling guilty, you have just shifted the blame from another person to yourself.

Another caution is that this Power Process is not a religion. Saying that you "create it all" does not mean that you have divine powers. It is simply a way to expand the choices you already have. This Power Process is easy to deny. Tell your friends about it, and they're likely to say, "What about world hunger? I didn't cause that. What about people who get cancer? Did they create that?"

These are good arguments—and they miss the point. Victims of rape, abuse, incest, and other forms of violence can still use "I create it all" to choose their response to the people and events that violated them.

Some people approach world hunger, imprisonment, and even cancer with this attitude: "Pretend for a moment that I *am* responsible for this. What will I do about it?" These people see problems in a new way, and they discover choices that other people miss.

"I create it all" is not always about disaster. It also works when life is going great. We often give credit to others for our good fortune when it's actually time to pat ourselves on the back. By choosing our behavior and thoughts, we can create A's, interesting classes, enjoyable relationships, material wealth, and ways to contribute to a better world.

Whenever tar-footed dogs are getting in the way of your education, remember this Power Process. When you use it, you instantly open up a world of choices. You give yourself power. ☒

career application

Hanae Niigata is a part-time receptionist at a large cardiovascular clinic. Her responsibilities include handling incoming calls, scheduling patient visits, maintaining medical records, and completing other tasks assigned by her office manager.

Hanae's career focus is health care. She has worked as a home health aide and is currently enrolled in school. Her goal is to complete an Associate in Science degree in nursing and work as a registered nurse.

Hanae has a reputation as a hard worker. Even in a noisy environment with frequent interruptions, she completes tasks that require attention to detail and sustained concentration. She catches errors on medical records that her coworkers tend to miss. In addition, Hanae is often the first person in the office to whom people turn when they have a problem to solve. Even in the most difficult circumstances, she can generate a list of options—including solutions that occur to no one else.

Today, the office manager asked Hanae to attend a two-hour course on a new telephone system soon to be installed in her office. She was told to take good notes so she could teach the other five receptionists. Hanae was shocked that the old system was being replaced. In her opinion, it was user-friendly.

As the training session began, Hanae diligently attempted to write down almost everything the instructor said. While doing so, she repeatedly found herself distracted by the thought that her manager was replacing a perfectly good phone system with some "sure-to-be-a-nightmare, high-tech garbage."

After completing the course, Hanae sat down with her manager to fill him in on the new system. As she thumbed through her notes, she realized they didn't make much sense to her, even though she had just finished writing them. She couldn't recall much of the course from memory either, leaving her with little information to share with her manager. ☒

Reflecting on this scenario

1. List two or three suggestions for Hanae that could make her note taking more effective. Be specific.

____

____

____

2. Refer to the article "100 transferable skills" on page 63. Identify a transferable skill that Hanae already has.

____

____

____

3. What behaviors lead you to conclude that Hanae has this skill?

____

____

____

4. Describe another skill that would be useful for Hanae to develop.

____

____

____

quiz

Name ______________________________ Date ____/____/____

1. What are the three major steps of effective note taking as explained in this chapter? Summarize each step in one sentence.

2. According to the text, neat handwriting and knowledge of outlining are requirements for effective notes. True or False? Explain your answer.

3. What are some advantages of sitting in the front and center of the classroom?

4. Instructors sometimes give clues that the material they are presenting is important. List at least three of these clues.

5. Postponing judgment while taking notes means that you have to agree with everything that the instructor says. True or False? Explain your answer.

6. Graphic signals include:
   (a) Brackets and parentheses.
   (b) Stars and arrows.
   (c) Underlining and connecting lines.
   (d) Equal signs and greater- and less-than signs.
   (e) All of the above.

7. Describe the two types of key words. Then write down at least five key words from this chapter.

8. Briefly summarize the four A's technique for taking notes during meetings.

9. Describe at least three strategies for reviewing notes.

10. According to the text, the Power Process: "I create it all" means that:
   (a) We control everything that happens to us.
   (b) We can choose our thoughts about what happens to us.
   (c) We can choose our behaviors as we respond to what happens to us.
   (d) Both b and c.
   (e) None of the above.

learning styles application

The questions below will "cycle" you through four styles, or modes, of learning as explained in the article "Learning styles: Discovering how you learn" in Chapter One. Each question will help you explore a different mode. You can answer the questions in any order.

what if *Create an original format for taking notes. Think about how you can modify or combine the note-taking systems discussed in this chapter. Describe your format here.*

why *Describe a situation in school or at work in which you could benefit by taking more effective notes.*

how *Of the note-taking techniques in this chapter that you like and intend to apply, choose one and describe when and where you will use it.*

what *Think back to the major note-taking options discussed in this chapter: the Cornell method, mind mapping, outlining, concept mapping, or some combination. Choose one system that you intend to apply and briefly summarize its key features.*

master student profile

FAYE WATTLETON

(1943–) Was president of Planned Parenthood Federation of America from 1978 until 1992. She is currently the founder and president of the Center for the Advancement of Women.

I ***don't ever recall not wanting to*** be a nurse, or not saying I wanted to be a nurse. This was, in part, certainly my mother's influence. She wanted me to be a missionary nurse. It wasn't sufficient just to be a nurse, I had to commit to a religious cause as well. Missionary nurses work in church hospitals, in Africa and all over the world. I suspect this was suggested to me before I even understood the power of suggestion, and I always grew up saying I was going to be a nurse. I earned two degrees in nursing, but never practiced as a nurse. In the broadest sense of the word, you can say I have nursed all the time, but not in the technical sense. After undergraduate school, I taught nursing for two years. Then I went to graduate school at Columbia University and earned my master's degree. Following that I moved to Dayton, Ohio, to work in a public health department. There, I was asked to join the board of the local Planned Parenthood. Two years later, I became executive director of the local chapter. Then, seven years later, I became the national president of the organization.

I'm sure the suggestion to become a nurse was colored by the limitation on women's options in those years. Women were nurses, social workers, or teachers. I don't ever remember being explicitly told, "Oh, you can't be that because you're a girl." It just was . . . . It was never conveyed to me there were any limitations on what I could do and what my work could be, although

I'm sure the idea that I be a nurse, as opposed to a doctor or something else, was due to the limitations on the role of women at that time.

Even though we lived in a working class community, there wasn't as much integration, so blacks of all economic levels lived in the black community. My father was a laborer, and my mother was a seamstress, but I went to nursery school with our doctor's son. The doctor's family lived a few blocks from us. This was before the Civil Rights movement, and before blacks moved into white or integrated neighborhoods. That experience also played a very important role in my sense of who I am ethnically, as well as what the possibilities were for me. We lived next door to professionals, as well as the housepainter who had the most beautiful house on the block because he painted and decorated it beautifully.

I try to find the best people I can in various specialties so I can learn from them. I want people who are better than me in their specialties, maybe not better than me in running the whole shebang, but better than me in the communications field or legal field. Stitching everything together to make it work as a [piece of] machinery is, for me, the challenge and the excitement.

I try very hard to listen. If there is conflict, I want to hear what the other side says. . . . As long as I feel there is mutual respect, it does not hurt me to listen to someone with whom I am really in conflict, to hear what they are saying even if I disagree. If it's a conflict I really want to resolve, I try to find ways we can come to mutual points of agreement. One thing I always believe is if you talk long enough you can almost always reach a resolution. Just the process of talking has a de-fanging influence. I have great faith in human beings finding ways to relate if they have enough contact with each other.

For more biographical information on Faye Wattleton, visit the Master Student Hall of Fame on the *From Master Student to Master Employee* Website.

6 Tests

MASTER STUDENT MAP

why this chapter matters . . .

Adopting a few simple techniques can make a major difference in how you cope with pressure—and improve your performance during test taking.

how you can use this chapter . . .

Predict test questions and use your study time more effectively.

Harness the power of cooperative learning by studying with other people.

Learn to look on an F as *feedback* rather than *failure*.

As you read, ask yourself what if . . .

I could let go of stress over tests—or anything else?

what is included . . .

FROM THE DESK OF . . .

I found filling out forms to secure my job as a highway engineer professional a lot like taking a test—I was so nervous the night before. As I prepared for my interview and for filling out paperwork, I was able to reduce my "test anxiety" by staying focused, getting a good night's sleep, and eating a healthy breakfast. In the end, I got the job.

—RAYMOND PEREZ, JR.

Disarm tests

On the surface, tests don't look dangerous. Yet sometimes we treat them like land mines. Suppose a stranger walks up to you on the street and asks, "Does a finite abelian P-group have a basis?" Would you break out in a cold sweat? Would your muscles tense up? Would your breathing become shallow?

Probably not. Even if you have never heard of a finite abelian P-group, you are likely to remain coolly detached. However, if you find the same question on a test and if you have never heard of a finite abelian P-group, your hands might get clammy.

Grades (A to F) are what we use to give power to tests. And there are lots of misconceptions about what grades are. Grades are not a measure of intelligence or creativity. They are not an indication of our ability to contribute to society. Grades are simply a measure of how well we do on tests.

Grades are not a measure of self-worth. Yet we tend to give test scores the power to determine how we feel about ourselves. Common thoughts include "If I fail a test, I am a failure" or "If I do badly on a test, I am a bad person." The truth is that if you do badly on a test, you are a person who did badly on a test. That's all.

Carrying around misconceptions about tests and grades can put undue pressure on your performance. It's like balancing on a railroad track. Many people can walk along the rail and stay balanced for long periods. Yet the task seems entirely different if the rail is placed between two buildings, 52 stories up.

It is easier to do well on exams if you don't put too much pressure on yourself. Academic tests are not a matter of life and death. Scoring low on important tests—entrance tests for college or medical school, bar exams, CPA exams—usually means only a delay.

Tests have an equivalent in the workplace, commonly known as a performance review. Like tests, performance reviews offer feedback. These meetings can help you discover your strengths as an employee and set goals for behavior change. Remember that the techniques for managing test anxiety presented later in this chapter also work for managing stress related to performance reviews—or any other aspect of your job.

Whether the chance of doing poorly on a test or performance review is real or exaggerated, worrying about it can become paralyzing. Use the strategies in this chapter to enhance your memory and regain your perspective. Keep the railroad track on the ground.

journal entry 16

Discovery/Intention Statement

Mentally re-create a time when you had difficulty taking a test. Do anything that helps you re-experience this event. You could draw a picture of yourself in this situation, list some of the questions you had difficulty answering, or tell how you felt after finding out your score on the test. Briefly describe that experience in the space below.

I discovered that I . . .

____

____

____

Now wipe your mental slate clean and declare your intention to replace it with a new scenario. Describe how you want your experience of test taking to change. For example, you might write: "I intend to walk into every test I take feeling well rested and thoroughly prepared."

I intend to . . .

____

____

____

Preview this chapter, looking for at least five strategies that can help you accomplish your goal. List those strategies below and note the page numbers where you can find out more about them.

Strategy	*Page number*

What to do *before* the test

Do daily reviews. Daily reviews include short pre- and post-class reviews of lecture notes. Also conduct brief daily reviews with textbooks: Before reading a new assignment, scan your notes and the sections you underlined in the previous assignment. In addition, use the time you spend waiting for the bus or doing the laundry to conduct short reviews.

Concentrate daily reviews on two kinds of material. One is material you have just learned, either in class or in your reading. Second is material that involves simple memorization—equations, formulas, dates, definitions.

Begin to review on the first day of class. Most instructors outline the whole course at that time. You can even start reviewing within seconds after learning. During a lull in class, go over the notes you just took. Immediately after class, review your notes again.

Do weekly reviews. Review each subject at least once a week, allowing about one hour per subject. Include reviews of assigned reading and lecture notes. Look over any mind map summaries or flash cards you have created. Also practice working on sample problems.

Do major reviews. Major reviews are usually conducted the week before finals or other critical exams. They help integrate concepts and deepen understanding of material presented throughout the term. These are longer review periods—two to five hours at a stretch with sufficient breaks. Remember that the effectiveness of your review begins to drop after an hour or so unless you give yourself a short rest.

After a certain point, short breaks every hour might not be enough to refresh you. That's when it's time to quit. Learn your limits by being conscious of the quality of your concentration.

During long sessions, study the most difficult subjects when you are the most alert: at the beginning of the session.

Schedule reviews. Schedule specific times in your calendar for reviews. Start reviewing key topics at least five days before you'll be tested on them. This allows plenty of time to find the answers to questions and close any gaps in your understanding.

Create study checklists. Study checklists are used the way a pilot uses a preflight checklist. Pilots go through a standard routine before they take off. They physically mark off each item: test flaps, check magnetos, check fuel tanks, adjust instruments, check rudder. A written list helps them to be sure they don't miss anything. Once they are in the air, it's too late. Taking an exam is like flying a plane. Once the test begins, it's too late to memorize that one equation you forgot to include in your review.

Make a checklist for each subject. List reading assignments by chapters or page numbers. List dates of lecture notes. Write down various types of problems you will need to solve. Write down other skills to master. Include major ideas, definitions, theories, formulas, and equations. For math and science tests, choose some problems and do them over again as a way to review for the test.

Remember that a study checklist is not a review sheet; it is a to-do list. Checklists contain the briefest possible description of each item to study.

Create mind map summary sheets. There are several ways to make a mind map as you study for tests. Start by creating a map totally from memory. You might be surprised by how much you already know. After you have gone as far as you can using recall alone, go over your notes and text and fill in the rest of the map. Another option is to go through your notes and pick out key words. Then, without looking at your notes, create a mind map of everything you can recall about each key word. Finally, go back to your notes and fill in material you left out.

Create flash cards. Three-by-five flash cards are like portable test questions. On one side of the cards, write the questions. On the other, write the answers. It's that simple. Always carry a pack of flash cards with you, and review them whenever you have a minute to spare. Use flash cards for formulas, definitions, theories, key words from your notes, axioms, dates, foreign language phrases, hypotheses, and sample problems. Create flash cards regularly as the term progresses. Buy an inexpensive card file to keep your flash cards arranged by subject.

Monitor your reviews. Each day that you prepare for a test, assess what you have learned and what you still want to learn. See how many items you've covered from your study checklist. Look at the tables of contents in your textbooks and write an "X" next to the sections that you've summarized. This helps you gauge the thoroughness of your reviews and alert you to areas that still need attention.

Take a practice test. Write up your own questions and take this practice test several times before the actual exam. You might type this "test" so that it looks like the real thing. If possible, take your practice test in the same room where you will take the actual test.

Also meet with your instructor to go over your practice test. Ask whether your questions focus on appropriate topics and represent the kind of items you can expect to see. The instructor might decline to give you any of this information. More often, instructors will answer some or all of your questions about the test.

Get copies of old exams. Copies of previous exams for the class might be available from the instructor, the instructor's department, the library, or the counseling office. Old tests can help you plan a review strategy. One caution: If you rely on old tests exclusively, you might gloss over material the instructor has added since the last test. Also check your school's policy about making past tests available to students. Some might not allow it. ☒

How to cram . . . even though you shouldn't

Know the limitations of cramming and be aware of its costs. Cramming won't work if you've neglected all of the reading assignments, or if you've skipped most of the lectures and daydreamed through the rest. The more courses you have to cram for, the less effective cramming will be. Also, cramming is not the same as learning: You won't remember what you cram. The purpose of cramming is only to make the best of the situation.

Make choices. Pick out a *few* of the most important elements of the course and learn those backward, forward, and upside down. For example, devote most of your attention to the topic sentences, tables, and charts in a long reading assignment.

Make a plan. After you've chosen what elements you want to study, determine how much time to spend on each one.

Recite and recite again. The key to cramming is repetition. Go over your material again and again.

Don't "should" yourself. Avoid telling yourself that you *should* have studied earlier, you *should* have read the assignments, or you *should* have been more conscientious. Instead, write an Intention Statement about how you plan to change your study habits. Lighten up. Our brains work better when we aren't criticizing ourselves. Give yourself permission to be the fallible human being you are.

Ways to predict test questions

Predicting test questions can do more than get you a better grade. It can also keep you focused on the purpose of a course and help you design your learning strategies. Making predictions can be fun, too—especially when they turn out to be accurate.

Ask about the nature of the test. Eliminate as much guesswork as possible. Ask your instructor to describe upcoming tests. Do this early in the term so you can be alert for possible test questions throughout the course. Some questions to ask are:

- What course material will the test cover—readings, lectures, lab sessions, or a combination?
- Will the test be cumulative, or will it cover just the most recent material you've studied?
- Will the test focus on facts and details or major themes and relationships?
- Will the test call on you to solve problems or apply concepts?
- Will you have choices about which questions to answer?
- What types of questions will be on the test—true/false, multiple choice, short-answer, essay?

Note: In order to study appropriately for essay tests, find out how much detail the instructor wants in your answers. Ask how much time you'll be allowed for the test and how long the essay answers should be (number of pages, blue books, or word limit). Having that information before you begin studying will help you gauge your depth for learning the material.

Put yourself in your instructor's shoes. If you were teaching the course, what kinds of questions would you put on an exam? You can also brainstorm test questions with other students—a great activity for study groups.

Look for possible test questions in your notes and readings. Have a separate section in your notebook labeled "Test questions." Add several questions to this section after every lecture and assignment. You can also create your own code or graphic signal—such as a *T!* in a circle—to flag possible test questions in your notes. Use the same symbol to flag review questions and problems in your textbooks that could appear on a test.

Look for clues to possible questions during class. During lectures, you can predict test questions by observing what an instructor says and how he says it. Instructors often give clues. They might repeat important points several times, write them on the board, or return to them in later classes.

Gestures can indicate critical points. For example, your instructor might pause, look at notes, or read passages word for word.

Notice whether your teacher has any strong points of view on certain issues. Questions on those issues are likely to appear on a test. Also pay attention to questions the instructor poses to students, and note questions that other students ask.

When material from reading assignments is covered extensively in class, it is likely to be on a test. For science courses and other courses involving problem solving, work on sample problems using different variables.

Save all quizzes, papers, lab sheets, and graded materials of any kind. Quiz questions have a way of reappearing, in slightly altered form, on final exams. If copies of previous exams and other graded materials are available, use them to predict test questions.

Apply your predictions. To get the most value from your predictions, use them to guide your review sessions.

Remember the obvious. Be on the lookout for these words: *This material will be on the test.*[1] ⊠

For suggestions on ways to predict a variety of test questions, go to the *From Master Student to Master Employee* Website.

Cooperative learning:

Working in teams

Education often seems like competition. We compete for entrance to school, for scholarships and grades while we're in school, and for jobs when we leave school. In that climate, it's easy to overlook the power of cooperation.

Forming study groups and joining committees develops your ability to work in teams—a key transferable skill. In the workplace, projects often combine the efforts of many people. For example, manufacturing a single car calls for the contribution of designers, welders, painters, electricians, marketing executives, computer programmers, and many others. Learning to work in teams now, while you are in school, can help you expand your learning styles and advance in your career.

As social animals, humans draw strength from groups. In addition to offering camaraderie, study groups can lift your mood on days when you just don't feel like working. If you skip a solo study session, no one else will know. If you declare your intention to study with others who are depending on you, your intention gains strength.

Study groups are especially important if going to school has thrown you into a new culture. Joining a study group with people you already know can help ease the transition. To multiply the benefits of working with study groups, seek out people of other cultures, races, and ethnic groups. You can get a whole new perspective on the world, along with some valued new friends. And you can experience what it's like to be part of a diverse team—an important asset in today's job market.

Form a study group

Choose a focus for your study group. Many students assume that the purpose of a study group is to help its members prepare for a test. That's one valid purpose—and there are others.

Through his research on cooperative learning, psychologist Joe Cuseo has identified several kinds of study groups.[2] For instance, *test review* groups compare answers and help group members discover sources of errors. *Note-taking* groups focus on comparing and editing notes, often meeting directly after the day's class. *Research* groups meet to help group members find, evaluate, and take notes on background materials for papers and presentations. *Reading* groups can be useful for courses in which test questions are based largely on textbooks. Meet with classmates to compare the passages you highlighted and the notes you made in the margins of your books.

Look for dedicated students. Find people you are comfortable with and who share your academic goals. Look for students who pay attention, participate in class, and actively take notes. Invite them to join your group.

Limit groups to four people. Research on cooperative learning indicates that four people is an ideal group size.[3] Larger ones can be unwieldy.

Balance common interests with diversity. Studying with friends is fine, but if your common interests are pizza and jokes, beware of getting together to study.

Include people in your group who face academic or personal challenges similar to your own. For example, if you are divorced and have two toddlers at home, you might look for other single parents who have returned to school.

Also include people who face challenges that are different from your own. Choose people with similar educational goals who have different backgrounds and methods of learning. Each of you can gain by seeing the material from a new perspective.

Hold a planning session. Ask two or three people to get together for a snack and talk about group goals, meeting times, and other logistics. You don't have to make an immediate commitment.

As you brainstorm about places to meet, aim for a quiet meeting room with plenty of room to spread out materials. Also set clear starting and stopping times for meetings. Knowing that you have only an hour or two to get something done can help you be more productive.

Do a trial run. Test the group first by planning a one-time session. If that session works, plan another. After a few successful sessions, you can schedule regular meetings.

Conduct your group

Set an agenda for each meeting. At the beginning of each meeting, reach agreement on what you intend to do. Set a time limit for each agenda item and determine a quitting time. End each meeting with assignments for all members to complete before the next meeting.

Assign roles. To make the most of your time, ask one member to lead each group meeting. The leader's role is to keep the discussion focused on the agenda and ask for contributions from all members. Assign another person to act as recorder. This person will take notes on the meeting, recording possible test questions, answers, and main points from group discussions. Rotate both of these roles so that every group member takes a turn.

Teach each other. Teaching is a great way to learn something. Turn the material you're studying into a list of topics and assign a specific topic to each person, who will then teach it to the group.

When you're done presenting your topic, ask for questions or comments. Prompt each other to explain ideas more clearly, find gaps in understanding, consider other points of view, and apply concepts to settings outside the classroom. Here's where you tap into the power of cooperative learning. This kind of freewheeling conversation doesn't happen when you study by yourself.

Test each other. During your meeting, take a practice test created from questions contributed by group members. When you're finished, compare answers. Or turn testing into a game by pretending you're on a television game show. Use sample test questions to quiz each other.

Compare notes. Make sure that you all heard the same thing in class and that you all recorded the important information. Ask others to help explain material in your notes that is confusing to you.

Work in groups of two at a computer to review a course. One person can operate the keyboard while the other person dictates summaries of lectures and assigned readings. Together, both group members can check facts by consulting textbooks, lecture notes, and class handouts.

Create wall-size mind maps or concept maps to summarize a textbook or series of lectures. Work on large sheets of butcher paper, or tape together pieces of construction paper. When doing a mind map, assign one branch of the mind map to each member of the study group. Use a different colored pen or marker for each branch. (For more information on concept maps and mind maps, see Chapter Five: Notes.)

Pair off to do "book reports." One person can summarize a reading assignment. The other person can act as an interviewer on a talk show, posing questions and asking for further clarification.

Monitor effectiveness. On your meeting agenda, include an occasional discussion about your group's effectiveness. Are you meeting consistently? Is the group helping members succeed in class?

As a group, brainstorm ways to get unprepared members involved in the group. Reel in a dominating member by reminding him that everyone's voice needs to be heard.

To resolve conflict among group members, keep the conversation constructive. Focus on solutions. Move from vague complaints ("You're never prepared") to specific requests ("Will you commit to bring 10 sample test questions next time?"). Asking a "problem" member to lead the next meeting might make an immediate difference.

Ask for group support in personal areas. Other people might have insight into problems such as transportation, childcare, finances, and time management. Study groups can support you in getting what you want in many areas of life. Promote your success in school by refusing to go it alone.

journal entry 17

Intention Statement

In the space below, outline a plan to form a study group. Explain the steps you will take to get the group organized and set a first meeting date. Also describe the reward you anticipate for acting on this intention.

I intend to . . .

____

____

____

____

____

20 memory techniques

Use the following techniques to develop a flexible, custom-made memory system that serves you well at test time.

1 Be selective. As you dig into your textbooks and notes, make choices about what is most important to learn. Imagine that you are going to create a test on the material and consider the questions you would ask.

2 Make it meaningful. One way to create meaning is to learn from the general to the specific. Before you begin your next reading assignment, skim it to locate the main idea. If you're ever lost, step back and look at the big picture. The details might make more sense.

3 Create associations. Think about your favorite courses. They probably relate to subjects that you already know something about. If you know a lot about the history of twentieth-century music, for example, then you'll find it easier to remember facts about twenty-first century music.

Even when you're tackling a new subject, you can build a mental store of basic background information—the raw material for creating associations. Preview reading assignments, and complete those readings before you attend lectures. Before taking upper-level courses, master the prerequisites.

4 Learn actively. When you sit at your desk, sit up straight. Sit on the edge of your chair, as if you were about to spring out of it and sprint across the room.

Also experiment with standing up when you study. It's harder to fall asleep in this position. Some people insist that their brains work better when they stand. Pace back and forth and gesture as you recite material out loud. Use your hands. Get your body moving.

This includes your mouth. During a lecture, ask questions. With your textbooks, read key passages out loud. Use a louder voice for the main points.

Many courses in higher education lean heavily toward abstract concepts—lectures, papers, and reading. These courses might not offer chances to actively experiment with ideas or test them in concrete experience.

Create those opportunities yourself. For example, your introductory psychology book probably offers some theories about how people remember information. Choose one of those theories and test it on yourself. See if you can discover a new memory technique.

5 Relax. When you're relaxed, you absorb new information quickly and recall it with greater ease and accuracy. Students who can't recall information under the stress of a final exam can often recite the same facts later when they are relaxed.

Being relaxed is not the same as being drowsy, zoned out, or asleep. Relaxation is a state of alertness, free of tension, during which your mind can play with new information, roll it around, create associations with it, and apply many of the other memory techniques. You can be active *and* relaxed.

6 Create pictures. Draw diagrams. Make cartoons. Use these images to connect facts and illustrate relationships. Associations within and among abstract concepts can be "seen" and recalled more easily when they are visualized. The key is to use your imagination.

For example, Boyle's law states that at a constant temperature, the volume of a confined ideal gas varies inversely with its pressure. Simply put, cutting the volume in half doubles the pressure. To remember this concept, you might picture someone "doubled over" using a bicycle pump. As she increases the pressure in the pump by decreasing the volume in the pump cylinder, she seems to be getting angrier. By the time she has doubled the pressure (and halved the volume), she is boiling ("Boyle-ing") mad.

7 Recite and repeat. When you repeat something out loud, you anchor the concept in two different senses. First, you get the physical sensation in your throat, tongue, and lips when voicing the concept. Second, you hear it. The combined result is synergistic, just as it is when you create pictures. That is, the effect of using two different senses is greater than the sum of their individual effects.

8 Write it down. Writing a note to yourself helps you remember an idea, even if you never look at the note again. You can extend this technique by writing down an idea not just once, but many times.

Writing engages a different kind of memory than speaking. Writing prompts us to be more logical, coherent, and complete. Written reviews reveal gaps in knowledge that oral reviews miss, just as oral reviews reveal gaps that written reviews miss.

Finally, writing is physical. Your arm, your hand, and your fingers join in. Remember, learning is an active process—you remember what you *do*.

9 Engage your emotions. You're more likely to remember course material when you relate it to a goal—whether academic, personal, or career—that you feel strongly about. This is one reason why it pays to be specific about what you want. The more goals you have and the more clearly they are defined, the more channels you create for incoming information.

10 Overlearn. One way to fight mental fuzziness is to learn more than you need to know about a subject simply to pass a test. You can pick a subject apart, examine it, add to it, and go over it until it becomes second nature.

This technique is especially effective for problem solving. Do the assigned problems, and then do more problems. Find another textbook and work similar problems. Then make up your own problems and solve them.

11 Escape the short-term memory trap. Short-term memory can fade after a few minutes, and it rarely lasts more than several hours. A short review within minutes or hours of a study session can move material from short-term memory into long-term memory. That quick minireview can save you hours of study time when exams roll around.

12 Use your times of peak energy. Study your most difficult subjects during the times when your energy peaks. Many people can concentrate more effectively during daylight hours. The early morning hours can be especially productive, even for those who hate to get up with the sun. Observe the peaks and

critical thinking exercise 20

REHEARSE FOR SUCCESS

Sit up in a chair, legs and arms uncrossed. Close your eyes, let go of all thoughts, and focus on your breathing for a minute or two.

Then relax various parts of your body, beginning with your feet. Relax your toes, your ankles. Move up to your calves and thighs. Relax your buttocks. Relax the muscles of your lower back, abdomen, and chest. Relax your hands, arms, and shoulders. Relax your neck, jaw, eyelids, and scalp.

When you are completely relaxed, imagine yourself in an exam room. It's the day of the test. Visualize taking the test successfully. The key is detail. See the test being handed out. Notice your surroundings. Hear the other students shift in their seats. Feel the desk, the pen in your hand, and the exam in front of you. See yourself looking over the exam calmly and confidently. You discover that you know all of the answers.

Stay with this image for a few minutes. Next, imagine yourself writing quickly. Watch yourself turn in the test with confidence. Finally, imagine receiving the test grade. It is an A. Savor the feeling.

As soon as you realize you are feeling anxious about an upcoming test, begin using this technique. The more you do this visualization, the better it can work.

A version of this Critical Thinking Exercise is available online.

valleys in your energy flow during the day and adjust study times accordingly.

13 Distribute learning. As an alternative to marathon study sessions, experiment with shorter, spaced-out sessions. You might find that you can get far more done in three two-hour sessions than in one six-hour session.

You can get more done if you take regular breaks. You can even use the breaks as minirewards. After a productive study session, give yourself permission to log on and check your e-mail, listen to a song, or play 10 minutes of hide-and-seek with your kids.

There is an exception to this idea of allowing time for consolidation. When you are so engrossed in a textbook that you cannot put it down, when you are consumed by an idea for a term paper and cannot think of anything else—keep going. The master student within you has taken over. Enjoy the ride.

14 Be aware of attitudes. People who think history is boring tend to have trouble remembering dates and historical events. People who believe math is difficult often have a hard time recalling mathematical equations and formulas. All of us can forget information that contradicts our opinions.

If you think a subject is boring, remind yourself that everything is related to everything else. Look for connections that relate to your own interests.

For example, consider a person who is fanatical about cars. She can rebuild a motor in a weekend and has a good time doing so. From this apparently specialized interest, she can explore a wide realm of knowledge. She can relate the workings of an engine to principles of physics, math, and chemistry. Computerized parts in newer cars can lead her to the study of data processing. She can research how the automobile industry has changed our cities and helped create suburbs, a topic that includes urban planning, sociology, business, economics, psychology, and history. Being aware of attitudes is not the same as fighting them or struggling to give them up. Just notice attitudes and be willing to put them on hold.

Mnemonic devices

It's pronounced *ne-mon'-ik*. The word refers to tricks that can increase your ability to recall everything from grocery lists to speeches.

There is a catch. Mnemonic devices have limitations: They don't always help you understand or digest material. And they rely only on rote memorization.

Even so, mnemonic devices can be powerful. Some examples are creative sentences and rhymes and songs.

New words. Acronyms are words created from the initial letters of a series of words. Examples include NASA (**N**ational **A**eronautics and **S**pace **A**dministration) and laser (**l**ight **a**mplification by **s**timulated **e**mission of **r**adiation).

You can make up your own acronyms to recall series of facts. A common mnemonic acronym is Roy G. Biv, which has helped thousands of students remember the colors of the visible spectrum (**r**ed, **o**range, **y**ellow, **g**reen, **b**lue, **i**ndigo, and **v**iolet). IPMAT helps biology students remember the stages of cell division (**i**nterphase, **p**rophase, **m**etaphase, **a**naphase, and **t**elophase).

Creative sentences. Acrostics are sentences that help you remember a series of letters that stand for something. For example, the first letters of the words in the sentence "Every good boy does fine" (E, G, B, D, and F) are the music notes of the lines of the treble clef staff.

Rhymes and songs. Madison Avenue advertising executives spend billions of dollars a year on commercials designed to burn their messages into your memory. Coca-Cola's song, "It's the Real Thing," once stood for Coca-Cola, despite the soda's artificial ingredients.

Rhymes have been used for centuries to teach basic facts. "*I* before *e*, except after *c*" has helped many a student on spelling tests.

15 Elaborate. According to Harvard psychologist Daniel Schacter, all courses in memory improvement are based on this single technique. *Elaboration* means consciously encoding new information. Repetition is a basic way to elaborate. However, current brain research indicates that other types of elaboration are more effective for long-term memory.[4]

One technique is to ask questions about incoming information: Does this remind me of something or someone I already know? Is this similar to a technique that I already use? Where and when can I use this information?

The same idea applies to more complex material. When you meet someone new, for example, ask yourself: Does she remind me of someone else? Or when doing the Learning Styles Applications in this book, ask how they relate to the Master Student Map that opens each chapter.

16 **Intend to remember.** To instantly enhance your memory, form the simple intention to *learn it now* rather than later. The intention to remember can be as powerful as any single memory technique.

17 **Remember something else.** When you are stuck and can't remember something that you're sure you know, remember something else that is related to it. During an economics exam, if you can't remember anything about the aggregate demand curve, recall what you do know about the aggregate supply curve. If you cannot recall specific facts, remember the example that the instructor used during her lecture. A brainstorm is a good memory jog. If you are stumped when taking a test, start writing down lots of answers to related questions, and—pop!—the answer you need is likely to appear.

18 **Notice when you do remember.** Everyone has a different memory style. Some people are best at recalling information they've read. Others have an easier time remembering what they've heard, seen, or done.

To develop your memory, notice when you recall information easily and ask yourself what memory techniques you're using naturally. Also notice when it's difficult to recall information. Be a reporter. Get the facts and then adjust your learning techniques. And remember to congratulate yourself when you do remember.

19 **Use it before you lose it.** To remember something, access it a lot. Read it, write it, speak it, listen to it, apply it—find some way to make contact with the material regularly. Each time you do so, you widen the neural pathway to the material and make it easier to recall the next time.

Study groups are especially effective because they put you on stage. The friendly pressure of knowing that you'll teach the group helps focus your attention.

20 **Adopt the attitude that you never forget.** Instead of saying, "I don't remember," you can say, "It will come to me." The latter statement implies that the information you want is encoded in your brain and that you can retrieve it—just not right now.

Use positive affirmations that support you in developing your memory: "I recall information easily and accurately." "At any time I choose, I will be able to recall key facts and ideas." "My memory serves me well." Or even "I never forget!" ⊠

Remembering names

New friendships, job contacts, and business relationships all start with remembering names.

Recite and repeat in conversation. When you hear a person's name, repeat it. Immediately say it to yourself several times without moving your lips. You can also repeat the name out loud in a way that does not sound forced or artificial: "I'm pleased to meet you, Maria."

Ask the other person to recite and repeat. You can let other people help you remember their names. After you've been introduced to someone, ask that person to spell the name and pronounce it correctly for you. Most people will be flattered by the effort you're making to learn their names.

Visualize. After the conversation, construct a brief visual image of the person. For a memorable image, make it unusual. Imagine the name painted in hot pink fluorescent letters on the person's forehead.

Admit you don't know. Admitting that you can't remember someone's name can actually put people at ease. Most of them will sympathize if you say, "I'm working to remember names better. Yours is right on the tip of my tongue. What is it again?"

Introduce yourself again. Most of the time we assume introductions are one-shot affairs. If we miss a name the first time around, our hopes for remembering it are dashed. Instead of giving up, reintroduce yourself: "We met earlier. I'm Jesse. Please tell me your name again."

Use associations. Link each person you meet with one characteristic that you find interesting or unusual. For example, you could make a mental note: "Vicki Cheng—long, black hair" or "James Washington—horn-rimmed glasses." To reinforce your associations, write them on 3 × 5 cards as soon as you can.

Use technology. After you meet new people, enter their names as contacts in your e-mail or database software. If you get a business card, enter phone numbers, e-mail addresses, and other contact information as well.

What to do during the *TEST*

Prepare yourself for the test by arriving early. That often leaves time to do a relaxation exercise. While you're waiting for the test to begin and talking with classmates, avoid the question "How much did you study for the test?" This question might fuel anxious thoughts that you didn't study enough.

As you begin

Ask the teacher or test administrator if you can use scratch paper during the test. (If you use a separate sheet of paper without permission, you might appear to be cheating.) If you *do* get permission, use this paper to jot down memory aids, formulas, equations, facts, or other material you know you'll need and might forget. An alternative is to make quick notes in the margins of the test sheet.

Pay attention to verbal directions given as a test is distributed. Then scan the whole test immediately. Evaluate the importance of each section. Notice how many points each part of the test is worth and estimate how much time you'll need for each section, using its point value as your guide. For example, don't budget 20 percent of your time for a section that is worth only 10 percent of the points.

Read the directions slowly. Then reread them. It can be agonizing to discover that you lost points on a test merely because you failed to follow the directions. When the directions are confusing, ask to have them clarified.

Now you are ready to begin the test. If necessary, allow yourself a minute or two of "panic" time. Notice any tension you feel, and apply one of the techniques explained in the article "Let go of test anxiety" later in this chapter.

Answer the easiest, shortest questions first. This gives you the experience of success. It also stimulates associations and prepares you for more difficult questions. Pace yourself and watch the time. If you can't think of an answer, move on. Follow your time plan.

If you are unable to determine the answer to a test question, keep an eye out throughout the test for context clues that may remind you of the correct answer or that provide you with evidence to eliminate wrong answers.

Multiple choice questions

- *Answer each question in your head first.* Do this before you look at the possible answers. If you come up with an answer that you're confident is right, look for that answer in the list of choices.
- *Read all possible answers before selecting one.* Sometimes two answers will be similar and only one will be correct.
- *Test each possible answer.* Remember that multiple choice questions consist of two parts: the stem (an incomplete statement at the beginning) and a list of possible answers. Each answer, when combined with the stem, makes a complete statement that is either true or false. When you combine the stem with each possible answer, you are turning each multiple choice question into a small series of true/false questions. Choose the answer that makes a true statement.
- *Eliminate incorrect answers.* Cross off the answers that are clearly not correct.

True/false questions

- *Read the entire question.* Separate the statement into its grammatical parts—individual clauses and phrases—and then test each one. If any part is false, the entire statement is false.

- *Look for qualifiers.* These include words such as *all, most, sometimes,* or *rarely.* Absolute qualifiers such as *always* or *never* generally indicate a false statement.
- *Find the devil in the details.* Double-check each number, fact, and date in a true/false statement. Look for numbers that have been transposed or facts that have been slightly altered. These are signals of a false statement.
- *Watch for negatives.* Look for words such as *not* and *cannot.* Read the sentence without these words and see if you come up with a true or false statement. Then reinsert the negative words and see if the statement makes more sense. Watch especially for sentences with two negative words. As in math operations, two negatives cancel each other out: *We cannot say that Chekhov never succeeded at short story writing* means the same as *Chekhov succeeded at short story writing.*

Computer-graded tests

- Make sure that the answer you mark corresponds to the question you are answering.
- Check the test booklet against the answer sheet whenever you switch sections and whenever you come to the top of a column.
- Watch for stray marks; they can look like answers.
- If you change an answer, be sure to erase the wrong answer completely.

Open-book tests

- Carefully organize your notes, readings, and any other materials you plan to consult when writing answers.
- Write down any formulas you will need on a separate sheet of paper.
- Bookmark the table of contents and index in each of your textbooks. Place Post-it Notes and Index Flags or paper clips on other important pages of books (pages with tables, for instance).
- Create an informal table of contents or index for the notes you took in class.
- Predict which material will be covered on the test and highlight relevant sections in your readings and notes.

Short-answer/fill-in-the-blank tests

- Concentrate on key words and facts. Be brief.
- Overlearning material can really pay off. When you know a subject backward and forward, you can answer this type of question almost as fast as you can write.

Matching tests

- Begin by reading through each column, starting with the one with fewer items. Check the number of items in each column to see if they're equal. If they're not, look for an item in one column that you can match with two or more items in the other column.
- Look for any items with similar wording and make special note of the differences between these items.

What to do when you get stuck on a test question

- **Read it again.** Eliminate the simplest sources of confusion, such as misreading the question.
- **Skip the question for now.** This advice is simple—and it works. Let your subconscious mind work on the answer while you respond to other questions.
- **Look for answers in other test questions.** A term, name, date, or other fact that escapes you might appear in another question on the test itself.
- **Treat intuitions with care.** In quick-answer questions (multiple choice, true/false), go with your first instinct as to which answer is correct. If you think your first answer is wrong because you misread the question, do change your answer.
- **Rewrite the question.** See if you can put a confusing question into your own words. Doing so might release the answer.
- **Free-write.** On scratch paper or in the margins of your test booklet, record any response to the test question that pops into your head. Instead of just sitting there, stumped, you're doing something—a fact that can reduce anxiety. Writing might also trigger a mental association that answers the question.
- **Write a close answer.** Answer the question as best as you can, even if you don't think your answer is fully correct. This technique might help you get partial credit for short-answer questions, essay questions, and problems on math or science tests.

- When matching individual words with phrases, first read a phrase. Then look for the word that logically completes the phrase.
- Cross out items in each column when you are through with them.

Essay questions

Managing your time is crucial to answering essay questions. Note how many questions you have to answer and monitor your progress during the test period. Writing shorter answers and completing all of the questions on an essay test will probably yield a better score than leaving some questions blank.

Find out what an essay question is asking—precisely. If a question asks you to *compare* the ideas of Sigmund Freud and Karl Marx, you are on a one-way trip to No Credit City no matter how eloquently you *explain* them.

Before you write, make a quick outline. An outline can help speed up the writing of your detailed answer, you're less likely to leave out important facts, and if you don't have time to finish your answer, your outline could win you some points. To use test time efficiently, keep your outline brief. Focus on key words to use in your answer.

Introduce your answer by getting to the point. General statements such as "There are many interesting facets to this difficult question" can cause acute irritation for teachers grading dozens of tests.

One way to get to the point is to begin your answer with part of the question. Suppose the question is "Discuss how increasing the city police budget might or might not contribute to a decrease in street crime." Your first sentence might be "An increase in police expenditures will not have a significant effect on street crime for the following reasons." Your position is clear. You are on your way to an answer.

When you expand your answer with supporting ideas and facts, start with the most solid points. Be brief and avoid filler sentences.

Write on one side of the paper only. If you write on both sides of the paper, writing will show through and obscure the writing on the other side. If necessary, use the blank side to add points you missed. Leave a generous left-hand margin and plenty of space between your answers, in case you want to add to them later. Be sure to also write legibly.

Finally, if you have time, review your answers for grammar and spelling errors, clarity, and legibility. ☒

Words to watch for in essay questions

The following words are commonly found in essay test questions. They give you precise directions about what to include in your answer. Get to know these words well. When you see them on a test, underline them. Also look for them in your notes. Locating such key words can help you predict test questions.

Analyze: Break into separate parts and discuss, examine, or interpret each part. Then give your opinion.

Compare: Examine two or more items. Identify similarities and differences.

Contrast: Show differences. Set in opposition.

Criticize: Make judgments. Evaluate comparative worth. Criticism often involves analysis.

Define: Explain the exact meaning—usually, a meaning specific to the course or subject. Definitions are usually short.

Describe: Give a detailed account. Make a picture with words. List characteristics, qualities, and parts.

Discuss: Consider and debate or argue the pros and cons of an issue. Write about any conflict. Compare and contrast.

Explain: Make an idea clear. Show logically how a concept is developed. Give the reasons for an event.

Prove: Support with facts (especially facts presented in class or in the text).

Relate: Show the connections between ideas or events. Provide a larger context for seeing the big picture.

State: Explain precisely.

Summarize: Give a brief, condensed account. Include conclusions. Avoid unnecessary details.

Trace: Show the order of events or the progress of a subject or event.

Notice how these words differ. For example, *compare* asks you to do something different than *contrast*. Likewise, *criticize* and *explain* call for different responses. If any of these terms are still unclear to you, look them up in an unabridged dictionary.

Review these key words and other helpful vocabulary terms by using the online flash cards on the *From Master Student to Master Employee* Website.

Student Website

The test isn't over until . . .

Many students believe that a test is over as soon as they turn in the answer sheet. Consider another point of view: You're not done with a test until you know the answer to any question that you missed—and why you missed it.

This point of view offers major benefits. Tests in many courses are cumulative. In other words, the content included on the first test is assumed to be working knowledge for the second test, mid-term, or final exam. When you discover what questions you missed and understand the reasons for lost points, you learn something—and you greatly increase your odds of achieving better scores later in the course.

To get the most value from any test, take control of what you do at two critical points: the time immediately following the test, and the time when the test is returned to you.

Immediately following the test. After finishing a test, your first thought might be to nap, snack, rent a DVD, or go out with friends to celebrate. Restrain those impulses for a short while so that you can reflect on the test. The time you invest now carries the potential to raise your grades in the future.

To begin with, sit down in a quiet place and take a few minutes to write some Discovery Statements related to your experience of taking the test. Doing this while the test is still fresh in your mind increases the value of this technique. Describe how you felt about taking the test, how effective your review strategies were, and whether you accurately predicted the questions that appeared on the test.

Follow up with an Intention Statement or two. State what, if anything, you will do differently to prepare for the next test. The more specific you are, the better. If the test revealed any gaps in your knowledge, list follow-up questions to ask in class.

When the test is returned. When a returned test includes a teacher's comments, view this document as a treasure-trove of intellectual gold.

First, make sure that the point totals add up correctly and double-check for any other errors in grading. Even the best teachers make an occasional mistake.

Next, ask these questions:

- On what material did the teacher base test questions—readings, lectures, discussions, or other class activities?
- What types of questions appeared in the test—objective (such as matching items, true/false questions, or multiple choice), short-answer, or essay?
- What types of questions did you miss?
- Can you learn anything from the instructor's comments that will help you prepare for the next test?

Also see if you can correct any answers that lost points. To do this, carefully analyze the source of your errors and find a solution. Consult the chart in this article for help.

Source of test error	Possible solutions
Study errors–studying material that was not included on the test, or spending too little time on material that *did* appear on the test	• Ask your teacher about specific topics that will be included on a test. • Practice predicting test questions. • Form a study group with class members to create mock tests.
Careless errors, such as skipping or misreading directions	• Read and follow directions more carefully–especially when tests are divided into several sections with different directions. • Set aside time during the next test to proofread your answers.
Concept errors–mistakes made when you do not understand the underlying principles needed to answer a question or solve a problem	• Look for patterns in the questions you missed. • Make sure that you complete all assigned readings, attend all lectures, and show up for laboratory sessions. • Ask your teacher for help with specific questions.
Application errors–mistakes made when you understand underlying principles but fail to apply them correctly	• Rewrite your answers correctly. • When studying, spend more time on solving sample problems. • Predict application questions that will appear in future tests and practice answering them.
Test mechanics errors–missing more questions in certain parts of the test than others, changing correct answers to incorrect ones at the last minute, leaving items blank, miscopying answers from scratch paper to the answer sheet	• Set time limits for taking each section of a test and stick to them. • Proofread your test answers carefully. • Look for patterns in the kind of answers you change at the last minute. • Change answers only if you can state a clear and compelling reason to do so.

The high costs of cheating

Cheating on tests can be a tempting choice. One benefit is that we might get a good grade without having to study.

Instead of studying, we could spend more time watching TV, partying, sleeping, or doing anything that seems like more fun. Another benefit is that we could avoid the risk of doing poorly on a test—which could happen even if we *do* study.

Also remember that cheating carries costs. Here are some to consider.

Risk of failing the course or expulsion from college. The consequences for cheating are serious. Cheating can result in failing the assignment, failing the entire course, getting suspended, or getting expelled from college entirely. Documentation of cheating may also prevent you from being accepted to other colleges.

We learn less. While we might think that some courses offer little or no value, it is more likely that we can create value from any course. If we look deeply enough, we can discover some idea or acquire some skill to prepare us for future courses or a career after graduation.

We lose time and money. Getting an education costs a lot of money. It also calls for years of sustained effort. Cheating sabotages our purchase. We pay full tuition and invest our energy without getting full value for it.

Fear of getting caught promotes stress. When we're fully aware of our emotions about cheating, we might discover intense stress. Even if we're not fully aware of our emotions, we're likely to feel some level of discomfort about getting caught.

Violating our values promotes stress. Even if we don't get caught cheating, we can feel stress about violating our own ethical standards. Stress can compromise our physical health and overall quality of life.

Cheating on tests can make it easier to violate our integrity again. Human beings become comfortable with behaviors that they repeat. Cheating is no exception.

Think about the first time you drove a car. You might have felt excited—even a little frightened. Now driving is probably second nature, and you don't give it much thought. Repeated experience with driving creates familiarity, which lessens the intense feelings you had during your first time at the wheel.

We can experience the same process with almost any behavior. Cheating once will make it easier to cheat again. And if we become comfortable with compromising our integrity in one area of life, we might find it easier to compromise in other areas.

Cheating lowers our self-concept. Whether or not we are fully aware of it, cheating sends us the message that we are not smart enough or responsible enough to make it on our own. We deny ourselves the celebration and satisfaction of authentic success.

An alternative to cheating is to become a master student. Ways to do this are described on every page of this book.

Have some FUN!

Contrary to popular belief, finals week does not have to be a drag.

In fact, if you have used techniques in this chapter, exam week can be fun. You will have done most of your studying long before finals arrive. You can feel confident and relaxed.

When you are well prepared for tests, you can even use fun as a technique to enhance your performance. The day before a final, go for a run or play a game of basketball. Take in a movie or a concert. Watch TV. A relaxed brain is a more effective brain. If you have studied for a test, your mind will continue to prepare itself even while you're at the movies.

Get plenty of rest, too. There's no need to cram until 3 a.m. when you have reviewed material throughout the term.

On the first day of finals, you can wake up refreshed, have a good breakfast, and walk into the exam room with a smile on your face. You can also leave with a smile on your face, knowing that you are going to have a fun week. It's your reward for studying regularly throughout the term.

If this kind of exam week sounds inviting, you can begin preparing for it right now.

If you freeze during tests and flub questions when you know the answers, you might be suffering from test anxiety.

Let go of test anxiety

A little tension before a test is good. That tingly, butterflies-in-the-stomach feeling you get from extra adrenaline can sharpen your awareness and keep you alert. You can enjoy the benefits of a little tension while you stay confident and relaxed. Sometimes, however, tension is persistent and extreme. It causes loss of sleep, appetite, and sometimes even hair. That kind of tension is damaging. It is a symptom of test anxiety, and it can prevent you from doing your best on exams.

Other symptoms include nervousness, fear, dread, irritability, and a sense of hopelessness. Boredom can also be a symptom of test anxiety. Frequent yawning immediately before a test is a common reaction. Though it suggests boredom, yawning is often a sign of tension. It means that oxygen is not getting to the brain because the body is tense. A yawn is one way the body increases its supply of oxygen.

You might experience headaches, an inability to concentrate, or a craving for food. For some people, test anxiety makes asthma or high blood pressure worse. During an exam, symptoms can include confusion, panic, mental blocks, fainting, sweaty palms, and nausea.

Symptoms after a test include the following.

Mock indifference: "I answered all the multiple choice questions as 'none of the above' because I was bored."
Guilt: "Why didn't I study more?"
Anger: "The teacher never wanted me to pass this stupid course anyway."
Blame: "If only the textbook weren't so dull."
Depression: "After that test, I don't see any point in staying in school."

Test anxiety can be serious. It can also be managed.

Test anxiety has two components: mental and physical. The mental component of stress includes all of your thoughts and worries about tests. The physical component includes bodily sensations and tension.

The following techniques can help you deal with the mental and physical components of stress in any situation, from test anxiety to stage fright.

Dealing with thoughts

Yell "Stop!" When you notice that your mind is consumed with worries and fears, that your thoughts are spinning out of control, mentally yell "Stop!" If you're in a situation that allows it, yell it out loud.

This action is likely to bring your focus back to the present moment and allow you to redirect your thoughts. Once you've broken the cycle of worry or panic, you can use any of the following techniques.

Daydream. When you fill your mind with pleasant thoughts, there is no room left for anxiety. If you notice yourself worrying about an upcoming test, replace visions of doom with images of something you like to do. Daydream about being with a special friend or walking alone in a favorite place.

Visualize success. Most of us live up—or down—to our own expectations. If we spend a lot of time mentally rehearsing what it will be like to fail a test, our chances of doing so increase. Instead, you can take time to rehearse

F is for feedback, not failure

When some students get an F on an assignment, they interpret that letter as a message: "You are a failure." That interpretation is not accurate. Getting an F means only that you failed a test—not that you failed your life.

From now on, imagine that the letter *F* when used as a grade represents another word: *feedback.* An F is an indication that you didn't understand the material well enough. It's a message to do something differently before the next test or assignment.

If you interpret F as *failure*, you don't get to change anything. But if you interpret F as *feedback*, you can change your thinking and behavior in ways that promote your success.

what it will be like to succeed. Be specific. Create detailed pictures, actions, and even sounds as part of your visualization. If you are able to visit the room where you will take the test, mentally rehearse while you are actually in this room.

Focus. Focus your attention on a specific object. Examine details of a painting, study the branches on a tree, or observe the face of your watch (right down to the tiny scratches in the glass). During an exam, take a few seconds to listen to the sounds of concentration—the squeaking of chairs, the scratching of pencils, the muted coughs. Touch the surface of your desk and notice the texture. Concentrate all of your attention on one point. Don't leave room in your mind for anxiety-related thoughts.

Praise yourself. Talk to yourself in a positive way. Many of us take the first opportunity to belittle ourselves: "Way to go, dummy! You don't even know the answer to the first question on the test." We wouldn't dream of treating a friend this way, yet we do it to ourselves.

An alternative is to give yourself some encouragement. Treat yourself as if you were your own best friend. Consider telling yourself, "I am very relaxed. I am doing a great job on this test."

Consider the worst. Rather than trying to put a stop to your worrying, consider the very worst thing that could happen. Take your fear to the limit of absurdity.

Imagine the catastrophic problems that might occur if you were to fail the test. You might say to yourself, "Well, if I fail this test, I might fail the course, lose my financial aid, and get kicked out of school. Then I won't be able to get a job, so the bank will repossess my car, and I'll start drinking." Keep going until you see the absurdity of your predictions. After you stop chuckling, you can backtrack to discover a reasonable level of concern. Your worry about failing the entire course if you fail the test might be justified. At that point ask yourself, "Can I live with that?" Unless you are taking a test in parachute packing and the final question involves jumping out of a plane, the answer will almost always be yes. (If the answer is no, use another technique. In fact, use several other techniques.)

The cold facts are hardly ever as bad as our worst fears. Shine a light on your fears, and they become more manageable.

Zoom out. When you're in the middle of a test or another situation in which you feel distressed, zoom out. Think the way film directors do when they dolly a camera out and away from an action scene. In your mind, imagine that you're floating away and viewing the situation as a detached outside observer.

If you're extremely distressed, let your imagination take you even farther. See yourself rising above the scene so that your whole community, city, nation, or planet is within view.

From this larger viewpoint, ask yourself whether this situation is worth worrying about. A negative response is not a license to belittle or avoid problems; it is permission to gain some perspective.

Another option is to zoom out in time. Imagine yourself one week, one month, one year, one decade, or one century from today. Assess how much the current situation will matter when that time comes.

Dealing with the physical sensations of anxiety

Breathe. You can calm physical sensations within your body by focusing your attention on your breathing. Concentrate on the air going in and out of your lungs. Experience it as it passes through your nose and mouth.

Do this for two to five minutes. If you notice that you are taking short, shallow breaths, begin to take longer and deeper breaths. Imagine your lungs to be a pair of bagpipes. Expand your chest to bring in as much air as possible. Then listen to the plaintive chords as you slowly release the air.

Scan your body. Simple awareness is an effective technique to reduce the tension in your body.

Sit comfortably and close your eyes. Focus your attention on the muscles in your feet and notice if they are relaxed. Tell the muscles in your feet that they can relax.

Move up to your ankles and repeat the procedure. Next go to your calves and thighs and buttocks, telling each group of muscles to relax.

Do the same for your lower back, diaphragm, chest, upper back, neck, shoulders, jaw, face, upper arms, lower arms, fingers, and scalp.

Tense and relax. If you are aware of a particularly tense part of your body or if you discover tension when you're scanning your body, you can release this tension with the tense-relax method.

To do this, find a muscle that is tense and make it even more tense. If your shoulders are tense, pull them back, arch your back, and tense your shoulder muscles even more tightly. Then relax. The net result is that you can be aware of the relaxation and allow yourself to relax even more.

You can use the same procedure with your legs, arms, abdomen, chest, face, and neck. Clench your fists, tighten your jaw, straighten your legs, and tense your abdomen all at once. Then relax and pay close attention to the sensations of relaxation. By paying attention, you can learn to re-create these sensations whenever you choose.

Use guided imagery. Relax completely and take a quick fantasy trip. Close your eyes, free your body of tension, and imagine yourself in a beautiful, peaceful, natural setting. Create as much of the scene as you can. Be specific. Use all of your senses.

For example, you might imagine yourself at a beach. Hear the surf rolling in and the seagulls calling to each other. Feel the sun on your face and the hot sand between your toes. Smell the sea breeze. Taste the salty mist from the surf. Notice the ships on the horizon and the rolling sand dunes. Use all of your senses to create a vivid imaginary trip.

Some people find that a mountain scene or a lush meadow scene works well. You can take yourself to a place you've never been or re-create an experience out of your past. Find a place that works for you and practice getting there. When you become proficient, you can return to it quickly for trips that might last only a few seconds.

With practice, you can use this technique even while you are taking a test.

Describe it. Focus your attention on your anxiety. If you are feeling nauseated or if you have a headache, concentrate on that feeling. Describe it to yourself. Tell yourself how large it is, where it is located in your body, what color it is, what shape it is, what texture it is, how much water it might hold if it had volume, and how heavy it is.

Be with it. As you describe your anxiety in detail, don't resist it. When you completely experience a physical sensation, it will often disappear. People suffering from severe and chronic pain have used this technique successfully.

Exercise aerobically. This is one technique that won't work in the classroom or while you're taking a test. Yet it is an excellent way to reduce body tension. Exercise regularly during the days that you review for a test. See what effect this has on your ability to focus and relax during the test.

Do some kind of exercise that will get your heart beating at twice your normal rate and keep it beating at that rate for 15 or 20 minutes. Aerobic exercises include rapid walking, jogging, swimming, bicycling, basketball, and anything else that elevates your heart rate and keeps it elevated.

Get help. When these techniques don't work, when anxiety is serious, get help. If you become withdrawn, have frequent thoughts about death or suicide, get depressed and stay depressed for more than a few days, or have prolonged feelings of hopelessness, see a counselor.

Depression and anxiety are common among students. Suicide is the third leading cause of death among young adults between the ages of 15 and 24.[5] This is tragic and unnecessary. Many schools have counselors available. If not, the student health service or another office can refer you to community agencies that provide free or inexpensive counseling. You can also get emergency assistance over the phone. Most phone books contain listings for suicide prevention hot lines and other emergency services. ☒

20 THINGS I LIKE TO DO

One way to relieve tension is to mentally yell "Stop!" and substitute a pleasant daydream for the stressful thoughts and emotions you are experiencing.

In order to create a supply of pleasant images to recall during times of stress, conduct an eight-minute brainstorm about things you like to do. Your goal is to generate at least 20 ideas. Time yourself and write as fast as you can in the space below.

When you have completed your list, study it. Pick out two activities that seem especially pleasant and elaborate on them by creating a mind map. Write down all of the memories you have about that activity.

You can use these images to calm yourself in stressful situations.

journal entry 18

Discovery/Intention Statement

Do a timed, four-minute brainstorm of all the reasons, rationalizations, justifications, and excuses you have used to avoid studying. Be creative. List your thoughts in the space below by completing the following Discovery Statement.

I discovered that I . . .

Next, review your list, pick the excuse that you use the most, and circle it. In the space below, write an Intention Statement about what you will do to begin eliminating your favorite excuse. Make this Intention Statement one that you can keep, with a timeline and a reward.

I intend to . . .

journal entry 19

Discovery Statement

Explore your feelings about tests. Complete the following sentences.

As exam time gets closer, one thing I notice that I do is . . .

When it comes to taking tests, I have trouble . . .

The night before a test, I usually feel . . .

The morning of a test, I usually feel . . .

During a test, I usually feel . . .

After a test, I usually feel . . .

When I get a test score, I usually feel . . .

An online version of this Journal Entry is available on the *From Master Student to Master Employee* Website.

Student Website

Getting ready for math tests

Many students who could succeed in math shy away from the subject. Some had negative experiences in past courses. Others believe that math is only for gifted students.

At some level, however, math is open to all students. There's more to this subject than memorizing formulas and manipulating numbers. Imagination, creativity, and problem-solving skills are important, too.

Consider a three-part program for math success. Begin with strategies for overcoming math anxiety. Next, boost your study skills. Finally, let your knowledge shine during tests.

Overcome math anxiety

Many schools offer courses in overcoming math anxiety. Ask your advisor about resources on your campus. Also experiment with the following suggestions.

Connect math to life. Think of the benefits of mastering math courses. You'll have more options for choosing a major and career. Math skills can also put you at ease in everyday situations—calculating the tip for a waiter, balancing your checkbook, working with a spreadsheet on a computer. If you follow baseball statistics, cook, do construction work, or snap pictures with a digital camera, you'll use math. And speaking the language of math can help you feel at home in a world driven by technology.

Pause occasionally to get an overview of the branch of math that you're studying. What's it all about? What basic problems is it designed to solve? How is this knowledge applied in daily life? For example, many architects, engineers, and space scientists use calculus daily.

Take a First Step. Math is cumulative. Concepts build upon each other in a certain order. If you struggled with algebra, you may have trouble with trigonometry or calculus.

To ensure that you have an adequate base of knowledge, tell the truth about your current level of knowledge and skill. Before you register for a math course, locate assigned texts for the prerequisite courses. If that material seems new or difficult for you, see the instructor. Ask for suggestions on ways to prepare for the course.

Remember that it's OK to continue your study of math from your current level of ability, whatever that level might be.

Notice your pictures about math. Sometimes what keeps people from succeeding at math is their mental picture of mathematicians. They see a man dressed in a baggy plaid shirt and brown wingtip shoes. He's got a calculator on his belt and six pencils jammed in his shirt pocket.

These pictures are far from the truth. Succeeding in math won't turn you into a nerd. Actually, you'll be able to enjoy school more, and your friends will still like you.

Mental pictures about math can be funny, and they can have serious effects. If math is seen as a field for white males, then women and people of color get excluded. Promoting math success for all students helps to overcome racism and sexism.

Change your conversation about math. When students fear math, they often say negative things to themselves about their abilities in these subjects. Many times this self-talk includes statements such as *I'll never be fast enough at solving math problems.* Or *I'm good with words, so I can't be good with numbers.*

Get such statements out in the open and apply some emergency critical thinking. You'll find two self-defeating assumptions lurking there: *Everybody else is better at math and science than I am.* And *Since I don't understand a math concept right now, I'll never understand it.* Both of these are illogical.

Replace negative beliefs with logical, realistic statements that affirm your ability to succeed in math: *Any confusion I feel now can be resolved. I learn math without comparing myself to others.* And *I ask whatever questions are needed to aid my understanding.*

Choose your response to stress. Math anxiety is seldom just "in your head." It can also register as sweaty palms, shallow breathing, tightness in the chest, or a mild headache. Instead of trying to ignore these sensations, just notice them without judgment. Over time, simple awareness decreases their power.

In addition, use stress management techniques. "Let go of test anxiety" on page 196 offers a bundle of them.

No matter what you do, remember to breathe. You can relax in any moment just by making your breath slower and deeper. Practice doing this while you study math. It will come in handy at test time.

Boost study skills for math

Choose teachers with care. Whenever possible, find a math teacher whose approach to math matches your learning style. Try several teachers until you find one whom you enjoy.

Another option is to ask around. Maybe your academic advisor can recommend math teachers. Also ask classmates to name their favorite math teachers—and to explain the reasons for their choices.

Perhaps only one teacher is offering the math course you'll need. Use the following suggestions to learn from this teacher regardless of her teaching style.

Take math courses back to back. Approach math in the same way that you learn a foreign language. If you take a year off in between Spanish I and Spanish II, you won't gain much fluency. To master a language, you take courses back to back. It works the same way with math, which is a language in itself.

Form a study group. During the first week of each math course, organize a study group. Ask each member to bring five problems to group meetings, along with solutions. Also exchange contact information so that you can stay in touch via e-mail, phone, and instant messaging.

Avoid short courses. Courses that you take during summer school or another shortened term are condensed. You might find yourself doing far more reading and homework each week than you do in longer courses. If you enjoy math, the extra intensity can provide a stimulus to learn. But if math is not your favorite subject, then give yourself extra time. Enroll in courses with more calendar days.

Participate in class. Success in math depends on your active involvement. Attend class regularly. Complete homework assignments *when they're due*—not just before the test. If you're confused, get help right away from an instructor, tutor, or study group. Instructor's office hours, free on-campus tutoring, and classmates are just a few of the resources available to you. Also support class participation with time for homework. Make daily contact with math.

Ask questions fearlessly. It's a cliché, and it's true: In math, there are no dumb questions. Ask whatever questions will aid your understanding. Keep a running list of them and bring the list to class.

Make your text top priority. Math courses are often text-driven. Class activities closely follow the book. This makes it important to complete your reading assignments. Master one concept before going on to the next, and stay current with your reading. Be willing to read slowly and reread sections as needed.

Read actively. To get the most out of your math texts, read with paper and pencil in hand. Work out examples. Copy diagrams, formulas, and equations. Use chapter summaries and introductory outlines to organize your learning.

From time to time, stop, close your book, and mentally reconstruct the steps in solving a problem. Before you memorize a formula, understand the basic concepts behind it.

Practice solving problems. To get ready for math tests, work *lots* of problems. Find out if practice problems or previous tests are on file in the library, in the math department, or with your math teacher.

Isolate the types of problems that you find the most difficult. Practice them more often. Be sure to get help with these *before* exhaustion or frustration sets in.

To prepare for tests, practice working problems fast. Time yourself. This is a great activity for math study groups.

Approach problem solving with a three-step process. During each step, apply an appropriate strategy. For ideas, see the chart on the next page.

Use tests to show what you know

Practice test taking. Part of preparing for any math test is rehearsal. Instead of passively reading through your text or scanning class notes, do a practice test:

- Print out a set of practice problems and set a timer for the same length of time as your testing period.
- Whenever possible, work these problems in the same room where you will take the actual test.

- Use only the kinds of supporting materials—such as scratch paper or lists of formulas—that will be allowed during the test.
- As you work problems, use deep breathing or another technique to enter a more relaxed state.

Ask appropriate questions. If you don't understand a test item, ask for clarification. The worst that can happen is that an instructor or proctor will politely decline to answer your question.

Write legibly. Put yourself in the instructor's place and imagine the prospect of grading stacks of illegible answer sheets. Make your answers easy to read. If you show your work, underline key sections and circle your answer.

Do your best. There are no secrets involved in getting ready for math tests. Master some stress management techniques, do your homework, get answers to your questions, and work sample problems. If you've done those things, you're ready for the test and deserve to do well. If you haven't done all those things, just do the best you can.

Remember that your personal best can vary from test to test, and even day to day. Even if you don't answer all test questions correctly, you can demonstrate what you *do* know right now.

During the test, notice when solutions come easily. Savor the times when you feel relaxed and confident. If you ever feel math anxiety in the future, these are the times to remember.[6]

1: Prepare

- Read each problem two or three times, slowly and out loud whenever possible.
- Consider creating a chart with three columns labeled *What I already know, What I want to find out,* and *What connects the two.* This third column is the place to record a formula that can help you solve the problem.
- Determine which arithmetic operations (addition, subtraction, multiplication, division) or formulas you will use to solve the problem.
- See if you can estimate the answer before you compute it.

2: Compute

- Reduce the number of unknowns as much as you can. Consider creating a separate equation to solve each unknown.
- When solving equations, carry out the algebra as far as you can before plugging in the actual numbers.
- Cancel and combine. For example, if the same term appears in both dividend and divisor, they will cancel each other out.
- Remember that it's OK to make several attempts at solving the problem before you find an answer.

3: Check

- Plug your answer back into the original equation or problem and see if it works out correctly.
- Ask yourself if your answer seems likely when compared to your estimate. For example, if you're asked to apply a discount to an item, that item should cost less in your solution.
- Perform opposite operations. If a problem involves multiplication, check your work by division; add, then subtract; factor, then multiply; find the square root, then the square; differentiate, then integrate.
- Keep units of measurement clear. Say that you're calculating the velocity of an object. If you're measuring distance in meters and time in seconds, the final velocity should be in meters per second.

Discovery/Intention Statement

Most of us can recall a time when learning became associated with anxiety. For many of us, this happened early in math courses.

One step toward getting past this anxiety is to write a math autobiography. Recall specific experiences in which you first felt stress related to this subject. Where were you? How old were you? What were you doing, thinking, and feeling? Who else was with you? What did those people say or do?

Describe one of these experiences in the space below.

Now recall any incidents in your life that gave you *positive* feelings about math. Describe one of these incidents briefly in the space below.

Now sum up any discoveries you made while describing these two sets of experiences.

I discovered that my biggest barrier to learning math is . . .

I discovered that the most satisfying aspect of doing math is . . .

Finally, prepare to take positive action. List three things you can do to succeed more consistently with math. Include a specific time frame for taking each action.

Action 1: I intend to . . .

Action 2: I intend to . . .

Action 3: I intend to . . .

Staying healthy under pressure

One key strategy for improving your performance under pressure goes beyond memory techniques or other study skills. This strategy involves taking care of your body.

Human bodies are incredible. They often continue to operate despite abuse. We run them too hard or let them sit idle for years. We pollute our bodies with junk food and expose them to illness. Yet we expect them to run flawlessly—even during stressful situations such as tests or long days at work.

If you want your body to perform at peak levels while you're in school or on the job, then fuel it with healthful food. Energize it with exercise. Rest it with sleep and stress management. Also make conscious choices about how you consume chemicals. These are transferable skills that can lengthen your life—and maybe even save it.

Fuel it

The following guidelines are adapted from *Dietary Guidelines for Americans 2005*, from the U.S. Department of Agriculture and U.S. Department of Health and Human Services.[7]

Choose a variety of fruits, vegetables, and whole grains. Eating plenty of fruits, vegetables, and grains of different kinds may help protect you against many chronic diseases.

Keep food safe to eat. Wash hands and cooking surfaces often.

Choose a diet that is low in saturated fat, trans fat, and cholesterol and moderate in total fat. Limit solid fats, such as butter, hard margarines, lard, and partially hydrogenated shortenings.

Choose beverages and foods to moderate your intake of sugars. Don't let soft drinks or other sweets crowd out other foods you need to maintain health. Drink water often.

Choose and prepare foods with little salt. Many people can reduce their chances of developing high blood pressure by consuming less salt.

If you drink alcoholic beverages, do so in moderation. Excess alcohol raises your risk for motor vehicle crashes, other injuries, high blood pressure, stroke, violence, suicide, and certain types of cancer. If you choose to drink alcoholic beverages, consume them only in moderation—up to one drink per day for women or two drinks per day for men. Drink with meals to slow alcohol absorption.

Two risks related to alcohol use are substance abuse and addiction. Substance abuse is compulsive use of alcohol or other drugs. This is a real problem in higher education. In a recent survey, 31 percent of college students met criteria for a diagnosis of alcohol abuse. Six percent met criteria for alcohol dependence.[8]

Some people will stop abusing a substance when the consequences get serious enough. Other people don't stop. They continue their self-defeating behaviors, no matter what the consequences for themselves, their friends, or their families. At that point the problem goes beyond abuse. It's addiction.

Many people find that they cannot treat addiction on their own. Two broad options exist for getting help. One is the growing self-help movement. The other is formal treatment. People recovering from addiction often combine the two.

If you're addicted to alcohol or another drug, consider taking a First Step: Acknowledge your lack of control over the drug once you start using it. Then go to your doctor or campus health service and ask for help.

Move it

Physical activity helps to control weight, prevent heart disease, control cholesterol levels and diabetes, and slow the bone loss that comes with aging. Exercise

Keep your brain fit for life

Your brain is an organ that needs regular care. Higher education gives you plenty of chances to exercise that organ. Don't let those benefits fade after you leave school. To keep your memory sharp and learn successfully for the rest of your life, adopt habits to keep your brain lean and fit. Consider these research-based suggestions from the Alzheimer's Association.[9]

Challenge your brain with new experiences. If you sit at a desk most of the workday, take a dance class. If you seldom travel, start reading maps of new locations and plan a cross-country trip. Seek out museums, theaters, concerts, and other cultural events. Even after you graduate, consider learning another language or taking up a musical instrument. New experiences give your brain a workout, much like sit-ups condition your abs.

Exercise. Physical activity promotes blood flow to the brain. It also reduces the risk of diabetes and other diseases that can impair brain function.

Eat well. A diet rich in dark-skinned fruits and vegetables boosts your supply of antioxidants—natural chemicals that nourish your brain. Examples of these foods are raisins, blueberries, blackberries, strawberries, raspberries, kale, spinach, Brussels sprouts, alfalfa sprouts, and broccoli. Avoid foods that are high in saturated fat and cholesterol, which increase the risk of Alzheimer's disease.

Nourish your social life. Having a network of supportive friends can reduce stress levels. In turn, stress management helps to maintain connections between brain cells. Stay socially active by working, volunteering, and joining clubs.

Protect your heart. In general, what's good for your heart is good for your brain. Protect both organs by eating well, exercising regularly, managing your weight, staying tobacco-free, and getting plenty of sleep. These habits reduce your risk of heart attack, stroke, and other cardiovascular conditions that interfere with blood flow to the brain.

also lowers the risk of certain cancers and helps to reduce anxiety and depression.

Do something you enjoy. You could start by walking briskly for at least 15 minutes every day. Increase that time gradually and add a little jogging or running. Other options include stair climbing, swimming, bicycling, rope jumping, and dancing. You can even burn calories by gardening, raking leaves, and working around the house.

Once you're in reasonable shape, you can stay there by doing aerobic activity on most days of the week. An hour of daily activity is ideal, but do whatever you can. Some activity is better than none. Look for exercise facilities on campus. School can be a great place to get in shape.

Before beginning any vigorous exercise program, consult a health care professional. This is critical if you are overweight, over age 60, in poor condition, or a heavy smoker, or if you have a history of health problems.

Rest it

A lack of sleep can decrease your immunity to illness and impair your performance in school and at work. Excess stress can have similar effects.

Promote sound sleep. As a student, you might be tempted to cut back drastically on your sleep once in a while. All-nighters before final exams are an example. If you indulge in them, read Chapter Three for some time-management ideas. Depriving yourself of sleep is a choice you can avoid.

Sometimes, getting to sleep isn't easy, even when you feel tired. If you have trouble falling asleep, experiment with the following suggestions:

- Exercise daily. For many people, this promotes sounder sleep. However, finish exercising at least several hours before you want to go to sleep.
- Avoid naps during the daytime.
- Monitor your caffeine intake, especially in the afternoon and evening.

Manage stress. Stress is both mental and physical. It includes thoughts that promote fear along with unpleasant sensations such as muscle tension. Turn to "Let go of test anxiety" on page 196 for ways to deal with both elements of stress.

If these techniques don't work within a few weeks, get help. See your doctor or a counselor at your student health service.

Make performance reviews work for you

Performance reviews are First Steps—opportunities to get feedback about how you're doing at work. Like tests, they are occasions when your knowledge and skills are evaluated. Unlike tests, the results can range from getting a large raise to getting fired.

Performance reviews usually take place in a meeting with your direct supervisor. Meetings follow various formats, and many organizations have their own systems for rating performance. Yet the basic idea in any case is for you to walk away with answers to three questions: What am I doing well? What could I do better? and How can I develop the skills to do better?

Some employees approach performance reviews with the same level of enthusiasm that they feel about getting a root canal. It's possible to take a different attitude. When handled with skill, performance reviews are tools for taking charge of your career.

Set goals early. Your organization may schedule performance reviews only once or twice per year. Yet effective performance review is a continuous process. For optimum results, begin this process on your first day at work. When you start a new job, meet with your direct supervisor to define exactly what "effective performance" means for you.

Here's where your skills at goal setting can be a lifesaver (see Chapter Two). Set work-related goals that you can achieve. State them in specific, measurable terms, as explained later in this article. Whenever possible, include a specific date to meet each goal. Put your goals in writing and share them with your supervisor.

Prepare for the review. As the date of your performance review approaches, anticipate the kind of questions your supervisor will ask. For example:

- What was your biggest accomplishment since your last performance review?
- In light of your stated goals, how did you feel about your performance?
- What prevented you from performing well or meeting any of your goals?
- What can you do to overcome those obstacles?
- What can coworkers and managers do to help you overcome those obstacles?

Keep the tone positive. When you meet with your supervisor, refer to your list of goals and note which ones you met. Take time to celebrate your accomplishments and set new goals.

If you missed a goal, talk about how that happened. Instead of focusing on failure or placing blame, take a problem-solving approach. If you made a mistake, talk about what you learned from the experience and what you intend to do differently in the future. Revise the goal and create a new plan for achieving it.

Effective performance reviews include time for you to *give* feedback as well as receive it. Discuss what you like about your job and what you would like to change. If meeting your goals calls for extra resources or changes in your job description, then ask for them.

Instead of complaining about working conditions, make suggestions. "My office is way too noisy for me to be productive" is a complaint. "Let's set up a quiet room in our building where people can go to do work that requires long periods of concentration" is a suggestion. Suggestions are easier to hear than complaints and naturally lend themselves to follow-up action.

Create a focused plan for personal development. Performance reviews often end with a development plan that includes specific ways to improve performance. Standard advice from many self-development "experts" is to focus this plan on identifying your greatest personal weakness and changing that right away.

Consider throwing this advice out the window for three reasons. First, tackling your biggest weakness first can feel threatening and lead to procrastination. Second, this weakness may be hard to change before your next performance review. And third, eliminating this weakness might affect your life outside work but have little or no impact on your career.

Instead, focus your development plan on goals that you can actually achieve in the near future, leading to clear benefits at work. David B. Peterson and Mary Dee Hicks, authors of *Development First: Strategies for Self-Development*, suggest that you start by completing the following sentences. Use them as seeds for Discovery and Intention Statements:

- "If I were better at . . ., I would excel relative to my peers."
- "If I improved . . ., I would fix an ongoing problem."
- "In my performance reviews and other feedback, I have been told more than once that I could improve . . . ."
- "In the future, my organization will need people who are good at . . . ."
- "As I dream about what I want to do some day, the main things I need to learn are . . . ."[10]

Set a timer for one hour and list as many responses to these prompts as possible. Then, after a day or two, come back to your list. Choose one idea as your top priority goal for the next three months. That way, your development plan will have a clear focus.

Choose new behaviors and monitor them. Next, give your personal development plan even more power. Translate your goal into concrete behaviors. Ask yourself: What exactly will I *do* differently based on my goal? And how will I *monitor* this behavior?

If you did the Time Monitor/Time Plan exercise in Chapter Three, you already have some experience with monitoring your behavior. You can monitor your progress toward any goal, no matter how ambitious. To monitor listening skills, for example, you could count the number of times each day that you interrupt other people. To monitor how well you focus attention at work, you could count the number of breaks you take during the workday. And to monitor your skill at meeting people, you could record the number of times each month that you introduce yourself to a new coworker.

Remember that the point of monitoring your behavior is not to become a cold-blooded measurement machine. Rather, the idea is to make a change that really makes a difference over the long term. The behaviors that we measure are the ones most likely to change.

As you monitor your behavior, suspend all self-judgment. Just record the facts. If you deviate from your plan, just look for the next opportunity to practice your new behavior.

Act on your plan every day. For your development plan, choose a behavior that you can do every day at work. Also describe how you will record the measurements that you make while monitoring your behavior. For instance, you could tally the number of your work breaks on a 3 × 5 card that you carry in your pocket or purse.

To get the most value from your personal development plan, do a daily debriefing on your way home from work. This can take only a minute or two. Estimate how often you're succeeding at changing your behavior. Make any adjustments to your plan that seem necessary. Then set a clear intention about when and where you will practice a new behavior at work tomorrow.

Using the above strategies will help you translate performance reviews into permanent behavior change. By creating a continuous cycle of planning and monitoring, you set yourself up for long-term success at work.

Based on this feedback about performance in your current job, you can define the next job you want. Every performance review can be one more step to the career of your dreams.

celebrate mistakes

Most of us are haunted by the fear of failure. We dread the thought of making mistakes or being held responsible for a major breakdown. We shudder at the missteps that could cost us grades, careers, money, or even relationships.

It's possible to take an entirely different attitude toward mistakes. Rather than fearing them, we could actually celebrate them.

Celebration allows us to notice the mistake. This article is not an argument in favor of *making* mistakes in the first place. Rather, the intention is to encourage shining a light on mistakes so that we can examine them and fix them. Mistakes that are hidden cannot be corrected.

Mistakes are valuable feedback. Mistakes are part of the learning process. Not only are mistakes usually more interesting than most successes—they're often more instructive.

Mistakes demonstrate that we're taking risks. People who play it safe make few mistakes. Making mistakes is evidence that we're stretching to the limit of our abilities—growing, risking, and learning.

Mistakes happen only when we're committed to making things work. Imagine a school where there's no concern about quality and effectiveness. Teachers usually come to class late. Residence halls are never cleaned, and scholarship checks are always late. The administration is in chronic debt, students seldom pay tuition on time, and no one cares. In this school, the word *mistake* would have little meaning. Mistakes become apparent only when people are committed to improving an institution. Mistakes go hand in hand with a commitment to quality. ☒

Notable failures

If you ever get a low score on a test or make a mistake at work, remember to keep it in perspective. Many people before you have failed miserably before succeeding brilliantly. Consider a few examples.

In his first professional race, cyclist **Lance Armstrong** finished last.

The first time **Jerry Seinfeld** walked on-stage at a comedy club as a professional comic, he looked out at the audience and froze.

When **Lucille Ball** began studying to be an actress in 1927, she was told by the head instructor of the John Murray Anderson Drama School, "Try any other profession."

In high school, actor and comic **Robin Williams** was voted "Least Likely to Succeed."

Walt Disney was fired by a newspaper editor because "he lacked imagination and had no good ideas."

R. H. Macy failed seven times before his store in New York City caught on.

Emily Dickinson had only seven poems published in her lifetime.

Decca Records turned down a recording contract with the **Beatles** with the unprophetic evaluation, "We don't like their sound. Groups of guitars are on their way out."

In 1954, Jimmy Denny, manager of the Grand Ole Opry, fired **Elvis Presley** after one performance.

Babe Ruth is famous for his past home run record, but for decades he also held the record for strikeouts. **Mark McGwire** broke that record.

After **Carl Lewis** won the gold medal for the long jump in the 1996 Olympic Games, he was asked to what he attributed his longevity, having competed for almost 20 years. He said, "Remembering that you have both wins and losses along the way. I don't take either one too seriously."

"I've missed more than 9,000 shots in my career," **Michael Jordan** said. "I've lost almost 300 games. Twenty-six times I've been trusted to take the game winning shot . . . and missed. I've failed over and over and over again in my life. That is why I succeed."[11]

power process

DETACH

This Power Process helps you release the powerful, natural student within you. It is especially useful whenever negative emotions are getting in the way of your education.

Attachments are addictions. When we are attached to something, we think we cannot live without it, just as a drug addict feels he cannot live without drugs. We believe our well-being depends on maintaining our attachments.

We can be attached to just about anything: expectations, ideas, objects, self-perceptions, people, results, rewards. The list is endless.

One person, for example, might be so attached to his car that he takes an accident as a personal attack. Pity the poor unfortunate who backs into this person's car. He might as well back into the owner himself.

Another person might be attached to his job. His identity and sense of well-being depend on it. He could become suicidally depressed if he gets fired.

We can be addicted to our emotions as well as to our thoughts. We can identify with our anger so strongly that we are unwilling to let it go. We can also be addicted to our pessimism and be reluctant to give it up. Rather than perceive these emotions as liabilities, we can see them as indications that it's time to practice detachment.

Most of us are addicted, to some extent, to our identities: We are Americans, veterans, high achievers, bowlers, loyal friends, business owners, humanitarians, devoted parents, dancers, hockey fans, or birdwatchers. If we are attached to these roles, they can dictate who we think we are.

When these identities are threatened, we might fight for them as if we were defending our lives. The more addicted we are to an identity, the harder we fight to keep it.

Ways to recognize an attachment

When we are attached and things don't go our way, we might feel irritated, angry, jealous, confused, fatigued, bored, frightened, or resentful.

Suppose you are attached to getting an A on your physics test. You feel as though your success in life depends on getting an A. It's not just that you want an A. You *need* an A. During the exam, the thought "I must get an A" is in the back of your mind as you begin to work a problem. And the problem is difficult. The first time you read it, you have no idea how to solve it. The second time around, you aren't even sure what it's asking. The more you struggle to understand it, the more confused you get. To top it all off, this problem is worth 40 percent of your score.

As the clock ticks away, you work harder, getting more stuck, while that voice in your head gets louder: "I must get an A. I MUST get an A. I MUST GET AN A!"

At this point, your hands begin to sweat and shake. Your heart is pounding. You feel nauseated. You can't concentrate. You flail about for the answer as if you were drowning. You look up at the clock, sickened by the inexorable sweep of the second hand. You are doomed.

Now is a time to detach.

Ways to use this process

Detachment can be challenging. In times of stress, it might seem like the most difficult thing in the world to do. You can practice a variety of strategies to help you move toward detachment.

Practice observer consciousness. This is the quiet state above and beyond your usual thoughts, the place where you can be aware of being aware. It's a tranquil spot, apart from your emotions. From here, you can observe yourself objectively, as if you were someone else. Pay attention to your emotions and physical sensations. If you are confused and feeling stuck, tell yourself, "Here I am, confused and stuck." If your palms are sweaty and your stomach is one big knot, admit it.

Practice perspective. Put current circumstances into a broader perspective. View personal issues within the larger context of your community, your nation, or your planet. You will likely see them from a different point of view. Imagine the impact your present problems will have 20 or even 100 years from now.

Take a moment to consider the worst that could happen. During that physics exam, notice your attachment to getting an A. Realize that even flunking the test will not ruin your life. Seeing this helps you put the test in perspective.

Practice breathing. Calm your mind and body with breathing or relaxation techniques.

Note: It might be easier to practice these techniques when you're not feeling strong emotions. Notice your thoughts, behaviors, and feelings during neutral activities such as watching television or taking a walk.

Practice detaching. The key is to let go of automatic emotional reactions when you don't get what you want.

Rewrite the equation

To further understand this notion of detaching, we can borrow an idea from mathematics. An equation is a set of symbols joined by an equals sign (=) that forms a true statement. Examples are $2 + 2 = 4$ and $a + b = c$.

Equations also work with words. In fact, our self-image can be thought of as a collection of equations. For example, the thought "I am capable" can be written as the equation "I = capable." "My happiness depends on my car" can be written as "happiness = car." The statement "My well-being depends on my job" becomes "well-being = job." Each equation is a tip-off to an attachment. When we're upset, a closer look often reveals that one of our attachments is threatened. The person who believes that his happiness is equal to his current job will probably be devastated if his company downsizes and he's laid off.

Once we discover a hidden equation, we can rewrite it. In the process, we can watch our upsets disappear. The person who gets laid off can change his equation to "my happiness = my happiness." In other words, his happiness does not have to depend on any particular job.

People can rewrite equations under the most extreme circumstances. A man dying from lung cancer spent his last days celebrating his long life. One day his son asked him how he was feeling.

"Oh, I'm great," said the man with cancer. "Your mom and I have been having a wonderful time just rejoicing in the life that we have had together."

"Oh, I'm glad you're doing well," said the man's son. "The prednisone you have been taking must have kicked in again and helped your breathing."

"Well, not exactly. Actually, my body is in terrible shape, and my breathing has been a struggle these last few days. I guess what I'm saying is that my body is not working well at all, but I'm still great."

The dying man rewrote the equation "I = my body." He knew that he had a body and that he was more than his body. This man lived this Power Process and gave his son—the author of this book—an unforgettable lesson about detachment.

Some cautions

Giving up an addiction to being an A student does not mean giving up being an A student. And giving up an addiction to a job doesn't mean getting rid of the job. It means not investing your entire well-being in the grade or the job. Keep your desires and goals alive and healthy while detaching from the compulsion to reach them.

Notice also that detachment is different from denial. Denial implies running away from whatever you find unpleasant. In contrast, detachment includes accepting your emotions and knowing the details of them—down to every last thought and physical sensation involved. It's OK to be angry or sad. Once you accept and fully experience your emotions, you can more easily move beyond them.

Being detached is not the same as being apathetic. We can be 100 percent detached and 100 percent involved at the same time. In fact, our commitment toward achieving a particular result is usually enhanced by being detached from it.

Detach and succeed

When we are detached, we perform better. When we think everything is at stake, the results might suffer. Without anxiety and the need to get an A on the physics test, we are more likely to recognize the problem and remember the solution.

This Power Process is useful when you notice that attachments are keeping you from accomplishing your goals. Behind your attachments is a master student. By detaching, you release that master student. Detach. ☒

career application

During his senior year of high school, Chang Lee read about the favorable job market for medical assistants.

He set a goal to enroll in a local community college and earn his A.A. degree in medical assisting. This was a logical choice for Chang. His mother worked as a psychiatric nurse, and he'd always been interested in health care. He figured that his degree would equip him with marketable skills and a way to contribute to society.

Chang's choice paid off. He excelled in classes. With his career goal in mind, he often asked himself: *How could I use this information to become a better medical assistant?*

During his second year of college, Chang landed an internship with a large medical clinic near campus. The clinic offered him a job after he graduated, and he accepted.

Chang enjoyed the day-to-day tasks of medical assisting. He helped doctors run medical tests and perform physical exams. In addition, he ordered lab work and updated medical records.

After three months on the job, Chang was on a first-name basis with many of the clinic's regular patients. No matter how busy the clinic's schedule, Chang made time for people. When they finished describing their symptoms, he frequently asked, "Is there anything else that's on your mind?" Then he listened without interrupting. Chang's ability to put people at ease made him popular with patients, who often asked specifically to see him.

The only part of his job that Chang dreaded was performance reviews, which took place twice during each year of employment. Even though he was respected by coworkers, Chang felt nervous whenever the topic of evaluating work performance came up. "It just reminds me too much of final exams during school," he said. "I like my job and I try to do it well every day. Having a performance review just raises my anxiety level and doesn't really benefit me." ☒

Reflecting on this scenario

1. Refer to "100 transferable skills" on page 63, then list a transferable skill that Chang demonstrates in this scenario.

2. How would you describe Chang's learning style?

3. List three strategies from this chapter that Chang could use to create value from performance reviews.

quiz

Name ______________________________ Date ____/____/____

1. According to the text, test scores measure your accomplishments in a course. True or False? Explain your answer.

2. When answering multiple choice questions, it is better to read all of the possible answers before answering the question in your head. True or False? Explain your answer.

3. The presence of absolute qualifiers, such as *always* or *never*, generally indicates a false statement. True or False? Explain your answer.

4. Briefly explain the differences between a daily review and a major review.

5. Define the term *study checklist* and give three examples of what to include on such checklists.

6. Describe how *detachment* differs from *denial.*

7. Study groups can focus on
   (a) Comparing and editing class notes.
   (b) Doing research to prepare for papers and presentations.
   (c) Finding and understanding key passages in assigned readings.
   (d) Creating and taking practice tests.
   (e) All of the above.

8. Define the term *personal development plan*. Also describe some elements to include in such a plan.

9. Describe at least three techniques for dealing with the thoughts connected to test anxiety.

10. Describe at least three techniques for dealing with the physical feelings connected to test anxiety.

learning styles application

The questions below will "cycle" you through four styles, or modes, of learning as explained in the article "Learning styles: Discovering how you learn" in Chapter One. Each question will help you explore a different mode. You can answer the questions in any order.

what if *Explain how a suggestion for managing test anxiety can help you manage stress in a situation that you face outside school.*

why *Name at least one benefit you could experience—in addition to better grades—by taking tests more effectively.*

how *Of the techniques that you gained from this chapter, choose one that you will use on your next test. Describe exactly how you intend to apply the technique.*

what *List three new techniques for reviewing course material or taking tests that you gained from reading this chapter.*

master student profile

CHRISTOPHER REEVE

(1952–2004) Was left paralyzed after a horseback riding accident in 1995. This on-screen Superman and real-life hero was a tireless activist who helped raise millions of dollars for spinal cord research before his death in 2004.

Soon I realized that I'd have to leave Kessler [hospital] at some point. A tentative date was set for sometime between Thanksgiving and mid-December. I thought: God, I've totally given up on breathing. So what am I going to do, stay on a ventilator for the rest of my life? . . .

I announced that on the first Monday of November, I was going to try again to breathe on my own. At 3:30 in the afternoon of November 2, Bill Carroll, Dr. Kirshblum, Dr. Finley, and Erica met me in the PT room. And I remember thinking: This is it. I've got to do something, I have simply got to. I don't know where it's going to come from, but I've got to produce some air from someplace.

Dr. Finley said, "We're going to take you off the ventilator. I want you to try to take ten breaths. If you can only do three, then that's the way it is, but I want you to try for ten. And I'm going to measure how much air you move with each breath, and let's just see where you are. Okay?"

And I took ten breaths. I was lying on my back on the mat. My head moved as I struggled to draw in air; I wasn't able to move my diaphragm at all, just my chest, neck, and shoulder muscles in an intense effort to bring some air into my lungs. I was only able to draw in an average of 50 cc's with each attempt. But at least it was something. I had moved the dial.

We came back the next day, and now I was really motivated. I prepared

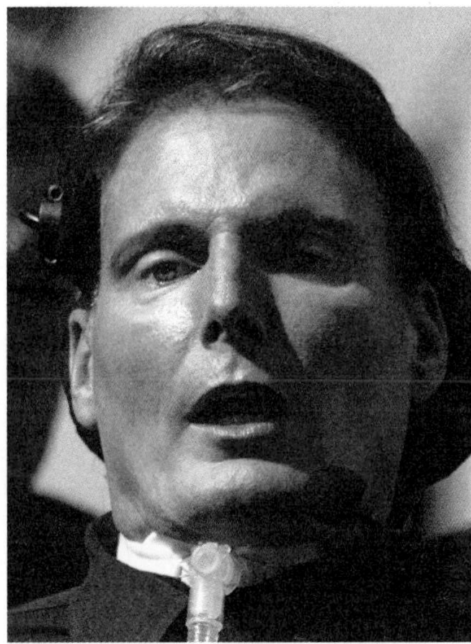

myself mentally by imagining my chest as a huge bellows that I could open and close at will. I told myself over and over again that I was going home soon and that I couldn't leave without making some real progress. Dr. Finley asked me to take another ten breaths for a comparison with yesterday's numbers. I took the ten breaths, and my average for each one was 450 cc's.

They couldn't believe it. I thought to myself: All right. Now we're getting somewhere.

At 3:30 the next day I was in place and ready to begin. . . . Finally I was really taking charge. When Dr. Finley arrived once again he asked me to take ten breaths. This time the average was 560 cc's per breath. A cheer broke out in the room. . . .

After that Erica and I worked alone. Every day we would breathe. I went from seven minutes to twelve to fifteen. Just before I left Kessler on the thirteenth of December, I gave it everything I had, and I breathed for thirty minutes. . . . The previous summer, still adjusting to my new circumstances, I had given up. But by November I had the motivation to go forward. . . .

Juice [Reeve's aide] had often told me, "You've been to the grave two times this year, brother. You're not going there again. You are here for a reason." He thought my injury had meaning, had a purpose. I believed, and still do, that my injury was simply an accident. But maybe Juice and I are both right, because I have the opportunity now to make sense of this accident. I believe that it's what you do after an accident that can give it meaning.

I began to face my new life. On Thanksgiving in 1995, I went home to Bedford to spend the day with my family. In the driveway, when I saw our home again, I wept. Dana held me. At the dinner table, when each of us in turn spoke a few words about what we were thankful for, Will said, "Dad."

For more biographical information on Christopher Reeve, visit the Master Student Hall of Fame on the *From Master Student to Master Employee* Website.

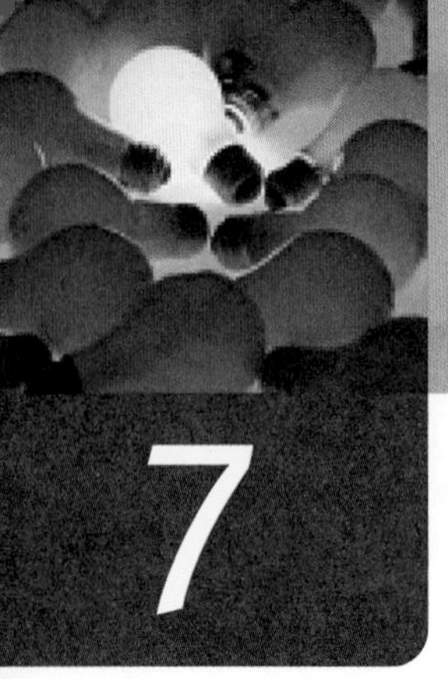

7 Thinking

MASTER STUDENT MAP

why this chapter matters ...

The ability to think helps you succeed in school and promotes many skills that transfer to the workplace—including reading, writing, speaking, and listening.

how you can use this chapter ...

Learn to create and refine ideas.
Choose attitudes that promote your success.
Avoid common mistakes in thinking.
Enhance your success in problem solving.
Apply thinking skills to practical decisions such as career planning and ethical choices.

As you read, ask yourself what if ...

I could solve problems more creatively and make decisions in every area of life with more confidence?

what is included ...

FROM THE DESK OF . . .

When developing Websites, I am essentially solving a client's problem. When a potential client comes to me, they believe that they have a problem and that a Website will solve it. My job is to unearth whether the problem they think they have is in fact the real problem, and whether or not a Website is the appropriate solution.

—KIM GARLAND, WEBSITE DESIGNER AND DEVELOPER

Critical thinking: A survival skill

Society depends on persuasion. Advertisers want us to spend money on their products. Political candidates want us to "buy" their stands on the issues. Teachers want us to agree that their classes are vital to our success. Parents want us to accept their values. Authors want us to read their books. Broadcasters want us to spend our time in front of the radio or television, consuming their programs and not those of the competition. The business of persuasion has an impact on all of us.

A typical American sees thousands of television commercials each year. And that's just one medium of communication. Add to that the writers and speakers who enter our lives through radio shows, magazines, books, billboards, brochures, Internet sites, and fund-raising appeals—all with a product, service, cause, or opinion for us to embrace.

This leaves us with hundreds of choices about what to buy, where to go, and who to be. It's easy to lose our heads in the crosscurrent of competing ideas—unless we develop skills in critical thinking. When we think critically, we can make choices with open eyes.

Uses of critical thinking

Critical thinking underlies reading, writing, speaking, and listening. These are the basic elements of communication—a process that occupies most of our waking hours.

Critical thinking promotes social change. Consider that the institutions in any society—courts, governments, schools, businesses—are the products of a certain way of thinking. Any organization draws its life from certain assumptions about the most effective goals and ways to meet them. Before the institution can change, those assumptions need to be loosened up or reinvented. In many ways, the real location of an institution is inside our heads.

Critical thinking uncovers bias and prejudice. This is a First Step toward communicating with people of other races, ethnic backgrounds, and cultures.

Critical thinking reveals long-term consequences. Crises occur when our thinking fails to keep pace with reality. An example is the world's ecological crisis, which arose when people polluted the earth, air, and water without considering the long-term consequences. Imagine how different our world would be if our leaders had thought like the first female chief of the Cherokees. Asked about

journal entry 21

Discovery/Intention Statement

Think back to a time when you felt unable to choose among several different solutions to a problem or several stands on a key issue in your life. In the space below, describe this experience.

I discovered that . . .

___

___

___

Now scan this chapter to find useful suggestions for decision making, problem solving, and critical thinking. Note below at least four techniques that look especially promising to you.

Strategy	*Page number*

Finally, declare a time that you intend to explore these techniques in more detail, along with a situation coming up during this term in which you could apply them.

I intend to improve my thinking skills by . . .

___

___

___

___

___

___

___

the best advice her elders had given her, she replied, "Look forward. Turn what has been done into a better path. If you are a leader, think about the impact of your decision on seven generations into the future."

Critical thinking reveals nonsense. Novelist Ernest Hemingway once said that anyone who wants to be a great writer must have a built-in, shockproof "crap" detector.[1] That inelegant comment points to a basic truth: As critical thinkers, we are constantly on the lookout for thinking that's inaccurate, sloppy, or misleading.

Critical thinking is a skill that will never go out of style. At various times in human history, nonsense has been taken for the truth. For example, people believed that:

- Illness results from an imbalance in the four vital fluids: blood, phlegm, water, and bile.
- Caucasians are inherently more intelligent than people of other races.
- Women are incapable of voting intelligently.
- We will never invent anything smaller than a transistor. (That was before the computer chip.)
- Computer technology will usher in the age of the paperless office.

The critical thinkers of history courageously challenged such ideas. These men and women pointed out that—metaphorically speaking—the emperor had no clothes.

Critical thinking is a path to freedom from half-truths and deception. You have the right to question everything that you see, hear, and read. Acquiring this ability is a major goal of a liberal education.

Critical thinking as thorough thinking

For some people, the term *critical thinking* has negative connotations. If you prefer, use *thorough thinking* instead. Both terms point to the same activities: sorting out conflicting claims, weighing the evidence, letting go of personal biases, and arriving at reasonable conclusions. This adds up to an ongoing conversation—a constant process, not a final product.

We live in a culture that values quick answers and certainty. This is often at odds with effective thinking. Thorough thinking is the ability to examine and re-examine ideas that might seem obvious. This kind of thinking takes time and the willingness to say three subversive words: "I don't know."

Thorough thinking is also the willingness to change our opinions as we continue to examine a problem. This calls for courage and detachment. Just ask anyone who has given up a cherished point of view in light of new evidence.

Skilled students are thorough thinkers. They distinguish between opinion and fact. They ask probing questions and make detailed observations. They uncover assumptions and define their terms. They make assertions carefully, basing them on sound logic and solid evidence. Almost everything that we call *knowledge* is a result of these activities. This means that critical thinking and learning are intimately linked.

It's been said that human beings are rational creatures. Yet no one is born a thorough thinker. This is a learned skill. Use the suggestions in this chapter to claim the thinking powers that are your birthright. The critical thinker is one aspect of the master student who lives inside you.

Becoming a critical thinker

Critical thinking is a path to intellectual adventure. Though there are dozens of possible approaches, the process boils down to *asking and answering questions.*

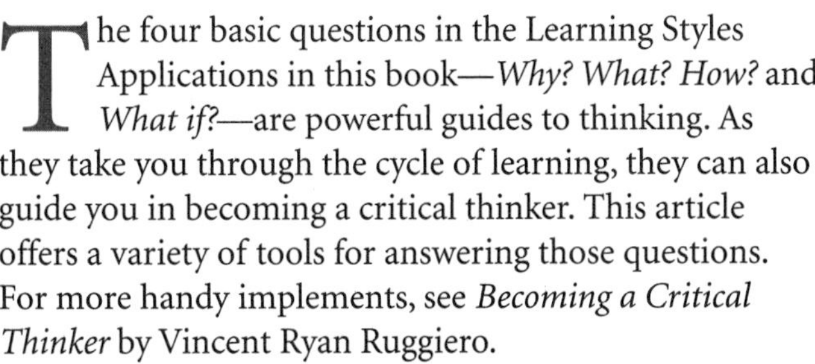

The four basic questions in the Learning Styles Applications in this book—*Why? What? How?* and *What if?*—are powerful guides to thinking. As they take you through the cycle of learning, they can also guide you in becoming a critical thinker. This article offers a variety of tools for answering those questions. For more handy implements, see *Becoming a Critical Thinker* by Vincent Ryan Ruggiero.

1 *Why* am I considering this issue? Critical thinking and personal passion go together. Begin critical thinking with a question that matters to you. Seek a rationale for your learning. Understand why it is important for you to think about a specific topic. You might want to arrive at a new conclusion, make a prediction, or solve a problem. By finding a personal connection with an issue, your interest in acquiring and retaining new information increases.

2 *What* are various points of view on this issue? Imagine Karl Marx, Cesar Chavez, and Donald Trump assembled in one room to choose the most desirable economic system. Picture Mahatma Gandhi, Winnie Mandela, and General George Patton lecturing at a United Nations conference on conflict resolution. Visualize Fidel Castro, George W. Bush, and Mother Teresa in a discussion about distributing the world's resources equitably. When seeking out alternative points of view, let such events unfold in your mind.

Dozens of viewpoints exist on every important issue—reducing crime, ending world hunger, preventing war, educating our children, and countless other concerns. In fact, few problems have any single, permanent solution. Each generation produces its own answers to critical questions, based on current conditions. Our search for answers is a conversation that spans centuries. On each question, many voices are waiting to be heard.

You can take advantage of this diversity by seeking out alternative views with an open mind. When talking to another person, be willing to walk away with a new point of view—even if it's the one you brought to the table, supported with new evidence.

Examining different points of view is an exercise in analysis, which you can do with the suggestions that follow.

Define terms. Imagine two people arguing about whether an employer should limit health care benefits to members of a family. To one person, the word *family* means a mother, father, and children; to the other person, the word *family* applies to any long-term, supportive relationship between people who live together. Chances are, the debate will go nowhere until these people realize that they're defining the same word in different ways.

Conflicts of opinion can often be resolved—or at least clarified—when we define our key terms up front. This is especially true with abstract, emotion-laden terms such as *freedom, peace, progress,* or *justice.* Blood has been shed over the meaning of these words. Define them with care.

Look for assertions. A speaker's or writer's key terms occur in a larger context called an assertion. An *assertion* is a complete sentence that directly answers a key question. For example, consider this sentence from the article "The meaning of mastery" in Chapter One: "A master is a person who has attained a level of skill that goes beyond technique." This sentence is an assertion that answers an important question: How do we recognize a master?

Look for at least three viewpoints. When asking questions, let go of the temptation to settle for just a single answer. Once you have come up with an answer, say to yourself, "Yes, that is one answer. Now what's another?" Using this approach can sustain honest inquiry, fuel creativity, and lead to conceptual breakthroughs. Be prepared: The world is complicated, and critical thinking is a complex business. Some of your answers might contradict others. Resist the temptation to have all of your ideas in a neat, orderly bundle.

Practice tolerance. One path to critical thinking is tolerance for a wide range of opinions. Taking a position on important issues is natural. When we stop having an opinion on things, we've probably stopped breathing.

The problem occurs when we become so attached to our current viewpoints that we refuse to consider alternatives. Many ideas that are widely accepted in western cultures—for example, civil liberties for people of color and women's right to vote—were once considered dangerous. Viewpoints that seem outlandish today might become widely accepted a century, a decade, or even a year from now. Remembering this can help us practice tolerance for differing beliefs and, in doing so, make room for new ideas that might alter our lives.

3 *How* well is each point of view supported?

Uncritical thinkers shield themselves from new information and ideas. As an alternative, you can follow the example of scientists, who constantly search for evidence that contradicts their theories. The following suggestions can help.

Look for logic and evidence. The aim of using logic is to make statements that are clear, consistent, and coherent. As you examine a speaker's or writer's assertions, you might find errors in logic—assertions that contradict each other or assumptions that are unfounded.

Also assess the evidence used to support points of view. Evidence comes in several forms, including facts, expert testimony, and examples. To think critically about evidence, ask questions such as:

- Are all or most of the relevant facts presented?
- Are the facts consistent with each other?
- Are facts presented accurately—or in a misleading way?
- Are enough examples included to make a solid case for the viewpoint?
- Do the examples truly support the viewpoint?
- Are the examples typical? That is, could the author or speaker support the assertion with other examples that are similar?
- Is the expert credible—truly knowledgeable about the topic?

Consider the source. Look again at that article on the problems of manufacturing cars powered by natural gas. It might have been written by an executive from an oil company. Check out the expert who disputes the connection between smoking and lung cancer. That "expert" might be the president of a tobacco company.

This is not to say that we should dismiss the ideas of people who have a vested interest in stating their opinions. Rather, we can take their self-interest into account as we consider their ideas.

Understand before criticizing. Polished debaters can sum up their opponents' viewpoints—often better than the people who support those viewpoints themselves. Likewise, critical thinkers take the time to understand a statement of opinion before agreeing or disagreeing with it.

Effective understanding calls for listening without judgment. Enter another person's world by expressing her viewpoint in your own words. If you're conversing with that person, keep revising your summary until she agrees that you've stated her position accurately. If you're reading an article, write a short summary of it. Then scan the article again, checking to see if your synopsis is on target.

Watch for hot spots. Many people have mental "hot spots"—topics that provoke strong opinions and feelings. Examples are abortion, homosexuality, gun control, and the death penalty.

To become more skilled at examining various points of view, notice your own particular hot spots. Make a clear intention to accept your feelings about these topics and to continue using critical thinking techniques.

One way to cool down our hot spots is to remember that we can change or even give up our current opinions without giving up ourselves. That's a key message behind the Power Processes "Ideas are tools" and "Detach." These Power Processes remind us that human beings are much more than the sum of their current opinions.

Be willing to be uncertain. Some of the most profound thinkers have practiced the art of thinking by using a magic sentence: "I'm not sure yet."

Those are words that many people do not like to hear. Our society rewards quick answers and quotable sound bites. We're under considerable pressure to utter the truth in 10 seconds or less.

In such a society, it is courageous and unusual to take the time to pause, to look, to examine, to be thoughtful, to consider many points of view—and to be unsure. When a society adopts half-truths in a blind rush for certainty, a willingness to embrace uncertainty can move us forward.

One trait of skilled thinkers is that they monitor their understanding. When reading, thinking, or listening, they pause periodically to ask: *Am I really understanding this? If not, where is my understanding breaking down?* These questions can lead to breakthrough insights. And they are possible only with people who are willing to admit uncertainty.

4 *What if* I could combine various points of view or create a new one? Finding the truth is like painting a barn door by tossing an open can of paint at it. Few people who throw at the door miss it entirely. Yet no one can cover the whole door in a single toss.

People who express a viewpoint are seeking the truth. And no reasonable person claims to cover the whole barn door—to understand the whole truth about anything. Instead, each viewpoint can be seen as one approach among many possible alternatives. If you don't think that any one opinion is complete, combine different perspectives on the issue. Experiment with the following strategies.

Create a critical thinking "spreadsheet." When you consult authorities with different stands on an issue, you might feel confused about how to sort, evaluate, and combine their points of view. To overcome confusion, create a critical thinking "spreadsheet." List the authorities across the top of a page and key questions down the left side. Then indicate each authority's answer to each question, along with your own answers.

For example, the spreadsheet below clarifies different points of view on the issue of whether to outlaw boxing.

You could state your own viewpoint by combining your answers to the questions in the above spreadsheet: "I favor legalized boxing. While boxing poses dangers, so do other sports. And like other sports, the risk of injury can be reduced when boxers get proper training."

Creating a critical thinking spreadsheet automatically prompts you to ask certain questions: *What does this idea or fact remind me of? How does it relate to what I've heard or read about this subject in the past?* The answers can lead you to intuitive leaps and unexpected connections. This has been described as the "high country of the mind," the place where creative thinkers dwell.

Write about it. Thoughts can move at blinding speed. Writing slows down that process. Gaps in logic that slip by us in thought or speech are often exposed when we commit the same ideas to paper. Writing down our thoughts allows us to compare, contrast, and combine points of view more clearly—and therefore to think more thoroughly.

Accept your changing perspectives. Researcher William Perry found that students in higher education move through stages of intellectual development.[2] In earlier stages, students tend to think there is only one correct viewpoint on each issue, and they look to their

	Medical doctor	Former boxer	Sports journalist	Me
Is boxing a sport?	No	Yes	Yes	Yes
Is boxing dangerous?	Yes	Yes	Yes	Yes
Is boxing more dangerous than other sports?	Yes	No	Yes	No
Can the risk of injury be overcome by proper training?	No	No	No	Yes

Source: Vincent Ryan Ruggiero, *Becoming a Critical Thinker,* Fifth Edition. Copyright © 2006 by Houghton Mifflin Company. Reprinted with permission.

instructors to reveal that truth. Later, students acknowledge a variety of opinions on issues and construct their own viewpoints.

Monitor changes in your thinking processes as you combine viewpoints. Distinguish between opinions that you accept from authorities and opinions that are based on your own use of logic and your search for evidence. Also look for opinions that result from objective procedures (such as using the *Why? What? How?* and *What if?* questions in this article) and personal sources (using intuition or "gut feelings").

Remember that the process of becoming a critical thinker will take you through a variety of stages. Give yourself time, and celebrate your growing mastery.

Attitudes of a critical thinker

The American Philosophical Association invited a panel of 46 scholars from the United States and Canada to come up with answers to the following two questions: "What is college-level critical thinking?" and "What leads us to conclude that a person is an effective critical thinker?"[3] After two years of work, this panel concluded that critical thinkers share the attitudes summarized in the following chart.

Attitude	Sample statement
Truth-seeking	"Let's follow this idea and see where it leads, even if we feel uncomfortable with what we find out."
Open-minded	"I have a point of view on this subject, and I'm anxious to hear yours as well."
Analytical	"Taking a stand on the issue commits me to take some new action."
Systematic	"The speaker made several interesting points, and I'd like to hear some more evidence to support each one."
Self-confident	"After reading the book for the first time, I was confused. I'll be able to understand it after studying the book some more."
Inquisitive	"When I first saw that painting, I wanted to know what was going on in the artist's life when she painted it."
Mature	"I'll wait until I gather some more facts before reaching a conclusion on this issue."

Attitudes, affirmations, and visualizations

"I have a bad attitude." Some of us say this as if we were talking about having the flu. An attitude is certainly as strong as the flu, but it isn't something we have to succumb to or accept.

Some of us see our attitudes the way we see our height or eye color: "I might not like it, but I might as well accept it."

Acceptance is certainly a worthwhile approach to things we cannot change. When it comes to attitudes, acceptance is not necessary—attitudes can change. We don't have to live our lives with an attitude that doesn't work.

Attitudes are powerful. They create behavior. If your attitude is that you're not very interesting at a party, then your behavior will probably match your attitude, and you might act like a bore. If your attitude is that you are fun at a party, then your behavior is more likely to be playful. Soon you are the life of the party. All that has to change is attitude.

I'M A GREAT STUDENT!

Success in school starts with attitudes. They include your self-concept—the way you currently think about your abilities and potentials. Some attitudes will help you benefit from all the money and time you invest in higher education. Other attitudes will render your investment worthless.

You can change your attitudes through regular practice with affirmations and visualizations.

Affirm it. An affirmation is a statement describing what you want. The most effective affirmations are personal, positive, and written in the present tense.

Affirmations have an almost magical power. They are used successfully by athletes and actors, executives and ballerinas, and thousands of people who have succeeded in their lives. Affirmations can change your attitudes and behaviors.

To use affirmations, first determine what you want, then describe yourself as if you already have it. To get what you want from your education, you could write, "I, Malika Jones, am a master student. I take full responsibility for my education. I learn with joy, and I use my experiences in each course to create the life that I want."

If you decide that you want a wonderful job, you might write, "I, Susan Webster, have a wonderful job. I respect and love my colleagues, and they feel the same way about me. I look forward to going to work each day."

Or if money is your desire, you might write, "I, John Henderson, am rich. I have more money than I can spend. I have everything I want, including a six-bedroom house, a new sports car, a 200-watt sound system, and a large-screen television with a satellite dish receiver."

What makes the affirmation work is detail. Use brand names, people's names, and your own name. Involve all of your senses—sight, sound, smell, taste, touch. Take a positive approach. Instead of saying, "I am not fat," say, "I am slender."

Once you have written the affirmation, repeat it. Practice saying it out loud several times a day. This works best if you say it at a regular time, such as just before you go to sleep or just after you wake up.

Sit in a chair in a relaxed position. Take a few deep and relaxing breaths, and then repeat your affirmation with emotion. It's also effective to look in a mirror while saying the affirmation. Keep looking and repeating until you are saying your affirmation with conviction.

Visualize it. It would be difficult to grow up in our culture without hearing the maxim that "practice makes perfect." The problem is that most of us limit what we consider to be practice. Effective practice can occur even when we are not moving a muscle.

You can improve your golf swing, tennis serve, or batting average while lying in bed. You can become a better driver, speaker, or cook while sitting silently in a chair. In line at the grocery store, you can improve your ability to type or to take tests. This is all possible through visualization—the technique of seeing yourself be successful.

Here's one way to begin. Decide what you want to improve, and write down what it would look like, sound like, and feel like to have that improvement in your life. If you are learning to play the piano, write down briefly what you would see, hear, and feel if you were playing skillfully. If you want to improve your relationships with your children, write down what you would see, hear, and feel if you were communicating with them successfully.

A powerful visualization involves other senses besides seeing. Feel the physical sensations. Hear the sounds. Note any smells, tastes, textures, or qualities of light that accompany the scene in your mind.

Once you have a sketch of what it would be like to be successful, practice it in your imagination—successfully. As you play out the scenario, include as many details as you can. Always have your practices be successes. Whenever

Attitude replacements

You can use affirmations to replace a negative attitude with a positive one. There are no limitations, other than your imagination and your willingness to practice. Here are some sample affirmations. Modify them to suit your individual hopes and dreams, and then practice them. The article "Attitudes, affirmations, and visualizations" explains ways to use these attitude replacements.

I, ______, am healthy.

I, ______, have abundant energy and vitality throughout the day.

I, ______, exercise regularly.

I, ______, work effectively with many different kinds of people.

I, ______, eat wisely.

I, ______, plan my days and use time wisely.

I, ______, have a powerful memory.

I, ______, take tests calmly and confidently.

I, ______, have a sense of self-worth that is independent of my test scores.

I, ______, am a great speller.

I, ______, fall asleep quickly and sleep soundly.

I, ______, am smart.

I, ______, learn quickly.

I, ______, am creative.

I, ______, am aware of and sensitive to other people's moods.

I, ______, have relationships that are mutually satisfying.

I, ______, work hard and contribute to other people through my job.

I, ______, am wealthy.

I, ______, know ways to play and have fun.

I, ______, am attractive.

I, ______, focus my attention easily.

I, ______, like myself.

I, ______, am liked by other people.

I, ______, am a worthwhile person even though I am ______.

I, ______, have a slim and attractive body.

I, ______, am relaxed in all situations, including ______.

I, ______, make profitable financial investments.

I, ______, have an income that far exceeds my expenses.

I, ______, live a life of abundance and prosperity.

I, ______, always live my life in positive ways for the highest good of all people.

To hear an online version of these affirmations, visit the *From Master Student to Master Employee* Website.

Student Website

you toss the basketball, it swishes through the net. Every time you invite someone out on a date, the person says yes. Each test the teacher hands back to you is graded an A. Practice at least once a day.

You can also use visualizations to replay errors. When you make a mistake, replay it in your imagination. After a bad golf shot, stop and imagine yourself making that same shot again, this time very successfully. If you just had a discussion with your roommate that turned into a fight, replay it successfully. Get all of your senses involved. See yourselves calmly talking things over together. Hear the words and feel the pleasure of a successful interaction.

Visualizations and affirmations can restructure your attitudes and behaviors. Be clear about what you want—and then practice it.

I am a Loving Parent!

critical thinking exercise 22

REPROGRAM YOUR ATTITUDE

Affirmations and visualizations can be employed successfully to reprogram your attitudes and behaviors. Use this critical thinking exercise to change your approach to any situation in your life.

Step 1

Pick something in your life that you would like to change. It can be related to anything—relationships, work, money, or personal skills. Below, write a brief description of what you choose to change.

____

____

____

Step 2

Add more details about the change you described in Step 1. Write down how you would like the change to come about. Be outlandish. Imagine that you are about to ask your fairy godmother for a wish that you know she will grant. Be detailed in your description of your wish.

____

____

____

Step 3

Here comes the fairy godmother. Use affirmations and visualizations to start yourself on the path to creating exactly what you wrote about in Step 2. Below, write at least two affirmations that describe your dream wish. Also, briefly outline a visualization that you can use to picture your wish. Be specific, detailed, and positive.

____

____

____

Step 4

Put your new attitudes to work. Set up a schedule to practice them. Let the first time be right now. Then set up at least five other times and places that you intend to practice your affirmations and visualizations.

I intend to relax and practice my affirmations and visualizations for at least five minutes on the following dates and at the time(s) and location(s) given.

Date	*Time*	*Location*
1.		
2.		
3.		
4.		
5.		

Complete this exercise online. Student Website

Gaining skill at *decision making*

We make decisions all the time, whether we realize it or not. Even avoiding decisions is a form of decision making. The student who puts off studying for a test until the last minute might really be saying, "I've decided this course is not important" or "I've decided not to give this course much time." In order to escape such a fate, decide right now to experiment with the following suggestions.

Recognize decisions. Decisions are more than wishes or desires. There's a world of difference between "I wish I could be a better student" and "I will take more powerful notes, read with greater retention, and review my class notes daily." Decisions are specific and lead to focused action. When we decide, we narrow down. We give up actions that are inconsistent with our decision. Deciding to eat fruit for dessert instead of ice cream rules out the next trip to the ice cream store.

Establish priorities. Some decisions are trivial. No matter what the outcome, your life is not affected much. Other decisions can shape your circumstances for years. Devote more time and energy to the decisions with big outcomes.

Base your decisions on a life plan. The benefit of having long-term goals for our lives is that they provide a basis for many of our daily decisions. Being certain about what we want to accomplish this year and this month makes today's choices more clear.

Clarify your values. When you know specifically what's important to you, making decisions becomes easier. As part of a long-term plan for your life, define your values and put them in writing. Saying that you value education is fine. Now give that declaration some teeth. For instance, declare your intention to practice continuous learning as a way to upgrade your career skills.

Choose an overall strategy. Every time you make a decision, you choose a strategy—even when you're not aware of it. Effective decision makers can articulate and choose from among several strategies. For example:

- *Find all of the available options and choose one deliberately.* Save this strategy for times when you have a relatively small number of options, each of which leads to noticeably different results.
- *Find all of the available options and choose one randomly.* This strategy can be risky. Save it for times when your options are basically similar and fairness is the main issue.
- *Limit the options, then choose.* When deciding which search engine to use on the World Wide Web, visit many sites and then narrow the list down to two or three that you choose.

Use time as an ally. Sometimes we face dilemmas—situations in which any course of action leads to undesirable consequences. In such cases, consider putting a decision on hold. Wait it out. Do nothing until the circumstances change, making one alternative clearly preferable to another.

Use intuition. Some decisions seem to make themselves. A solution pops into our mind and we gain newfound clarity. Using intuition is not the same as forgetting about the decision or refusing to make it. Intuitive decisions usually arrive after we've gathered the relevant facts and faced a problem for some time.

Evaluate your decision. Hindsight is a source of insight. After you act on a decision, observe the consequences over time. Reflect on how well your decision worked and what you might have done differently.

Think *choices*. This final suggestion involves some creative thinking. Consider that the word *decide* derives from the same roots as *suicide* and *homicide*. In the spirit of those words, a decision forever "kills" all other options. That's kind of heavy. Instead, use the word *choice* and see if it frees up your thinking. When you *choose*, you express a preference for one option over others. However, those options remain live possibilities for the future. Choose for today, knowing that as you gain more wisdom and experience, you can choose again.

Four ways to solve problems

Think of problem solving as a process with four P's: Define the *problem*, generate *possibilities*, create a *plan*, and *perform* your plan.

1 **Define the problem.** To define a problem effectively, understand what a problem is—a mismatch between what you want and what you have. Problem solving is all about reducing the gap between these two factors.

Start with what you have. Tell the truth about what's present in your life right now, without shame or blame. For example: "I often get sleepy while reading my physics assignments, and after closing the book I cannot remember what I just read."

Next, describe in detail what you want. Go for specifics: "I want to remain alert as I read about physics. I also want to accurately summarize each chapter I read."

Remember that when we define a problem in limiting ways, our solutions merely generate new problems. As Einstein said, "The world we have made is a result of the level of thinking we have done thus far. We cannot solve problems at the same level at which we created them."[4]

This idea has many applications for success in school. An example is the student who struggles with note taking. The problem, she thinks, is that her notes are too sketchy. The logical solution, she decides, is to take more notes, and her new goal is to write down almost everything her instructors say. No matter how fast and furiously she writes, she cannot capture all of the instructors' comments.

Consider what happens when this student defines the problem in a new way. After more thought, she decides that her dilemma is not the *quantity* of her notes but their *quality*. She adopts a new format for taking notes, dividing her note paper into two columns. In the right-hand column, she writes down only the main points of each lecture. And in the left-hand column, she notes two or three supporting details for each point.

Over time, this student makes the joyous discovery that there are usually just three or four core ideas to remember from each lecture. She originally thought the solution was to take more notes. What really worked was taking notes in a new way.

2 **Generate possibilities.** Now put on your creative thinking hat. Open up. Brainstorm as many possible solutions to the problem as you can. At this stage, quantity counts. As you generate possibilities, gather relevant facts. For example, when you're faced with a dilemma about what courses to take next term, get information on class times, locations, and instructors. If you haven't decided which summer job offer to accept, gather information on salary, benefits, and working conditions.

3 **Create a plan.** After rereading your problem definition and list of possible solutions, choose the solution that seems most workable. Think about specific actions that will reduce the gap between what you have and what you want. Visualize the steps you will take to make this solution a reality and arrange them in chronological order. To make your plan even more powerful, put it in writing.

4 **Perform your plan.** This step gets you off your chair and out into the world. Now you actually *do* what you have planned. Ultimately, your skill in solving problems lies in how well you perform your plan. Through the quality of your actions, you become the architect of your own success.

Note that the four P's of this problem-solving process closely parallel the four key questions listed in the article "Becoming a critical thinker":

Define the **problem**	**What** is the problem?
Generate **possibilities**	**What if** there are several possible solutions?
Create a **plan**	**How** would this possible solution work?
Perform your plan	**Why** is one solution more workable than another?

When facing problems, experiment with these four P's, and remember that the order of steps is not absolute. Also remember that any solution has the potential to create new problems. If that happens, cycle through the four P's of problem solving again.

Finding "aha!"

Creativity fuels critical thinking

This chapter offers you a chance to practice two types of critical thinking: convergent thinking and divergent thinking.

Convergent thinking involves a narrowing-down process. Out of all the possible viewpoints on an issue or alternative solutions to a problem, you choose the one that is the most reasonable or that provides the most logical basis for action.

Some people see convergent thinking and critical thinking as the same thing. However, there's more to critical thinking. Before you choose among viewpoints, generate as many of them as possible. Open up alternatives and consider all of your options. Define problems in different ways. Keep asking questions and looking for answers. This opening-up process is called *divergent* or *creative thinking*.

Creative thinking provides the basis for convergent thinking. In other words, one path toward having good ideas is to have *lots* of ideas. Then you can pick and choose from among them, combining and refining them as you see fit.

Choose when to think creatively. The key is to make conscious choices about what kind of thinking to do in any given moment. Generally speaking, creative thinking is more appropriate in the early stages of planning and problem solving. Feel free to dwell in this domain for a while. If you narrow down your options too soon, you run the risk of missing an exciting solution or of neglecting a novel viewpoint.

Remember that creative thinking and convergent thinking take place in a continuous cycle. After you've used convergent thinking to narrow down your options, you can return to creative thinking at any time to generate new ones.

Cultivate "aha!" Central to creative thinking is something called the "aha!" experience. Nineteenth-century poet Emily Dickinson described aha! this way: "If I feel physically as if the top of my head were taken off, I know that is poetry." Aha! is the burst of creative energy heralded by the arrival of a new, original idea. It is the sudden emergence of an unfamiliar pattern, a previously undetected relationship, or an unusual combination of familiar elements. It is an exhilarating experience.

Aha! does not always result in a timeless poem or a Nobel Prize. It can be inspired by anything from playing a new riff on a guitar to figuring out why your car's fuel pump doesn't work. A nurse might notice a patient's symptom that everyone else missed. That's an aha! An accountant might discover a tax break for a client. That's an aha! A teacher might devise a way to reach a difficult student. Aha!

Follow through. The flip side of aha! is following through. Thinking is both fun and work. It is effortless and uncomfortable. It's the result of luck and persistence. It involves spontaneity and step-by-step procedures, planning and action, convergent and creative thinking.

Companies that depend on developing new products and services need people who can find aha! and do something with it. The necessary skills include the ability to spot assumptions, weigh evidence, separate fact from opinion, organize thoughts, and avoid errors in logic. All of this can be demanding work. Just as often, it can be energizing and fun.

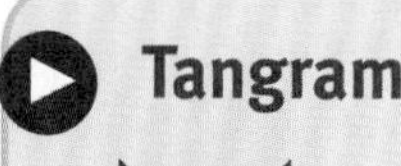

Tangram

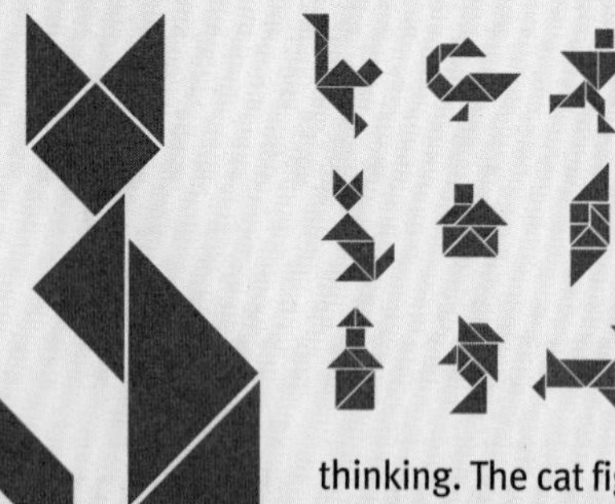

A tangram is an ancient Chinese puzzle game that stimulates the "play instinct" so critical to creative thinking. The cat figure here was created by rearranging seven sections of a square. Hundreds of images can be devised in this manner. Playing with tangrams allows us to see relationships we didn't notice before.

The rules of the game are simple: Use these seven pieces to create something that wasn't there before. Be sure to use all seven. You might start by mixing up the pieces and seeing whether you can put them back together to form a square.

Make your own tangram by cutting pieces like those above out of poster board. When you come up with a pattern you like, trace around the outside edges of it and see if a friend can discover how you did it.

Ways to *create ideas*

Anyone can think creatively. Use the following techniques to generate ideas about everything, whether you're studying math problems, remodeling a house, or writing a bestseller. With practice, you can set the stage for creative leaps, jump with style, and land on your feet with brand-new ideas in hand.

Conduct a brainstorm. Brainstorming is a technique for finding solutions, creating plans, and discovering new ideas. When you are stuck on a problem, brainstorming can break the logjam. For example, if you run out of money two days before payday every week, you can brainstorm ways to make your money last longer. You can brainstorm ways to pay for your education. You can brainstorm ways to find a job.

The purpose of brainstorming is to generate as many solutions as possible. Sometimes the craziest, most outlandish ideas, while unworkable in themselves, can lead to new ways to solve problems. Use the following steps to try out the brainstorming process.

- *Focus on a single problem or issue.* State your focus as a question. Open-ended questions that start with the words *what, how, who, where,* and *when* often make effective focusing questions.
- *Relax.* Creativity is enhanced by a state of relaxed alertness. If you are tense or anxious, use relaxation techniques such as those described in "Let go of test anxiety" in Chapter Six.
- *Set a quota or goal for the number of solutions you want to generate.* Goals give your subconscious mind something to aim for.
- *Set a time limit.* Use a clock to time it to the minute. Digital sports watches with built-in stopwatches work well. Experiment with various lengths of time. Both short and long brainstorms can be powerful.
- *Allow all answers.* Brainstorming is based on attitudes of permissiveness and patience. Accept every idea. If it pops into your head, put it down on paper. Quantity, not quality, is the goal. Avoid making judgments and evaluations during the brainstorming session. If you get stuck, think of an outlandish idea and write it down. One crazy idea can unleash a flood of other, more workable solutions.
- *Brainstorm with others.* This is a powerful technique. Group brainstorms take on lives of their own. Assign one member of the group to write down solutions. Feed off the ideas of others, and remember to avoid evaluating or judging anyone's idea during the brainstorm.
- *Avoid groupthink.* Sometimes brainstorming sessions backfire or fizzle out. The problem might

be groupthink—allowing the most verbal people to dominate the session and ignoring unpopular but worthy solutions just to come to a decision quickly. This can limit the number of options that the group creates. To avoid this situation, ask all members of the group for contributions and avoid discussing any of the options until the session is over.

After your brainstorming session, evaluate the results. Toss out any truly nutty ideas, but not before you give them a chance.

Focus and let go. Focusing and letting go are alternating parts of the same process. Intense focus taps the resources of your conscious mind. Letting go gives your subconscious mind time to work. When you focus for intense periods and then let go for a while, the conscious and subconscious parts of your brain work in harmony.

Focusing attention means being in the here and now. To focus your attention on a project, notice when you pay attention and when your mind starts to wander. And involve all of your senses. For example, if you are having difficulty writing a paper at a computer, practice focusing by listening to the sounds as you type. Notice the feel of the keys as you strike them. When you know the sights, sounds, and sensations you associate with being truly in focus, you'll be able to repeat the experience and return to your paper more easily.

Be willing to recognize conflict, tension, and discomfort. Notice them and fully accept them rather than fight against them. Look for the specific thoughts and body sensations that make up the discomfort. Allow them to come fully into your awareness, and then let them pass.

You might not be focused all of the time. Periods of inspiration might last only seconds. Be gentle with yourself when you notice that your concentration has lapsed. In fact, that might be a time to let go. "Letting go" means not forcing yourself to be creative. Practice focusing for short periods at first, then give yourself a break. Take a nap when you are tired. Thomas Edison took frequent naps. Then the light bulb clicked on.

Cultivate creative serendipity. The word *serendipity* was coined by the English author Horace Walpole from the title of an ancient Persian fairy tale, "The Three Princes of Serendip." The princes had a knack for making lucky discoveries. Serendipity is that knack, and it involves more than luck. It is the ability to see something valuable that you weren't looking for.

History is full of serendipitous people. Country doctor Edward Jenner noticed "by accident" that milkmaids seldom got smallpox. The result was his discovery that mild cases of cowpox immunized them. Penicillin was also discovered "by accident." Scottish scientist Alexander Fleming was growing bacteria in a laboratory petri dish. A spore of *Penicillium notatum,* a kind of mold, blew in the window and landed in the dish, killing the bacteria. Fleming isolated the active ingredient. A few years later, during World War II, it saved thousands of lives. Had Fleming not been alert to the possibility, the discovery might never have been made.

You can train yourself in the art of serendipity. Keep your eyes open. You might find a solution to an accounting problem in a Saturday morning cartoon. You might discover a topic for your term paper at the corner convenience store. Multiply your contacts with the world. Resolve to meet new people. Join a study or discussion group. Read. Go to plays, concerts, art shows, lectures, and movies. Watch television programs you normally wouldn't watch.

Also expect discoveries. One secret for success is being prepared to recognize "luck" when you see it.

Keep idea files. We all have ideas. People who treat their ideas with care are often labeled "creative." They not only recognize ideas but also record them and follow up on them.

One way to keep track of ideas is to write them down on 3 × 5 cards. Invent your own categories and number the cards so you can cross-reference them. For example, if you have an idea about making a new kind of bookshelf, you might file a card under "Remodeling." A second card might also be filed under "Marketable Ideas." On the first card, you can write down your ideas, and on the second, you can write "See card #321—Remodeling."

Include in your files powerful quotations, random insights, notes on your reading, and useful ideas that you encounter in class. Collect jokes, too.

Keep a journal. Journals don't have to be exclusively about your own thoughts and feelings. You can record observations about the world around you, conversations with friends, important or offbeat ideas—anything.

To fuel your creativity, read voraciously, including newspapers and magazines. Keep a clip file of interesting articles. Explore beyond mainstream journalism. There are hundreds of low-circulation specialty magazines and online news journals that cover almost any subject you can imagine.

Keep letter-size file folders of important correspondence, magazine and news articles, and other material. You can also create idea files on a computer using word processing, outlining, or database software.

Safeguard your ideas, even if you're pressed for time. Jotting down four or five words is enough to capture the essence of an idea. You can write down one quotation in a minute or two. And if you carry 3 × 5 cards in a pocket or purse, you can record ideas while standing in line or sitting in a waiting room.

Review your files regularly. Some amusing thought that came to you in November might be the perfect solution to a problem in March.

Collect and play with data. Look from all sides at the data you collect. Switch your attention from one aspect to another. Examine each fact, and avoid getting stuck on one particular part of a problem. Turn a problem upside down by picking a solution first and then working backward. Ask other people to look at the data. Solicit opinions.

Living with the problem invites a solution. Write down data, possible solutions, or a formulation of the problem on 3 × 5 cards and carry them with you. Look at them before you go to bed at night. Review them when you are waiting for the bus. Make them part of your life and think about them frequently.

Look for the obvious solutions or the obvious "truths" about the problem—then toss them out. Ask yourself: "Well, I know X is true, but if X were *not* true, what would happen?" Or ask the reverse: "If that *were* true, what would follow next?"

Put unrelated facts next to each other and invent a relationship between them, even if it seems absurd at first. In *The Act of Creation,* novelist Arthur Koestler says that finding a context in which to combine opposites is the essence of creativity.[5]

Make imaginary pictures with the data. Condense it. Categorize it. Put it in chronological order. Put it in alphabetical order. Put it in random order. Order it from most to least complex. Reverse all of those orders. Look for opposites.

It has been said that there are no new ideas—only new ways to combine old ideas. Creativity is the ability to discover those new combinations.

Create while you sleep. A part of our mind works as we sleep. You've experienced this directly if you've ever fallen asleep with a problem on your mind and awakened the next morning with a solution. For some of us, the solution appears in a dream or just before falling asleep or waking up.

You can experiment with this process. Ask yourself a question as you fall asleep. Keep pencil and paper or a recorder near your bed. The moment you wake up, begin writing or speaking and see if an answer to your question emerges.

Many of us have awakened from a dream with a great idea, only to fall asleep and lose it forever. To capture your ideas, keep a notebook by your bed at all times. Put the notebook where you can find it easily.

There is a story about how Benjamin Franklin used this suggestion. Late in the evenings, as he was becoming drowsy, he would sit in his rocking chair with a rock in his right hand and a metal bucket on the floor beneath the rock. The moment he fell asleep, the rock would fall from his grip into the bottom of the bucket, making a loud noise that awakened him. Having placed a pen and paper nearby, he immediately wrote down what he was thinking. Experience taught him that his thoughts at this moment were often insightful and creative.

Refine ideas and follow through. Many of us ignore this part of the creative process. How many great moneymaking schemes have we had that we never pursued? How many good ideas have we had for short stories that we never wrote? How many times have we said to ourselves, "You know, what they ought to do is attach two handles to one of those things, paint it orange, and sell it to police departments. They'd make a fortune." And we never realize that we are "they."

Genius resides in the follow-through—the application of perspiration to inspiration. One powerful tool you can use to follow through is the Discovery and Intention Journal Entry system. First write down your idea in a Discovery Statement, and then write what you intend to do about it in an Intention Statement. You also can explore the writing techniques discussed in Chapter Eight: Communicating as a guide for refining your ideas.

Another way to refine an idea is to simplify it. And if that doesn't work, mess it up. Make it more complex.

Finally, keep a separate file in your ideas folder for your own inspirations. Return to it regularly to see if there is anything you can use. Today's defunct term paper idea could be next year's A in speech class.

Create success strategies. Use creative thinking techniques to go beyond the pages of this book and create your own ways to succeed in school. Read other books on success. Interview successful people. Reflect on any of your current behaviors that help you do well in school. Change any habits that fail to serve you.

If you have created a study group with people from one of your classes, set aside time to talk about ways to succeed in any class. Challenge each other to practice your powers of invention. Test any new strategies you create and report to the group on how well they're working for you.

Trust the process. Learn to trust the creative process—even when no answers are in sight. We are often reluctant to look at problems if no immediate solution is at hand. Trust that a solution will show up. Frustration and a feeling of being stuck are often signals that a solution is imminent.

Sometimes solutions break through in a giant AHA! More often they come in a series of little aha!s. Be aware of what your aha!s look, feel, and sound like. That sets the stage for even more flights of creative thinking.

Create on your feet

A popular trend in executive offices is the "stand-up" desk—a raised working surface at which you stand rather than sit.

Standing has advantages over sitting for long periods. You can stay more alert and creative when you're on your feet. One theory is that our problem-solving ability improves when we stand due to increased heart rate and blood flow to the brain.

Standing can ease lower-back pain, too. Sitting for too long aggravates the spine and its supporting muscles.

This is a technique with tradition. If you search the Web for stand-up desks, you'll find models based on desks used by Thomas Jefferson, Winston Churchill, and writer Virginia Woolf. Consider setting your desk up on blocks or putting a box on top of your desk so that you can stand while writing, preparing speeches, or studying. Discover how long you can stand comfortably while working, and whether this approach works for you.

Uncovering *assumptions*

Consider the following argument:

> Orca whales mate for life.
> Orca whales travel in family groups.
> Science has revealed that Orca whales are intelligent.
> Therefore, Orca whales should be saved from extinction.

One idea underlies this line of thought:

> Any animal that displays significant human characteristics deserves special protection.

Whether or not you agree with this argument, consider for a moment the process of making assumptions. Assumptions are assertions that guide our thinking and behavior. Often these assertions are unconscious. People can remain unaware of their most basic and far-reaching assumptions—the very ideas that shape their lives.

Spotting assumptions can be tricky because they are usually unstated and offered without evidence. And scores of assumptions can be held at the same time. Those assumptions might even contradict each other, resulting in muddled thinking and confused behavior. This makes uncovering assumptions a feat worthy of the greatest detective.

Letting assumptions remain in our subconscious can erect barriers to our success. Take the person who says, "I don't worry about saving money for the future. I think life is meant to be enjoyed today—not later." This statement rests on at least two assumptions: *saving money is not enjoyable*, and *we can enjoy ourselves only when we're spending money.*

It would be no surprise to find out that this person runs out of money near the end of each month and depends on cash advances from high-interest credit cards. She is shielding herself from some ideas that could erase her debt: Saving money can be a source of satisfaction, and many enjoyable activities cost nothing.

The stakes in uncovering assumptions are high. Prejudice thrives on the beliefs that certain people are inferior or dangerous due to their skin color, ethnic background, or sexual orientation. Those beliefs have led to flawed assumptions such as *mixing the blood of the races will lead to genetically inferior offspring* and *racial integration of the armed forces will lead to the destruction of morale.*

When we remain ignorant of our assumptions, we also make it easier for people with hidden agendas to do our thinking for us. Demagogues and unethical advertisers know that unchallenged assumptions are potent tools for influencing our attitudes and behavior.

Take this claim from an advertisement: "Successful students have large vocabularies, so sign up today for our seminar on word power!" Embedded in this sentence are several assumptions. One is that a cause-and-effect relationship exists between a large vocabulary and success in school. Another is that a large vocabulary is the single or most important factor in that success. This claim also assumes that the advertiser's seminar is the best way to develop your vocabulary. In reality, none of these assumptions is necessarily true.

Assertions and opinions flow from our assumptions. Heated conflict and hard feelings often result when people argue on the level of opinions—forgetting that the real conflict lies at the level of their assumptions.

An example is the question about whether the government should fund public works programs that create jobs during a recession. People who advocate such programs might assume that creating such jobs is an appropriate task for the federal government. On the other hand, people who argue against such programs might assume that the government has no business interfering with the free workings of the economy. There's little hope of resolving this conflict of opinion unless we deal with something more basic: our assumptions about the proper role of government.

You can follow a three-step method for testing the validity of any viewpoint. First, look for the assumptions—the assertions implied by that viewpoint. Second, write down these assumptions. Third, see if you can find any exceptions to them. This technique helps detect many errors in logic.

Ways to *fool* yourself

Common mistakes in logic

Logic is a branch of philosophy that seeks to distinguish between effective and ineffective reasoning. Students of logic look for valid steps in an *argument*, or a series of assertions. The opening assertions of the argument are the premises, and the final assertion is the conclusion.

Over the last 2,500 years, specialists in logic have listed some classic land mines in the field of logic—common mistakes in thinking that are called *fallacies*. The study of fallacies could fill a year-long course. Following are twelve examples to get you started. Knowing about them before you string together a bunch of assertions can help you avoid getting fooled.

1 Jumping to conclusions. Jumping to conclusions is the only exercise that some lazy thinkers get. This fallacy involves drawing conclusions without sufficient evidence. Take the bank officer who hears about a student failing to pay back an education loan. After that, the officer turns down all loan applications from students. This person has formed a rigid opinion on the basis of hearsay. Jumping to conclusions—also called *hasty generalization*—is at work here.

2 Attacking the person. This mistake in logic is common at election time. An example is the candidate who claims that her opponent has failed to attend church regularly during the campaign. People who indulge in personal attacks are attempting an intellectual sleight of hand to divert our attention from the truly relevant issues.

3 Appealing to authority. A professional athlete endorses a brand of breakfast cereal. A famous musician features a soft drink company's product in a rock video. The promotional brochure for an advertising agency lists all of the large companies that have used its services.

In each case, the people involved are trying to win your confidence—and your dollars—by citing authorities. The underlying assumption is usually this: *Famous people and organizations buy our product. Therefore, you should buy it too.* Or: *You should accept this idea merely because someone who's well known says it's true.*

Appealing to authority is usually a substitute for producing real evidence. It invites sloppy thinking. When our only evidence for a viewpoint is an appeal to authority, it's time to think more thoroughly.

4 Pointing to a false cause. The fact that one event follows another does not necessarily mean that the two events have a cause-and-effect relationship. All we can actually say is that the events might be correlated. For example, as children's vocabularies improve, they can get more cavities. This does not mean that cavities are the result of an improved vocabulary. Instead, the increase in cavities is due to other factors, such as physical maturation and changes in diet or personal care.

5 Thinking in all-or-nothing terms. Consider these statements: *Doctors are greedy. . . . You can't trust politicians. . . . Students these days are in school just to get high-paying jobs; they lack idealism. . . . Homeless people don't want to work.*

These opinions imply the word *all*. They gloss over individual differences, claiming that all members of a group are exactly alike. They also ignore key facts, for instance, that some doctors volunteer their time at free medical clinics and that many homeless people are children who are too young to work. All-or-nothing thinking is one of the most common errors in logic.

6 Basing arguments on emotion. The politician who ends every campaign speech with flag waving and slides of her mother eating apple pie is staking her future on appeals to emotion. So is the candidate who paints a grim scenario of the disaster and ruination that will transpire unless she is elected. Get past the fluff and histrionics to see if you can uncover any worthwhile ideas.

7 Faulty analogy. An *analogy* states a similarity between two things or events. Some arguments rest on analogies that hide significant differences. On June 25, 1987, the Associated Press reported an example: U.S. Representative Tom DeLay opposed a bill to ban chlordane, a pesticide that causes cancer in laboratory animals. Supporting this bill, he argued, is like banning cars because they kill people. DeLay's analogy was faulty. Banning automobiles would have a far greater impact on society than banning a single pesticide, especially if safer pesticides are available.

8 Creating a straw man. The name of this fallacy comes from the scarecrow traditionally placed in gardens to ward off birds. A scarecrow works because it looks like a man. Likewise, a person can attack ideas that *sound like* his opponent's ideas but are actually absurd. For example, some legislators attacked the Equal Rights Amendment by describing it as a measure to abolish separate bathrooms for men and women. In fact, supporters of this amendment proposed no such thing.

9 Begging the question. Speakers and writers "beg the question" when their colorful language glosses over an idea that is unclear or unproven. Consider this statement: *Support the American tradition of individual liberty and oppose mandatory seat belt laws!* Anyone who makes such a statement "begs" (fails to answer) a key question: Are laws that require drivers to use seat belts actually a violation of individual liberty?

10 Confusing fact and opinion. Facts are statements verified by direct observation or compelling evidence that creates widespread agreement. In recent years, some politicians argued for tax cuts on the grounds that the American economy needed to create more jobs. However, it's not a fact that tax cuts automatically create more jobs. This statement is almost impossible to verify by direct observation, and there's evidence against it.

11 Creating a red herring. When hunters want to throw a dog off a trail, they can drag a smoked red herring (or some other food with a strong odor) over the ground in the opposite direction. This distracts the dog, who is fooled into following a false trail. Likewise, people can send our thinking on false trails by raising irrelevant issues. Case in point: In 2006, some people who opposed a presidential campaign by U.S. Senator Barack Obama emphasized his middle name: Hussein. This was an irrelevant attempt to link the senator to Saddam Hussein, the dictator and former ruler of Iraq.

12 Appealing to tradition. Arguments based on this fallacy take a classic form: *Our current beliefs and behaviors have a long history; therefore, they are correct.* This argument has been used to justify the divine right of kings, feudalism, witch burnings, slavery, child labor, and a host of other traditions that are now rejected. Appeals to tradition ignore that fact that unsound ideas can survive for centuries before human beings realize that they are being fooled.

Thinking critically *about information on the* Internet

Sources of information on the Internet range from the reputable (such as the Library of Congress) to the flamboyant (such as the *National Enquirer*). This fact underscores the need for thinking critically about everything you see online. People are free to post *anything* on the Internet, including outdated facts as well as intentional misinformation. Taking a few simple precautions when you surf the Internet can keep you from crashing onto the rocky shore of misinformation.

Look for overall quality. Examine the features of the Website in general. Notice the effectiveness of the text and visuals as a whole. Also note how well the site is organized and whether you can navigate the site's features with ease. Look for the date that crucial information was posted, and determine how often the site is updated.

Next, take a more detailed look at the site's content. Examine several of the site's pages and look for consistency of facts, quality of information, and competency with grammar and spelling. Are the links easy to follow?

Also evaluate the site's links to related Web pages. Look for links to pages of reputable organizations. Click on a few of those links. If they lead you to dead ends, this might indicate a site that's not updated often—one that's not a reliable source for late-breaking information.

Look at the source. Think about the credibility of the person or organization that posts a Website. Look for a list of author credentials and publications.

Notice evidence of bias or special interest. Perhaps the site's sponsoring organization wants you to buy a service, a product, or a point of view. If so, determine whether this fact colors the ideas and information posted on the Website.

The domain in the Uniform Resource Locator (URL) for a Website can give you clues about sources of information and possible bias. For example, distinguish among information from a for-profit commercial enterprise (URL ending in .com); a nonprofit organization (.org); a government agency (.gov); and a school, college, or university (.edu).

Reputable sites usually include a way for you to contact the author or sponsoring organization outside the Internet, including a mailing address and phone number. If you question a site, ask a librarian or your professor for help in evaluating it.

Note: Peer-edited sites such as Wikipedia do not employ editors to screen out errors and scrutinize questionable material before publication. Do not use these cites when researching a paper or presentation.

Look for documentation. When you encounter an assertion on a Web page or some other Internet resource, note the types and quality of the evidence offered. Look for credible examples, quotations from authorities in the field, documented statistics, or summaries of scientific studies. Also look for source notes, bibliographies, or another way to find the original sources of information on your own.

critical thinking exercise 23

EVALUATE SEARCH SITES

Access several popular search sites on the Web, such as:

Alta Vista	**www.altavista.com**
Ask.com	**www.ask.com**
Dogpile	**www.dogpile.com**
Excite	**www.excite.com**
Google	**www.google.com**
HotBot	**www.hotbot.com**
Yahoo!	**www.yahoo.com**

Then choose a specific topic that you'd like to research—preferably one related to a paper or other assignment that you will complete this term. Identify keywords for this topic and enter them in several search sites. (Open up a different window or tab in your browser for each site.) Be sure to use the same keywords each time that you search.

Next, evaluate the search sites by comparing the results that you got. Based on this evaluation, keep a list of your favorite search sites.

Overcome stereotypes *with critical thinking*

The word *stereotype* originally referred to a method used by printers to produce duplicate pages of text. This usage still rings true. When we stereotype, we gloss over individual differences and assume that every member of a group is the same.

People are stereotyped on the basis of their race, ethnic group, religion, political affiliation, geographic location, job, age, gender, IQ, height, or hobby. We stereotype people based on everything from the color of their hair to the year of their car.

Stereotypes involve general statements about groups of people. In themselves, general statements are neither good nor bad. In fact, they are essential. Mentally sorting people, events, and objects into groups allows us to make sense of the world. But when we make general statements that divide the people of the world into "us" versus "them," we create stereotypes and put on the blinders of prejudice.

You can take several steps to free yourself from stereotypes.

Look for errors in thinking. Some of the most common errors in stereotyping are:

- *Selective perception.* Stereotypes can literally change the way we see the world. If we assume that homeless people are lazy, for instance, we tend to notice only the examples that support our opinion. Stories about homeless people who are too young or too ill to work will probably escape our attention.
- *Self-fulfilling prophecy.* When we interact with people based on stereotypes, we set them up in ways that confirm our thinking. For example, when people of color were denied access to higher education based on stereotypes about their intelligence, they were deprived of opportunities to demonstrate their intellectual gifts.
- *Self-justification.* Stereotypes can allow people to assume the role of a victim and to avoid taking responsibility for their own lives. An unemployed white male might believe that affirmative action programs are making it impossible for him to get a job—even as he overlooks his own lack of experience or qualifications.

Test your generalizations about people through action. You can do this by actually meeting people of other cultures. It's easy to believe almost anything about certain groups of people as long as we never deal directly with individuals. Inaccurate pictures tend to die when people from different cultures study together, work together, and live together. Consider joining a school or community organization that will put you in contact with people of other cultures. Your rewards will include a more global perspective and an ability to thrive in a multicultural world. ✕

critical thinking exercise 24

EXAMINE ASSUMPTIONS ABOUT DIVERSITY

On separate paper, write down the first words that come to mind when you hear the terms listed below. Do this now.

musician
homeless people
football players
computer programmers
disabled person
retired person
adult learner

Next, exchange your responses to this exercise with a friend. Did you discover stereotypes or other examples of bias? What counts as evidence of bias? Summarize your answers here.

Thinking critically about career planning

One practical way to develop transferable skills in critical thinking is to apply them to career planning.

In conversations about career planning, you might hear statements such as the following:

1. The best way to plan a career is to enter a "hot" field with a lot of job openings.
2. I should choose a major that's directly related to my career.
3. I should have a clear idea of what I want to do *before* I go to the career planning center at my school.
4. I'm just a freshman, so it's too early to think about career planning.
5. Once I send out résumés or post them on the Internet, I can sit back and watch the job offers roll in.
6. Money is the main factor to consider when responding to job offers.

Listed below are *opposites* of the ideas stated above—statements that are reworded in a positive, proactive way. Consider ways that they could apply to your life.

1 I can plan a career in a field that I enjoy. Even in fields that are highly competitive, there are openings for qualified people. And the careers that are "hot" with plenty of job openings today may be "cool" by the time you graduate. In a constantly changing job market, following your own interests and values can be just as reliable as chasing current trends.

2 I can choose a major that interests me and balance it with activities to enhance my career. Students who are drawn to liberal arts sometimes deny their interests in favor of a more "lucrative" major. In many cases this is unnecessary. For example, Ted Turner majored in classical literature—a choice that appalled his father. Turner later established sports and media empires that turned him into a billionaire. And he's not unusual. Surveys indicate that nearly half of America's chief executive officers chose liberal arts majors.[6]

It's true that some careers require a specific undergraduate major. However, many careers are open to people with a variety of majors. To multiply your career options, choose a major that you love. Then round out your education with internships, service learning, and work-study assignments that create job contacts for the future.

3 I can use career-planning services to gain clarity about my future. Career-planning services are *designed* for people who have not yet chosen a career. Besides, your tuition dollars are helping to pay for these services. Make an appointment to use them today.

4 I can benefit by planning my career right now. Effective career planning and job hunting take time. Plan now to take career inventories, research the job market, do information interviews, set up internships, start a résumé, and practice job interviewing skills. Many graduates will tell you that they wish they'd started these things as freshmen.

5 I can find fulfilling work by using a variety of job-hunting methods. When you send out a résumé or post one on the Internet, you could be competing with hundreds of other candidates for the same jobs. Remember, it's not a résumé that gets you a job—it's a job interview. Skilled job hunters use a variety of methods, such as doing information interviews and joining professional associations. These activities help people develop a large network of contacts in their career field.

6 I can make powerful career choices by considering money along with other factors. Salary ranges are important, and they're only part of the picture. Job satisfaction also hinges on factors such as location, company culture, length of the workweek, relationships with coworkers, opportunities for advancement, and chances to make a worthwhile contribution. When weighing job offers, consider these factors as well. ☒

Making ethical decisions at work

One of the most important transferable skills you can develop is ethical decision making and acting with integrity. It pays to think through potential issues now.

Heed signs of trouble

One key to avoiding problems is staying alert to signs of impending ethical problems. You might find it easier to stop unethical behavior in its early stages—before it becomes habitual or widespread.

According to *Setting the Standard*, published by the Office of Ethics and Business Conduct at Lockheed Martin Corporation, you're probably walking on thin ethical ice when you hear the following statements as justifications for taking a certain action:

- "It doesn't matter how it gets done as long as it gets done."
- "Everyone does it."
- "Shred that document."
- "We can hide it."
- "No one will get hurt."
- "We didn't have this conversation."[7]

Consider three classic ethical theories

Some philosophers and religious teachers say that right and wrong choices are determined by universal rules that apply to all people at all times. Others hold that a given behavior might be ethical in some situations but unethical in others. This debate has focused on three elements of behavior:

Intention. Suppose that a consultant plans to take one of her clients out for dinner and drinks with the intention of seducing him afterward. The client cancels at the last minute, so the supervisor never gets a chance to act on her plan. According to some theorists, the consultant is ethically at fault for her goal even though she never had the opportunity to achieve it. This argument rests on the idea that our intentions shape our character as much as our behaviors.

Consequences. According to this theory, a supervisor might argue that he can ethically lay off two people in his department without two weeks' notice—if doing so lowers costs enough to save the jobs of four people across the company as a whole during a financial crisis. This is sometimes called "the greatest good for the greatest number" school of ethics.

Action. Some ethicists deny that either intentions or consequences are a reliable guide to making ethical decisions. We can seldom be sure of another person's intentions, and often we cannot accurately predict the consequences of an action. For this reason, some ethicists focus on the action itself. These people argue that ethical behavior is consistent with enduring, universal principles for behavior. An example is the Golden Rule: Do unto others as you would have them do unto you.

Create an ethics checklist

Start with a working definition of ethics as using moral standards to guide your behavior. Next, turn your personal moral standards into a checklist of pointed questions that you can use to make choices in daily life. Though there is no formula for making ethical decisions, you can gain clarity with questions that can be answered yes or no. Following is a sample checklist:

Is this action legal?	[ ] Yes [ ] No
Is this action consistent with my organization's mission, goals, and policies?	[ ] Yes [ ] No
Is this action consistent with my personal values?	[ ] Yes [ ] No
If I continue to make choices such as this, will I be happy with the kind of person I become?	[ ] Yes [ ] No
Will this action stand the test of time? Will I be able to defend this action tomorrow, next month, and next year?	[ ] Yes [ ] No
In taking this action, am I setting an example that I wish others to follow?	[ ] Yes [ ] No
Am I willing to make this decision public—to share it wholeheartedly with my boss, my family, and my friends? Would I feel confident if an article about my decision was published in tomorrow's newspaper?	[ ] Yes [ ] No
Has everyone who will be affected by this decision had the chance to voice their concerns?	[ ] Yes [ ] No

power process

FIND A BIGGER PROBLEM

Most of the time we view problems as barriers. They are a source of inconvenience and annoyance. They get in our way and prevent us from having happy and productive lives. When we see problems in this way, our goal becomes to eliminate problems.

This point of view might be flawed. For one thing, it is impossible to live a life without problems. Besides, they serve a purpose. They are opportunities to participate in life. Problems stimulate us and pull us forward.

Seen from this perspective, the goal becomes not to eliminate problems, but to find problems that are worthy of us. Worthy problems are those that draw on our talents, move us toward our purpose, and increase our skills. The challenge is to tackle those problems that provide the greatest benefits for others and ourselves. Viewed in this way, problems give meaning to our lives.

Problems fill the available space

Problems seem to follow the same law of physics that gases do: They expand to fill whatever space is available. If your only problem is to write a follow-up letter to a job interview, you can spend the entire day thinking about what you're going to say, writing the letter, finding a stamp, going to the post office—and then thinking about all of the things you forgot to say. If, on that same day, you also need to go food shopping, the problem of the letter shrinks to make room for a trip to the grocery store. If you want to buy a car, too, it's amazing how quickly and easily the letter and the grocery shopping tasks are finished. One way to handle little problems is to find bigger ones. Remember that the smaller problems still need to be solved. The goal is to solve them in less time and with less energy.

Bigger problems are plentiful

Bigger problems are not in short supply. Consider world hunger. Every minute of every day, people die because they don't have enough to eat. Also consider nuclear war, which threatens to end life on the planet. Child abuse, environmental pollution, terrorism, human rights violations, drug abuse, street crime, energy shortages, poverty, and wars throughout the world await your attention and involvement. You can make a contribution.

Play full out

Considering bigger problems does not have to be depressing. In fact, it can be energizing—a reason for getting up in the morning. Taking on a huge project can provide a means to channel your passion and purpose.

Some people spend vast amounts of time in activities they consider boring: their jobs, their hobbies, their relationships. They find themselves going through the motions, doing the same walk-on part day after day without passion or intensity. American author Henry David Thoreau described this kind of existence as "lives of quiet desperation."

Playing full out suggests another possibility: We can spend much of our time fully focused and involved. We can experience efficiency and enthusiasm as natural parts of our daily routines. Energy and vitality can accompany most of our activities.

When we take on a bigger problem, we play full out. We do justice to our potentials. We then love what we do and do what we love. We're awake, alert, and engaged. Playing full out means living our lives as if our lives depended on it.

You can make a difference

Perhaps a little voice in your mind is saying, "That's crazy. I can't do anything about global problems" or "Everyone knows that hunger has always been around and always will be, and there is nothing anyone can do about it." These thoughts might prevent you from taking on bigger problems.

Realize that you *can* make a difference. Your thoughts and actions can change the quality of life on the planet.

This is your life. It's your school, your city, your country, and your world. Own it. Inhabit it. Treat it with the same care that you would a prized possession.

One way to find problems that are worthy of your talents and energies is to take on bigger ones. Take responsibility for problems that are bigger than you are sure you can handle. Then notice how your other problems dwindle in importance—or even vanish.

Worthy problems are those that draw on our talents, move us toward our purpose, and increase our skills.

critical thinking exercise 25

FIX-THE-WORLD BRAINSTORM

This exercise works well with four to six people. Pick a major world problem such as hunger, nuclear proliferation, poverty, terrorism, overpopulation, or pollution. Then conduct a 10-minute brainstorm about the steps an individual could take to contribute to solving the problem.

Use the brainstorming techniques explained earlier in this chapter. Remember not to evaluate or judge the solutions during the process. The purpose of a brainstorm is to generate a flow of ideas and record them all.

After the brainstorming session, discuss the process and the solutions that it generated. Did you feel any energy from the group? Was a long list of ideas generated? Are several of them worth pursuing?

career application

Maria Sanchez graduated with an associate's degree in legal assistance and has been working for two years as a paralegal at a large law firm.

Maria's work is supervised by an attorney who is ultimately responsible for the documents she produces. As a paralegal, she cannot set legal fees, give legal advice, or present cases in court. Except for these restrictions, however, she does many of the same things that lawyers do. Maria's current job centers on legal research—identifying laws, judicial decisions, legal articles, and other materials that are relevant to her assigned cases.

Maria is one of three paralegals who work with her supervising attorney. Recently she applied for a new paralegal job that opened up in the firm. In addition to legal research, this job involves drafting legal arguments and motions to be filed in court. Getting this job would mean a promotion and a raise for Maria.

Maria has formally applied for the job and expressed strong interest in it. She believes that her chances are excellent. One of the paralegals she works with is not interested in the job, and she knows that the other one plans to announce next month that she's quitting the firm to attend law school.

One day, Maria finds the first draft of an e-mail that her supervisor has printed out and accidentally placed in a stack of legal documents for Maria to file. The e-mail is a note of congratulations that offers the new paralegal job to the person who plans to quit. ☒

Reflecting on this scenario

1. Does Maria face an ethical dilemma in this situation? Explain your answer.

____

____

____

____

____

____

2. Review the guidelines for decision making given in this chapter—particularly the suggestions for ethical decision making. Choose one and explain how Maria could apply it.

____

____

____

____

____

____

3. This chapter includes a suggestion that you create your own checklist for ethical decision making. (If you have not done this, do it now.) Does your checklist offer any guidelines for Maria? If so, explain.

____

____

____

____

____

____

quiz

Name ____ Date _____/_____/_____

1. List four questions that can guide you on your path to becoming a critical thinker.

2. Explain what is meant in this chapter by *aha!*

3. Define *serendipity* and give an example.

4. List and briefly describe three ways to create ideas.

5. List three questions you could ask yourself when making an ethical decision at work.

6. According to the text, *critical thinking* and *thorough thinking* are two distinct and different activities. True or False? Explain your answer.

7. Define *all-or-nothing thinking* and give an example.

8. Explain the suggestion "watch for hot spots" and describe its connection to critical thinking.

9. Name at least one fallacy involved in this statement: "Everyone who's ever visited this school has agreed that it's the best in the state."

10. List the four suggested steps for problem solving and give an example of each step.

learning styles application

The questions below will "cycle" you through four styles, or modes, of learning as explained in the article "Learning styles: Discovering how you learn" in Chapter One. Each question will help you explore a different mode. You can answer the questions in any order.

what if *Explain how you would modify a technique from this chapter to make it a more effective tool for decision making—or describe an original technique of your own.*

why *Think of a major decision you face right now and put it into the form of a question. Possible examples are: "What major will I declare?" or "What is my top priority goal for this year?"*

how *Briefly describe how you will use a technique from this chapter to make a major decision.*

what *List a technique from this chapter that could help you make a major decision you face right now (such as the decision you listed under* Why?*).*

master student profile

IRSHAD MANJI

(1969–) Controversial journalist, broadcaster, and author of The Trouble with Islam, *uses her "Muslim voice of reform, to concerned citizens worldwide" in an effort to explore faith and community, and the diversity of ideas.*

It's to be expected that an author with a book on the verge of publication will lose her cool over a last-minute detail or two. Some might get nervous that their facts won't hold up and run a paranoid, final check. Others might worry about what to wear to their book party. When Irshad Manji's book was about to hit the stands, her concern was a bit different. She feared for her life.

Certain her incendiary book *The Trouble with Islam* would set off outrage in the Muslim community, she called the police, told them she was working on a book that was highly critical of Islam, and asked if they could advise her on safety precautions.

They came to visit her Toronto apartment building several times and suggested she install a state-of-the-art security system, bulletproof windows, and hire a counterterrorism expert to act as her personal bodyguard.

In her short, plucky book she comes down hard on modern-day Islam, charging that the religion's mainstream has come to be synonymous with literalism. Since the 13th century, she said, the faith hasn't encouraged—or tolerated—independent thinking (or as its known in the faith, *ijtihad*).

The book, which is written like a letter, is both thoughtful and confrontational. In person, Ms. Manji embodied the same conflicting spirit. She was affable and wore a broad smile. Her upbeat, nervous energy rose to the task of filling in every potentially awkward pause. (One of her favorite factoids: "Prophet Mohammed was quite a feminist.")

Her journey scrutinizing Islam started when she was an 8-year-old and taking weekly religious classes at a *madrasa* (religious school) in suburban Vancouver. Her anti-Semitic teacher Mr. Khaki never took her questions seriously; he merely told her to accept everything because it was in the Koran. She wanted to know why she had to study it in Arabic, which she didn't understand, and was told the answers were "in the Koran."

Her questioning ended up getting her kicked out of school at 14, and she embarked on a 20-year-long private study of the religion. While she finds the treatment poured on women and foreigners in Islamic nations indefensible, she said that she continues to be a believer because the religion provides her with her values. "And I'm so glad I did because it was then I came to realize that there was this really progressive side of my religion and it was this tradition of critical thinking called *ijtihad*. This is what allows me to stay within the faith."

She calls herself a "Muslim refusenik" because she remains committed to the religion and yet she doesn't accept what's expected of Muslim women. As terrorist acts and suicide bombings refuse to subside, she said it's high time for serious reform within the Islamic faith.

She said many young Muslim supporters are still afraid to come out about their support of her. "Even before 9/11 it was the young Muslims who were emerging out of these audiences and gathering at the side of the stage. They'd walk over and say, 'Irshad, we need voices such as yours to help us open up this religion of ours because if it doesn't open up, we're leaving the mosques.'"

She wants Muslims to start thinking critically about their religion and to start asking more questions. "Most Muslims have never been introduced to the possibility, let alone the virtue, of asking questions about our holy book," she said. "We have never been taught the virtue of interpreting the Koran in different ways."

From Lauren Mechling, "The Trouble with Writing About Islam," as appeared in *New York Sun*, November 26, 2004. Reprinted with permission.

8 Communicating

MASTER STUDENT MAP

why this chapter matters . . .

Your communication abilities are as important to your success in the workplace as your technical skills.

how you can use this chapter . . .

Listen, speak, and write more effectively.
Prevent and resolve conflict with other people.
Build satisfying relationships with people of many cultures.

As you read, ask yourself what if . . .

I could align my words and my actions in ways that transform my life?

what is included . . .

FROM THE DESK OF . . .

Getting involved on campus in extracurricular activities helped to prepare me for working with people and forming sustaining relationships. I've transferred these practices to the workplace. As treasurer of one of the organizations I belonged to, I learned how to work in groups to accomplish goals, and I was able to practice taking charge of different types of situations.

—ROSS JACKSON, HELP DESK TECHNICIAN

Consulting projects are almost always executed in teams. . . . A great team player is able to leverage every individual's capabilities to maximize the team's performance.

—ERICA VOLINI, CONSULTING MANAGER

Communicating in a diverse world

According to the National Association of Colleges and Employers, what interviewers look for most of all in job applicants is skill in communicating—the ability to write and speak clearly and persuasively. And this is the skill that they find most consistently missing in new graduates.[1]

Communication can be defined as the process of creating shared meaning. When two people agree about the meaning of an event, they stand on common ground. They've communicated.

However, communication is a constant challenge. When people speak or listen, they don't exchange meaning. They exchange only symbols—words, images, gestures. And symbols are open to interpretation. This means that communication is always flawed to some extent. We can never be sure that the message we send is the message that others receive.

Also remember that no two people are alike. We are diverse. Adapting to diversity is a challenge that's *always* present in communication. The people sitting next to you in class or at work may come from many countries. Each of them has a separate bundle of life experiences.

In the workplace, you might face even greater diversity. Your coworkers might span three, four, or even five generations. Their race, ethnic group, religion, sexual orientation, and level of physical ability might differ greatly from yours.

According to the U.S, Census Bureau, one-third of Americans are now "minorities."[2] In addition, you will join an international workplace. American companies in the twenty-first century will buy from the world and sell to the world. You might work on project teams with people located in another city, state, or country.

Misunderstandings between people of different cultures can add noise to their interactions. In communication theory, the term *noise* refers to any factor that distorts meaning. When noise is present, the channels of communication start to close. Noise can be external (a lawn mower outside a classroom) or internal (fear, anger, false assumptions, or lack of information).

Communication ultimately works best when each of us has plenty of time to receive what others send *and* the opportunity to send a complete message when it's our turn. This is more challenging than it sounds. When emotions run high, people can totally forget when it's their job to receive and when it's their turn to send. Everyone talks and nobody listens.

Reaching common ground with other people presents a constant challenge. Yet with practice we can overcome many of the difficulties inherent in human communication. Look for dozens of ways to do that in the pages that follow. ☒

journal entry 22

Discovery/Intention Statement

Think of a time when you experienced an emotionally charged conflict with another person. Were you able to resolve this dispute effectively? If so, list below the strategies you used.

I discovered that I . . .

____

____

Now scan this chapter for ideas that can help you get your feelings and ideas across more skillfully in similar situations. List at least four ideas here, along with the page numbers where you can read more about them.

Strategy	*Page number*

Describe an upcoming situation in which you intend to apply these techniques. If possible, choose a situation that will occur within the next week.

I intend to . . .

____

____

____

____

____

Choosing to *listen*

Effective listening is not easy. It calls for concentration and energy. It's worth it. People love a good listener. The best salespeople, managers, coworkers, teachers, parents, and friends are the best listeners.

To listen well, begin from a clear intention. *Choose* to listen well. Once you've made this choice, you can use the following techniques to be even more effective at listening. Notice that these techniques start with nonverbal listening. They continue with suggestions for verbal responses that can help you fully receive a speaker's message.

Nonverbal listening

Be quiet. Silence is more than staying quiet while someone is speaking. Allowing several seconds to pass before you begin to talk gives the speaker time to catch his breath and gather his thoughts. He might want to continue. Someone who talks nonstop might fear he will lose the floor if he pauses.

If the message being sent is complete, this short break gives you time to form your response and helps you avoid the biggest barrier to listening—listening with your answer running. If you make up a response before the person is finished, you might miss the end of the message, which is often the main point.

Maintain eye contact. Look at the other person while he speaks. Doing this demonstrates your attentiveness and helps keep your mind from wandering. Your eyes also let you observe the speaker's body language and behavior. If you avoid eye contact, you can fail to see *and* fail to listen.

This idea is not an absolute. Maintaining eye contact is valued more in some cultures than others. Also, some people learn primarily by hearing; they can listen more effectively by turning off the visual input once in a while.

Display openness. You can display openness through your facial expression and body position. Uncross your arms and legs. Sit up straight. Face the other person and remove any physical barriers between you, such as a pile of books.

Send acknowledgments. Let the speaker know periodically that you are still there. Words and nonverbal gestures of acknowledgment convey to the speaker that you are interested and that you are receiving his message. Examples include "Umhum," "OK," "Yes," and head nods.

These acknowledgments do not imply your agreement. When people tell you what they don't like about you, your head nod doesn't mean that you agree. It just indicates that you are listening.

Release distractions. Even when your intention is to listen, you might find your mind wandering. Thoughts about what *you* want to say or something you want to do later might claim your attention. There's a simple solution: Notice your wandering mind without judgment. Then bring your attention back to the act of listening.

Suspend judgments. Listening and agreeing are two different activities. As listeners, our goal is to fully receive another person's message. This does not mean that we're obligated to agree with the message. Once you're confident that you accurately understand a speaker's point of view, you are free to agree or disagree with it. The key to effective listening is understand *before* evaluating.

Verbal listening

Choose when to speak. When listening to another person, we often interrupt with our own stories, opinions, suggestions, and comments. Consider the following dialogue:

"Oh, I'm so excited. I just found out that I've been nominated to be in *Who's Who in American Musicians.*"

"Yeah, that's neat. My Uncle Elmer got into *Who's Who in American Veterinarians.* He sure has an interesting job. One time I went along when he was treating a cow, and you'll never believe what happened next. . . ."

To avoid this kind of conversation, delay your verbal responses. This does not mean that you remain totally silent while listening. It means that you wait for an *appropriate* moment to respond.

Watch your nonverbal responses, too. A look of "Good grief!" from you can deter the other person from finishing his message.

Feed back meaning. Sometimes you can help a speaker clarify her message by paraphrasing it. This does not mean parroting what she says. Instead, briefly summarize. Psychotherapist Carl Rogers referred to this technique as *reflection.*[3]

Feed back what you see as the essence of that person's message: "Let me see if I understood what you said . . ." or "What I'm hearing you say is. . . ." Often, the other person will say, "No, that's not what I meant. What I said was. . . ."

There will be no doubt when you get it right. The sender will say, "Yeah, that's it," and either continue with another message or stop sending when he knows you understand.

When you feed back meaning, be concise. This is not a time to stop the other person by talking on and on about what you think you heard.

Notice verbal *and* nonverbal messages. You might point out that the speaker's body language seems to be the exact opposite of his words. For example: "I noticed you said you are excited, but you look bored."

Keep in mind that the same nonverbal behavior can have various meanings across cultures. Someone who looks bored might simply be listening in a different way.

Listen for requests. An effective way to listen to complaints is to look for the request hidden in them. "This class is a waste of my time" can be heard as "Please tell me what I'll gain if I participate actively in class." "The instructor talks too fast" might be asking "What strategies can I use to take notes when the instructor covers material rapidly?"

Viewing complaints as requests gives us more choices. Rather than responding with defensiveness ("What does he know anyway?"), resignation ("It's always been this way and always will be"), or indifference ("It's not my job"), we can decide whether to grant the request (do what will alleviate the other's difficulty) or help the person translate his own complaint into an action plan.

Allow emotion. In the presence of full listening, some people will share things that they feel deeply about. They might cry, shake, or sob. If you feel uncomfortable when this happens, see if you can accept the discomfort for a little while longer. Emotional release can bring relief and trigger unexpected insights.

Ask for more. Full listening with unconditional acceptance is a rare gift. Many people have never experienced it. They are used to being greeted with resistance, so they habitually stop short of saying what they truly think and feel. Help them shed this habit by routinely asking, "Is there anything more you want to say about that?" This sends the speaker a message that you truly value what she has to say.

Be careful with questions and advice. Questions are directive. They can take conversations in a new direction, which may not be where the speaker wants to go. Ask questions only to clarify the speaker's message. Later, when it's your turn to speak, you can introduce any topic that you want.

Also be cautious about advice. Unsolicited advice can be taken as condescending or even insulting. Skilled listeners recognize that people are different, and they do not assume that they know what's best for someone else.

Take care of yourself. People seek good listeners, and there are times when you don't want to listen. You might be distracted with your own concerns. Be honest. Don't pretend to listen. You can say, "What you're telling me is important, and I'm pressed for time right now. Can we set aside another time to talk about this?" It's OK not to listen.

Choosing to speak

We have been talking with people for years, and we usually manage to get our messages across. There are times, though, when we don't. Often, these times are emotionally charged.

Sometimes we feel wonderful or rotten or sad or scared, and we want to express it. Emotions can get in the way of the message. However, you can send almost any message through tears, laughter, fist pounding, or hugging.

Begin with a sincere intention to reach common ground with your listener. Then experiment with the suggestions that follow.

Replace "You" messages with "I" messages. It can be difficult to disagree with someone without his becoming angry or your becoming upset. When conflict occurs, we often make statements about the other person, or "You" messages:

"You are rude."
"You make me mad."
"You must be crazy."
"You don't love me anymore."

This kind of communication results in defensiveness. The responses might be:

"I am not rude."
"I don't care."
"No, *you* are crazy."
"No, *you* don't love *me*!"

"You" messages are hard to listen to. They label, judge, blame, and assume things that might or might not be true. They demand rebuttal. Even praise can sometimes be an ineffective "You" message. "You" messages don't work.

When communication is emotionally charged, psychologist Thomas Gordon suggests that you consider limiting your statements to descriptions about yourself.[4] Replace "You" messages with "I" messages:

"You are rude" might become "I feel upset."
"You make me mad" could be "I feel angry."
"You must be crazy" can be "I don't understand."
"You don't love me anymore" could become "I'm afraid we're drifting apart."

Suppose a friend asks you to pick him up at the airport. You drive 20 miles and wait for the plane. No friend. You decide your friend missed his plane, so you wait three hours for the next flight. No friend. Perplexed and worried, you drive home. The next day, you see your friend downtown.

"What happened?" you ask.
"Oh, I caught an earlier flight."
"You are a rude person," you reply.

Look for the facts, the observable behavior. Everyone will agree that your friend asked you to pick him up, that he did take an earlier flight, and that you did not receive a call from him. But the idea that he is rude is not a fact—it's a judgment.

He might go on to say, "I called your home and no one answered. My mom had a stroke and was rushed to Valley View. I caught the earliest flight I could get." Your judgment no longer fits.

When you saw your friend, you might have said, "I waited and waited at the airport. I was worried about you. I didn't get a call. I feel angry and hurt. I don't want to waste my time. Next time, you can call me when your flight arrives, and I'll be happy to pick you up."

"I" messages don't judge, blame, criticize, or insult. They don't invite the other person to counterattack with more of the same. "I" messages are also more accurate. They report our own thoughts and feelings.

At first, "I" messages might feel uncomfortable or seem forced. That's OK. Use the five ways to say "I" explained below.

Remember that questions are not always questions. You've heard these "questions" before. A parent asks, "Don't you want to look nice?" Translation: "I wish you'd cut your hair, lose the blue jeans, and put on a tie." Or how about this question from a spouse: "Honey, wouldn't you love to go to an exciting hockey game tonight?" Translation: "I've already bought tickets."

We use questions that aren't questions to sneak our opinions and requests into conversations. "Doesn't it upset you?" means "It upsets me," and "Shouldn't we hang the picture over here?" means "I want to hang the picture over here."

Communication improves when we say, "I'm upset" and "Let's hang the picture over here."

Choose nonverbal messages. How you say something can be more important than what you say. Your tone of voice and gestures add up to a silent message that you send. This message can support, modify, or contradict your words. Your posture, the way you dress, how often you shower, and even the poster hanging on your wall can negate your words before you say them.

Most nonverbal behavior is unconscious. We can learn to be aware of it and choose our nonverbal messages. The key is to be clear about our intention and purpose. When we know what we want to say and are committed to getting it across, our inflections, gestures, and words work together and send a unified message.

Notice barriers to sending messages. Sometimes fear stops us from sending messages. We are afraid of other people's reactions, sometimes justifiably. Being truthful doesn't mean being insensitive to the impact that our messages have on others. Tact is a virtue; letting fear prevent communication is not.

Assumptions can also be used as excuses for not sending messages. "He already knows this," we tell ourselves.

Predictions of failure can be barriers to sending, too. "He won't listen," we assure ourselves. That statement might be inaccurate. Perhaps the other person senses that we're angry and listens in a guarded way. Or perhaps he is listening and sending nonverbal messages we don't understand.

Or we might predict, "He'll never do anything about it, even if I tell him." Again, making assumptions can defeat your message before you send it.

Five ways to say "I"

An "I" message can include any or all of the following five elements. Be careful when including the last two because they can contain hidden judgments or threats.

Observations. Describe the facts—the indisputable, observable realities. Talk about what you—or anyone else—can see, hear, smell, taste, or touch. Avoid judgments, interpretations, or opinions. Instead of saying, "You're a slob," say, "Last night's lasagna pan was still on the stove this morning."

Feelings. Describe your own feelings. It is easier to listen to "I feel frustrated" than to "You never help me." Stating how you feel about another's actions can be valuable feedback for that person.

Wants. You are far more likely to get what you want if you say what you want. If someone doesn't know what you want, he doesn't have a chance to help you get it. Ask clearly. Avoid demanding or using the word *need*. Most people like to feel helpful, not obligated. Instead of saying, "Do the dishes when it's your turn, or else!" say, "I want to divide the housework fairly."

Thoughts. Communicate your thoughts, and use caution. Beginning your statement with the word "I" doesn't make it an "I" message. "I think you are a slob" is a "You" judgment in disguise. Instead, say, "I'd have more time to study if I didn't have to clean up so often."

Intentions. The last part of an "I" message is a statement about what you intend to do. Have a plan that doesn't depend on the other person. For example, instead of "From now on we're going to split the dishwashing evenly," you could say, "I intend to do my share of the housework and leave the rest."

It's easy to make excuses for not communicating. If you have fear or some other concern about sending a message, be aware of it. Don't expect the concern to go away. Realize that you can communicate even with your concerns. You can choose to make them part of the message: "I am going to tell you how I feel, and I'm afraid that you will think it's stupid."

Talking to someone when you don't want to could be a matter of educational survival. A short talk with an advisor, a teacher, a friend, or a family member might solve a problem that could jeopardize your education.

Speak candidly. When we brood on negative thoughts and refuse to speak them out loud, we lose perspective. And when we keep joys to ourselves, we diminish our satisfaction. A solution is to share regularly what we think and feel. Psychotherapist Sidney Jourard referred to such openness and honesty as *transparency* and wrote eloquently about how it can heal and deepen relationships.[5]

Sometimes candid speaking can save a life. For example, if you think a friend is addicted to drugs, telling him so in a supportive, nonjudgmental way is a sign of friendship.

Imagine a community in which people freely and lovingly speak their minds—without fear or defensiveness. That can be your community.

This suggestion comes with a couple of caveats. First, there is a big difference between speaking candidly about your problems and griping about them. Gripers usually don't seek solutions. They just want everyone to know how unhappy they are. Instead, talk about problems as a way to start searching for solutions.

Second, avoid bragging. Other people are turned off by constant references to how much money you have, how great your girlfriend is, how numerous your social successes are, or how much status your family enjoys. There is a difference between sharing excitement and being obnoxious.

Ask for support. One of the central messages of this book is that you are not alone. You can draw on the talent, strength, and wisdom of others.

Consider creating a team of people who help each other succeed. Such a team can develop naturally from a study group that works well. Ask members if they would be willing to accept and receive support in achieving a wide range of academic and personal goals. Meet regularly to do goal-setting exercises from this book and brainstorm success strategies.

After you have a clear statement of your goals and a plan for achieving them, let family members and friends know. When appropriate, let them know how they can help. You may be surprised at how often people respond to a genuine request for support.

journal entry 23

Discovery/Intention Statement

Think about one of your relationships for a few minutes. It can involve a parent, sibling, spouse, child, friend, hairdresser, or anyone else. In the space below, write down some things that are not working in the relationship. What bugs you? What do you find irritating or unsatisfying?

I discovered that . . .

____

____

____

____

____

____

____

____

Now think for a moment about what you want from this relationship. More attention? Less nagging? More openness, trust, financial security, or freedom? Choose a suggestion from this chapter and describe how you could use it to make the relationship work.

I intend to . . .

____

____

____

____

____

____

____

____

Communicating across cultures

Skill at communicating with people of different cultures begins with learning about yourself. You see the world through a unique set of lenses. See if you can switch lenses—that is, learn to see familiar events in a new way.

For example, think of a time when you were in the midst of a conflict among several people. Now mentally put yourself inside the skin of another person in that conflict. Ask: How would I view this situation if I were that person? Or if I were a person of the opposite gender? Or if I were member of a different racial or ethnic group? Or if I were older or younger?

Now shift gears for a different experiment: See if you can recall times when you were favored due to your gender, race, or age. Describe these to another person or summarize them briefly in writing. Next, see if you can recall times when you were excluded or ridiculed based on one of those *same* characteristics.

Exercises such as these can help you discover ways to identify with a wider range of people. Then you can translate the resulting insights into new behaviors. For example, if you're a younger student and habitually form study groups with people who are about the same age as you, then make it your intention to invite an adult learner to your group's next meeting. When choosing whether to join a campus organization, take into account the diversity of its membership. And before you make a statement about anyone who differs significantly from you, ask yourself: "Is what I'm about to say accurate, or is it based on a belief that I've held for years but never examined?"

The above suggestions illustrate ways to apply the cycle of discovery, intention, and action to learning to communicate across cultures. You can take this process deeper with any of the following suggestions.

Learn about other cultures. People from different cultures read differently, write differently, think differently, eat differently, and learn differently than you. Knowing this from the beginning, you can be more effective with your classmates, coworkers, and neighbors.

Cultures differ in a variety of dimensions. One of the most important dimensions is *style.* Just as we speak of learning styles, we can talk about communication styles, relationship styles, and other styles. Differing styles exist in every aspect of life—family structure, religion, relationships with authority, and more.

One key to understanding styles is to look for several possible interpretations of any behavior. For example:

- When Americans see a speaker who puts his hands in his pockets, they seldom attribute any meaning to this behavior. But in many countries—such as Germany, Indonesia, and Austria—this is considered rude.
- Americans seldom see men walking arm-in-arm down the street. In Italy, however, this is common.
- During a conversation, you might prefer having a little distance between yourself and another person. But in Iran, people may often get so close to you that you can feel their breath.[6]

These examples could be extended to cover many areas—posture, eye contact, physical contact, facial expressions, and more. And the various ways of interpreting these behaviors are neither right nor wrong. They simply represent differing styles in making meaning out of what we see.

You might find yourself fascinated by the styles that make up a particular culture. Consider learning as much about it as possible. Immerse yourself in that culture. Read novels, see plays, go to concerts, listen to music, look at art, take courses, learn another language. Find opportunities to speak with members of that culture. Your quest for knowledge will be an opening to new conversations.

Look for common ground. Students in higher education often find that they worry about many of the same things—including tuition bills, the quality of dormitory food, and the shortage of on-campus parking spaces. More important, our fundamental goals as human beings—such as health, physical safety, and economic security—are desires that cross culture lines.

Practice looking for common ground. You can cultivate friends from other cultures. Do this through volunteering, serving on committees, or any other activity in which people from other cultures are also

- Use gestures to accompany your words.
- Since English courses for non-native speakers often emphasize written English, write down what you're saying. Print your message in capitalized block letters.
- Stay calm and avoid sending nonverbal messages that you're frustrated.

If you're unsure about how well you're communicating, ask questions: "I don't know how to make this idea clear for you. How might I communicate better?" "When you look away from me during our conversation, I feel uneasy. Is there something else we need to talk about?" "When you don't ask questions, I wonder if I am being clear. Do you want any more explanation?" Questions such as these can get cultural differences out in the open in a constructive way.

Look for individuals, not group representatives. Sometimes the way we speak glosses over differences among individuals and reinforces stereotypes. For example, a student worried about her grade in math expresses concern over "all those Asian students who are skewing the class curve." Or a white music major assumes that her African American classmate knows a lot about jazz or hip-hop music. We can avoid such errors by seeing people as individuals—not spokespersons for an entire group.

involved. Then your understanding of other people unfolds in a natural, spontaneous way.

The key is to honor the differences among people while remembering what we have in common. Diversity is not just about our differences—it's about our similarities. On a biological level, less than 1 percent of the human genome accounts for visible characteristics such as skin color. In terms of our genetic blueprint, we are more than 99 percent the same.[7]

Speak and listen with cultural sensitivity. After first speaking to someone from another culture, don't assume that you've been understood or that you fully understand the other person. The same action can have different meanings at different times, even for members of the same culture. Check it out. Verify what you think you have heard. Listen to see if what you spoke is what the other person received.

If you're speaking to someone who doesn't understand English well, keep the following ideas in mind:

- Speak slowly and distinctly.
- To clarify your statement, don't repeat individual words over and over again. Restate your entire message in simple, direct language. Avoid slang.

Find a translator, mediator, or model. People who move with ease in two or more cultures can help us greatly. Diane de Anda, a professor at the University of California, Los Angeles, speaks of three kinds of people who can communicate across cultures. She calls them *translators, mediators,* and *models.*[8]

A *translator* is someone who is truly bicultural—a person who relates skillfully to people in a mainstream culture and people from a contrasting culture. This person can share her own experiences in overcoming discrimination, learning another language or dialect, and coping with stress. She can point out differences in meaning between cultures and help resolve conflict.

Mediators are people who belong to the dominant or mainstream culture. Unlike translators, they might not be bicultural. However, mediators value diversity and are committed to cultural understanding. Often they are teachers, counselors, tutors, mentors, or social workers.

Models are members of a culture who are positive examples. Models include students from any racial or cultural group who participate in class and demonstrate effective study habits. Models can also include entertainers, athletes, and community leaders.

Your school might have people who serve these functions, even if they're not labeled translators, mediators, or models. Some schools have mentor or "bridge" programs that pair new students with teachers of the same race or culture. Students in these programs get coaching in study skills and life skills; they also develop friendships with possible role models. Ask your student counseling service about such programs.

Be willing to accept feedback. Members of another culture might let you know that some of your words or actions had a meaning other than what you intended. Perhaps a comment that seems harmless to you is offensive to them. And they may tell you directly about it.

Avoid responding to such feedback with comments such as "Don't get me wrong," "You're taking this way too seriously," or "You're too sensitive." Instead, listen without resistance. Open yourself to what others have to say. Remember to distinguish between the *intention* of your behavior from its actual *impact* on other people. Then take the feedback you receive and ask how you can use it to communicate more effectively in the future.

Speak up against discrimination. You might find yourself in the presence of someone who tells a racist joke, makes a homophobic comment, or utters an ethnic slur. When this happens, you have a right to state what you observe, share what you think, and communicate how you feel. Depending on the circumstance, you might say:

- "That's a stereotype and we don't have to fall for it."
- "Other people are going to take offense at that. Let's tell jokes that don't put people down."
- "I realize that you don't mean to offend anybody, but I feel hurt and angry by what you just said."
- "As members of the majority culture around here, we can easily forget how comments like that affect other people."
- "I know that an African American person told you that story, but I still think it's racist and creates an atmosphere that I don't want to be in."

This kind of speaking may be the most difficult communicating you ever do. And, if you *don't* do it, you give the impression that you agree with biased speech.

In response to your candid comments, many people will apologize and express their willingness to change. Even if they don't, you can still know that you practiced integrity by aligning your words with your values.

Change the institution. None of us are individuals living in isolation. We live in systems that can be racist. As a student, you might see people of color ignored in class. You might see people of a certain ethnic group passed over in job hiring or underrepresented in school organizations. And you might see gay and lesbian students ridiculed or even threatened with violence. One way to stop these actions is to point them out.

You can speak more effectively about what you believe by making some key distinctions. Remember that:

- *Stereotypes* are errors in thinking—inaccurate ideas about members of another culture.
- *Prejudice* refers to positive or negative feelings about others, which are often based on stereotypes.
- *Discrimination* takes places when stereotypes or prejudice get expressed in policies and laws that undermine equal opportunities for all cultures.

Federal civil rights laws, as well as the written policies of most schools, ban racial and ethnic discrimination. If your school receives federal aid, it must set up procedures that protect students against such discrimination. Find out what those procedures are and use them, if necessary.

When it comes to ending discrimination, you are in an environment where you can make a difference. Run for student government. Write for school publications. Speak at rallies. Express your viewpoint. This is training for citizenship in a multicultural world.

Managing conflict

Conflict management is one of the most practical skills you'll ever learn. Here are strategies that can help.

These strategies fall into two categories. The first one is about dealing with the *content* of a conflict—defining the problem, exploring viewpoints, and discovering solutions. The second is about finding a *process* for resolving any conflict, no matter what the content. To bring these strategies to life, think of ways to use them in managing a conflict that you face right now.

Focus on content

Back up to common ground. As a first step in managing conflict, back up to common ground. List all of the points on which you are *not* in conflict: "I know that we disagree about how much to spend on a new car, but we do agree that the old one needs to be replaced." Often, such comments put the problem in perspective and pave the way for a solution.

State the problem. Using "I" messages, as explained earlier in this chapter, state the problem. Tell people what you observe, feel, think, want, and intend to do. Allow the other people in a particular conflict to do the same.

You might have different perceptions of the problem. That's fine. Let the conflict come into clear focus. It's hard to fix something unless people agree on what's broken.

Remember that the way you state the problem largely determines the solution. Defining the problem in a new way can open up a world of possibilities. For example, "We need a new car" is a problem statement that dictates one solution. "We need a way to get around town" opens up more options, such as using public transportation, taxi services, and rental cars.

State all points of view. If you want to defuse tension or defensiveness, set aside your opinions for a moment. Take the time to understand the other points of view. Sum up those viewpoints in words that the other parties can accept. When people feel that they've been heard, they're often more willing to listen.

Ask for complete communication. In times of conflict, we often say one thing and mean another. So before responding to what the other person says, use active listening. Check to see if you have correctly received that person's message: "What I'm hearing you say is. . . . Did I get it correctly?"

Focus on solutions. After stating the problem, dream up as many solutions as you can. Then evaluate the solutions you brainstormed. Choose one solution that is most acceptable to everyone involved and implement it. If it works, pat yourselves on the back. If not, make changes or implement a new solution.

Focus on process

Commit to the relationship. The thorniest conflicts usually arise between people who genuinely care for each other. Begin by affirming your commitment to the other person: "I care about you, and I want this relationship to last. So I'm willing to do whatever it takes to resolve this problem." Also ask the other person for a similar commitment.

Allow strong feelings. Permitting conflict can also mean permitting emotion. Being upset is all right. Feeling angry is often appropriate. Crying is OK. Allowing other people to see the strength of our feelings can help resolve the conflict. When we express and release resentment, we might discover genuine compassion in its place.

Notice your need to be "right." Some people approach conflict as a situation where only one person wins. That person has the "right" point of view. Everyone else loses.

See if you can define the conflict as a problem to be solved—not a contest to be won. Explore the possibility that you might be mistaken. There might be more than one acceptable solution. Let go of being "right" and aim for being effective at resolving conflict instead.

Slow down the communication. In times of great conflict, people often talk all at once. Words fly like speeding bullets and no one listens. Chances for conflict resolution take a nosedive.

When this happens, choose either to listen or to talk—not both at the same time. Just send your message. Or just receive the other person's message. Usually, this slows down the pace and allows everyone to become more levelheaded.

Communicate in writing. What can be difficult to say to another person face to face might be effectively communicated in writing. When people in conflict write letters or e-mails to each other, they automatically apply many of the suggestions in this article. Writing is a way to slow down the communication and ensure that only one person at a time is sending a message.

Get an objective viewpoint. One way to get an objective viewpoint is to use a mediator. Even an untrained mediator—someone who's not a party to the conflict—can do much to decrease tension. Mediators can help everyone get their point of view across. The mediator's role is not to give advice but to keep the discussion on track and moving toward a solution.

Learn to say no—gracefully. All your study plans can go down the drain when a friend says, "Time to party." Sometimes, succeeding in school means replying with a graceful and firm *no.* You can do this in a graceful way:

- *Think critically about assumptions.* An inability to say no can spring from the assumption that you'll lose friends if you state what you really want. But consider this: If you cannot say no, then you are not in charge of your time. You will not have friendships based on equality. True friends will respect your wishes.
- *Plan your refusal.* You might find it easier to say no when you don't have to grasp for words. Choose some key words and phrases in advance. For example: "I'd prefer not to right now." "That doesn't work for me today." "Thanks for asking; my schedule for today is full." Or "I'll go along next time when my day is clear."
- *Avoid apologies or qualifiers.* People give away their power when they couch their noes in phrases such as "I'm sorry but I just don't know if I want to." Or "Would you get upset if I said no?" You don't have to apologize for being in charge of your life. It's OK to say no.

Allow for cultural differences. People respond to conflict in different ways, depending on their cultural background. Some stand close, speak loudly, and make

critical thinking exercise 26

WRITE AN "I" MESSAGE

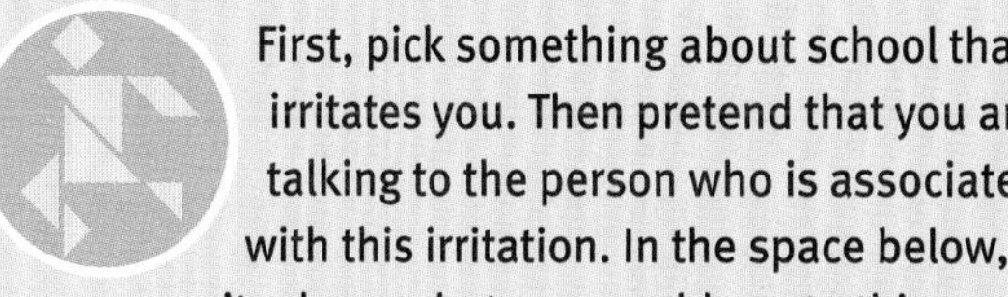

First, pick something about school that irritates you. Then pretend that you are talking to the person who is associated with this irritation. In the space below, write down what you would say to this person as a "You" message.

Now write the same complaint as an "I" message. Include at least the first three elements suggested in "Five ways to say 'I.' "

direct eye contact. Other people avert their eyes, mute their voices, and increase physical distance.

When it seems to you that other people are sidestepping or escalating a conflict, consider whether your reaction is based on cultural bias. Also remember to:

- *Check your temper.* People from other cultures might shrink from displays of sudden, negative emotion—for example, shouting or pointing.
- *Deliver your criticisms in private.* People in many Asian and Middle Eastern cultures place value on "saving face" in public.
- *Give the other person space.* Here the word *space* has two definitions. The first is physical space, meaning that standing close to people can be seen as a gesture of intimidation. The second is conversation space. Give people time to express their point of view. Allowing periods of silence might help.
- *Address people as equals.* For example, don't offer the other person a chair so that she can sit while you stand and talk. Conduct your conversation at eye level rather than from a position of superiority. Also refer to people by their first names only if you use *your* first name.
- *Stick to the point.* When feeling angry or afraid, you might talk more than usual. A person from another culture—especially one who's learning your language—might find it hard to take in everything you're saying. Pause from time to time so that others can ask clarifying questions.

Agree to disagree. Sometimes we say all we have to say and the conflict still remains, staring us right in the face. What's left is to recognize that honest disagreement is a fact of life. We can peacefully coexist with other people—and respect them—even though we don't agree on some issues. Conflict can be accepted even when it is not resolved.

See the conflict within you. When we're angry or upset, we can take a minute to look inside. Perhaps we were ready to take offense, waiting to pounce on something the other person said. Perhaps, without realizing it, we did something to create the conflict. Or maybe the other person is simply saying what we don't want to admit is true.

When these things happen, we can shine a light on our own thinking. A simple spot check might help the conflict disappear—right before our eyes. ☒

The economies of the world are gradually becoming one. Some time during the first third of this century, goods and services from China, India, and Japan could represent one-half of the world's gross domestic product.[9] Twenty percent of jobs in the United States are currently linked to international trade, and this percentage is expected to increase.[10]

As American companies look for ways to gain overseas market share, they will look for people who enter this global environment with ease. Diversity in the workplace will be seen as good for people—and good for business.

People of all races and cultures can use several strategies to reach common ground at work.

Join a diverse workplace

Expect differences

To begin, remember an obvious fact: People differ. Obvious as it is, this fact is easy to forget. Most of us unconsciously judge others by a single set of standards—our own. That can lead to communication breakdown. Consider some examples:

- A man in Costa Rica works for a multinational company. He turns down a promotion that would take his family to California. This choice mystifies the company's executives. Yet the man has grandparents who are in ill health, and leaving them behind would be taboo in his country.
- A Native American woman avoids eye contact with her superiors. Her coworkers see her as aloof. However, she comes from a culture where people seldom make eye contact with their superiors.
- A Caucasian woman from Ohio travels to Mexico City on business. She shows up promptly for a 9 a.m. meeting and finds that it starts 30 minutes late and goes an hour beyond its scheduled ending time. She's entered a culture with a flexible sense of time.
- An American executive schedules a meeting over dinner with people from his company's office in Italy. As soon as the group orders food, the executive launches into a discussion of his agenda items. He notices that his coworkers from Italy seem unusually silent, and he wonders if they feel offended. He forgets that they come from a culture where people ease into business discussions slowly—only after building a relationship through "small talk."

To prevent misunderstandings, remember that culture touches every aspect of human behavior, ranging from the ways people greet one another to the ways they resolve conflict. Differences in culture could affect any encounter you have with another person. Expecting differences up front helps you keep an open mind.

Mind the details

Pay attention to details that people from any culture will use to form first impressions of you. Lydia Ramsey, author of *Manners That Sell: Adding the Polish That Builds Profits*, suggests the following practices. You might find them especially useful if you travel overseas for your job:

- Shake hands appropriately. While the handshake is a near-universal form of greeting, people do it differently across the world. You might have been coached to take a firm grip, make eye contact, pump twice, and then let go. In other countries, however, people might prefer a lighter grip or longer contact. When traveling to the Middle East, you might even be greeted with a kiss or hug. Observe closely to discover the norm.
- When in doubt, dress up. Americans are relatively informal about workplace fashion. In many cultures, there are no "casual days." Formal business wear is expected every day. Dress up unless it's clearly OK to do otherwise.
- Treat business cards carefully. In many cultures, the way that you exchange cards conveys your respect for others. When someone gives you a card, take a second to look at it. Then offer your thanks and

place the card in a folder or briefcase with other work-related documents. Don't stash it quickly in a pocket or purse.

- Respect titles and names. Though Americans like to do business on a first-name basis, this is acceptable in some cultures only among family members. Avoid misunderstandings by using last names and job titles when you greet people in work settings.[11]

Use language with care

Even people who speak the same language sometimes use simple words that can be confused with each other. For instance, giving someone a "mickey" can mean pulling a practical joke—or slipping a drug into someone's drink. We can find it tough to communicate simple observations, let alone abstract concepts.

You can help by communicating simply and directly. When meeting with people who speak English as a second language, think twice before using figures of speech or slang expressions. Stick to standard English and enunciate clearly.

Also remember that nonverbal language differs across cultures. For example, people from India may shake their head from side to side to indicate agreement, not disagreement. And the hand signal that signifies *OK* to many Americans—thumb and index finger forming a circle—is considered obscene in Brazil.

Put messages in context

When speaking to people of another culture, you might find that words carry only part of an intended message. In many countries, strong networks of shared assumptions form a context for communication.

As an example, people from some Asian and Arabic countries might not include every detail of an agreement in a written contract. These people often place a high value on keeping verbal promises. Spelling out all the details in writing might be considered an insult. Knowing such facts can help you prevent and resolve conflicts in the workplace.

Test for understanding

To promote cross-cultural understanding, look for signs that your message got through clearly. Ask questions without talking down to your audience: *Am I making myself clear? Is there anything that doesn't make sense?* Watch for nonverbal cues of understanding, such as a nod or smile.

Learn about another culture

You can also promote cross-cultural understanding through the path of knowledge. Consider learning everything you can about another culture. Read about that culture and take related classes. Cultivate friends from that culture and take part in their community events. Get a feel for the customs, music, and art that members of the group share. If appropriate, travel abroad to learn more. Also ask about foreign language training your company may offer to the staff.

Follow up with action at work. Join project teams with diverse members. Experiencing diversity firsthand can be a positive experience when you're working with others to meet a common goal.

Expand networks

People with narrow circles of relationships can be at a disadvantage when trying to change jobs or enter a new field. For maximum flexibility in your career path, stay connected to people of your own culture—*and* cultivate contacts with people of other cultures.

Counter bias and discrimination

In the United States, laws dating back to the Equal Pay Act of 1963 and Title VII of the Civil Rights Act of 1964 ban discrimination in nearly all aspects of the work world, from hiring and firing to transfers and promotions. Congress set up the Equal Employment Opportunity Commission (EEOC) to enforce these laws. You can get more information through the EEOC Website at **http://www.eeoc.gov**.

If you think that you've been the subject of discrimination, take time to examine the facts. Before filing a lawsuit, exhaust other options. Start by bringing the problem to your supervisor, your company's equal employment officer, or someone from the EEOC.

Stereotypes based on race, ethnic group, gender, and disability are likely to fade as the workplace becomes more diverse. As they do, disprove stereotypes through your behavior. Set high standards for yourself and meet them. Seek out key projects that make you visible in the organization, and then perform effectively. These are useful success strategies for anyone in the workplace.

Also keep records of your performance. Log your achievements. Ask for copies of your performance evaluations and make sure they're accurate. Having a stack of favorable evaluations can help you make your case when bringing a complaint or resolving conflict.

Be willing to bridge gaps

Simply being *willing* to bridge culture gaps can be just as crucial as knowing about another group's customs or learning their language. People from other cultures might sense your attitude and be willing to reach out to you.

Begin by displaying some key attributes of a critical thinker. Be open-minded and willing to suspend judgment. Notice when you make assumptions based on another person's accent, race, religion, or gender. Become willing to discover your own biases, listen fully to people with other points of view, enter new cultural territory, and even feel uncomfortable at times.

It's worth it. Bridging to people of other cultures means that you gain new chances to learn, make contacts, increase your career options, and expand your friendships. The ability to work with people of many cultures is a marketable skill—and a way to enlarge your world.

critical thinking exercise 27

ENTER THE GLOBAL ECONOMY

In his classic book *The World Is Flat: A Brief History of the Twenty-First Century*, Thomas Friedman describes a new world economy driven by two major forces—globalization and technology.[12] He argues that the world economy is becoming "flat" in the sense of offering a more level playing field. The Internet and workflow software allow people across the world to collaborate on team projects. Digital technology also allows American employers to outsource jobs by hiring people in other countries to fill them. Take a few minutes to think about how you can succeed in this new world. One option is to develop your communication skills. For example, you might choose to learn a second language that could help you travel overseas on business. You could learn to communicate across cultures by joining a project team that involves a diverse group of people. Or you could plan to take courses in sales or public speaking. Having these skills could make it more difficult for an employer to ship your job overseas to someone sitting behind a computer.

In the space below, brainstorm what *you* could do to prosper in a "flat" global economy. Fill the space below and continue on additional paper as needed.

____

____

____

____

____

____

Now, review the list you just created and choose the idea that interests you most—one that has the potential to make a real difference in your long-term career plan. In the space below, write a goal based on this idea and list three action steps you can take to meet this goal.

____

____

____

____

____

____

V.I.P.S (VERY IMPORTANT PERSONS)

Step 1 Under the column below titled "Name," write the names of at least seven people who have positively influenced your life. They might be relatives, friends, teachers, coworkers, or perhaps persons you have never met. (Complete each step before moving on.)

Step 2 In the next column, rate your gratitude for this person's influence (from 1 to 5, with 1 being a little grateful and 5 being extremely grateful).

Step 3 In the third column, rate how fully you have communicated your appreciation to this person (again, 1 to 5, with 1 being not communicated and 5 being fully communicated).

Step 4 In the final column, put a U to indicate the persons with whom you have unfinished business (such as an important communication that you have not yet sent).

	Name	*Grateful (1–5)*	*Communicated (1–5)*	*U*
1.				
2.				
3.				
4.				
5.				
6.				
7.				

Step 5 Now select two persons with U's beside their names and write them a letter. Express the love, tenderness, and joy you feel toward them. Tell them exactly how they have helped change your life and how glad you are that they did.

Step 6 You also have an impact on others. Make a list of people whose lives you have influenced. Consider sharing with these people why you enjoy being a part of their lives.

Create high-performing teams

Working in teams helps you to develop several transferable skills. One is sociability—taking an interest in people, valuing what they think, and understanding how they feel. Another is understanding social systems in organizations and operating effectively in them. Teamwork also gives you a chance to practice all the communication skills explored in this chapter.

In the workplace, teams abound. To research their book *When Teams Work Best,* Frank LaFasto and Carl Larson studied 600 teams. These ranged from the Mount Everest climbing team to the teams that produced the Boeing 747 airplane—the world's largest aircraft and a product of 75,000 blueprints.[13]

LaFasto and Larson found that empowered teams set their own goals, plan their own schedule, and make decisions democratically. They also design their workspace and choose their own members.

You might wonder how to make all this happen. One answer is to take your cue from the word *empowered* and review the Power Processes included throughout this book. Following are ways you can use several of them to supercharge your next team project.

Discover what you want

When forming a team, look for a fit between individual goals and the team's mission. Team members might want formal recognition for taking part in the project and meeting its objectives. People naturally ask, "What's in this for me?" Provide answers to that question. Emphasize the chance to develop marketable skills by joining the team.

Equally important is ensuring that the organization knows what it wants from the team. To promote effective results, define your team's purpose, its expected results, and how it will be held accountable. Also ask for enough support—in terms of time, money, and other resources—to produce those results. To get down to specifics, ask four questions based on the Master Student Map that begins each chapter of this book:

- *Why* is this project being done?
- *What* would a successful outcome for this project look like?
- *How* are we going to create a bridge from our current reality to that successful outcome?
- *What if* we truly made this outcome a high priority? What is the very next action that each of us would take to make it happen?

Ideas are tools

Teams tend to fizzle when they create new ideas that meet with immediate skepticism or outright rejection. After proposing changes to a company's existing policies and procedures, team members might face resistance: "This suggestion will never work." "That's just not the way we do things around here." "We can't break with tradition." These responses are examples of groupthink, which happens when a team automatically rules out new options simply because they're . . . well, *new.*

Managers can prevent this outcome by asking pointed questions before a team convenes its first meeting: Are we truly interested in change? Are we willing to act on what the team recommends? Or are we just looking for a team to reinforce our current practices?

People who want a team to succeed will treat its ideas as tools. Instead of automatically looking for what's wrong with a proposal, look for potential applications. Even a proposal that seems outlandish at first might become workable with a few modifications. In an empowered team, all ideas are welcome, problems are freely admitted, and any item is open for discussion.

Be here now

Concentration and focused attention are attributes of effective students—and effective teams. When a team tries to tackle too many problems or achieve too many goals, it gets distracted. Members can forget the team's purpose and lose their enthusiasm for the project. You can help restore focus by asking: "What is the single most important goal that our team can meet?" and "What is the single most important thing we can do *now* to meet that goal?"

Another source of team distraction is a member who doesn't perform—someone who comes to meetings unprepared, consistently fails to complete individual assignments, or attacks new ideas. Effective teams have a leader who focuses the group on its agenda and tactfully asks nonperforming members to change their behavior.

Love your problems

Many teams develop problems—lack of clarity about their mission, missed goals, personality conflicts, and more. Team members can learn to love each problem as a stimulus for learning.

As you create team projects, make time for mileposts in the learning cycle. Cycle through the following steps several times during the life of your team:

- *Reflecting*—setting goals, assigning tasks to individual team members, and meeting regularly to discuss what's working well about the team and what can be improved.
- *Doing*—carrying out assigned tasks and meeting due dates specified in the work plan.
- *Experiencing*—observing the results of the team's actions, remaining sensitive to the feelings of coworkers and customers.
- *Thinking*—abstracting core insights from the team's experience and looking for ways to apply those insights to the whole organization.

To promote team success, combine the learning styles of individual members in complementary ways. If you're skilled at reflecting, for example, find someone who excels at doing. Also seek people who can reflect on the team's experience and think in more abstract ways. Pooling different styles allows you to draw on everyone's strengths.

Notice your pictures

During much of the previous century, many large businesses and nonprofit organizations were organized as hierarchies with multiple layers—executives, middle-level managers, supervisors, and employees. People who worked for such a company had jobs with clearly defined and limited responsibilities. Collaborations among employees in different departments were rare.

Teams present a different picture of how to operate a workplace. And old pictures die hard. Companies may give lip service to the idea of teams and yet fall back into traditional practices. Managers might set up teams but offer little training to help people function in this new working environment.

You can prepare for this situation now. While you are in school, seize opportunities to work collaboratively. Form study groups. Enroll in classes that include group projects. Show up for your next job with teamwork skills. At the same time, remember that some of your coworkers may not share your assumptions about the value of teams. By demonstrating your abilities, you help them to form new pictures. ⊠

Three paths to clear writing

Writing is essential to career success. Companies crank out documents daily: contracts, budgets, project plans, grant proposals, reports, marketing campaigns, advertisements, e-mails, job descriptions, and more. Employers value people who write well—and report that these people are hard to find.[14]

This article outlines a three-phase process for the kind of writing you'll do in higher education:

- Getting ready to write
- Writing a first draft
- Revising your draft

Following that are suggestions for common writing tasks in the workplace.

Getting ready to write

Schedule and list writing tasks. You can divide the ultimate goal—a finished paper—into smaller steps. Estimate how long it will take to complete each step. Start with the date your paper is due and work backward to the present. Say that the due date is December 1 and you have about three months to write the paper. Schedule November 20 as your targeted completion date, plan what you want to get done by November 1, then list what you want to get done by October 1. Remember to set a due date for your first draft, followed by second and third drafts. Allow plenty of time for revision.

Select a topic and working title. Using your instructor's guidelines for the paper, write down a list of topics that interest you. Write as many of these as you can think of in two minutes. Then choose one.

The most common pitfall is selecting a topic that's too broad. "Harriet Tubman" is not a useful topic for your American history paper. Instead, consider "Harriet Tubman's activities as a Union spy during the Civil War." Your topic statement can function as a working title.

Write a thesis statement. Clarify what you want to say by summarizing it in one concise sentence. This sentence, called a *thesis statement*, refines your working title. It also helps in making a preliminary outline.

You might write a thesis statement such as "Harriet Tubman's activities with the Underground Railroad led to a relationship with the Union army during the Civil War." A statement that's clear and to the point can make your paper easier to write. Remember, you can always rewrite your thesis statement as you learn more about your topic.

A thesis statement is different from a topic statement. Like newspaper headlines, a thesis statement makes an assertion or describes an action. It is expressed in a complete sentence, including a verb. "Diversity" is a topic. "Cultural diversity is valuable" is a thesis statement.

Consider your purpose. Effective writing flows from a purpose. Discuss the purpose of your assignment with your instructor. Also think about how you'd like your reader or listener to respond after considering your ideas. Do you want him to think differently, to feel differently, or to take a certain action?

Your writing strategy is greatly affected by how you answer these questions. If you want someone to think differently, make your writing clear and logical. Support your assertions with evidence. If you want someone to feel differently, consider crafting a story. Write about a character your audience can empathize with, and tell how he resolves a problem that your audience can relate to. And if your purpose is to move the reader into action, explain exactly what steps to take and offer solid benefits for doing so.

To clarify your purpose, state it in one sentence. For example, "The purpose of this paper is to define the term *success* in such a clear and convincing way that I win a scholarship from Houghton Mifflin."

Do initial research. At this stage, the objective of your research is not to uncover specific facts about your topic. That comes later. First, you want to gain an overview of the subject. Discover the structure of your topic—its major divisions and branches. Say that you want to persuade the reader to vote for a certain candidate. Learn enough about this person to summarize his background and state his stands on key issues.

Outline. An outline is a kind of map. When you follow a map, you avoid getting lost. Likewise, an outline keeps you from wandering off the topic.

To start an outline, gather a stack of 3 × 5 cards and brainstorm ideas you want to include in your paper. Write one phrase or sentence per card.

Then experiment with the cards. Group them into separate stacks, each stack representing one major category. After that, arrange the stacks in order. Finally, arrange the cards within each stack in a logical order. Rearrange them until you discover an organization that you like.

If you write on a computer, consider using outlining software. These programs allow you to record and rearrange ideas on the screen. You can also use major and minor headings to mark the major sections and subsections of your paper.

After you write the first draft of your outline, test it. Make sure that each word relates directly to your statement of purpose.

Do in-depth research. You can find information about research skills in Chapter Four: Reading and in Chapter Five: Notes. Following are added suggestions.

Three-by-five cards work wonders when taking notes on books, articles, and other sources of information on your topic. Just write down one idea per card. This makes it easy to organize—and reorganize—your ideas.

Remember to create information cards *and* source cards. On information cards, record a quotation, paraphrase, or summary based on one of your sources. On source cards, record the details about your sources—title, author, and date and place of publication. Create one card for each source. Assign each source a code, such as a number or abbreviation. Include the source code and page number on information cards.

In addition to source cards and information cards, write idea cards. If you have a thought while you are researching, write it down on a card. Label these cards clearly as your own ideas.

An alternative to 3 × 5 cards is the computer. You can take notes in a word processing, outlining, or database program. Key in each quotation, paraphrase, or summary as a separate paragraph. Be sure to enclose quotations in quotation marks and include a source for each paragraph.

Writing a first draft

To create your draft, gather your notes and arrange them to follow your outline. Then write about the ideas in your notes. Write in paragraphs, one idea per paragraph. If you have organized your notes logically, related facts will appear close to each other.

Remember that the first draft is not for keeps. Don't worry about grammar, punctuation, or spelling as you write your first draft. Write as if you were explaining the subject to a friend. Let the words flow. It's perfectly all right to crank out a draft that you heavily rewrite or even throw away. The purpose of a first draft is merely to have something to work with—period.

Some people find that it works well to forget the word *writing.* Instead, they ease into the task with activities that help generate ideas. You can free-associate, cluster, meditate, daydream, doodle, draw diagrams, visualize the event you want to describe, talk into a voice recorder—anything that gets you started.

Revising your draft

An effective way to revise your paper is to read it out loud. The eyes tend to fill in the blanks in our own writing. The combination of voice and ears forces us to pay attention to the details.

Another technique is to have a friend look over your paper. This is never a substitute for your own review, but a friend can often see mistakes you miss.

Reading aloud and having a friend comment on your paper are techniques that can help you in each step of rewriting explained below.

Cut. Begin revising by looking for excess baggage. Avoid at all costs and at all times the really, really terrible mistake of using way too many unnecessary words, a mistake that some student writers often make when they sit down to write papers for the various courses in which they participate at the fine institutions of higher learning that they are fortunate enough to attend. (Example: The previous sentence could be edited to "Avoid unnecessary words.")

Paste. In deleting passages, you've probably removed some of the original transitions and connecting ideas from your draft. Imagine yourself with scissors and glue, cutting the paper into scraps—one scrap for each point. Then paste these points down in a new, more logical order.

Fix. Now it's time to look at individual words and phrases. In general, rely on nouns and verbs. Using too many adjectives and adverbs weakens your message and adds unnecessary bulk to your writing. Include details and be specific. Also, use the active voice ("The research team began a project") rather than the passive voice ("A project was initiated"). Finally, look closely for any spelling or grammar errors and fix them.

Prepare. In a sense, any paper is a sales effort. If you hand in a paper with wrinkled jeans, its hair tangled and unwashed, and its shoes untied, your instructor is less likely to buy it. To avoid this situation, format your paper following accepted standards for margin widths, endnotes, title pages, and other details. Ask your instructor for specific instructions on how to list the sources you used in writing your paper.

Writing for the workplace

The skills that you develop in writing for teachers will also help you write clearly for coworkers. Remember, however, that readers at work are often pressed for time and impatient. Do them a courtesy by using the following strategies.

Get to the point, pronto! Don't worry about warming up to your point with an introduction. Put your main idea in the first paragraph—if possible, the first sentence. If your document will go over two pages, then add a summary at the top. Keep it to one paragraph and place the key "take away" idea there.

Answer key questions. Put yourself in your reader's place. She may be reading your document after a long day of meetings and still have ten items on her to-do list. When she sees your report, she's likely to ask: What's the problem you're addressing? What's your solution? And why should I care? Organize your document so that it directly answers such questions in a logical order.

Make it clear how you want readers to respond. You might want them to schedule a meeting, approve your budget, give a green light to your project plan, or give you a raise. Whatever your purpose, make sure that your request is polite and clear.

Let your text breathe. Allow white space between paragraphs. For long documents, include each of your main points in a newspaper-style headline. For ideas that come in a series, use numbered or bulleted lists.

Write e-mail that gets results. Be conscious of the amount of e-mail that busy people receive. Send e-mail messages only to the people who need them, and only when necessary.

Write an informative subject line. Rather than offering a generic description of your message, include a capsule summary—a complete sentence with the main point.

Above all, think short. Keep your subject line short, your paragraphs short, and your message as a whole short.

Before hitting the Send button, review what you've written. Every message you send says something about your attention to detail. Keep the tone professional—more formal than the instant messaging you do with friends.

Use Reply All carefully. Use this feature only when everyone who received a message truly needs to know your response. People will appreciate your help in keeping their incoming messages to a minimum.

Avoiding plagiarism

Using another person's words or pictures without giving proper credit is called *plagiarism.* Plagiarism amounts to stealing someone else's work and claiming it as your own—the equivalent of cheating on a test.

Higher education consists of a community of scholars who trust each other to speak and write with integrity. Plagiarism undermines this trust. The consequences of plagiarism can range from a failing grade to expulsion from school.

To avoid plagiarism, cite a source for each phrase, sequence of ideas, or visual image created by another person. Clearly distinguish your own ideas from the ideas of others. There are several ways to ensure that you do this consistently.

Identify direct quotes. If you use a direct quote from another writer or speaker, put that person's words in quotation marks. If you do research online, you might find yourself copying sentences or paragraphs from a Web page and pasting them directly into your notes. *This is the same as taking direct quotes from your source.* To avoid plagiarism, identify such passages in an obvious way. Besides enclosing them in quotation marks, you could format them in a different font or color.

Paraphrase carefully. Instead of using a direct quote, you might choose to paraphrase an author's words. Paraphrasing means restating the original passage in different words, usually making it shorter and simpler. Students who copy a passage word for word and then just rearrange or delete a few phrases are running a serious risk of plagiarism. Consider this paragraph:

> *Higher education also offers you the chance to learn how to learn. In fact, that's the subject of this book. Employers value the person who is a "quick study" when it comes to learning a new job. That makes your ability to learn a marketable skill.*

Following is an improper paraphrase of that passage:

> *With higher education comes the chance to learn how to learn. Employers value the person who is a "quick study" when it comes to learning a new job. Your ability to learn is a marketable skill.*

A better paraphrase of the same passage would be:

> *The author notes that when we learn how to learn, we gain a skill that is valued by employers.*

Cite a source for paraphrases, just as you do for direct quotes.

When you use the same sequence of ideas as one of your sources—even if you have not paraphrased or directly quoted—cite that source.

Note details about each source. For books, these details include the author, title, the name and location of the publisher, publication date, and page number. For articles from print sources, record the title and the name of the magazine as well. If you found the article in an academic or technical journal, also record the volume and number of the publication. A librarian can help identify these details.

If your source is a Web page, record as many identifying details as you can find—author, title, sponsoring organization, URL, publication date, and revision date. In addition, list the date that you accessed the page.

Cite your sources as endnotes or footnotes to your paper. Ask your instructor for examples of the format to use.

Submit only your own work. Turning in materials that have been written or revised by someone else puts your education at risk.

Note: Out of a concern for avoiding plagiarism, some students go overboard in crediting their sources. You do not need to credit wording that's wholly your own. Nor do you need to credit general ideas, such as the suggestion that people use a to-do list to plan their time. When you use your own words to describe such an idea, there's no need to credit a source. But if you borrow someone else's words or images to explain the idea, do give credit.

Mastering public speaking

Some people tune out during a speech. Just think of all the times you have listened to instructors, lecturers, and politicians. Remember all the wonderful daydreams you had during their speeches.

Your audiences are like you. The way you plan and present your speech can determine the number of audience members who will stay with you until the end. Polishing your speaking and presentation skills can also help you think on your feet and communicate clearly. These are skills that you can use in any course and in any career you choose.

Analyze your audience

Developing a speech is similar to writing a paper. Carefully analyze your audience by using the strategies in the chart on page 270.

As you analyze your audience, also consider the diversity of its members. Choose words carefully to avoid any hint of stereotypes based on race, ethnic group, sexual orientation, or gender.

To gain acceptance for your ideas, find common ground with your audience. Certain values cut across cultures and come close to being universal. These include the desires for safety, economic security, recognition, enjoyment, fairness, friendship, and love. See if you can link the purpose and content of your speech to these core values.

Plan to avoid expressions that might confuse people who speak English as a second or third language. English expressions such as "a picture paints a thousand words" or "he's having a bad hair day" don't translate well into other languages. Screen your speaking for such phrases and look for other ways to get your point across.

Organize your presentation

Consider the length of your presentation. Plan on delivering about 100 words per minute. This is only a general guideline, however, so time yourself as you practice your presentation.

Aim for a lean presentation—enough words to make your point but not so many that your audience becomes restless. Leave your listeners wanting more. When you speak, be brief and then be seated.

Speeches are usually organized in three main parts: the introduction, the main body, and the conclusion.

If your topic is new to listeners . . .	• Explain why your topic matters to them. • Relate the topic to something that listeners already know and care about. • Define any terms that listeners might not know.
If listeners already know about your topic . . .	• Acknowledge this fact at the beginning of your speech. • Find a narrow aspect of the topic that may be new to listeners. • Offer a new perspective on the topic, or connect it to an unfamiliar topic.
If listeners disagree with your thesis . . .	• Tactfully admit your differences of opinion. • Reinforce points on which you and your audience agree. • Build credibility by explaining your qualifications to speak on your topic. • Quote expert figures that agree with your thesis—people whom your audience is likely to admire. • Explain that their current viewpoint has costs for them, and that a slight adjustment in their thinking will bring significant benefits.
If listeners may be uninterested in your topic . . .	• Explain how listening to your speech can help them gain something that matters deeply to them. • Explain ways to apply your ideas in daily life.

Write the introduction. Rambling speeches with no clear point or organization put audiences to sleep. Solve this problem with your introduction. The following introduction, for example, reveals the thesis and exactly what's coming. The speech will have three distinct parts, each in logical order:

> *Dog fighting is a cruel sport. I intend to describe exactly what happens to the animals, tell you who is doing this, and show you how you can stop this inhumane practice.*

Whenever possible, talk about things that hold your interest. Include your personal experiences and start with a bang! Consider this introduction to a speech on the subject of world hunger:

> *I'm very honored to be here with you today. I intend to talk about malnutrition and starvation. First, I want to outline the extent of these problems, then I will discuss some basic assumptions concerning world hunger, and finally I will propose some solutions.*

You can almost hear the snores from the audience. Following is a rewrite:

> *More people have died from hunger in the past five years than have been killed in all of the wars, revolutions, and murders in the past 150 years. Yet there is enough food to go around. I'm honored to be here with you today to discuss solutions to this problem.*

Though some members of an audience begin to drift during any speech, most people pay attention for at least the first few seconds. Highlight your main points in the beginning sentences of your speech.

Draft your introduction and then come back to it after you've written the rest of your speech. In the process of creating the main body and conclusion, your thoughts about the purpose and main points of your speech might change. You might even want to write the introduction last.

Write the main body. The main body of your speech is the content, which accounts for 70 to 90 percent of most speeches. In the main body, you develop your ideas in much the same way that you develop a written paper.

Transitions are especially important. Give your audience a signal when you change points, using meaningful pauses and verbal emphasis as well as transitional phrases: "On the other hand, until the public realizes what is happening to children in these countries . . ." or "The second reason hunger persists is. . . ."

In long speeches, recap from time to time. Also preview what's to come. Use facts, descriptions, expert opinions, and statistics to hold your audience's attention.

Write the conclusion. At the end of the speech, summarize your points and draw your conclusion. You started with a bang; now finish with drama. The first and last parts of a speech are the most important. Make it clear to your audience when you've reached the end. Avoid endings such as "This is the end of my speech." A simple standby is "So in conclusion, I want to reiterate three points: First. . . ." When you are finished, stop talking.

Create speaking notes. Some professional speakers recommend writing out your speech in full, then putting key words or main points on a few 3 × 5 cards. Number the cards so that if you drop them, you can quickly put them in order again. As you finish the information on each card, move it to the back of the pile. Write information clearly and in letters large enough to be seen from a distance.

The disadvantage of the 3 × 5 card system is that it involves card shuffling. Some speakers prefer to use standard outlined notes. Another option is mind mapping. Even an hour-long speech can be mapped on one sheet of paper. You can also use memory techniques to memorize the outline of your speech.

Prepare effective visuals. Presentations often include visuals such as overhead transparencies, flip charts, or slides created with presentation software. These visuals can reinforce your main points and help your audience understand how your presentation is organized. In addition, visuals can serve as your speaking notes.

Use visuals to *complement* rather than *replace* your speaking. If you use too many visuals—or visuals that are too complex—your audience might focus on them and forget about you. To avoid this fate:

- Limit the amount of text on each visual. Stick to key words presented in short sentences and bulleted or numbered lists. Use a consistent set of plain fonts that are large enough for all audience members to see.
- Stick with a simple, coherent color scheme. Use light-colored text on a dark background, or dark text on a light background.
- Use consistent terminology in your speaking, your handouts, and your visuals. Inconsistency can lead people to feel lost or to question your credibility.
- Proofread your visuals for spelling and other mechanical errors.

Overcome fear of public speaking

While you may not be able to eliminate fear of public speaking, you can take steps to reduce and manage it.

Prepare thoroughly. Research your topic thoroughly. Knowing your topic inside and out can create a baseline of confidence.

Accept your physical sensations. You've probably experienced physical sensations that are commonly associated with stage fright: dry mouth, pounding heart, sweaty hands, muscle jitters, shortness of breath, and a shaky voice. One immediate way to deal with such sensations is to simply notice them. Tell yourself, "Yes, my hands are clammy. Yes, my stomach is upset. Also, my face feels numb." Trying to deny or ignore such facts can increase your fear. When you fully accept sensations, however, they start to lose power.

Focus on content, not delivery. Michael Motley, a professor at the University of California, Davis, distinguishes between two orientations to speaking. People with a *performance orientation* believe that speakers must captivate their audiences by using formal techniques that differ from normal conversation. In contrast, speakers with a *communication orientation* see public speaking simply as an extension of one-to-one conversation. The goal is not to perform but to communicate your ideas to an audience in the same ways that you would explain them to a friend.[15]

Adopting a communication orientation can reduce your fear of public speaking. Instead of thinking about yourself, focus on your message. Your audiences are more interested in *what* you have to say than *how* you say it. Give them valuable ideas and information that they can use.

Practice your presentation

The key to successful public speaking is practice.

Use your "speaker's voice." When you practice, do so in a loud voice. Your voice sounds different when you talk loudly, and this can be unnerving. Get used to it early on.

Practice in the room in which you will deliver your speech. Hear what your voice sounds like over a sound system. If you can't practice your speech in the actual room, at least visit the site ahead of time. Also make sure that the materials you will need for your speech, such as an overhead projector and screen, will be available when you want them.

Make a recording. Many schools have recording equipment available for student use. Use it while you practice, then view the finished recording to evaluate your presentation.

Listen for repeated phrases. Examples include *you know, kind of, really,* plus any little *uh*'s, *umm*'s, and *ah*'s. To get rid of these, tell yourself that you intend to notice every time they pop up in your daily speech. When you hear them, remind yourself that you don't use those words anymore.

Keep practicing. Avoid speaking word for word, as if you were reading a script. When you know your material well, you can deliver it in a natural way. Practice your presentation until you could deliver it in your sleep. Then run through it a few more times.

Deliver your presentation

Before you begin, get the audience's attention. If people are still filing into the room or adjusting their seats, they're not ready to listen. When all eyes are on you, then begin.

Project your voice. When you speak, talk loudly enough to be heard. Avoid leaning over your notes or the podium.

Maintain eye contact. When you look at people, they become less frightening. Remember, too, that it is easier for the audience to listen to someone when that person is looking at them. Find a few friendly faces around the room and imagine that you are talking to each person individually.

Notice your nonverbal communication. Be aware of what your body is telling your audience. Contrived or staged gestures will look dishonest. Be natural. If you don't know what to do with your hands, notice that. Then don't do anything with them.

Notice the time. You can increase the impact of your words by keeping track of the time during your speech. Better to end early than run late.

Pause when appropriate. Beginners sometimes feel that they have to fill every moment with the sound of their voice. Release that expectation. Give your listeners a chance to make notes and absorb what you say.

Have fun. Chances are that if you lighten up and enjoy your presentation, so will your listeners.

Reflect on your presentation

Review and reflect on your performance. Did you finish on time? Did you cover all of the points you intended to cover? Was the audience attentive? Did you handle any nervousness effectively?

Welcome evaluation from others. Most of us find it difficult to hear criticism about our speaking. Be aware of resisting such criticism and then let go of your resistance. Listening to feedback will increase your skill.

For more strategies on overcoming fear of public speaking, visit the *From Master Student to Master Employee* Website.

Making the grade in group presentations

When preparing group presentations, you can use three strategies for making a memorable impression.

Get organized. As soon as you get the assignment, select a group leader and exchange contact information. Schedule specific times and places for planning, researching, writing, and practicing your presentation.

At your first meeting, write a to-do list including all of the tasks involved in completing the assignment. Distribute tasks fairly, paying attention to the strengths of individuals in your group. For example, some people excel at brainstorming, while others prefer researching.

As you get organized, remember how your presentation will be evaluated. If the instructor doesn't give grading criteria, create your own. One powerful way to get started is to define clearly the topic and thesis, or main point, of your presentation. Then support your thesis by looking for the most powerful facts, quotations, and anecdotes you can find.

Get coordinated. Coordinate your presentation so that you have transitions between individual speakers. Practice making those transitions smooth.

Also practice using visuals such as flip charts, posters, DVDs, videotapes, or slides. To give visuals their full impact, make them appropriate for the room where you will present. Make sure that text is large enough to be seen from the back of the room. For bigger rooms, consider using presentation software or making overhead transparencies.

Get cooperation. Presentations that get top scores take teamwork and planning—not egos. Communicate with group members in an open and sensitive way. Contribute your ideas and be responsive to the viewpoints of other members. When you cooperate, your group is on the way to scoring well.

Joining online communities

Online communities create value. Websites such as MySpace and Facebook are known as places to share news, photos, and personal profiles. You can also use such sites to form study groups, promote special events, and make job contacts.

Activity in online communities can also have unexpected consequences. You might find examples of hate speech or threats of violence. And some users find that embarrassing details from their online profiles come back to haunt them years later.

You can use simple strategies to stay in charge of your safety and integrity any time that you connect with people online.

Post only what you want made public. Don't post anything that could embarrass you later. Act today to protect the person that you become four or five years from now.

To avoid unwanted encounters with members of online communities, also avoid posting private information. This includes your home or school address, your phone number, class schedule, and birth date.

Be honest. After you've chosen what information to post, make sure that it's accurate. False information can lead to expulsion from a community. For example, MySpace administrators can delete profiles of people who lie about their age.[16]

Use privacy features. Many online communities offer options for blocking messages from strangers, including instant messages and friendship invitations. For more information, look for a link on each site titled Frequently Asked Questions or Security Features.

In addition, respect the privacy of other members. If you want to post something on their site, send a message asking for permission first.

Be cautious about meeting community members in person. Because people can give misleading or false information about themselves online, avoid meeting them in person. If you do opt for a face-to-face meeting, choose a public place and bring along a friend whom you trust.

Report malicious content. If you find online content that you consider offensive or dangerous, report it to site administrators. In many online communities, you can do this anonymously.

Set reasonable limits to online activity. People who update their site daily may be sending an unintended message—that they spend too much time online. Don't let time spent on MySpace, Facebook, or similar sites distract you from meeting personal and academic goals.

Developing interpersonal intelligence calls for speaking with and listening to real people, away from the computer. People who cancel a meeting or try to break up with a partner through text messaging are not developing that intelligence. True friends know when to go offline and head across campus to resolve a conflict, or go back home to support a family member.

Remember "netiquette." Certain kinds of exchanges can send the tone of online communications into the gutter. To promote a cordial online community, abide by the following guidelines:

- Avoid typing passages in ALL UPPERCASE LETTERS. This is the online equivalent of shouting.
- Don't dish out spam—unsolicited messages, often meant to advertise a product or service, that are sent indiscriminately to large numbers of computer users.
- Can the sarcasm. Use humor with caution. A joke that's funny when you tell it in person might fall flat or even offend someone when you put it in writing and send it down the computer lines.
- Put out flames. *Flaming* takes place when someone sends an online message tinged with sarcasm or outright hostility. To create positive relationships when you're online, avoid sending such messages. If you get one, do not respond in kind.

The cornerstone of netiquette is to remember that the recipient on the other end is a human being. Whenever you're at the keyboard typing messages, ask yourself one question: "Would I say this to the person's face?"

power process

EMPLOY YOUR WORD

When you speak and give your word, you are creating—literally. Your speaking brings life to your values. In large part, others know who you are by the words you speak and the agreements you make. You can learn who you are by observing which commitments you choose to make and which ones you choose to avoid.

Your word makes things happen. Circumstances, events, and attitudes fall into place. The resources needed to accomplish whatever was promised become available. When you give your word, all this comes about.

The person you are right now is, for the most part, a result of the choices and agreements you've made in your life up to this point. Your future is determined largely by the choices and agreements you will make from this point on. By making and keeping agreements, you employ your word to create your future.

The world works by agreement

There are over 6 billion people on planet earth. We live on different continents and in different nations, and communicate in different languages. We have diverse political ideologies and subscribe to various social and moral codes.

This complex planetary network is held together by people keeping their word. Agreements minimize confusion, prevent social turmoil, and keep order. Projects are finished, goods are exchanged, and treaties are made. People, organizations, and nations know what to expect when agreements are kept. When people keep their word, the world works. Agreements are the foundation of many things that we often take for granted. Language, our basic tool of communication, works only because we agree about the meanings of words. A pencil is a pencil only because everyone agrees to call a thin, wood-covered column of graphite a pencil. We could just as easily call them ziddles. Then you might hear someone say, "Do you have an extra ziddle? I forgot mine."

Money exists only by agreement. If we leave a $100 Monopoly bill (play money) on a park bench next to a real $100 bill (backed by the United States Treasury), one is more likely to disappear than the other. The only important difference between the two pieces of paper is that everyone agrees that one can be exchanged for goods and services and the other cannot. Shopkeepers will sell merchandise for the "real" $100 bill because they trust a continuing agreement.

Relationships work by agreement

Relationships are built on agreements. They begin with our most intimate personal contacts and move through all levels of families, organizations, communities, and nations.

When we break a promise to be faithful to a spouse, to help a friend move to a new apartment, or to pay a bill on time, relationships are strained and the consequences can be painful. When we keep our word, relationships are more likely to be satisfying and harmonious. Expectations of trust and accountability develop. Others are more likely to keep their promises to us.

Perhaps our most important relationship is the one we have with ourselves. Trusting ourselves to keep our word is enlivening. As we experience success, our self-confidence increases.

When we commit to complete a class assignment and then keep our word, our understanding of the subject improves. So does our grade. We experience satisfaction and success. If we break our word, we create a gap in our learning, a lower grade, and possibly negative feelings.

Ways to make and keep agreements

Being cautious about making agreements can improve the quality of our lives. Making only those promises that we fully intend to keep improves the likelihood of reaching our goals. We can ask ourselves what level of commitment we have to a particular promise.

At the same time, if we are willing to take risks, we can open new doors and increase our possibilities for success. The only way to ensure that we keep all of our agreements is either to make none or to make only those that are absolutely guaranteed. In either case, we are probably cheating ourselves. Some of the most powerful promises we can make are those that we have no idea how to keep. We can stretch ourselves and set goals that are both high and realistic.

If we break an agreement, we can choose to be gentle with ourselves. We can be courageous, quickly admit our mistake to the people involved, and consider ways to deal with the consequences.

Examining our agreements can improve our effectiveness. Perhaps we took on too much—or too little. Perhaps we did not use all the resources that were available to us—or we used too many. Perhaps we did not fully understand what we were promising. When we learn from both our mistakes and our successes, we can become more effective at employing our word.

Move up the ladder of powerful speaking

The words used to talk about whether or not something will happen fall into several different levels. We can think of each level as one rung on a ladder—the ladder of powerful speaking. As we move up the ladder, our speaking becomes more effective.

Obligation. The lowest rung on the ladder is *obligation.* Words used at this level include *I should, he ought to, someone better, they need to, I must,* and *I had to.* Speaking this way implies that people and circumstances other than ourselves are in control of our lives. When we live at the level of obligation, we often feel passive and helpless to change anything.

Note: When we move to the next rung, we leave behind obligation and advance to self-responsibility. All of the rungs work together to reinforce this characteristic.

Possibility. The next rung up is *possibility.* At this level, we examine new options. We play with new ideas, possible solutions, and alternative courses of action. As we do, we learn that we can make choices that dramatically affect the quality of our lives. We are not the victims of circumstance. Phrases that signal this level include *I might, I could, I'll consider, I hope to,* and *maybe.*

Preference. From possibility we can move up to *preference.* Here we begin the process of choice. The words *I prefer* signal that we're moving toward one set of possibilities over another, perhaps setting the stage for eventual action.

By making and keeping agreements, you employ your word to create your future.

Passion. Above preference is a rung called passion. Again, certain words signal this level: *I want to, I'm really excited to do that, I can't wait.* Possibility and passion are both exciting places to be. Even at these levels, though, we're still far from action. Many of us want to achieve lots of things and have no specific plan for doing so.

Planning. Action comes with the next rung—*planning.* When people use phrases such as *I intend to, my goal is to, I plan to,* and *I'll try like mad to,* they're at the level of planning. The Intention Statements you write in this book are examples of planning.

Promising. The highest rung on the ladder is *promising.* This is where the power of your word really comes into play. At this level, it's common to use phrases such as these: *I will, I promise to, I am committed, you can count on it.* This is where we bridge from possibility and planning to action. Promising brings with it all of the rewards of employing your word.

career application

After Mark Hyland earned his associate degree in dental hygiene, he applied to work with his family's dentist. He got the job the day after he graduated.

Mark welcomed the chance to apply the skills he'd gained in school. He examined patients' teeth and gums. He removed stains and plaque. Mark asked if he could expand his job duties to include taking and developing dental X-rays. The dentist who hired him agreed.

Everyone in the dental office admitted that Mark's technical skills were superb. His communication skills were another matter. Several long-term patients complained that Mark's manner was condescending—even harsh at times.

One day, the dentist who hired Mark overheard him talking to a patient.

"You can't expect to have white teeth if you drink coffee," Mark told the patient.

The patient tried to make light of the situation. "Oh well," she said, "we all have our vices, and. . . ."

"Yeah, but it's your teeth we're talking about here," Mark said, interrupting her. "Tea is just as bad, and hot chocolate is even worse. On top of that, you've got a lot of plaque on your upper teeth. Do you *ever* floss?"

The dentist winced. He feared he was about to lose a valued patient. On the other hand, he'd known Mark for years and counted his parents as friends. He wanted to meet with Mark and give him feedback about his "chair-side manner." Yet the dentist knew that this conversation would be awkward for both of them. He found this meeting an easy thing to put off. ✖

Reflecting on this scenario

1. Review the suggestions given in this chapter for creating "I" messages. Then write an "I" message that the dentist could use to express his concerns with Mark.

____

____

____

2. List at least two other suggestions for sending or receiving messages that the dentist could use.

____

____

____

3. List at least two suggestions for Mark to use when communicating with patients.

____

____

____

4. Review the article "100 transferable skills" on page 63. Then list three skills that could benefit Mark and the dentist in this scenario.

____

____

____

quiz

Name ______________________________ Date ____/____/____

1. Reword the following complaint as a request: "You always interrupt when I talk!"

2. List the five possible parts of an "I" message (the five ways to say "I").

3. Rewrite the following statement as an "I" message: "You never listen to me!"

4. Briefly summarize the differences among translators, mediators, and models as explained in the text.

5. Give an example of how a Power Process from this book could be used to create an effective workplace team.

6. List three strategies for resolving conflict between people from different cultures.

7. Which of the following is an effective thesis statement? Explain your answer.
   (a) Two types of thinking.
   (b) Critical thinking and creative thinking go hand in hand.
   (c) The relationship between critical thinking and creative thinking.

8. Define *plagiarism* and explain ways to avoid it.

9. List three techniques for overcoming fear of public speaking.

10. What characteristic distinguishes the top five rungs of the ladder of powerful speaking from the bottom rung?

learning styles application

The questions below will "cycle" you through four styles, or modes, of learning as explained in the article "Learning styles: Discovering how you learn" in Chapter One. Each question will help you explore a different mode. You can answer the questions in any order.

what if *After reading this chapter, will you generally approach conflict management in a different way? Briefly explain your answer.*

why *Think of a conflict you are experiencing right now with an important person in your life. (If you cannot think of one, recall a conflict you've experienced in the past.) Do you think that any of the suggestions in this chapter could help you resolve this conflict? Briefly explain your answer.*

how *Describe when and where you plan to use a suggestion from this chapter to resolve a conflict with another person.*

what *Choose a specific suggestion from this chapter that could help you resolve a conflict you are experiencing right now with another person.*

master student profile

CESAR CHAVEZ

(1927–1993) Leader of the United Farm Workers (UFW), organized strikes, boycotts, and fasts to improve conditions for migrant workers.

A *few men and women have* engraved their names in the annals of change through nonviolence, but none have experienced the grinding childhood poverty that Chavez did after the Depression-struck family farm on the Gila River was foreclosed in 1937. Chavez was 10. His parents and the five children took to the picking fields as migrant workers.

Chavez's faith sustained him, but it is likely that it was both knowing and witnessing poverty and the sheer drudgery and helplessness of the migrant life that drove him.

He never lost the outreach that he had learned from his mother, who, despite the family's poverty, told her children to invite any hungry people in the area home to share what rice, beans and tortillas the family had.

He left school to work. He attended 65 elementary schools but never graduated from high school. . . .

It was in the fields, in the 1950s, that Chavez met his wife, Helen. The couple and their eight children gave much to "La Huelga," the strike call that became the UFW trademark, from their eventual permanent home near Bakersfield. Chavez did not own the home . . . but paid rent out of his $900 a month as a union official.

Yet, in the fields in the 1930s, something happened that changed Chavez's life. He was 12 when a Congress of Industrial Organizations union began organizing dried-fruit industry workers, including his father and uncle. The young boy learned about strikes, pickets and organizing.

For two years during World War II, Chavez served in the U.S. Navy; then it was back to the fields and organizing. There were other movements gaining strength in the United States during those years, including community organizing.

From 1952 to 1962, Chavez was active outside the fields, in voter registration drives and in challenging police and immigration abuse of Mexicans and Mexican-Americans.

At first, in the 1960s, only one movement had a noticeable symbol: the peace movement. By the time the decade ended, the United Farm Workers, originally established as the National Farm Workers Association, gave history a second flag: the black Aztec eagle on the red background.

In eight years, a migrant worker son of migrants helped change a nation's perception through nonviolent resistance. It took courage, imagination, and the ability to withstand physical and other abuse.

The facts are well-known now. During the 1968 grape boycott, farmers and growers fought him, but Chavez stood firm. Shoppers hesitated, then pushed their carts past grape counters without buying. The growers were forced to negotiate.

The UFW as a Mexican-American civil rights movement in time might outweigh the achievements of the UFW as a labor movement, for Chavez also represented something equally powerful to urban Mexican-Americans and immigrants—a nonviolent leader who had achieved great change from the most humble beginnings.

Word of Chavez's death spread to the union halls decorated with the Virgin of Guadalupe and UFW flag, to the fields, to the small towns and larger cities. And stories about the short, compact man with the ready smile, the iron determination, the genuine humility and the deep faith were being told amid the tears.

For more biographical information on Cesar Chavez, visit the Master Student Hall of Fame on the *From Master Student to Master Employee* Website.

9 Money

MASTER STUDENT MAP

why this chapter matters . . .

Money issues are frequently cited as reasons for quitting school, and this outcome can be prevented.

how you can use this chapter . . .

Discover the details about how money flows in and out of your life.

Experiment with ways to increase your income and decrease expenses.

Gain strategies for saving, investing, and reducing debt.

as you read, ask yourself what if . . .

I could adopt habits that will free me from money worries for the rest of my life?

what is included . . .

FROM THE DESK OF . . .

I look at the money I'm spending as an investment. Some people invest in real estate or a house. Well, they can take away your house, but they can never take away your education.

—CYNTHIA DAMOND

Freedom from money worries

"I can't afford it" is a common reason that students give for dropping out of school. "I don't know how to pay for it" or "I don't think it's worth it" are probably more accurate ways to state the problem.

Money produces more unnecessary conflict and worry than almost anything else. And it doesn't seem to matter how much money a person has. People who earn $10,000 a year never have enough. People who earn $100,000 a year might also say that they never have enough. Money worries can upset people no matter how much they have.

When you entered higher education, you took a big step in your financial life. If you're returning to school after years away from the classroom, you might be reducing your hours at work—and sacrificing income—in order to study and attend classes. If you've just graduated from high school, you might be taking out long-term loans to pay for your education.

No matter what your age, you can transform your relationship to money with one idea: *Most money problems result from spending more than is available.* It's that simple, even though often we do everything we can to make the problem much more complicated.

The solution also is simple: *Don't spend more than you have.* If you are spending more than you have, then increase your income, decrease your spending, or do both. This idea has never won a Nobel Prize in economics, but you won't go broke applying it.

There is a big payoff in making money management seem more complicated than it really is. If we don't understand money, then we don't have to be responsible for it. After all, if you don't know how to change a flat tire, then you don't have to be the one responsible for fixing it. It works the same way with money.

Using the strategies in this chapter could free you from money worries. That's a bold statement—perhaps even outrageous. But what if it's true? Approach this idea with an open mind.

The strategies you're about to learn are not complicated. In fact, they're not even new. They're all based on the cycle of discovery, intention, and action that you've already practiced in this book. With these strategies and the abilities to add and subtract, you have everything you need to manage money.

There are three main steps in money management:

- First, tell the truth about how much money you have and how much you spend (discovery).
- Second, commit to spend no more than you have (intention).
- Finally, apply the suggestions for earning more money, spending less money, or both (action).

If you do those three things consistently, you can eventually say goodbye to most money worries. This does not necessarily mean you will have all the money you could ever desire. It does mean controlling money instead of letting money control you.

journal entry 24

Discovery/Intention Statement

Reflect on your overall experience of money. List any statements you've made about your financial life during the last month—anything from "I never have enough" to "I have some extra money to invest and I'm wondering where to put it." Write your statements here:

When speaking about my money life, I discovered that I . . .

____

____

____

____

Scan this chapter again with an eye for strategies that could help you increase your income, decrease your expenses, or both. List three money strategies that you'd consider using right away.

I intend to . . .

____

____

____

____

THE MONEY MONITOR/MONEY SUMMARY PLAN

Many of us find it easy to lose track of money. It likes to escape when no one is looking. And usually no one is looking. That's why the simple act of noticing the details about money can be so useful—even if this is the only idea from this chapter that you ever apply.

Use this exercise as an opportunity to discover how money flows in and out of your life. The goal is to record all the money you receive and spend over the course of one month. This sounds like a big task, but it's simple. All it requires is your commitment to carry a pen and a piece of paper and to use them, even when it's inconvenient.

There's a payoff for this action—plugging the leaks in your financial life. With increased awareness of income and expenses, you can make choices about money that will change your life. Here's how to begin.

1. Tear out the Money Monitor and Money Summary Plan forms on the following pages. Make photocopies of these forms to use each month. Each form has a different purpose.

The Money Monitor is designed for recording the details about what you earn and spend each day of the month.

At the end of the month, use the entries from your Money Monitor to fill out the Money Summary Plan. This form helps you do two things. One is to get a big picture of the money that flows in and out of your life each month. The other is to plan specific changes in your monthly income and expenses.

2. Use the Money Monitor on a daily basis. You can fill out this form in a few minutes each day. The key is to carry the form with you and get into the habit of using it. There are just two things to remember:

- *Each time you receive income, note the details.* Record the date and a brief description of the source on the Money Monitor form. Write the amount of income received in the "In" column.
- *Each time you spend money, note the details.* Record the date of each expense on your Money Monitor, along with a brief description of it. Then write the amount of the expense in the "Out" column.

Following are some examples of income and expenses:

Date	Description	In	Out
4/1	Paycheck from part-time job	150	
4/3	Coffee from Café Caffeine		2.56
4/4	DVD rental		5
4/5	Scholarship check	300	

3. On the last day of the month, fill out your Money Summary Plan. Complete the following steps:

- *Fill in specific categories of income and expenses across the second row of the form.* Choose categories that apply to you—enough to create an accurate and meaningful summary of your monthly income and expenses. Some people get that with five or ten categories. Others like to have more.

  Examples of income categories are gifts, loans, scholarships and grants, veteran's benefits, wages and salary, contributions from family members, refunds, and withdrawals from a savings or investment account.

  For expenses, sample categories include cash, clothing, education, entertainment, groceries, health care, housing, restaurant purchases, phone bills, transportation, and utilities.

  You may need a few months to fine-tune your list of categories. Keep experimenting until you get a list that works. Also remember that your categories will change over time as your sources of income and types of expenses change.

- *Summarize your income for the month.* Take each amount that you listed in the "In" column of your Money Monitor and write that amount under an appropriate income category. Add the amounts in each column to come up with a total for each category of income.

- *Summarize your expenses for the month.* Take the amounts you listed in the "Out" column of your Money Monitor and list each one under an appropriate expense category. Add the amounts in each column to come up with a total for each category of expense.

  Remember to split expenses when necessary. For example, you might write one check each month to cover the cost of your cable television and Internet access. This one transaction could fall into two expense categories—entertainment (the cable television charge) and education (since access to the Internet is essential for your class work). Under "Entertainment," list the amount of your check that goes for cable television; under "Education," list the amount that goes to Internet access.

- *Note your plans for next month.* Take a moment to congratulate yourself for the sustained effort you've made so far. You're actively collecting and analyzing the data needed to take conscious control of your financial life. No matter how the numbers add up, you are now on the path to financial freedom.

  Take the next step on that path by making financial choices for the upcoming month. Reflect on the totals for each of your income and expense categories. If you anticipate that the total for a category will remain the same next month, write an "S" under "Plan." If you want to increase the total, write "+." And if you want to decrease the total, write "−."

Following is an excerpt from a sample Money Summary Plan. Notice that this student plans to reduce her spending for clothes, food eaten out, and movies and DVD rentals. However, she plans to increase the total she spends on food prepared at home, figuring that she'll save money by eating out less.

Note: The Money Monitor and Money Summary Plan represent one method for tracking your income and expenses. Of course, there are other options. For example, you can use money software such as Quicken or Microsoft Money.

Or simply use 3 × 5 cards. Every time you receive money or buy something, write the date, description, and amount on a card. (Be sure to use a separate card for each amount.) At the end of the month, sort your cards into income and expense categories and then total the amounts for each category. Use this information to fill out your Money Summary Plan.

Income						**Expenses**					
Wages	Scholarship	Gift	Family contribution			Rent	Phone	Clothes	Food-At home	Food-Eating out	Movies/ DVD rental
150	300		200			450	35.99	25	35.06	2.56	5
150								10	25.99	1.80	5
150									14.43	1.80	5
150									11.32	10.36	5
									20.00	25.05	
									40.00		
Total: 600	Total: 300	Total:	Total: 200	Total:	Total:	Total: 450	Total: 35.99	Total: 35	Total: 146.80	Total: 41.57	Total: 20
Plan: S	Plan: S	Plan: S	Plan: S	Plan:	Plan:	Plan: S	Plan: S	Plan: −	Plan: +	Plan: −	Plan: −

MONEY MONITOR

Date	Description	In	Out

MONEY MONITOR

Date	Description	In	Out

MONEY SUMMARY PLAN FOR____________ (month/year)

Income						Expenses					
Total:						Total:					
Plan:						Plan:					

MONEY SUMMARY PLAN FOR____________ (month/year)

Income						Expenses					
Total:						Total:					
Plan:						Plan:					

Discovery/Intention Statement

Now that you've experimented with the process of monitoring your money life, take a few moments to reflect on what you're learning and create your future with money. Complete the following statements.

After monitoring my income and expenses for one month, I was surprised to discover that . . .

When it comes to money, I am skilled at . . .

When it comes to money, I am *not* so skilled at . . .

I could increase my income by . . .

I could spend less money on . . .

After thinking about the most powerful step I can take right now to improve my finances, I intend to . . .

Make more money

For many people, making more money is the most appealing way to fix a broken budget. This approach is reasonable, and it has a potential problem: When their income increases, many people continue to spend more than they make. This means that money problems persist, even at higher incomes. You can avoid this dilemma by managing your expenses no matter how much money you make.

If you do succeed at controlling your expenses over the long term, then increasing your income is definitely a way to build wealth. Among the ways to make more money are to focus on your education, work while you're in school, and do your best at every job.

Focus on your education. Your most important assets are not your house, your car, or your bank accounts—they are your skills.

That's why your education is so important. Right now, you're developing knowledge, experience, and abilities that you can use to create income for the rest of your life.

Once you graduate and land a job in your chosen field, continue your education. Look for ways to gain additional skills or certifications that lead to higher earnings and more fulfilling work assignments.

Work while you're in school. If you work while you're in school, you can earn more than money. You'll gain experience, establish references, and expand your contacts in the community. And regular income in any amount can make a difference in your monthly cash flow.

Many students work full-time or part-time jobs. Work and school don't have to conflict, especially if you plan carefully (see Chapter Three) and ask for your employer's support.

On most campuses, there is a person in the financial aid office whose job is to help students find work while they're in school. See that person. In addition, check into career planning and job placement services at your school. Using these resources can greatly multiply your job options.

Most jobs are never advertised. In fact, a key source of information about new jobs is people—friends, relatives, coworkers, and fellow students. Ask around.

In addition, make a list of several places where you would like to work. Then go to each place on your list and tell someone that you would like a job. She might say that she doesn't have a job available. No problem. Ask to be considered for future job openings. Then check back periodically.

Another option is to start your own business. Consider a service you could offer—anything from lawn mowing to computer consulting. Students can boost their income in many ways, such as running errands, giving guitar lessons, walking pets, and house-sitting. Charge reasonable rates, provide impeccable service, and ask your clients for referrals.

Self-employment during higher education can blossom into amazing careers. For example, David Filo and Jerry Yang started making lists of their favorite Websites while they were graduate students. They went on to create Yahoo!, which became the world's most popular site.[1]

Do your best at every job. Once you get a job, make it your intention to excel as an employee. A positive work experience can pay off for years by leading to other jobs, recommendations, and contacts.

See if you can find a job related to your chosen career. Even an entry-level job in your field can provide valuable experience. Once you've been in such a job for a while, explore the possibilities for getting a promotion—or a higher-paying job with another employer.

No matter what job you have, be as productive as possible. Look for ways to boost sales, increase quality, or accomplish tasks in less time.

To maximize your earning power, also keep honing your job-hunting and career-planning skills. You can find a wealth of ideas on these topics in Chapters Two and Ten.

Finally, keep things in perspective. If your job is lucrative and rewarding, great. If not, remember that almost any job can support you in reaching your educational goals and becoming a master student.

Start saving now. You can begin saving now even if you are in debt and living in a dorm on a diet of macaroni. Saving now helps you establish a habit that will really pay off in the future.

Take some percentage of every paycheck you receive and immediately deposit that amount in a savings account. To build money for the future, start by saving 10 percent of your income. Then see if you can increase that amount over time.

The first purpose of this savings account is to have money on hand for surprises and emergencies—anything from a big repair bill to a sudden job loss. For peace of mind, have an emergency fund equal to three to six months of living expenses.

Next, save for longer-term goals. Examples are a new car, a child's education, and your own retirement.

Keep your savings in liquid investments such as an FDIC-insured savings account at a bank. The word *liquid* means that you can withdraw the money immediately.

Other options for saving include certificates of deposit and Treasury securities (bills, notes, and bonds backed by the federal government). These are not as liquid as a savings account. However, they are low-risk ways to save for longer-term goals.

It's never too early to start thinking about your retirement. Many employers offer 401(k) retirement plans and will match employee contributions to these accounts. Perhaps you're lucky enough to work for an employer who offers a full range of benefits. In addition to retirement plans, these might include discounted insurance plans, tuition reimbursement, and more. Schedule a meeting with your supervisor or someone in the employee benefits department to explore your options.

Invest carefully. Investing in stocks, corporate bonds, and mutual funds can be risky. Do so only if you regularly save money and pay off the full balance on your credit cards each month. Even then, only invest money that you can afford to lose.

If you meet these criteria, then consider lower-risk investments such as Treasury securities, bonds, no-load mutual funds, and blue chip stocks.

Successful investing requires extensive homework. Educate yourself by taking a class about personal finance and getting coaching from an independent, certified financial planner.

No matter how you choose to invest, put time on your side. Invest as much as you can, as early as you can. This gives you the power of long-term compound interest. Say that you invest $500 in an account that earns 8 percent interest. In 30 years, that investment will grow to $5,031. Given the same interest rate and number of years, a $1,000 investment will grow to $10,063.

Save on insurance. Once you have life insurance, you can usually stay insured even if you develop a major illness. So, it's wise to insure your life now.

There are basically two kinds of life insurance: term and whole life. Term insurance is the least expensive. It pays if you die and that's it. Whole life is more expensive. It pays if you die, and it also accumulates money like a savings plan. However, you'll often get a higher return on your money if you buy the lower-priced term insurance and invest your extra dollars in something other than insurance.

Before you choose a policy, shop with more than one agent. Ask questions about anything you don't understand. If the agent can't answer your questions, then get another agent.

The same suggestions apply to buying any kind of insurance. Buy policies with higher deductibles to save on premiums. Ask for safe driver, nonsmoker, multiple policy, and good student discounts.

Getting affordable, comprehensive health insurance can be challenging. It's worth the effort. About half of the personal bankruptcies in the United States are due to health care costs.[2]

Many schools offer competitive health insurance for students. Find out what's available on your campus. ☒

Spend less money

Spend less than you earn. This principle does not require that you live like a miser, pinching pennies and saving used dental floss. Controlling your expenses is something you can do right away, and it's usually easier than increasing your income. Use some ideas from the following list and invent more of your own.

Look to big-ticket items. When you look for places to cut expenses, start with the items that cost the most. Choices about where to live, for example, can save you thousands of dollars. Sometimes a place a little farther from campus, or a smaller house or apartment, will be much less expensive. You can also keep your housing costs down by finding a roommate.

Another high-ticket item is a car. Take the cost of buying or leasing and then add expenses for parking, insurance, repairs, gas, maintenance, and tires. You might find that it makes more sense to use public transportation.

Look to small-ticket items. Decreasing the money you spend on low-cost purchases can make the difference between a balanced budget and rising debt. For example, three dollars spent at the coffee shop every day adds up to $1,095 over a year. That kind of spending can give anyone the jitters. Reduce or eliminate such small but regular purchases.

Consider the life energy you're spending. According to authors Joe Dominguez and Vicki Robin, money is what we accept in exchange for our life energy—our time and effort. These authors suggest that you calculate your real hourly wage as a way to measure your life energy.[3] This wage is the amount you're paid for each hour of work—minus work-related expenses, such as transportation and childcare. If you find out that a new DVD player will cost 50 hours of life energy, then you might reconsider how important this item is to you.

Do comparison shopping. Prices vary dramatically. Shop around, wait for off-season sales, and use coupons. Check out secondhand stores, thrift stores, and garage sales. Before plunking down the full retail price for a new item, also consider whether you could buy it used.

Be aware of quality. The cheapest product is not always the least expensive over the long run. Sometimes, a slightly more expensive item is the best buy because it will last longer.

Cook for yourself. This single suggestion could save many a sinking budget. Instead of eating out, head to the grocery store. Fresh fruits, fresh vegetables, and whole grains are not only better for you than processed food—they cost less.

Consume alcohol consciously. Each year, American college students spend over $5 billion on alcohol.[4] One cost-saving solution is to simply abstain. If you are of legal age and prefer to drink, then buy your own liquor rather than drinking in restaurants or bars. The markup on alcohol is enough to make you dizzy.

Conserve energy. To save money on utility bills, turn out the lights. Keep windows and doors closed in winter. Avoid loss of cool air in summer. In cool weather, dress warmly and keep the house at 68 degrees or less. In hot weather, take cool showers and baths. Leave air conditioning at 72 degrees or above.

Pay cash. To avoid interest charges, deal in cash. If you don't have the cash, don't buy. Buying on credit makes it more difficult to monitor spending. You can easily bust next month's budget with this month's credit card purchases.

Fix things yourself. Many repair or service jobs are easy when you take the time to look into them. Ask friends for help and buy them lunch or treat them to a movie in return. This is often cheaper—and more fun—than paying a repair shop.

Postpone purchases. If you plan to buy something, leave your checkbook or credit card at home when you first go shopping. Look at all the possibilities. Then go home and make your decision when you don't feel pressured.

Notice what you spend on "fun." Blowing your money on fun is fun. It is also a fast way to bust your budget. When you spend money on entertainment, ask yourself what the benefits will be and whether you could get the same benefits for less money. You can read magazines for free at the library. Most libraries also loan music tapes, videotapes, and DVDs for free.

Don't compete with big spenders. When you watch other people spend their money, remember that you don't know the whole story. Some students have parents with deep pockets. Others head to Mexico every year for spring break but finance the trips with high-interest credit cards.

If you find yourself feeling pressured to spend money so that you can keep up with other people, stop to think about how much it will cost over the long run. Maybe it's time to shop around for some new friends. ☒

critical thinking exercise 30

SHOW ME THE MONEY

See if you can create a financial gain from using *From Master Student to Master Employee* that is many times more than the cost of the book. Scan the entire text and look for suggestions that could help you save money or increase income in significant ways; for example:

- Use suggestions for career planning and job hunting in Chapters Two and Ten to find your next job more quickly—and start earning money sooner.
- Negotiate a higher salary for your next job. See the article "Use interviews to hire yourself an employer" on page 320.
- Using suggestions for goal setting from Chapter Two, create a detailed plan to acquire a skill that will make it easier for you to get a higher-paying job.

In the space below, write your ideas for creating more money from your experience of this book. Use additional paper as needed.

____

____

____

____

____

Take charge of your credit

A good credit rating will serve you for a lifetime. With this asset, you'll be able to borrow money any time that you need it.

A poor credit rating, on the other hand, can keep you from getting the car or house that you want. You might also have to pay higher insurance rates, and you could even be turned down for a job.

Borrow money only when truly necessary. If you do borrow, then make all of your payments, and make them on time. This is especially important for managing credit cards and student loans.

Use credit cards with caution

Credit cards often come with a hefty interest rate, sometimes as high as 20 percent. Imagine working five days a week and getting paid for only four: You'd lose one-fifth of your income. Likewise, when people rely on high-interest credit cards to get by from month to month, they can lose one-fifth of their monthly payments to interest charges.

In a 2000 survey by Nellie Mae, a student loan corporation, 78 percent of undergraduate students had credit cards. Their average credit card debt was $2,748. Suppose that a student with this debt used a credit card with an annual percentage rate of 18 percent. Also suppose that he pays only the minimum balance due each month. He'll be making payments for 15 years and will pay an additional $2,748 in interest fees.[5]

Credit cards do offer potential benefits. Having one means that you don't have to carry around a checkbook or large amounts of cash, and they're pretty handy in emergencies. Getting a card is one way to establish a credit record. And some cards offer rewards, such as frequent flier miles and car rental discounts.

Used unwisely, however, credit cards can leave us with a debt load that takes decades to repay. This can seriously delay other goals—paying off student loans, financing a new car, buying a home, or saving for retirement.

Scrutinize credit card offers. Beware of cards offering low interest rates. These rates are often only temporary. After a few months, they could double or triple. Also look for annual fees, late fees, and other charges buried in the fine print.

Be especially wary of credit card offers made to students. Remember that the companies who willingly dispense cards on campus are not there to offer an educational service. They are in business to make money by charging you interest.

Avoid cash advances. Due to their high interest rates and fees, credit cards are not a great source of spare cash. Even when you get cash advances on these cards from an ATM, it's still borrowed money. As an alternative, get a debit card tied to a checking account and use that card when you need cash on the go.

Check statements against your records. File your credit card receipts each month. When you get the bill for each card, check it against your receipts for accuracy. Mistakes in billing are rare, but they can happen. In addition, checking your statement reveals the interest rate and fees that are being applied to your account.

Pay off the balance each month. An unpaid balance is a sure sign that you are spending more money than you have. To avoid this outcome, keep track of how much you spend with credit cards each month. Then save an equal amount in cash. That way, you can pay off the card balance each month and avoid interest charges. Following this suggestion alone might transform your financial life.

If you do accumulate a large credit card balance, go to your bank and ask about ways to get a loan with a lower interest rate. Use this loan to pay off your credit cards. Then promise yourself never to accumulate credit card debt again.

Use just one credit card. To simplify your financial life and take charge of your credit, consider using only one card. Choose one with no annual fee and the lowest interest rate. Don't be swayed by offers of free T-shirts or coffee mugs. Consider the bottom line and be selective.

Get a copy of your credit report. A credit report is a record of your payment history and other credit-related items. You are entitled to get a free copy each year. Go to your bank and ask someone there how to do this. You can also request a copy online at **https://www.annualcreditreport.com.** This site was created by three nationwide consumer credit-reporting companies—Equifax, Experian, and TransUnion. Check your report carefully for errors or accounts that you did not open.

If you're in trouble . . .

Financial problems are common. Solve them in ways that protect you for the future.

Get specific data. Complete the Money Monitor/Money Summary Plan exercise included earlier in this chapter.

Be honest with creditors. Determine the amount you are sure you can repay each month and ask if that would work for your case.

Go for credit counseling. Most cities have agencies with professional advisors who can help straighten out your financial problems.

Change your spending patterns. If you have a history of overspending (or underearning), change *is* possible. This chapter is full of suggestions.

Manage student loans

You don't have to go broke to get an education. It's true that a college degree is one of the best investments you can make. And you can make this investment at varying levels of debt. Keep yours as low as possible.

The number of college graduates with more than $40,000 of student debt has increased tenfold since 1993. According to the Project on Student Debt, a nonprofit research group, this is more than most people can manage to repay in ten years (the standard repayment period).[6]

Choose schools with costs in mind. If you decide to transfer to another school, you can save thousands of dollars at the moment you sign your applications for admission. In addition to choosing schools on the basis of reputation, consider how much they cost and the financial aid packages that they offer.

Some students just resign themselves to high debt loads. "I'll go to the best school that accepts me, no matter how much it costs," they say. "I'll worry about the loans later." That line of reasoning can leave you with loan payments that lower your standard of living for decades.

The surest way to manage debt is to avoid it altogether. If you do take out loans, then borrow only the amount that you cannot get from other sources—scholarships, grants, employment, gifts from relatives, and personal savings.

Shop around for loans. Look into loans with fixed interest rates that are guaranteed by the federal government. Stafford loans are available to students at any income level. If your parents are helping to pay for your education, they can apply for PLUS loans.

In contrast, loans from private companies often have variable interest rates. Those rates can vary widely depending on the borrower's credit rating.

Look for loans with features that make repayment easier. Avoid loans with prepayment penalties (extra charges for paying off the loan before the final due date). Also remember that interest payments on some forms of debt, such as home equity loans, may be tax-deductible.

Some lenders will forgive part of a student loan if you agree to take a certain job for a few years, such as teaching in a public school in a low-income neighborhood or working as a nurse in a rural community. Ask someone in the financial aid office if she knows of such programs.

YOU can pay for SCHOOL

There's a saying: Knowledge is power. When it comes to financial aid, knowledge is money. Millions of dollars are waiting for people who take part in higher education. But the funds flow only when students know how to find them.

There are many ways to pay for school. The kind of help you get depends on your financial need. In general, financial need equals the cost of your schooling minus what you can reasonably be expected to pay.

Getting financial aid has little to do with "being poor." Your prospects for aid depend greatly on the costs of the school you attend. Do not assume that your application for financial aid will be rejected.

Financial aid includes money you don't pay back (grants and scholarships), money you do pay back (loans), and work-study programs. Most students who get financial aid receive a package that includes several examples of each type.

To find out more, visit your school's financial aid office on a regular basis. Also go online. Start with FinAid, a Website posted by the federal government, at **http://www.finaid.org.**

Once you've lined up financial aid, keep it flowing. Find out the requirements for renewing loans, grants, and scholarships. Remember that many financial aid packages depend on your making "satisfactory academic progress." Also, programs change constantly. Money may be limited and application deadlines are critical.

Scholarships, grants, and loans backed by the federal government are key sources of money for students. There are other resources as well. State governments often provide grants and scholarships. So do credit unions, service organizations such as Kiwanis International, and local chambers of commerce. Sometimes relatives will provide financial help.

Selling something, while it might be a last resort, is an option. Consider the money you have tied up in a car, motorcycle, piano, house, or hobby.

If you start every term wondering where you are going to get money for school, you are more likely to drop out. Determine how much you need to complete your education and where you will get it. A plan for paying for your entire education makes it easier to finish your degree.

Education is worth it

Education is a unique purchase—one of the few things you can buy that will last a lifetime. It can't rust, corrode, break down, or wear out. It can't be stolen, burned, repossessed, or destroyed. Once you have a degree, no one can take it away. That makes your education a safer investment than real estate, gold, oil, diamonds, or stocks.

To get in touch with the value of higher education, think about all the services and resources that your tuition money buys: academic advising to help you choose classes and select a major; access to the student health center and counseling services; career planning and job placement offices that you can visit even after you graduate; athletic, arts, and entertainment events at a central location; a student center where you can meet people and socialize.

If you live on campus, you also get a place to stay with meals provided, all for less than the cost of an average hotel room.

And, by the way, you get to attend classes.

Consider how much nonstudents would have to pay for such an array of services. You can see that higher education is a bargain.

The benefits go even further. A 2005 study released by the College Board reports that higher levels of education are associated with:

- Higher incomes for both men and women in all racial and ethnic groups. For male college graduates, median earnings are 60 percent higher than those for male high school graduates. For females, there is a 58 percent premium for having a college degree. And among 25- to 34-year-olds who work full-time, white, Hispanic, and black college graduates earn about 60 percent more than high school graduates from the same racial and ethnic groups.
- Higher levels of volunteer work and voting.
- Higher tax revenues for governments, which fund libraries, schools, parks, and other public goods.
- Lower levels of unemployment, incarceration, dependence on social services, and smoking rates.[7]

In short, education is a good deal for you and for society. It's worth investing in periodically to update your skills, reach your goals, and get more of what you want in life.

critical thinking exercise 31

EDUCATION BY THE HOUR

Determine exactly what it costs you to go to school. Fill in the blanks below using totals for a semester, quarter, or whatever term system your school uses.

Note: Include only the costs that relate directly to going to school. For example, under "Transportation," list only the amount that you pay for gas to drive back and forth to school—not the total amount you spend on gas for a semester.

Tuition	$______
Books	$______
Fees	$______
Transportation	$______
Clothing	$______
Food	$______
Housing	$______
Entertainment	$______
Other (such as insurance, medical costs, and childcare) expenses	$______
Subtotal	$______
Salary you could earn per term if you weren't in school	$______
Total (A)	$______

Now figure out how many classes you attend in one term. This is the number of your scheduled class periods per week multiplied by the number of weeks in your school term. Put that figure below:

Total (B) $______

Divide the **Total (B)** into the **Total (A)** and put that amount here:

$______

This is what it costs you to go to one class one time.

On a separate sheet of paper, describe your responses to discovering this figure. Also list anything you will do differently as a result of knowing the hourly cost of your education.

Complete this exercise online. *Student Website*

Using technology to manage money

If you own a computer, you can use it in a variety of ways to make peace with money. Consider the following options, including the suggestions for safe online transactions.

Sign up for direct deposit

Your employer might offer to deposit paychecks directly to a bank or credit union account. This saves you time—no waiting for checks to arrive, no waiting in line to make deposits in person, and no waiting for checks to clear.

Bank online

Many banks, credit unions, and brokerage firms now offer online services. These services typically allow you to view account activity, access account statements, transfer funds, and pay bills. You may have the choice of paying bills manually or setting up automatic payments. With either method, be sure to schedule payments at least five days before each bill's due date.

Use personal finance software

Products such as Quicken and Microsoft Money allow you to:

- Keep detailed records of activity related to your bank accounts, credit cards, mortgage, and investments.
- Reconcile your records with bank and credit card statements.

- Move money between accounts.
- Sort your income and expenses into categories.
- Organize records needed to prepare tax returns.
- Print reports and graphs that show your income and expenses.
- Compare your actual expenses to budgeted amounts.
- Receive notices of low balances and potential overdraft fees.
- Plan for major purchases and long-term financial goals, such as retirement.
- Create reminders for when bills are due.
- Print checks.

If you bank online, you can download account transactions directly from your bank's Website to your personal finance software. This reduces the time needed to enter data.

Avoid scams

Con artists have been around ever since money was invented. Today, they're active online, looking for high-tech ways to peddle their schemes. Don't fall for them.

One scheme is called *phishing*. It works like this: You receive an e-mail that looks as if it came from a bank or credit card company. The e-mail asks you to verify your account number, PIN, password, social security number, or other private information by clicking on a link.

If you get such a message, trash it. No reputable business asks for this kind of information via e-mail. People who forget this fact set themselves up for identity theft.

Guard your money data

To prevent other security breaches when managing money online:

- Keep account information, including your social security number, private.
- For money transactions, use Websites with an address (URL) that begins with **https://** rather than **http://.** The extra *s* stands for "secure," meaning that any data you send will be encrypted and nearly impossible to steal.
- Check the lower right-hand corner of your browser for an icon that looks like a closed lock. This also indicates a secure site.
- Don't manage your money on public computers. Other users could see your information displayed on the screen and watch the keyboard as you type in passwords.
- Don't let your Web browser store passwords and other login information for sites that you use to manage money. People who know how to access this information could hack in to your accounts.
- Take any financial documents you print out or receive in the mail and shred them before throwing them away.

Make responsible online purchases

Modern technology has created a new form of impulse buying—the "sip and click" transaction. The *New York Times* reported the story of a man who had several drinks and then decided to do some online shopping. He found a piece of jewelry advertised on a Website for $1,500 and bought it for his girlfriend. When he got his next credit card bill, he discovered that he'd misplaced the decimal point. The actual charge was $15,000.[8]

Avoid buying online with a brain that's offline. Shop sober. ⊠

You are ALREADY rich

Step back in time just a few centuries and imagine how a king, queen, or other wealthy person might have lived.

These people had enough to eat. Sometimes they even had feasts. In their food would be spices from the four corners of the earth. Guests would eat until they were stuffed. After the meal, they summoned entertainment with the snap of a finger.

Transportation was no problem. Horses were always ready and a driver would chauffeur the king or queen from kingdom to kingdom.

Dress was lavish. Monarchs wore the latest fashions. The king and queen got new clothes at least once a year and never had to wear anything that was full of holes.

Royal families often lived in castles. Sometimes these were drafty and chilly. Yet the inhabitants were safe from nature and usually safe from intruders.

True, infectious disease was common in those days, and life spans were shorter than they are now. Yet the richest people lived out their years in relative ease.

In short, these people lived a royal existence.

And they lacked central heating, air conditioners, refrigerators, stoves, public transportation, public parks, libraries, television, CDs, DVDs, computers, and many other comforts and conveniences that most of us enjoy today.

Some people don't say to themselves, "We live like royalty." They don't see the riches they possess right now. Through their selective perceptions, they create lives based on scarcity rather than abundance. They might roll their eyes if you tell them that real wealth is all about loving relationships, fulfilling work, and continuous opportunities to learn. Tell them that money worries are unnecessary and they might even get upset.

This article is not meant to upset anyone. The point is to consider a new way of thinking. Ideas such as "Wealth means more than having money" and "I am already rich" can change how you feel about money. They can open you up to new possibilities for making and saving money. And that can affect how much money you actually have.

Test this idea for yourself. For example, see if you can apply each of the Power Processes to your relationship with money. You can ease frustration by being here now, detaching, surrendering, letting go of your pictures of how much money you ought to have, loving your frustration to death, or looking at how you create your money problems. ⊠

Free fun

Sometimes it seems that the only way to have fun is to spend money. Not true. Search out free entertainment on campus and in your local community. Also remember that donating your time to community organizations can be a way to contribute to society—and have fun at the same time.

Beyond this, your imagination is the only limit on free fun. Some suggestions are listed below and more are on the Student Website. If you think that they're silly or boring, then create better ideas of your own.

- Browse a bookstore
- Donate blood
- Draw
- Exercise
- Find other people who share your hoby and start a club
- Give a haircut
- Give a massage

Practicing money skills at work

The expertise you develop now in monitoring money, increasing income, and decreasing expenses can help you succeed professionally. Look for ways to practice these skills on the job. The following examples can stimulate your thinking.

Develop financial literacy now. Your next job may require you to prepare budgets, keep money records, make financial forecasts, and adjust income and expenses in order to meet an organization's financial goals. The ability to handle such tasks successfully is called workplace financial literacy.

Think about the ways you'll be handling money in your chosen career. If you plan to become an architect, for example, you'll need to estimate costs for a building project, request bids from contractors, and then evaluate those bids. Find out more by interviewing people who work in your field. Ask them how they handle money on the job.

After listing the financial skills that you need, consider which courses you'll take to develop them. You might benefit from classes in business management or accounting.

Learn spreadsheet software. With spreadsheet programs such as Microsoft's Excel, you can enter data into charts with rows and columns and then apply various formulas. This makes it possible to create budgets, income reports, expense records, and investment projections. Master this software now and you'll have a marketable skill to add to your résumé.

Get continuing financial education at work. Stress related to personal finances can have a negative impact on an employee's productivity. Recognizing this, many companies offer free workshops topics. These include classes on retirement planning, insurance planning, investing, college funding, and estate planning.

Keep records of financial success on the job. Throughout your career, keep track of the positive outcomes you produce at work, including financial successes. Summarize these results in a sentence or two and add them to your résumé as well.

Whenever you deliver a project on time and on budget, write Discovery Statements about how you created that result. Follow up with Intention Statements about ways to be even more effective on your next project.

Consider income and expenses related to your career choices. Your career plan can include estimates of how much money you'll earn in various jobs in your field. In addition, think about the possible expenses involved in your career choice. If you're planning a career that requires graduate school, for example, then consider how you will pay for that education.

Perhaps advancement in your career calls for additional certifications or coursework. Examples are continuing education credits for teachers and board certifications for nurses and physicians. Start thinking now about how you'll meet such requirements.

An equally important consideration is your choice about where to locate after graduating from school. Given the high cost of living in certain cities, this choice can have a big impact on your personal finances.

Consider whether your career calls for living in a major metropolitan area with high housing and transportation costs. If so, then set salary goals that will help you cover such costs, with money to spare.

Define your values *align your actions*

If you're in a conversation with friends and introduce the topic of *values clarification*, you might notice a few eyes roll. Some people see values as warm, fuzzy, and unreal. To them, talking about values is like talking about corporate mission and vision statements—pleasant platitudes that have nothing to do with daily life.

Actually, values are as real as dollar bills. If you want an instant index of your values, look at your calendar and credit card statements. Values are the principles that influence our moment-to-moment choices, including choices about how we spend our time and how we spend our money.

Some people are guided by values that they automatically adopt from others or by values that remain largely unconscious. These people could be missing the opportunity to live a life that's truly of their own choosing.

Investing time and energy to define your values is a pivotal suggestion in this book. In fact, *From Master Student to Master Employee* is based on a particular value system. It underlies every suggestion in the book. This system includes the values of:

- Focused attention
- Self-responsibility
- Integrity
- Risk taking
- Contributing

You'll find these values and related ones directly stated in the Power Processes throughout the text. For example:

Discover what you want is about the importance of living a purpose-based life.
Ideas are tools points to the benefits of being willing to experiment with new ideas.
Love your problems (and experience your barriers) is about seeing difficulties as opportunities to develop new skills.
Be here now expresses the value of focused attention.
Notice your pictures and let them go is about adopting an attitude of open-mindedness.
I create it all is about taking responsibility for our beliefs and behaviors.
Detach reminds us that our core identity and value as a person does not depend on our possessions, our circumstances, or even our accomplishments.
Find a bigger problem is about offering our lives by contributing to others.
Employ your word expresses the value of making and keeping agreements.

In addition, most of the techniques and strategies that you read about in these pages have their source in values. The Time Monitor/Time Plan critical thinking exercise, for example, calls for focused attention. Even the simple act of sharing your notes with a student who missed a class is an example of contributing.

Start by monitoring your spending. This allows you to make financial choices that are consistent with your stated values. For example, take the person who says that he values health and then discovers that he spends $300 per month on alcohol and fast food. He concludes that there's a contradiction between his values and his behavior. Now he can redefine his values, change his spending habits, or do both.

Students can also think critically about the wisdom of owning expensive gadgets, such as a cell phone or MP3 player, but not buying a textbook or other resource needed for education. It's true that digital gadgets can deliver many hours of entertainment. Compare that benefit to the possibility of graduating with high grades, marketable skills, and increased earning power for the rest of your working life. Then ask yourself which option is more aligned with your personal statement of values.

Defining your values is powerful. And it doesn't guarantee any results. To achieve your goals, take actions that align with your values. Following this suggestion alone can permanently change your relationship with money—and transform your life.

power process

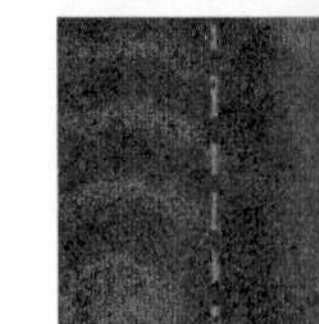

RISK BEING A FOOL

A powerful person has the courage to take risks. And taking risks means being willing to fail sometimes—even to be a fool. This idea can work for you because you already are a fool.

Don't be upset. All of us are fools at one time or another. There are no exceptions. If you doubt it, think back to that stupid thing you did just a few days ago. You know the one. Yes . . . *that* one. It was embarrassing and you tried to hide it. You pretended you weren't a fool. This happens to everyone.

People who insist that they have never been fools are perhaps the biggest fools of all. We are all fallible human beings. Most of us, however, spend too much time and energy trying to hide our foolhood. No one is really tricked by this—not even ourselves. And whenever we pretend to be something we're not, we miss part of life.

For example, many of us never dance because we don't want to risk looking ridiculous. We're not wrong. We probably would look ridiculous. That's the secret of risking being a fool.

It's OK to look ridiculous while dancing. It's all right to sound silly when singing to your kids. Sometimes it's OK to be absurd. It comes with taking risks.

Taking risks is not being foolhardy

Sometimes it's not OK to be absurd. This Power Process comes with a warning label: Taking risks does *not* mean escaping responsibility for our actions. "Risk being a fool" is not a suggestion to get drunk at a party and make a fool of yourself. It is not a suggestion to act the fool by disrupting class. It is not a suggestion to be foolhardy or to "fool around."

"Risk being a fool" means recognizing that foolishness—along with dignity, courage, cowardice, grace, clumsiness, and other qualities—is a human characteristic. We all share it. You might as well risk being a fool because you already are one, and nothing in the world can change that. Why not enjoy it once in a while? Consider the case of the person who won't dance because he's afraid he'll look foolish. This same person will spend an afternoon tripping over his feet on a basketball court. If you say that his jump shot from the top of the key looks like a circus accident, he might even agree.

"So what?" he might say. "I'm no Michael Jordan." He's right. On the basketball court, he is willing to risk looking like a fool in order to enjoy the game.

He is no Fred Astaire, either. For some reason, that bothers him. The result is that he misses the fun of dancing. (Dancing badly is as much fun as shooting baskets badly—and maybe a lot more fun.)

There's one sure-fire way to avoid any risk of being a fool, and that's to avoid life. The writer who never finishes a book will never have to worry about getting negative reviews. The center fielder who sits out every game is safe from making any errors. And the comedian who never performs in front of an audience is certain to avoid telling jokes that fall flat. The possibility of succeeding at any venture increases when we're comfortable with making mistakes—that is, with the risk of being a fool.

Look at courage in a new way

Again, remember the warning label. This Power Process does not suggest that the way to be happy in life is to do things badly. Courage involves the willingness to face danger and risk failure. Mediocrity is not the goal. The point is that mastery in most activities calls for the willingness to do something new, to fail, to make corrections, to fail again, and so on. On the way to becoming a good writer, be willing to be a bad writer.

Consider these revised clichés: Anything worth doing is worth doing badly at first. Practice makes improvement. If at first you don't fail, try again.

Most artists and athletes have learned the secret of being foolish. Comedians are especially well versed in this art. All of us know how it feels to tell a joke and get complete silence. We truly look and feel like fools. Professional comedians risk feeling that way for a living. Being funny is not enough for success in the comedy business. A comedian must have the courage to face failure.

The possibility of succeeding at any venture increases when we're comfortable with making mistakes—that is, with the risk of being a fool.

Courage is an old-fashioned word for an old-fashioned virtue. Traditionally, people have reserved that word for illustrious acts of exceptional people—the campaigns of generals and the missions of heroes.

This concept of courage is fine. At the same time, it can be limiting and can prevent us from seeing courage in everyday actions. Courage is the kindergartner who, with heart pounding, waves good-bye to his parents and boards the bus for his first day of school. Courage is the 40-year-old who registers for college courses after being away from the classroom for 20 years.

For a student, the willingness to take risks means the willingness to experiment with new skills, to achieve personal growth, and sometimes to fail. The rewards of risk taking include expanded creativity, more satisfying self-expression, and more joy.

An experiment for you

Here's an experiment you can conduct to experience the joys of risk taking. The next time you take a risk and end up doing something silly or stupid, allow yourself to be totally aware of your reaction. Don't deny it. Don't cover it up. Notice everything about the feeling, including the physical sensations and thoughts that come with it. Acknowledge the foolishness. Be exactly who you are. Explore all of the emotions, images, and sensations surrounding your experience.

Also remember that we can act independently of our feelings. Courage is not the absence of fear but the willingness to take risks even when we feel fear. We can be keenly homesick and still register for classes. We can tremble at the thought of speaking in public yet still walk up to the microphone.

When we fully experience it, the fear of taking risks loses its power. Then we have the freedom to expand and grow.

career application

Gordon McGinnis, assistant dean and director of student activities at Mountain State University, had vehemently banned credit card solicitations during his five-year tenure.

Over the years, a number of credit card companies and banks had approached him, offering deals to market their cards on campus that would generate good income for the university.

Yet Gordon had heard stories from his colleagues at other colleges of students cutting back on classes or dropping out to earn money to pay off debt. And bad credit histories often hurt students seeking their first jobs. Many of them had both student loan and credit card debt.

Gordon had tried to convince the business school to offer basic courses on this topic for students who weren't business majors. So far, he'd had no luck.

Despite his successes in keeping the credit card hawkers at bay, Gordon faced a new challenge when he got a call from Elsie Lombardi, the university's treasurer and vice president for finance. "I just got an offer I don't think we can refuse," began Elsie. "The credit card division at Highland Bank Corporation wants us to enter into an exclusive credit card marketing program with them. They'll pay us $5 million over the next three years to allow them to be the only bank card issuer allowed to market on campus."

"While we could really use the money, I'm afraid I'll have to say no," replied Gordon, "I'm philosophically opposed to marketing credit cards on campus."

"I didn't know you were a philosopher," said Elsie. "Listen, this is a service that students want in a world where, like it or not, plastic is important. Having a credit card helps students establish a credit history. And most students handle cards as responsibly as adults.

Gordon paused. "Those are good points, Elsie. And if there's one thing that we can agree on, it's that our student organizations could always use a financial boost. Tell you what: I'd like to sleep on this before making a decision. Would you give me 24 hours to sleep on this? I'll get back to you tomorrow."[9]

Reflecting on this scenario

1. Identify at least one transferable skill that Gordon demonstrates in this scenario.

   ____

   ____

   ____

2. Consider Gordon's chances of finding a win-win option in this scenario. Can you think of a way for Gordon to promote financial literacy among students *and* take advantage of the marketing program that Elsie wants? Summarize your ideas here.

   ____

   ____

   ____

quiz

Name ______________________________ Date _____/_____/_____

1. List five sources of money to help students pay for their education.

2. Describe at least three ways to decrease your expenses while you are in school.

3. How can you avoid getting into financial trouble when you use credit cards?

4. If you are in financial trouble, which of the following strategies is *least* likely to help?
   (a) Monitor your income and expenses.
   (b) Borrow additional money.
   (c) Be honest with creditors.
   (d) Go for credit counseling.
   (e) Change your spending patterns.

5. The text asserts that investing in your education is safer than investing in real estate, gold, oil, or stocks. List the reasons given for this assertion.

6. A First Step approach to managing money is to:
   (a) Admit that you probably don't have enough money.
   (b) Admit that money management is complicated.
   (c) Tell the truth about how much money you have and how much you spend.
   (d) All of the above
   (e) None of the above.

7. Privately owned companies generally offer better student loans than the federal government. True or False? Explain your answer.

8. The Power Process: "Risk being a fool" suggests that you sometimes take action without considering the consequences. True or False? Explain your answer.

9. Describe three strategies for increasing your income.

10. List three ways to make online transactions more secure.

learning styles application

The questions below will "cycle" you through four styles, or modes, of learning as explained in the article "Learning styles: Discovering how you learn" in Chapter One. Each question will help you explore a different mode. You can answer the questions in any order.

what if *After experimenting with your chosen strategy, describe any changes you'd like to make in the way you handle money in the future.*

why *Describe some aspect of your financial life that's not working as well as you'd like right now. For example, some people run out of money near the end of the month and rely on credit cards to make up the difference. Describe your own issue here.*

how *Commit to using one of the strategies you listed under* What? *Describe specifically what you will do to carry out this strategy.*

what *Consider the two basic options mentioned in this chapter for solving money problems: making more money and spending less money. Then list five specific strategies you could use to increase your income or decrease your expenses.*

master student profile

KAT JAMES

Profiled in What Should I Do with My Life?*—a book by Po Bronson about people who transformed their lives by asking that question.*

K*at James had never gone to* college, so she felt very lucky that the long boom years carried her up into the ranks of successful professionals. She worked for a public relations agency in London. The hours were long and demanding, and she'd often wonder, "What am I after? What do I want?" Her rote answer: someday, one of her clients would offer her a big salary and a Vice Presidency. She wanted to move up—or assumed she did. Didn't everyone? . . .

A year and a half ago, at a time when many people in high-tech felt lucky to have any job at all, Kat was offered a job running the P.R. department at one of the hottest telecoms in the UK. To convince her, they offered to *double* her salary. Double it!

At first she said yes, instinctively.

But the offer to double her salary had an unintended effect. It made it crystal clear that if she were to take this job, she would be doing it for the money. Not because it would be fun and interesting. For the money, plain and simple.

Over the next three weeks, she stalled. She told the telecom she was reconsidering.

She thought, *if I accept this, where will it end?*

This was not what she wanted the rest of her life.

. . . She had one thought. She barely let herself consider it. Ever since she was six years old, Kat had said that if money were no object,

and if status didn't matter, and if there were nothing in the way . . . she would be a landscape gardener.

Why not go do the thing she'd always wanted to do?

. . . A few days later, she went to a music festival, and between bands she had a Tarot card reading performed, somewhat as a joke. Kat didn't believe in that stuff. Up turned goddess cards and earth cards. The Tarot reader looked at these cards and pronounced, "You would be really good at tending people's gardens."

Wow! Was it that obvious, that a complete stranger could see this in her?

The next day, she recounted the amazing coincidence to a neighbor.

"Are you thinking about doing it?" the neighbor asked.

"I'm thinking," Kat said.

The neighbor said she had just thrown into the trash a catalog for courses at Brighton City College. "I'll go get it," she offered. Kat took the catalog into her house. The College offered an extensive horticulture program that awarded two-year vocational certification. The first class began the next week, and the enrollment session for the class *was that very afternoon.*

Guided by another in the string of coincidences, Kat went down to enroll immediately. She felt light and happy and excited about what she was doing.

Classes were from nine a.m. to five p.m., three days a week. A third of each day was spent in the classroom, two thirds outdoors. She loved it.

. . . Does she ever regret not taking that doubled salary?

She said many people in her shoes would have taken the double salary in order to save up for the leap into garden design, believing that money is the path to freedom. She didn't, and she's found that true freedom comes from the confidence she can live within her means, whatever those means may be.

For more information about Kat James, visit the Master Student Hall of Fame on the *From Master Student to Master Employee* Website.

10 Working

MASTER STUDENT MAP

why this chapter matters . . .

You can gain strategies to succeed as a job hunter and employee.

how you can use this chapter . . .

Learn effective strategies for job hunting.
Create résumés that lead to job interviews.
Go into job interviews fully prepared.
Build satisfying relationships with coworkers.

As you read, ask yourself

what if . . .

I could do work that expresses my core values and connects daily with my passions?

what is included . . .

FROM THE DESK OF . . .

By concentrating on a few key efforts such as sharing credit, showing grace under pressure, and promoting your ambition in appropriate ways, your day job can lead to the career of your dreams.

—STEPHEN VISCUSI, CEO, THE VISCUSI GROUP

The master employee

The title of this book—*From Master Student to Master Employee*—implies that these two types of mastery have something in common. To some people, this idea sounds half-baked. They separate life into two distinct domains: work and school. One is the "real" world. The other is the place where you attend classes to prepare for the real world.

Consider another point of view—the idea that success in higher education promotes success on the job.

There's some pretty hard-nosed evidence for this idea. One factor is that higher levels of education are correlated with higher levels of income. Another is that mastery in school and in work seems to rest on a common set of transferable skills.

Consider the Secretary's Commission on Achieving Necessary Skills (SCANS) issued by the U.S. Department of Labor.[1] According to this document, one crucial skill for the workplace is a personal quality called responsibility. This is demonstrated by any employee who:

- "Exerts a high level of effort and perseverance toward goal attainment.
- "Works hard to become excellent at doing tasks by setting high standards, paying attention to details, working well, and displaying a high level of concentration even when assigned an unpleasant task.
- "Displays high standards of attendance, punctuality, enthusiasm, vitality, and optimism in approaching and completing tasks."

A better definition of mastery would be hard to find. And if you've ever exerted a high level of effort to complete an assignment, paid attention to the details of a lecture, or displayed a high level of concentration while reading a tough textbook, then you've already demonstrated some key aspects of self-responsibility and mastery.

When you graduate from school, you don't leave your capacity for mastery locked inside a classroom. Excellence in one setting paves the way for excellence in other settings.

For example, a student who knows how to show up for class on time is ready to show up for work on time. The student who knows how to focus attention during a lecture is ready to focus attention during a training session at work. And a student who's worked cooperatively in a study group brings a lot of skills to the table when joining a workplace team. You can multiply this list by reflecting on each of the skills explained in this book.

A master employee embraces change, takes risks, and looks for chances to lead others while contributing to the quality of their lives. A master employee completes tasks efficiently, communicates openly and respectfully, and commits to lifelong learning. In developing a mastery of higher education, you'll do all this and more. *Master student* and *master employee* are names for qualities that already exist in you, waiting to be expressed as you embrace new ideas and experiment with new behaviors.

journal entry 26

Discovery/Intention Statement

Reflect on all the jobs you've held in your life. What aspect of working would you most like to change? Answers might include job hunting with less frustration, resolving conflicts with coworkers, building a better relationship with your boss, or coping with office politics. Describe the change that would make the biggest positive difference in your job satisfaction over the long run.

I discovered that I . . .

____

____

____

____

____

Now preview this chapter for ideas that could help you make the positive change you just described. List three to five suggestions below, along with the page numbers where you can read more about them.

Strategy	*Page number*

Use power tools for finding work

Tool #1: Upgrade your strategies

When applied to finding work, not all strategies are equal. People often find job searches less effective when they do the following things:

- Rely exclusively on want ads when looking for a job.
- Mail out a stack of résumés and cover letters and simply wait for a reply.
- Wait for a job to open up before contacting potential employers.
- Work only with employment agencies and human resources departments in large companies.

These methods are not all useless. Rather, problems arise when we rely on just one strategy and exclude others.

As an alternative, consider the following ideas. They can greatly increase your chances of finding the work you want:

- Make direct contact with a person who can hire you.
- Make such contacts even when the job you want is not yet open or even conceived.
- Cultivate a list of contacts, join professional associations, and meet people in your field.
- Use information interviews to research companies and meet people who support your career success.
- Approach a former employer with your updated résumé. Talk about the kind of positions you can apply for *now* with your recent degree.
- Join a support group for people who are looking for work.
- Write thank-you notes after an interview.
- Present yourself impeccably—everything from error-free résumés to well-polished shoes.

Tool #2: Meet employers right on campus

Many companies use campus interviews when they want to fill jobs with a recent graduate. In a survey conducted by the National Association of Colleges and Employers, campus recruitment topped the list of favored methods for recruiting new hires. (Second and third on the list were filling jobs from internships and asking employees for referrals.)[2]

Companies schedule campus interviews on specific dates. Check with your school's career center for details. The career center might also offer classes or workshops to help you prepare for these interviews.

Articles included later in this chapter give suggestions for writing a résumé and job interviewing. Before you leave a campus interview, consider asking these specific questions:

- Are you looking to fill current job openings? If so, what are they?
- How can I follow up on the status of my application?
- How can I find out about future job openings with your company?

Tool #3: Create your own job

Lists of job openings never include positions that are waiting to be created. With a little imagination and analysis, you can create a job or career where none exists.

Students have a long history of creating self-employment and small businesses to help pay the bills. Some examples are:

- Word processing for papers and theses
- Computer consulting
- Baby sitting and childcare
- Gardening and lawn care
- Doing minor house repairs and odd jobs
- Offering a delivery and errand service
- Pet care and dog walking
- Taking photographs or producing videos of weddings and parties
- Writing, editing, and proofreading on a freelance basis

You might use creative thinking to expand such enterprises into a lifelong career. All it takes is looking for an unmet need that you can respond to with a new product or service.

Another option is to redesign a job you already have. Sometimes companies allow employees to create new positions or businesses "within" a business.

Tool #4: Attend to the details

The whole process of finding work may hang on details such as getting to appointments on time, respecting an interviewer's schedule, and staying no longer than agreed.

To make your job search more effective, sweat the small stuff. Ask yourself: "What is one more thing I can do to make my job research more complete or my presentation more effective?" Keep taking that next step, however small. Each one takes you closer to finding the work you love.

Tool #5: Use technology to power your job search

Millions of people go online to research potential employers, find job openings, post résumés, and submit applications. While this technology offers many benefits, it can also lead to frustration: The haphazard organization of the Internet can make it hard for potential employers to find your résumé online. And many job openings are not listed on the Internet (or anywhere else for that matter).

This is not meant to disparage the Internet as a tool for job hunters and career planners. For more powerful job hunting, supplement the Internet with face-to-face contact. Get out and talk to people in your career field, including those who can hire you someday.

View the Internet as just one resource.

Tool #6: When job offers are scarce, stay flexible

Some people are lucky enough to graduate from higher education with a job offer or two in hand. However, many new graduates plan to spend their first weeks after the commencement party in an all-out job hunt.

If you're in this situation, you won't be alone. And if you've done career planning as suggested in Chapter Two, you'll have a head start on finding work.

Stay in contact with classmates who are job hunting or those who have just found jobs. These people, especially those with similar career interests, can be excellent sources of referrals.

Perhaps you'll find out about an entry-level job that's related to your chosen career—but not quite the job you envisioned. Consider the possible benefits of taking it. This choice might pay off if you're weeks or months into your job search, and if the position offers a chance to "step up" to a position that's more in tune with your career plan.

Tool #7: Cope with emotional ups and downs

Job hunting can pose psychological challenges. Your self-confidence can crack a little when people don't return your calls, or when job applications disappear into the void with no response.

Whatever your feelings, take a First Step about them. There's power in telling the truth to yourself and to a good listener. You can go into more depth by writing Discovery Statements about your changing moods.

Follow up with Intention Statements about the next strategies that you will use for your job search. One cornerstone of mental health is that you can *do* something constructive even when you *feel* sad or mad. Moving into action can change your mood and bring you closer to the job you've been waiting for.

REHEARSE YOUR JOB SEARCH

Imagine that you've completed your education as of today. Your next task is to find a job in a field of interest to you. The following questions will help you rehearse this job hunt.

If you are unsure of an answer, write down your best guess. Write your answers in the space below each question.

1. What kind of job will you apply for? If you choose self-employment, what product or service will you offer?

2. Where will you go to find a job? Will you approach an existing company or choose self-employment? If you opt for self-employment, how will you find potential customers or clients?

3. What kind of training, education, and experience is required for the kind of work that you want?

4. Next, visualize your job interview. Who will interview you? What questions will this person ask? What questions will you ask the interviewer?

5. Will this job be your "dream job"? If not, how long will it take you to find that ideal job?

Finally, review what you've just written. Does any of it suggest changes to make in your current course work or major? If so, describe the specific changes you intend to make.

Tell everyone you know

The art of networking

Networking means staying in touch with people to share career-planning ideas and track job openings. It's possible that more jobs are filled through networking than through any other method.

Following are ideas that can help you create a powerful network.

Start by listing contacts

A *contact* is often defined as someone who can help you implement your career plan. Such a person can give you inside information about job openings—or introduce you to someone else who knows about them. Contacts can also coach or mentor you. Sometimes they can hire you.

This definition makes for a broad list of possible contacts. They can include classmates, roommates, teachers, friends, relatives, and *their* friends. Also add former employers, current employers, staff members at your school's career center, members of your school's alumni association, and members of any professional organization to which you belong. Don't forget people who interviewed you for jobs in the past—even if they didn't hire you—and people who agreed to information interviews.

Start your contact list now. List each person's name, phone number, and e-mail address on a separate 3 × 5 card or Rolodex card. Another option is to keep your list on a computer, using word processing, database, or contact management software.

Whenever you speak to someone on your contact list, make brief notes about what you discussed. Also jot down any further actions you'll take to follow up on your discussion.

Craft your "pitch"

Develop a short statement of your career plans that you can easily share with people. For example: "After I graduate, I plan to work in the travel business. I'm looking for an internship in a travel agency that helps business people arrange international trips. I'm looking for agencies that take interns."

Focus on contribution

Networking is a two-way street. One purpose of networking is meeting people who will support you in meeting your career goals. An equally important purpose is assisting other people in meeting *their* goals.

This means developing the listening skills presented in Chapter Eight: Communicating. When you meet people, ask about their career plans. If they're willing to go into specifics, ask them what kind of work they'd like to be doing one year, five years, and even ten years from today. Then listen fully to what they say.

When you allow people to talk about the kind of jobs that excite them, you help them create a compelling and detailed vision for the future. This is a form of contribution. And when you can usefully put them in touch with someone you know, you add even more value to the relationship.

Get past the fear of competition

When told about networking, some people feel intimidated. They fear that others will steal or conceal job openings. *Why should I share this information with anybody?* goes the objection. *After all, we're competing with each other for the same jobs.*

Remember that few people in any network are actually going after the same jobs. Students majoring in education, for example, can work at many types of jobs, including noneducation jobs.

Also, any "competitor" could turn into a friend. Suppose someone in your network lands a job before you. This person might be in a position to recommend you for another job opening—or even to hire you.

Write a résumé that gets noticed

Your résumé is a living document that distills an essential part of your overall life plan. The attention you give to your résumé can pay you back hundreds of times over. Use a résumé to find a job that you love and a salary that matches your skills.

A résumé is a piece of persuasive writing, not a laundry list of previous jobs or a dry recitation of facts. This document has a purpose—to get you to the next step in the hiring process, usually an interview.

When writing a résumé, consider your audience. Picture a person who has a hundred résumés to plow through, and almost no time for it. She may spend only 30 seconds scanning each résumé before making a decision about who to call for interviews.

Your goal is to get past this first cut. Neatness, organization, and correct grammar and punctuation are essential. Meet these goals, and then make an even stronger impression with the following strategies.

Consider a standard format

There is no formula for a great résumé. Employers have many different preferences for what they want to see. Strike a reasonable balance by using a common format.

Begin with contact information—your name, mailing address, e-mail address, and phone number.

Next, describe your desired job, often called an *objective* or *goal.* Keep this to one sentence, and tailor it to the specific job for which you're applying.

Follow with the body of your résumé—major headings such as *experience* and *education.*

Write your "experience" section carefully. Here is where you give details about your past jobs, listed in order. This is the heart of a *chronological* résumé.

Employers pay special attention to this section. They read it with several questions in mind: How long did you stay at each job? Were your jobs related? Did you develop new skills and gain new responsibilities over time? What kind of contribution can you make to our company?

List details that answer these questions. Include your past job titles, names of your employers, and job duties. Whenever possible, use phrases that start with an active verb: "*supervised* three people," "*generated* leads for sales calls," "*wrote* speeches and *edited* annual reports," "*designed* a process that reduced production expenses by 20 percent."

Active verbs refer directly to your skills. Make them relevant to the job you're seeking, and tie them to specific accomplishments whenever possible. Be prepared to discuss these accomplishments during a job interview.

Your experience might include a variety of jobs in different fields. See if you can relate them to your objective. Say that your objective is to become a software engineer, and you spent the past three summers working at a bookstore. Perhaps your bookstore experience included customer service and training other employees. These are transferable skills, and they can be essential to people in your field. List them in your résumé.

Finish on a strong note. You might end your résumé with an intriguing statement ("I enjoy turning around departments with low morale") or a favorable quote from a coworker ("Julio regularly exceeded the requirements of his job").

Note: An alternative to the chronological format is the *functional* résumé. It highlights the functions, or skills, that you developed and used rather than the jobs you held. This format might be useful for people with limited experience or gaps in their work history.

Cut the fluff

Leave out information that could possibly eliminate you from the hiring process and send your résumé hurtling into the circular file. Some items to delete or question are these:

- Boilerplate language—stock wording or vague phrases such as "proven success in a high-stress environment," "highly motivated self-starter," or "a demonstrated capacity for strategic thinking."
- The date you're available to start a new job.
- Salary information, including what you've earned in the past and want to earn now.
- Details about jobs you held over 10 years ago.
- Reasons for leaving previous jobs.

Note that employers cannot legally discriminate against job applicants based on personal information such as age, national origin, race, religion, disability, and pregnancy status. Including this kind of information on your résumé might even hurt your job prospects. To learn more about types of job discrimination, access the U.S. Equal Employment Opportunity Commission (EEOC) at **http://www.eeoc.gov/types/index.html.** This Website also explains how to file a charge of discrimination.

Get feedback

Ask friends and family members if your résumé is persuasive and easy to understand. Also get feedback from someone at your school's career-planning center. Revise your résumé based on their comments. Then revise some more. Create sparkling prose that will intrigue a potential employer enough to call you for an interview.

Check your online presence

While you're preparing a résumé, take a break to type your name into a popular Internet search engine such as Google and see what results you get. Potential employers may do a similar search. If you've posted a blog or other online profile, make sure it's consistent with the image you want to present to employers.

Combine your résumé with other strategies

To get the most from your résumé, use it to supplement other job-hunting strategies. Research companies and do information interviews. Take part in internships and other work experiences in your chosen field. Create a career-planning support group and find a mentor.

Go ahead and contact potential employers directly—even if they don't have a job opening at the moment. Find people in organizations who have the power to hire you. Then use every job contact you have to introduce yourself to those people and schedule an interview. If you just send out résumés and neglect to make personal contacts, you may be disappointed.

Each time you meet with someone, leave your résumé behind. Then stay in touch. Periodically remind a potential employer of your existence. Send a short personal note: "Here's an updated résumé to put in my file." If the company doesn't have a file on you yet, chances are that somebody will start one. At that point, your name will start to stand out from the crowd. Your résumé is doing its job. 

For more information, visit the *From Master Student to Master Employee* Website.

Keys to scannable résumés

Write your résumé so that it's easy to skim. Make key facts leap off the page. Use short paragraphs and short sentences. Use bulleted lists for key points. Also avoid filling the page with ink. Instead, leave some blank space between the major sections of your résumé.

Many companies use a computerized scanning program to catalog résumés and fill positions by using keyword searches. Human resources associates can quickly retrieve and route résumés to fill positions by matching their specifications with your qualifications.

Including appropriate keywords on your résumé can help it stand out from others. Review job postings to find buzzwords in your field of interest. Include these words on your résumé.

Other things to keep in mind:

- Describe your experience with concrete terms. For example: "manager of mechanical engineering team" instead of "responsible for managing professionals."
- Use common headings such as: Objective, Experience, Education, Professional Experience, Affiliations, and Certifications.
- Get recognized by including specific positions and leadership roles you have held, related work experience, and degrees or certifications you have completed.

Print your scannable résumé on one side of an $8\frac{1}{2}$" × 11" sheet of plain white paper with an easy-to-read font and layout. If your résumé is more than one page in length, be sure your name and contact information appear on both sheets of paper. Avoid using italics, boldface, or underlining and other special text formatting.

Do not staple or fold your résumé. Instead, deliver it by hand or send it in an oversized envelope.

Sample résumés

Susan Chang
susangeorgia276@aol.com
2500 North Highland Avenue, Atlanta, GA 30306
770-899-8707

Work Experience:	**LAND Enterprises, Inc., Atlanta, GA** Administrative Assistant: January 2005–present • Responsible for supporting national sales manager and three district managers in creating reports for nationwide sales staff. • Create, prepare, and maintain Excel spreadsheets with weekly sales data. • Manage sales representative calendar of events in Lotus Notes database.
	Peachtree Bank, Alpharetta, GA Teller: May 2001–December 2004 • Responsible for receiving cash/checks for deposits, processing withdrawals, and accepting loan payments. • Communicated with customers and provided account balance and savings and loan information. • Provided friendly and prompt customer service.
Education:	**Macon State Community College, Macon, GA** AA—Communications and Information Technology; May 2007 Overall GPA—3.0
Volunteer:	**Macon Chamber of Commerce** Holiday Events Coordinator 2000–2006 • Maintained budget from Chamber of Commerce for annual holiday parties. • Solicited donations from local businesses to support monthly events.
Computer Skills:	Microsoft Word, Microsoft Excel, Microsoft Access, Lotus Notes, PowerPoint.
Personal:	Interested in writing poetry, playing team sports, and traveling.
References:	Available upon request.

Lamont Jackson
2250 First Avenue, #3 • New York, NY 10029 • (212) 222-5555
Lamont_Jackson44@hotmail.com

Objective

To obtain a position as a public relations associate that allows me to utilize my writing and communication skills.

Education

Rutgers University, New Brunswick, NJ
BA in English, minor in Business Communication; May 2007
Major GPA — 3.2; Minor GPA — 3.3

Experience

The Medium, Rutgers University, New Brunswick, NJ
Contributing Writer, August 2006 to May 2007

- Developed feature articles pertaining to faculty and student issues and community issues.
- Responsible for writing weekly sidebar featuring community service on and off campus.

Shandwick Public Relations, New York, NY
Intern, summer 2005

- Coordinated mass mailings of press releases to medical community biweekly.
- Conducted health surveys focusing on nutrition habits of senior citizens in the tristate area; organized all retrieved data of 1000 respondents.
- Handled telephone inquiries efficiently from clients and corporations represented by firm.

Activities

- Intramural Soccer Team, Spring 2007
- Habitat for Humanity, *Treasurer*, Fall 2005–Spring 2006
- Rutgers University Orientation Leader, Summer 2005

Skills

- Ability to perform on both PC and Macintosh platforms.
- Software knowledge that includes: Windows NT, Microsoft Office, Lotus Notes, Lotus 1-2-3, Quark, and beginning HTML.
- Fluency in Spanish — oral and written competency.

Honors

Rutgers University Dean's List, Fall 2004, Spring 2007

Sell your résumé with an effective cover letter

An effective cover letter can leave a prospective employer waiting with bated breath to read your résumé. An ineffective letter can propel your résumé to that nefarious stack of papers to be read "later." In some cases, a well-written letter alone can land you an interview.

Many cover letters are little more than a list of stock phrases. In essence, they say: "I want that job you listed. Here's my résumé. Read it, dude."

You can avoid this trap. Present your cover letter as a response to a specific job opening—not just a form letter. Also write with a tone that's professional *and* conversational. Avoid jargon such "attached please find my résumé for your perusal," or "I am writing in regard to the aforementioned position." Sound like a human being instead.

A three-part structure

Remember the primary question in an employer's mind: What do you have to offer us? Using a three-part structure can help you answer this question.

1 In your first sentence, address the person who can hire you and grab that person's attention. Make a statement that appeals directly to her self-interest. Write something that moves a potential employer to say, "We can't afford to pass this person up. Call him right away to set up an appointment."

To come up with ideas for your opening, complete the following sentence: "The main benefits that I can bring to your organization are. . . ." Another option: "My work experience ties directly to several points mentioned in your job description. First, ..."

Perhaps someone the employer knows told you about this job opening. Mention this person in your opening paragraph, especially if she has a positive reputation in the organization.

2 Next, build interest. Add a fact or two to back up your opening paragraph. Briefly refer to your experience and highlight one or two key achievements. If you're applying for a specific job opening, state this. If you're not, then offer an idea that will intrigue the employer enough to respond anyway.

3 Finally, take care of business. Refer the reader to your résumé. Then mention that you'll call at a specific point to follow up.

Correspondence quick tips

Use these additional suggestions for making your cover letter a "must read":

- Address your letter to a specific individual. Make sure to use the correct title and mailing address. Mistakes in such details could detract from your credibility.
- Use a simple typeface that is easy to read.
- Tailor each letter you write to the specific company and position you are applying for.
- Be honest. During an interview, an employer may choose to ask you questions about information you present in your résumé or cover letter. Be prepared to expand upon and support your statements. The ability to do this enhances your reputation as an ethical employee.
- Thank your reader for her time and consideration.
- Check for typographical, grammatical, and word usage errors. Do not rely on your computer to spell check.
- Ask someone to read your letter before you send it out. An extra pair of eyes may help you uncover errors.
- Use high-quality paper stock for your hard-copy letters.
- When sending cover letters via e-mail, use a meaningful subject header and a professional tone. Do not use emoticons like :-). Be sure to include your phone number in case the contact prefers to follow up with you via phone.
- When faxing a cover letter and résumé, indicate the total number of pages in the transmission.

Sample cover letters

Example 1

My recent experience makes me a candidate for your entry-level position as an editorial assistant for *Seventeen* magazine. I held three positions at my college's magazine, including Features Editor, Campus Correspondent, and Senior Copyeditor. In my senior year, I initiated a new section in our magazine, *Style File*, featuring local clothing and accessories stores. A similar *Style File* in your magazine from different cities across the nation would be an intriguing section for your readers.

I am proficient in both PC and MAC platforms, and have used the Microsoft Office Suite and Quark.

I will call you in a few days to schedule a time when we can talk in more detail. At that time I can share with you my writing portfolio.

Example 2

Your flyer announcing the position of Program Coordinator caught my attention immediately. This position interests me because I have the skills required to work on a diverse team. I am fluent in Spanish, French, and English and have had a long-standing interest in working with people from many cultures. My experience as a vendor in an Argentina zoo and my current job as unit manager at the UN Communications Center are two examples of the unique and relevant background I would bring to the position of Program Coordinator at the UC International House.

As a member of the International House, I also have a firsthand understanding of how residents feel about the activities and special events hosted by the office throughout the year. Because of this, I am in an excellent position to help plan a variety of activities residents will appreciate.

As directed in the job announcement, I am requesting an appointment for an interview on March 28, between 2 p.m. and 6 p.m., at a time convenient for you. Please contact me if another time is more appropriate. Thank you very much for your time and consideration.

Example 3

Your Chief Financial Officer, Elena Perez, told me recently that you were looking for an MIS director. Because of my background, she encouraged me to contact you directly. I am impressed with the growth of your company during the last two years. With that kind of expansion, I can understand your need to create a separate MIS department.

This position relates directly to my current experience for Murphy and Sons, LLP, as you will see from my résumé.

I welcome the opportunity to meet with you to discuss how my qualifications may best meet your needs. Thank you for your time and consideration.

Creating and using *portfolios*

In medieval times, artisans who wished to join a guild presented samples of their work. Furniture makers showed cabinets and chairs to their potential mentors. Painters presented samples of their sketches and portraits. Centuries later, people still value a purposeful collection of work samples. It is called a portfolio.

The word *portfolio* derives from two Latin terms: *port,* which means "to move," and *folio,* which means "papers" or "artifacts." True to these ancient meanings, portfolios are movable collections of papers and artifacts. Photographers, contractors, and designers regularly show portfolios filled with samples of their work.

Portfolios differ from résumés. A résumé lists facts, including your interests, skills, work history, and accomplishments. Although a portfolio might include these facts, it also includes tangible objects to verify the facts—anything from transcripts of your grades to a videotape that you produced. Résumés offer facts; portfolios provide artifacts.

To create a portfolio, experiment with a four-step process:

1. Collect and catalog artifacts.
2. Plan your portfolio.
3. Assemble your portfolio.
4. Present your portfolio.

Collect and catalog artifacts

An artifact is any object that's important to you and that reveals something about yourself. Examples include photographs, awards, recommendation letters, job descriptions for positions you've held, newspaper articles about projects you've done, lists of grants or scholarships you've received, programs from performances you've given, transcripts of your grades, or models you've constructed.

Taken together, your artifacts form a large and visible "database" that gives a picture of you—what you value, what you've done, and what skills you have. You can add to this database during every year of your life. From this constantly evolving collection of artifacts, you can create many portfolios for different purposes and different audiences.

Start collecting now. Write down the kinds of artifacts you'd like to save. Think about what will be most useful to you in creating portfolios for your courses and your job search. In some cases, collecting artifacts requires follow-up. You might call former instructors or employers to request letters of recommendation. Or you might track down newspaper articles about a service-learning project you did. Your responses to the journal entries and exercises in this book can also become part of your portfolio.

Plan your portfolio

When you're ready to create a portfolio for a specific audience, allow some time for planning. Begin with your purpose for creating the portfolio—for example, to demonstrate your learning or to document your work experience as you prepare for a job interview.

Also list some specifics about your audience. Write a description of anyone who will see your portfolio. List what each person already knows about you and predict what else these people will want to know. Answer their questions in your portfolio.

When you plan your portfolio, also think about how to order and arrange your artifacts. One basic option is a chronological organization. For example, start with work samples from your earliest jobs and work up to the present.

Another option is to structure your portfolio around key themes, such as your values or work skills. When preparing this type of portfolio, you can define *work* to include any time you used a job-related skill, whether or not you got paid.

Assemble your portfolio

With a collection of artifacts and a written plan, you're ready to assemble your portfolio. Arranging artifacts according to your design is a big part of this process. Also include elements to orient your audience members and guide them through your portfolio. Such elements can include:

- A table of contents.
- An overview or summary of the portfolio.
- Titles and captions for each artifact.
- An index to your artifacts.

Although many portfolios take their final form as a collection of papers, remember that this is just one possibility. You can also create a bulletin board, a display, or a case that contains your artifacts. You could even create a recording or a digital portfolio in the form of a personal Website.

Present your portfolio

Your audience might ask you to present your portfolio as part of an interview or oral exam. If that's the case, rehearse your portfolio presentation the way you would rehearse a speech. Write down questions that people might ask about your portfolio. Prepare some answers, then do a dry run. Present your portfolio to friends and people in your career field, and request their feedback.

That feedback will give you plenty of ideas about ways to revise your portfolio. Any portfolio is a living document. Update it as you acquire new perspectives and skills.

Artifacts for your portfolio

When looking for items to include in a portfolio, start with the following checklist. Then brainstorm your own list of additional possibilities.

- ❑ Brochures describing a product or service you've created, or workshops you've attended
- ❑ Certificates, licenses, and awards
- ❑ Computer disks with sample publications, databases, or computer programs you've created
- ❑ Course descriptions and syllabuses of classes you've taken or taught
- ❑ Formal evaluations of your work
- ❑ Job descriptions of positions you've held
- ❑ Letters of recommendation
- ❑ Lists of grants, scholarships, clients, customers, and organizations you've joined
- ❑ Newspaper and magazine articles about projects you've participated in
- ❑ Objects you've created or received—anything from badges to jewelry
- ❑ Plans—lists of personal and professional values, goals, action plans, completed tasks, project timelines, and lifelines
- ❑ Printouts of e-mail and Web pages (including your personal Web page)
- ❑ Programs from artistic performances or exhibitions
- ❑ Recordings (digital or voice), compact discs, or CD-ROMs
- ❑ Résumés or a curriculum vitae
- ❑ Sheet music or scores
- ❑ Transcripts of grades, test scores, vocational aptitude tests, or learning style inventories
- ❑ Visual art, including drawings, photographs, collages, and computer graphics
- ❑ Writing samples, such as class reports, workplace memos, proposals, policy and mission statements, bids, manuscripts for articles and books, and published pieces or bibliographies of published writing

Use interviews to hire yourself an employer

Job interviews can be exhilarating. They offer a way to meet people. They give you a chance to present your skills. They can expand your network of contacts. And they can lead directly to a job that you love.

If you've written a career plan and prepared a résumé, you've already done much of the preparation for a successful interview. You probably have specific ideas about *what* job skills you want to use and *where* you want to use them. By the time you get to a job interview, you'll be able to see if the job is something that you really want. An interview is a chance for you to assess a potential job and work environment. By interviewing, you're "hiring" yourself an employer.

Prepare for common questions

Job interviewers ask many questions. Most of them boil down to a few major concerns:

- Would we be comfortable working with you?
- How did you find out about us?
- How can you help us?
- Will you learn to do this job quickly?
- What makes you different from other applicants?

Before your interview, rehearse some answers to questions such as these. Answer each question directly. Know the main points you want to make, and be brief.

To make the most favorable impression on an interviewer, avoid canned answers. These are easy to detect. Remember that genuine enthusiasm for a job counts as much as carefully composed answers. Before convincing an employer that you want a job and can do the job, convince yourself. When you're authentic, it will show.

If you get turned down for the job after your interview, write a Discovery Statement that describes your feelings about this event. Also describe what you learned from the experience. Follow up with an Intention Statement that describes how you can interview more effectively next time. Every interview is a source of feedback about what works—and what doesn't work—when meeting with employers.

Start on a positive note and stay there

Many interviewers make their decision about an applicant early on. This can happen during the first five minutes of the interview.

With this in mind, start on a strong note. Do everything you can to create a positive impression early in the interview. Even if you're nervous, you can be outgoing and attentive. Explain how your research led you to the company. Focus on how you can contribute to the employer. Talk about skills or experiences that make you stand out from the crowd of other applicants.

One way to create a favorable first impression is through the way you look. Be well groomed. Wear clothing that's appropriate for the work environment.

Also monitor your nonverbal language. Give a firm handshake and make eye contact (without looking like a zombie). Sit in a way that says you're at ease with people and have a high energy level. During the interview, seize opportunities to smile or even tell an amusing story, as long as it's relevant and positive.

As the interview gets rolling, search for common ground. Finding out that you share an interest with an interviewer can make the conversation sail—and put you closer to a job offer. You can demonstrate interest through focused attention. Listen carefully to everything interviewers say. Few of them will mind if you take notes. This might even impress them.

As the interviewer speaks, listen for challenges that the company faces. Then paint yourself as someone who can help meet those challenges. Explain how you've solved similar problems in the past—and what you can do for the employer right now. To support your claims, mention a detail or two about your accomplishments and refer the interviewer to your résumé for more.

Once you hit a positive note, do everything possible to stay there. When speaking about other people, for example, be courteous. If you find it hard to say something positive about a previous coworker or supervisor, shift the focus back to the interviewer's questions.

Show that you know the value of time. If your interview is scheduled to end soon, mention this to the interviewer. Allow this person the option to end the conversation or extend the interview time.

When appropriate, take the initiative

The interviewer might be uncomfortable with her role. Few people have training in this skill. Interviewers may dominate the conversation, interrupt you, or forget what they want to ask.

When things like this happen, take the initiative. Ask for time to get your questions answered. Sum up your qualifications, and ask for a detailed job description.

Ask open-ended questions and listen

Come with your own list of questions for the interviewer. Skilled interviewers will leave time for these. Some questions you can consider asking are:

- If I take this job, what kind of training will it include?
- Does this job offer opportunities for advancement?
- Who would be my supervisor, and to whom does that person report?
- Who would be my direct coworkers, and can you tell me a little about them?
- Can I have short tour of the area where I'd be working?
- What would be the best way for me to follow up on this interview?

After you ask a question, give the interviewer plenty of time to talk. Listen at least 50 percent of the time.

If the interview has gone well, consider asking one more question: "Do you have any concerns about hiring me?" Some interviewers might see this as too bold. Others might see it as a perceptive question and give you an honest answer. The benefit is that you get a chance to address their concerns immediately. And the very fact that you asked this question could distinguish you from other applicants.

Give yourself a raise before you start work

Effective salary discussion can make a huge difference to your financial well-being. Consider the long-term impact of making just an extra $1,000 per year. Over the next decade, that's an extra $10,000 dollars in pretax income, even if you get no other raises.

It's possible to discuss salary too early in the interview process. Let the interviewer bring up this topic. In many cases, an ideal time to talk about salary is when the interviewer is ready to offer you a job. This often takes place during a second or even third interview. At this point the employer might be willing to part with some more money.

Many interviewers use a standard negotiating strategy: They come to the interview with a salary range in mind. Then they offer a starting salary at the lower end of that range.

This strategy holds an important message for you: Salaries are sometimes flexible. You do not have to accept the first salary offer.

When you finally get down to money, be prepared. Begin by knowing the income that you want. First, figure out how much money you need to maintain your desired standard of living. Then add some margin for comfort. If you're working a job that's comparable to the one you're applying for, consider adding 10 percent to your current salary. As you do this, take into account the value of any benefits the employer provides. Also consider stating a desired salary range at first rather than a fixed figure.

Find out the salary range for the job you want. This information might be available online. Start with America's Career InfoNet at **http://www.careerinfonet.org/** and click on Occupation Information. Also go to your favorite Internet search engine and key in the term *salary range.*

Other sources of salary information are friends who work in your field and notes from your information interviews. Another option is the obvious one—directly asking interviewers what salary range they have in mind.

Once you know that range, aim higher rather than lower. Name a figure toward the upper end and see how the interviewer responds. Starting high gives you some room to negotiate. See if you can get a raise now rather than later.

Salary negotiation gives you an opening to ask about benefits. Depending on the company and the job involved, these might include health insurance, life insurance, disability plans, use of a company car, reimbursement for travel expenses, retirement plans, and tuition reimbursement.

Use each *no* to come closer to *yes*

Almost everyone who's ever applied for a job knows the lines: "We have no job openings right now"; "We'll keep your résumé on file"; "There were many qualified applicants for this position"; "Even though you did not get the job, thanks for applying"; "Best of luck to you as you pursue other career opportunities."

Each of those statements is a different way of saying no. And they can hurt.

However, *no* does not have to be the final word. Focus on the future. If you're turned down for one job, consider ways to turn that *no* into a *yes* next time. Could you present yourself differently during the interview? Could you do more thorough research? Can you fine-tune your career goals? You might even ask the interviewer for suggestions. Also ask for referrals to other companies that might be hiring.

Think about what a job rejection really means. It's not an eternal judgment of your character. It only reflects what happened between you and one potential employer, often over just a few hours or even a few minutes. It means no for right now, for this job, for today—not for every job, forever.

Eventually an employer or client will hire you. It's just a matter of time before the inevitable *yes.* When you're turned down for a job, that is just one more *no* that's out of the way.

critical thinking exercise 33

PRACTICE ANSWERING AND ASKING QUESTIONS

Before your next job interview, also set up situations where you can practice answering common interview questions. Enroll a friend to play the part of an interviewer and ask you the following:

Tell me about yourself.
What are your most important strengths?
What are your most important areas for improvement?
Why do you want this job?
Why should I hire you?
Why did you leave your previous job?
What do you see yourself doing five years from now?
What was a key problem you faced on your last job, and how did you solve it?
How well do you get along with people?

You can prepare your answers to these questions by focusing on key words from the four learning styles questions explained in Chapter One. In other words, your job during an interview is to explain *Why* you are an ideal candidate for the job, *What* skills and experience you bring to the company, *How* well you will get along with other employees, and *What* specific benefits an employer can expect to gain *if* she hires you.

During your practice interview, keep your speaking brief and to the point. See if you can respond to each question in two minutes or less.

Be alert to any inconsistencies in your answers. For example, if you say that you're a "team player" but prefer to work independently, be prepared to explain. When you're done, ask your friend for feedback about your answers.

Succeeding as a new employee

Your first year at a new job represents a distinct stage in your life, especially if it's your first job after getting a degree. You're no longer a student. Nor are you a seasoned professional in your new position. You've left one world behind and your new world is still an unknown.

The way that you manage this year might affect your entire career. Coworkers' early impressions of you can create lasting attitudes. These attitudes influence your chances for advancement, with long-term effects on your job satisfaction and income. Make the most of this key transition period with the following strategies for succeeding as a new employee.

Prepare for culture clash

If you're a new graduate and just beginning your career, prepare for a radical change. After mastering the culture of higher education, you are in a game with entirely new rules. For example:

- You might be used to structured courses with lots of direction from teachers—and find yourself in an unstructured workplace with little direction from your supervisor.
- You might be used to a flexible schedule—and find yourself saddled with a tight "eight to five" schedule.
- You might thrive on mastering ideas and facts—and find yourself forced to master office politics.
- You might be used to focusing on your individual development—and now find yourself focusing on team results.
- You might be used to moving in groups of people who know about your academic accomplishments—and now find yourself among strangers.

One powerful way to prepare for this clash of cultures is to simply know that it's coming. In addition, review the Introduction to this book, including the article "Making the transition to higher education." The strategies presented there—such as admitting your feelings, giving yourself time, and taking constructive action—can help you make *any* transition, including the transition to a new job.

Focus on attitudes first

As a new employee, your first concern might be succeeding at job *tasks*. The top questions on your mind might be: "Am I really prepared to *do* this job?" and "Can I actually complete the projects that my boss gives me?"

Meanwhile, your boss's top concern might be *attitudes*. She's probably asking herself: "Is this new person open to coaching?" and "Will he fit in with our team?"

Remember that your boss scoped out your qualifications *before* you got hired. Because she hired you, she's probably confident that you can handle job tasks now or learn to do them within a reasonable period. To really shine as a new employee, shift your focus to "soft" skills—those that relate to personality and people.

People in Twelve Step programs such as Alcoholics Anonymous talk about the usefulness of HOW attitudes—Honesty, Openness, and Willingness. This is a useful acronym for succeeding as a new employee. It points to:

- Being honest when you don't understand directions—and being willing to ask questions.
- Being open to feedback about your performance—and being willing to change your behavior on the basis of the feedback.
- Being willing to complete the mundane tasks that are part of almost every job—and understanding what it means to "pay your dues."

If your boss could talk candidly about her desires for "new hires," she might say: "Send me someone with a positive attitude, a work ethic, and plenty of energy. We'll teach him everything else he needs to know."

Content skills help people get hired. However, it's the lack of transferable skills—such as listening well, speaking clearly, and thinking thoroughly—that can get them fired.

Decode the culture

Every organization, large or small, develops its own culture. One way to succeed in the workplace is to "decode" corporate cultures—the basic assumptions and shared values that shape human behavior in the workplace every day.

You can use this knowledge to prevent misunderstanding, resolve conflict, and forge lasting relationships.

Start by observing. Being culturally savvy starts with discovering "the way we do things around here"—the beliefs and behaviors that are widely shared by your coworkers. In terms of the cycle of learning explained in

Surviving your first day

You've landed a new job. Congratulations! Now prepare to walk into the office and make a place for yourself.

Well-meaning people may advise you to "just be yourself" when you show up for your first day of work. The following offers more specifics.

Dress the part. Many students cultivate an eclectic wardrobe that won't pass the test for a new job. And even employers with "casual days" prefer to meet new employees in standard business attire. Think back to what people in the office were wearing when you showed up for your job interview. To make a positive impression, put special effort into looking your best on your first day.

Arrive early. Don't underestimate the power of this simple suggestion. Arriving late for your first day of work sends mixed messages. To you, it may be a simple mistake. Your supervisor might interpret it as being careless or having an "attitude." Remove all possibility of misunderstanding by showing up with at least 15 minutes to spare.

Notice your "nonverbals." Remember to shake hands firmly and say hello in a friendly voice. Make eye contact and smile. Also check out your other nonverbal messages. In meetings, for example, check to see if your posture says, *I'm here now and paying attention to what you say.*

Remember names. Occasionally, we find ourselves in situations where we're introduced to many people at the same time: "Let's take a tour so you can meet all 32 people in this department."

When meeting a group of people, concentrate on remembering just two or three names. Free yourself from feeling obligated to remember everyone. Few of the people in mass introductions expect you to remember their names.

Another way to avoid memory overload is to limit yourself to learning just first names. Last names can come later.

In some cases, you might be able to get photos of the people you meet on your first day at work. For example, a small business where you apply for a job might have a brochure with employee pictures.

Ask for individual or group photos and write in the names if they're not included. You can use these photos as "flash cards" as you drill yourself on names.

Take notes. During your first day you'll cover lots of details. First, there's the obvious stuff—where to sit, where to park, where to eat, where to make photocopies, where to take breaks, where to go to the bathroom. Then there's the higher level stuff, such as phone numbers, and user IDs and passwords for Internet access.

Be prepared with paper and pen to write this stuff down. Besides aiding your memory, taking notes gives you something to do with your hands if you feel nervous.

Pack a briefcase. Companies just love to push paper at new employees—brochures, forms, maps, manuals, and more. When you receive this stuff, look at it for a few seconds. This communicates in a small and significant way that you pay attention to details. Then place the papers in a professional-looking folder or briefcase.

Go easy on yourself. Notice whether there's a self-critical voice in your head that's saying something like: "You're not fooling anyone—you really have no idea what you're doing here." No one else hears that voice. And no one expects you to perform to perfection on your first day. If you hear a self-critical voice, just notice it and let it go.

Do not say these words: "Wow, that's not how we did things at my last job." This invites an inevitable response: "Well, then why did you leave that job?" Expect procedures to differ from job to job, and look for chances to suggest improvements in the future.

Chapter One, this means that your efforts to decode corporate culture begin with the stage of reflective observation.

In other words, keep your eyes open. See what actions are rewarded and which are punished. Observe what people do and say to gain credibility in your organization.

You may disagree with what you see and find yourself making negative judgments about your coworkers. Start by noticing those judgments and letting them go. You cannot fully observe behaviors and judge them at the same time. Play the role of a social scientist and collect facts impartially.

Create theories about unwritten rules. Next, create theories about how people succeed in your organization. In terms of the learning cycle, this is the stage of abstract conceptualization. In particular, notice the unwritten "rules" that govern your workplace. Your coworkers may behave on the basis of beliefs such as:

- Never make the boss look bad.
- Some commitments are not meant to be kept.
- If you want to get promoted, then be visible.
- Everyone is expected to work some overtime.
- Before you try to change the rules around here, prove that you know what you're doing.
- Before we assign you to a big project, build a solid track record of small successes.

Once you understand the norms and standards of your company, you can consciously choose to accept them. Or you can challenge them by actively experimenting with new behaviors and immersing yourself in new experiences. In any case, changing any organization begins with a First Step—telling the truth about how it works right now.

Cope with office politics

The unspoken rules for getting recognized and rewarded are usually what people mean when they talk about *office politics*. One way to deal with office politics is to pretend they don't exist. The downfall of this strategy is that politics are a fact of life.

Another option is to be politically savvy—*and* still hold fast to your values. You can move through the echelons of power and meet ethical career goals at the same time. More specifically:

- *Grow "industry-smart."* Read trade journals and newsletters related to your field. Keep up with current developments. Speak the language shared by the decision makers in your organization.
- *Promote your boss.* During your first year with an organization, the single most important person in your work life could be your boss. This is the person who most closely monitors your performance. This is also the person who can become your biggest advocate. Find out what this person needs and wants. Learn about her goals and then assist her to meet them.
- *Get close to the power centers.* People who advance to top positions are often those who know the language of sales, marketing, accounting, and information technology. These departments are power centers. They directly affect the bottom line. You can enhance your company's profitability no matter what position you hold. Look for ways to save money and time. Suggest workable ways to streamline procedures or reduce costs. Focus on solutions to problems, no matter how small, and you'll play the ultimate political game—making a contribution.
- *Be visible.* To gain credibility in your organization, get involved in a high-profile project that you believe in. Then perform well. Go beyond the minimum standards. Meet the project goals—and deliver even more. Focus on solutions to problems, no matter how small, and you'll play the ultimate political game—making a contribution. ☒

Learning on the job

Besides a paycheck, the workplace offers constant opportunities for learning. Employers value the person who is a "quick study"—someone who can get up to speed at a new job in minimum time.

In addition, some of the information you acquired in school might become quickly outdated. Learning how to learn—a key transferable skill—is a necessity if you want to survive in the job market and advance in your career.

Let go of old ideas about learning. Educational literature is full of distinctions such as "theory versus application" and "beginning versus advanced." These distinctions are useful. But if you want to learn on the job, you can often benefit by letting them go. In workplace-based learning, for example:

- There is no "finish" line such as a graduation ceremony. Rather, you learn continuously, taking periodic progress checks to assess your current skills.
- Except in formal training programs, there are no course divisions. A new job might call on you to integrate knowledge of several subjects at once.
- There is no syllabus for learning a subject, with assignments carefully laid out in planned sequence. You might learn concepts in an "illogical" order as dictated by the day-to-day demands of a job.

Seize informal opportunities to learn. At work, your learning may take place in unplanned, informal ways. Look for opportunities to:

- Do self-directed reading on topics related to new job tasks.
- Observe people who demonstrate a skill that you would like to develop.
- Ask questions on the spot.
- Attend trade shows for new products or services offered by your company's competitors.
- Join professional organizations in your field that offer workshops and seminars.
- Make yourself into the company expert on a new product or procedure by digging into brochures, Websites, professional journals, technical manuals, and other sources of information that your coworkers may have overlooked.

Create a development plan. Some organizations require their employees to create a professional development plan. If your employer does not require such a plan, create one anyway. You can do this by answering several "W questions":

What skill or specialized base of knowledge is most essential for you to acquire now in order to do your job more effectively?

Who has acquired this knowledge or demonstrated this skill and would be willing to share their expertise? Perhaps one of these people would be willing to mentor you.

If learning your desired knowledge or skill requires experiences outside your work environment, **Where** will you go to pursue those experiences? Answers might include a night class at a local business school or a company-sponsored training session.

When would you like to demonstrate mastery of your new knowledge or skill? Give yourself a due date for meeting each professional development goal.

In addition, ask **How** you will know that you've mastered the new knowledge or skill. List specifically what you will say or do differently as a result of your development.

Finally, consider **What if**—what if the job promotions and other career possibilities that you gain help you to meet the goals in your development plan?

As you answer these questions, keep focused. If you try to develop too many skills at once, you might end with few gains over the long run. Consider setting and achieving one major development goal each year.

Act on your plan every day. Remember that the word *learning* is often defined as an enduring change in behavior. Focus on a new work-related behavior—such as creating a to-do list or overcoming procrastination—that will make a significant, positive, and immediate difference in your performance. Then do it. Every day, implement one new behavior or practice one new habit. In the workplace, learning means doing.

Working with a mentor

One strategy for planning your career and succeeding in the workplace is to find a mentor—a partner in your professional and personal development. Many people will be flattered to take on such a role in your life.

Start with a development plan. Before you ask someone to mentor you, reflect on your goals for this relationship. List the specific skills that you want to develop with a mentor's involvement.

For maximum clarity, put your development plan in writing. Consider using the Discovery and Intention Journal Entry system. Write Discovery Statements to list your current skills, recent examples of how you've used them, and insights from your mentor.

Whenever possible, create a way to measure your progress. For example, you could note the number of times you practice a new habit. Or you could summarize ratings from your performance reviews at work. Include these measurements in your Discovery Statements and share them with your mentor.

Follow up with Intention Statements that describe exactly what new behaviors you want to implement, along with ongoing updates to your development plan.

In your Intention Statements, include a timeline. Use your goal-setting skills to set due dates for acquiring new skills or producing new outcomes in your life. Also state when you want to begin and end the mentoring sessions. Keep in mind that many mentoring relationships are short-term, taking place over weeks or months rather than years.

Approach potential mentors. Identify several people who have demonstrated competence in the skills you want to gain, along with the energy and desire to take on a mentee—that is, you.

Next, contact each person on your list and mention that you're seeking a mentor. Summarize your development plan and timetable. Also suggest ways that you can create value for a mentor, such as helping that person complete a project or achieve one of *his* development goals. The more you give to the mentor relationship, the more you'll get out of it.

Accept your mentor's feedback. Remember that a mentor is not a boss, parent, or taskmaster. Instead, you're looking for coaching. A coach helps you clarify your goals and then offers nonjudgmental observations of your behavior, along with suggestions for improvement. However, the responsibility for your day-to-day performance and long-term development lies with you.

Schedule regular meetings with your mentor. During these meetings, put all your listening skills to work. Resist the temptation to debate, argue, or justify your behavior. Simply receive what your mentor has to say. Ask questions to clarify anything you don't understand.

Remember that when you asked for mentoring, you signed on for objective feedback and suggestions—including ideas you may have resisted in the past. A commitment to change implies the willingness to think, speak, and act in new ways. Stay open to suggestion.

Beyond listening, move into action. When your mentor offers an insight, look for an immediate way to apply it. Experiment with a new behavior every day.

Seek closure—and continue. When you've come to the end of a mentoring relationship, offer your thanks and celebrate your accomplishments. Solidify your learning by listing the top five insights or skills you gained.

In addition, choose your next step. List upcoming opportunities to practice your newly acquired skills.

Adapting to styles in the workplace

Sometimes learning styles clash in the workplace. When that happens, we have several options. One is to throw up our hands and resign ourselves to "personality conflicts." Another option is to recognize differences, accept them, and respect them as complementary ways to meet common goals. The more you can adapt to differences in style, the more likely you are to enjoy your job, forge positive work relationships, and meet your career goals.

Notice learning styles

You can learn a lot about other people's styles simply by observing them during the workday. For example, some people process new information by sitting quietly and reading or writing. When learning to use a new computer, they'll read the manual first. Others will skip the manual, unpack all the boxes, and start setting up equipment. And others might ask a more experienced colleague to guide them in person, step by step.

Accommodate learning styles

As you collaborate on projects with coworkers, encourage them to answer all four learning style questions.

Asking *Why?* means defining the purpose and desired outcomes of a project. Before moving into action, help participants answer the questions *What's in this for our organization?* and *What's in this for me?*

Asking *What?* means assigning major tasks, setting due dates for each task, and generating commitment to action. As you answer this question, allow for coworkers who excel at reflecting on experience and making predictions based on theories. When appropriate, provide handouts or give presentations that include visuals, bulleted lists, and step-by-step instructions. Visual learners and people who like organized information will appreciate it. Also schedule periods for questions and answers, which will draw in auditory learners.

Asking *How?* means carrying out assigned tasks, discussing what's working well, and brainstorming ways to improve performance. Here you can allow time for active experimentation and concrete experience.

Asking *What if?* means discussing what the team has learned from the project and ways to apply that learning to the larger organization. Other project teams can avoid any mistakes you made and build on your successes.

Deepen your experience of styles

Beyond noticing and accommodating styles is another dimension—learning to value individual differences and thrive on them.

Introduce a conversation about styles. Attend a workshop on styles and share what you learn.

When collaborating on projects, look for ways to complement each other's styles. Pooling different styles allows you to pool everyone's strengths and draw more powerful lessons from your collective experience.

Let people expand their styles. Style is both stable and dynamic. People gravitate toward the kinds of tasks and relationships that they've succeeded at in the past. They can also broaden their styles by acquiring new behaviors.

Use the above suggestions as starting points for developing your own strategies. The point is to expect differences in style—and to make conscious choices about working with them.

Dealing with sexism and sexual harassment

Sexism and sexual harassment are real. Incidents that are illegal or violate organizational policies occur throughout the year at schools and workplaces.

Until the early nineteenth century, women in the United States were banned from attending colleges and universities. Today they make up the majority of first-year students in higher education, yet they still encounter bias based on gender.

This bias can take many forms. For example, instructors might gloss over the contributions of women. Students in philosophy class might never hear of a woman named Hypatia, an ancient Greek philosopher and mathematician. Those majoring in computer science might never learn about Rear Admiral Grace Murray Hopper, who pioneered the development of a computer language named COBOL. And your art history textbook might not mention the Mexican painter Frida Kahlo or the American painter Georgia O'Keeffe.

Though men can be subjects of sexism and sexual harassment, women are more likely to experience this form of discrimination. Even the most well-intentioned people might behave in ways that hurt or discount women. Sexism is a factor when:

- Instructors use only masculine pronouns—*he, his,* and *him*—to refer to both men and women.
- Career counselors hint that careers in mathematics and science are not appropriate for women.
- Students pay more attention to feedback from a male teacher than from a female teacher.
- Women are not called on in class, their comments are ignored, or they are overly praised for answering the simplest questions.
- Examples given in a textbook or lecture assign women only to traditionally "female" roles, such as wife, mother, day care provider, elementary school teacher, or nurse.
- People assume that middle-aged women who return to school have too many family commitments to study adequately or do well in their classes.

Many kinds of behavior—both verbal and physical—can be categorized as sexual harassment. This kind of discrimination involves unwelcome sexual conduct. Examples of such conduct in a school setting are:

- Sexual advances.
- Any other unwanted touch.
- Sexual graffiti.
- Displaying or distributing sexually explicit materials.
- Sexual gestures or jokes.
- Pressure for sexual favors.
- Talking about personal sexual activity.
- Spreading rumors about someone's sexual activity or rating someone's sexual performance.

Sexual Harassment: It's Not Academic, a pamphlet from the U.S. Department of Education, quotes a woman who experienced sexual harassment in higher education: "The financial officer made it clear that I could get the money I needed if I slept with him."[3] That's an example of *quid pro quo harassment.* This legal term applies when students believe that an educational decision depends on submitting to unwelcome sexual conduct. *Hostile environment harassment* takes place when such incidents are severe, persistent, or pervasive.

People can be harassed due to many dimensions of diversity besides gender. Examples include sexual orientation, size, and religion.

The feminist movement has raised awareness about all forms of harassment. We can now respond to such incidents in the places we live, work, and go to school. Specific strategies follow.

Point out sexist language and behavior. When you see examples of sexism, point them out. Your message can be more effective if you use "I" messages instead of personal attacks, as explained in Chapter Eight: Communicating.

Indicate the specific statements and behaviors that you consider sexist.

For example, you could rephrase a sexist comment so that it targets another group, such as Jews or African Americans. People might spot anti-Semitism or racism more readily than sexism.

Keep in mind that men can also be subjected to sexism, ranging from antagonistic humor to exclusion from jobs that have traditionally been done by women.

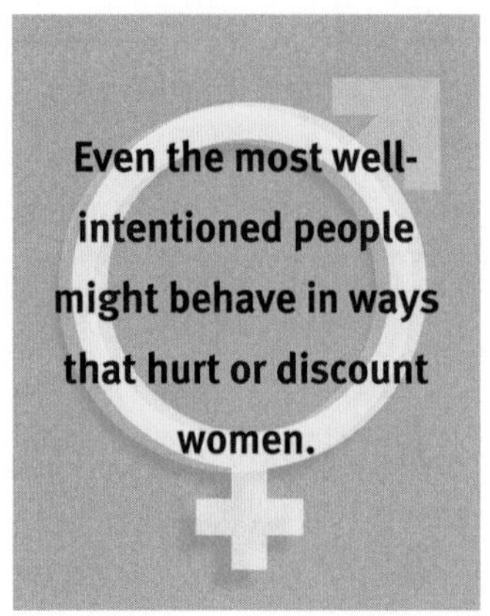

Observe your own language and behavior. Looking for sexist behavior in others is effective. Detecting it in yourself can be just as powerful. Write a Discovery Statement about specific comments that could be interpreted as sexist. Then notice if you say any of these things. Also ask people you know to point out occasions when you use similar statements. Follow up with an Intention Statement that describes how you plan to change your speaking or behavior.

You can also write Discovery Statements about the current level of intimacy (physical and verbal) in any of your relationships at home, work, or school. Be sure that any increase in the level of intimacy is mutually agreed upon.

Encourage support for women. Through networks, women can work to overcome the effects of sexism. Strategies include study groups for women, women's job networks, and professional organizations, such as Women in Communications. Other examples are counseling services and health centers for women, family planning agencies, and rape prevention centers. Check your school catalog and library to see if any of these services are available at your school.

If your school does not have the women's networks you want, you can help form them. Sponsor a one-day or one-week conference on women's issues. Create a discussion or reading group for the women in your class, department, residence hall, union, or neighborhood.

Set limits. Women, value yourselves. Recognize your right to an education without the distraction of inappropriate and invasive behavior. Trust your judgment about when your privacy or your rights are being violated. Decide now what kind of sexual comments and actions you're uncomfortable with—and refuse to put up with them.

Take action. If you are sexually harassed, take action. Title IX of the Education Amendments of 1972 prohibits sexual harassment and other forms of sex discrimination. The law also requires schools to have grievance procedures in place for dealing with such discrimination. If you believe that you've been sexually harassed, report the incident to a school official. This person can be a teacher, administrator, or campus security officer. Check to see if your school has someone specially designated to handle your complaint, such as an affirmative action officer or Title IX coordinator.

You can also file a complaint with the Office for Civil Rights (OCR), a federal agency that makes sure schools and workplaces comply with Title IX. In your complaint, include your name, address, and daytime phone number, along with the date of the incident and a description of it. Do this within 180 days of the incident. You can contact the OCR at 1-800-421-3481. Or go online to **http://wdcrobcolp01.ed.gov/CFAPPS/OCR/contactus.cfm**.

Your community might offer more resources to protect against sexual discrimination. Examples are public interest law firms, legal aid societies, and unions that employ lawyers to represent students. ☒

Loving your next job

Job disappointment has countless symptoms, including statements such as "My boss is a jerk," "I'm so bored," and "This is too hard."

Faced with such sentiments, there's a tempting short-term solution: "I quit." Sometimes that is a reasonable option. In many cases of job dissatisfaction, however, there are solutions that do less damage to your immediate income and your long-term job prospects.

Manage your expectations

Instead of changing jobs, consider changing the way you think. Perhaps you never expected to run the company within six months after joining it. Yet your expectations for your current job might still be unrealistic.

This suggestion can be especially useful if you've just graduated from school and find yourself working in an entry-level position in your field. Students who are used to stimulating class discussions and teachers with a passion for their subject might be shocked by the realities of the workplace: people who hide behind a cubicle and avoid human contact, managers with technical skills but no people skills, coworkers who get promoted on the basis of political favors rather than demonstrated skills.

If you're unhappy at work, review the Power Process: "Notice your pictures and let them go." Then ask which of your work-related pictures might be related to your upset. Perhaps you're operating on the basis of unrealistic "shoulds" such as:

- My first job after graduating *should* draw on all the skills I developed in school.
- Everyone I meet on a job *should* be interesting, competent, and kind.
- Every task that I perform at work *should* be enjoyable.
- My work environment *should* be problem-free.

See if you can replace the *should* in such statements with *can* or *could*. For example: "Even though I'm not using all my skills, I *can* use this job to learn about corporate culture and coping with office politics;" or "I *could* use this job to develop at least one skill that I can transfer to my next job."

Practice problem solving

Sometimes you can benefit by adjusting more than your attitude. Apply your transferable skills at problem solving. Write Discovery Statements about:

- How you felt when you started the job.
- When you started feeling unhappy with the job.
- Any specific events that triggered your dissatisfaction.

This writing can help you pinpoint the sources of job dissatisfaction. Possibilities include conflict with coworkers, a mismatch between your skills and the job requirements, or a mismatch between your personal values and the values promoted in the workplace. No matter what the source, you can brainstorm solutions. Ask friends and family members for help. If you're bored with work, propose a project that will create value for your boss and offer to lead it. If your supervisor seems unhappy with your performance, ask for coaching to do it better. If you feel stressed, review the stress-management techniques in Chapter Six: Tests, and choose at least one to use on a daily basis. If you're in conflict with a coworker, apply strategies for resolving conflict presented in Chapter Eight: Communicating. And if you want more challenging assignments, then ask for them.

Moving into action to solve the problem offers a reminder that you—not your boss or coworkers—are in charge of the quality of your life.

Focus on process

You can also take a cue from the term *Power Process.* Shift your focus from the content of your job to the process you use—from *what* you do to *how* you do it. Even if a task seems boring or beneath you, see if you can do it impeccably and with total attention. As you do, project a professional image in everything from the way you dress to the way you speak. One strategy for handling a dead-end job is to do it so well that you get noticed—and promoted to a new job.

Leadership as a way of life

Many people mistakenly think that leaders are only those with formal titles such as *supervisor* or *manager.* In fact, some leaders have no such titles. Some have never supervised others. Like Mahatma Gandhi, some people change the face of the world without ever reaching a formal leadership position.

It's impossible to escape leadership. Every time you speak, you lead others in some small or large way. Every time you take action, you lead others through your example. Every time you ask someone to do something, you are leading that person.

No one is born knowing how to lead. We acquire the skills over time. Begin now, while you are in higher education. Campuses offer continual opportunities to gain leadership skills. Volunteer for clubs, organizations, and student government. Look for opportunities to tutor or to become a peer advisor or mentor. No matter what you do, take on big projects—those that are worthy of your time and talents.

In its *Report on the American Workforce 2001,* the U.S. Department of Labor concluded that "the United States likely will continue to be a nation in which increasing racial and ethnic diversity is the rule, not the exception."[4] Translation: Your next boss or coworker could be a person whose life experience and view of the world differs radically from yours. Prepare to apply your leadership skills in a multicultural work force.

Millions of words have been written and spoken about diversity and the nature of effective leadership. James Kouzes and Barry Posner, authors of *The Leadership Challenge* and the *Student Leadership Practices Inventory,* offer a model that is both research-based and adapted for student leaders.[5] The following suggestions are based on the five fundamental practices of exemplary leadership included in this model.

Challenge the process

Every example of leadership that Kouzes and Posner describe involves people who set out to change the status quo. These people created new products, developed new services, started new businesses, founded new organizations, and passed new legislation. They contributed by recognizing good ideas early on and then tirelessly promoting them.

This calls for the willingness to be uncomfortable. Leadership is a courageous act. Leaders often are not appreciated or even liked. They can feel isolated, cut off from their colleagues. This can sometimes lead to self-doubt and even fear. Before you take on a leadership role, be aware that you might experience such feelings. But none of them needs to stop you from leading.

Also allow mistakes. The more you practice leadership, the more likely it is that you'll make mistakes. And the more influential you are, the more likely it is that your mistakes will have huge consequences. The chief financial officer for a large company can make a mistake that costs thousands or even millions of dollars. A physician's error could cost a life. At the same time, such leaders are in a position to make huge changes for the better—to save thousands of dollars or lives through their power, skill, and influence.

Inspire a shared vision

There's a biblical saying: "Without vision, the people perish." Long-term goals usually involve many intermediate steps. Unless we're reminded of the purpose for those day-to-day actions, our work can feel like a grind.

Keeping the vision alive helps spirits soar again. Leadership is the art of helping others lift their eyes to the horizon—keeping them in touch with the ultimate value and purpose of a project. When you lead a project, speak a lot about the end result and the potential value of what you're doing.

Enable others to act

"After reviewing over 2,500 personal-best cases, we developed a simple test to detect whether someone is on the road to becoming a leader," Kouzes and Posner write. "That test is the frequency of the use of the word *we*. Exemplary leaders enlist the support and assistance of all those who must make the project work."

A leader's vision has little power until people get behind it. That vision cannot be forced on anyone. Instead, leaders enlist wide support for new projects through the sheer force of enthusiasm. Their passion for a new project spreads to people at all levels of an organization.

In addition to sharing your passion, you can move people into action with several strategies:

- Make requests—lots of them. An effective leader is a request machine. Making requests—both large and small—is an act of respect. When we ask a lot from others, we demonstrate our respect for them and our confidence in their abilities.

- Delegate. Ask a coworker or classmate to take on a job that you'd like to see done. Ask the same of your family or friends. Delegate tasks to the mayor of your town, the governor of your state, and the leaders of your country. Take on projects that are important to you. Then find people who can lead the effort.

- Follow up. What we don't inspect, people don't respect. When other people agree to do a job for you, follow up to see how it is going. This can be done in a way that communicates your respect and interest—not your fear that the project might flounder.

Effective leaders also know that "we" goes beyond a small group of people at the top of an organization. Leaders involve everyone who will be affected by a change—managers, customers, clients, and citizens.

Today this calls on leaders to implement diversity policies—and to go beyond them by preventing *micro-inequities*. These are small, subtle behaviors that over time create an atmosphere of intolerance. They occur, for example, when a manager continually glances at her watch while talking to a person of color, when a team leader consistently mispronounces the name of an employee from another country, or when a supervisor habitually interrupts women who speak during a meeting.

You can avoid such micro-inequities simply by practicing the Power Process: "Be here now" with every person you interact with as a leader. When people speak, listen with full permission and full attention.

Model the way

"Be the change you want to see" is a useful motto for leaders. Perhaps you want to see integrity, focused attention, and productivity in the people around you. Begin by modeling these qualities yourself. It's easy to excite others about a goal when you are enthusiastic about it yourself. Having fun while being productive is contagious. If you bring these qualities to a project, others might follow suit.

Encourage the heart

As a leader, you can sustain enthusiasm for a project by constantly acknowledging others. Express genuine appreciation for the energy and creativity that others have put into their work. Take the time to be interested in what they have done and to care about the results they have accomplished. Thank and acknowledge them with your eyes, your words, and the tone of your voice.

Share credit. As a leader, give away the praise and acknowledgment that you receive. When you're congratulated for your performance, pass it on to others. Share the credit with the group.

When you're a leader, the results you achieve depend on the efforts of many others. Acknowledging that fact often is more than telling the truth—it's essential if you want to continue to count on their support in the future.

At times, leadership is a matter of trial and error and flying by the seat of your pants. As a leader, you might sometimes feel that you don't know what you're doing. That's OK. A powerful course of action can be discovered in midstream. You can *act* as a leader even when you don't *feel* like a leader. As a process of constant learning, leadership calls for all of the skills of master students.

Look for areas in which you can make a difference and experiment with these strategies. Right now there's something worth doing that calls for your leadership. Take action and others will join you.

journal entry 27

Discovery/Intention Statement

You can use this journal entry any time that you feel unhappy at work. Complete the following sentences, using additional paper as needed.

I discovered that:

- If I could change one thing about this job, I would . . .

____

____

____

____

- Something I *do* like about this job is . . .

____

____

____

____

- The transferable skills I am learning on this job include . . .

____

____

____

____

- I intend to make this job—or my next job—more satisfying by . . .

____

____

____

____

DISCOVERY WHEEL—COMING FULL CIRCLE

This book doesn't work. It is worthless. Only you can work. Only you can make a difference and use this book to become more effective at transferring skills from the classroom to the workplace.

The purpose of this book is to give you the opportunity to change your behavior. The fact that something seems like a good idea doesn't necessarily mean that you will put it into practice. This exercise gives you a chance to see what behaviors you have changed on your journey toward mastery.

Answer each question quickly and honestly. Record your results on the Discovery Wheel on this page and then compare it with the one you completed in Chapter One.

The scores on this Discovery Wheel indicate your current strengths and weaknesses. The Journal Entry that follows this Critical Thinking Exercise provides an opportunity to write about how you intend to change. As you complete this self-evaluation, keep in mind that your commitment to change allows you to become a master student and a master employee.

Your scores might be lower here than on your earlier Discovery Wheel. That's OK. Lower scores might result from increased self-awareness and honesty, and other valuable assets.

Note: The online version of this exercise does not include number ratings, so the results will be formatted differently than described here. If you did your previous Discovery Wheel online, do it online again. This will help you compare your two sets of responses more accurately

This statement is always or almost always true of me.

4 points
This statement is often true of me.

3 points
This statement is true of me about half the time.

2 points
This statement is seldom true of me.

1 point
This statement is never or almost never true of me.

Do this exercise online.

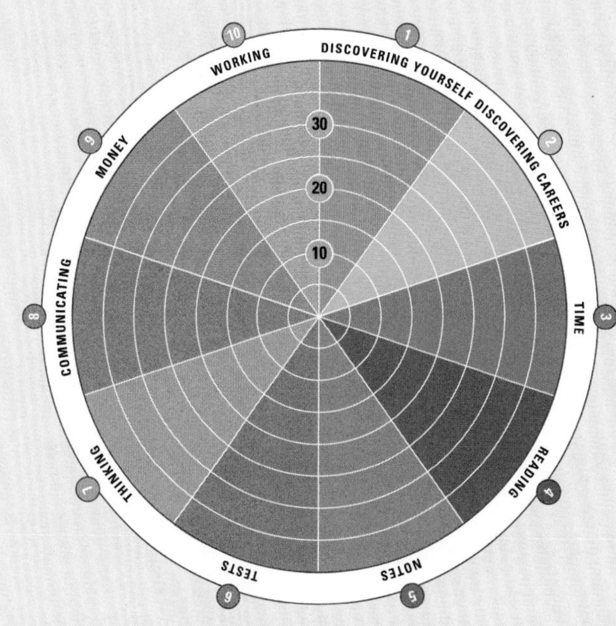

1. ______ I enjoy learning.
2. ______ I understand and apply the concept of multiple intelligences.
3. ______ I connect my courses to my purpose for being in school and the benefits I intend to get from my education.
4. ______ I regularly assess my personal strengths and areas for improvement.
5. ______ I am satisfied with how I am progressing toward achieving my goals.
6. ______ I use my knowledge of learning styles to support my success in school and at work.
7. ______ I am willing to consider any idea that can help me succeed in school—even if I initially disagree with that idea.
8. ______ I monitor my habits and change them in ways that support my success.

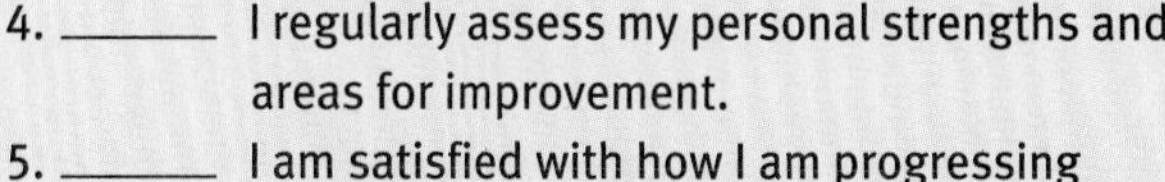

1. ______ I relate school to what I plan to do for the rest of my life.
2. ______ I plan my career with a detailed knowledge of my skills.
3. ______ I relate my career plan to my interests, attitudes, and core values.
4. ______ I can effectively use the library and the Internet to research possible careers.

5. ______ I use the career-planning services offered by my school.
6. ______ I am planning a career that contributes something worthwhile to the world.
7. ______ I have a written career plan and update it regularly.
8. ______ I use internships, extracurricular activities, information interviews, and on-the-job experiences to test and refine my career plan.

______ Total score (2) ***Career Planning***

1. ______ I set long-term goals and periodically review them.
2. ______ I set mid-term and short-term goals to support my long-term goals.
3. ______ I write a plan for each day and each week.
4. ______ I assign priorities to what I choose to do each day.
5. ______ I plan regular recreation time.
6. ______ I adjust my study time to meet the demands of individual courses.
7. ______ I have adequate time each day to accomplish what I plan.
8. ______ I effectively plan projects and manage time in work settings.

______ Total score (3) ***Time***

1. ______ I preview and review reading materials.
2. ______ When reading, I ask myself questions about the material.
3. ______ I underline or highlight important passages when reading.
4. ______ When I read textbooks or reports, I am alert and awake.
5. ______ I relate what I read to my life.
6. ______ I select a reading strategy to fit the type of material I'm reading.
7. ______ I take effective notes when I read.
8. ______ When I don't understand what I'm reading, I note my questions and find answers.

______ Total score (4) ***Reading***

1. ______ When I am in class, I focus my attention.
2. ______ I take notes in class and during meetings.
3. ______ I am aware of various methods for taking notes and choose those that work best for me.
4. ______ I distinguish major ideas from examples and other supporting material.
5. ______ I copy down material that the presenter writes on the board or overhead projector.
6. ______ I can put important concepts into my own words.
7. ______ My notes are valuable for review.
8. ______ I review notes within 24 hours.

______ Total score (5) ***Notes***

1. ______ I use techniques to enhance my memory.
2. ______ I manage my time during exams and am able to complete them.
3. ______ I am able to successfully predict test questions.
4. ______ I adapt my test-taking strategy to the kind of test I'm taking.
5. ______ I create value from any type of evaluation, including performance reviews.
6. ______ I start reviewing for tests at the beginning of the term and continue reviewing throughout the term.
7. ______ I manage stress and maintain my health even when I feel under pressure.
8. ______ My sense of personal worth is independent of my test scores.

______ Total score (6) ***Tests***

1. ______ I have flashes of insight and often think of solutions to problems at unusual times.
2. ______ I use brainstorming to generate solutions to a variety of problems.
3. ______ When I get stuck on a creative project, I use specific methods to get unstuck.
4. ______ I see problems and tough decisions as opportunities for learning and personal growth.
5. ______ I am open to different points of view and diverse cultural perspectives.
6. ______ I can support my points of view with sound logic and evidence.
7. ______ I use critical thinking to resolve ethical dilemmas.

8. ______ As I share my viewpoints with others, I am open to their feedback.

______ Total score (7) ***Thinking***

1. ______ I am candid with others about who I am, what I feel, and what I want.
2. ______ Other people tell me that I am a good listener.
3. ______ I can communicate my upset and resolve conflict without blaming others.
4. ______ I work effectively as a member of a project team.
5. ______ I am learning ways to thrive with diversity—attitudes and behaviors that will support my career success.
6. ______ I can effectively plan, research, draft, and revise a large writing assignment.
7. ______ I learn effectively from materials and activities that are posted online.
8. ______ I prepare and deliver effective speeches and presentations.

______ Total score (8) ***Communicating***

1. ______ I am in control of my personal finances.
2. ______ I can access a variety of resources to finance my education.
3. ______ I am confident that I will have enough money to complete my education.
4. ______ I take on debts carefully and repay them on time.
5. ______ I have long-range financial goals and a plan to meet them.
6. ______ I make regular deposits to a savings account.
7. ______ I pay off the balance on credit card accounts each month.
8. ______ I can have fun without spending money.

______ Total score (9) ***Money***

1. ______ In work settings, I look for models of success and cultivate mentors.
2. ______ My work creates value for my employer.
3. ______ I see working as a way to pursue my interests, expand my skills, and develop mastery.
4. ______ I support other people in their career planning and job hunting—and am willing to accept their support.
5. ______ I can function effectively in corporate cultures and cope positively with office politics.
6. ______ I create résumés and cover letters that distinguish me from other job applicants.
7. ______ I can accurately predict and prepare responses to questions asked by job interviewers.
8. ______ I see learning as a lifelong process that includes experiences inside and outside the classroom.

______ Total score (10) ***Working***

Filling in your Discovery Wheel

Using the total score from each category, shade in each section of the Discovery Wheel on page 335. Use different colors, if you want. For example, you could use green to denote areas you want to work on. When you have finished, complete the Journal Entry on page 338.

Discovery/Intention Statement

The purpose of this Journal Entry is to (1) review both of the Discovery Wheels you completed in this book, (2) summarize your insights from doing them, and (3) declare how you will use these insights to promote your continued success in the classroom and in the workplace.

Again, a lower score on the second Discovery Wheel does not necessarily indicate decreased personal effectiveness. Instead, the lower score could result from increased honesty and greater self-awareness.

	Chapter 1	*Chapter 10*
Self-Discovery	______	______
Career Planning	______	______
Time	______	______
Reading	______	______
Notes	______	______
Tests	______	______
Thinking	______	______
Communicating	______	______
Money	______	______
Working	______	______

Comparing the Discovery Wheel in this chapter with the Discovery Wheel in Chapter One, I discovered that I . . .

In the next six months, I intend to review the following articles from this book for additional suggestions I could use in the classroom:

In the next six months, I also intend to review the following articles for additional suggestions I could use in the workplace:

Keep your career plan alive

New jobs and career pathways are constantly being added to the workplace. To thrive in this world of constant change, create a career plan that includes lifelong learning and skill updating. Then put your plan into action.

Creating a plan and keeping it alive acknowledges a key fact: *You* are in charge of your career. No other person or organization can take on this task. Effective career planners routinely watch for new work opportunities, take responsibility for their long-term financial security, plan for job transitions, and expect to change careers. You can now benefit by ultimately thinking of yourself as self-employed—even when you work for someone else.

Keep thinking about what you want in all areas of your life, including your career. Then use a variety of techniques to transform your written plan into real change.

Display your goals. Without reminders, even skilled planners can forget their goals. One solution is to post written goals in prominent locations—the bathroom, bedroom, hall mirror, or office door. Also write goals on 3 × 5 cards and tape them to walls or store them next to your bed. Review the cards every morning and night.

You can make goals even more visible. Create an elaborate poster or collage that displays your life purpose. Use frames, color, graphics, and other visual devices to rivet your attention on your goals.

Add to your plan. Goals might pop into your mind at the oddest moments—while you're waiting in line, riding the bus, or stuck in rush-hour traffic. With a little preparation, you can capture those fleeting goals. Carry around a few 3 × 5 cards and a pen in your pocket or purse. (To quote an old advertisement, "Don't leave home without [them].") Or pack a small voice recorder with you. Speak your goals and preserve them for the ages.

Schedule time for career planning. Schedule regular times for career planning. This is an important appointment with yourself. Treat it as seriously as an appointment with your doctor.

Remember that planning does not have to take a lot of time. In just one hour or less, you can:

- Review and revise your career plan.
- Update your résumé.
- Visit the career center at your school.
- Do an information interview with someone working in a job related to your major.
- Brainstorm a list of places where you'd like to do an internship.
- Rehearse your answers to common questions asked during job interviews.
- Call or e-mail one of your contacts.

To get more benefit from planning and create the most options for your future, see career planning as a constant activity. This is not something to put off until your last year of school. Begin now.

Advertise your career plan. When it comes to achieving your goals, everyone you know is a potential ally. Take a tip from Madison Avenue and advertise. Tell friends and family members about what you plan to be, do, or have. Make your career plan public.

Enlist support. People might criticize your goals: "You want to promote world peace *and* become a millionaire? That's crazy." Remember that there are ways to deal with resistance.

One is to ask directly for support. Explain how much your goal means to you and what you'll do to achieve it. Mention that you're willing to revise your goal as circumstances change. Also *keep* talking about your vision. Goals that sound outlandish at first can become easier to accept over time.

Get coaching. You can hire a personal life coach to assist with goal setting and achievement. The principle is the same as hiring a personal trainer to set and meet fitness goals. A life coach engages you in a conversation about goals for all areas of your life—work, family, finances, education, spirituality, and more. To find such a person, key the words *life coach* into your favorite search site on the Web. National organizations for life coaches have their own sites, which can link you with resources in your own area.

Teach career planning. There's a saying: We teach what we most want to learn. You can turn this idea into an incentive for creating your future. Explain the process of career planning to friends and family. Volunteer to lead an informal seminar or workshop on this topic. If you have children, help them to set and meet goals.

Enjoy the rewards. Break large, long-term career goals into small tasks that you can finish in one hour or less. Savor the feeling that comes with crossing off items on a to-do list. Experience accomplishment often.

At least once each year, list the career goals that you achieved and celebrate. Do the same with goals in all areas of your life. Let the thrill of meeting one goal lead you to setting more.

critical thinking exercise 35

TRANSLATE YOUR CAREER GOALS INTO ACTION

1. Choose one goal from your career plan. List that goal here:

____

____

____

____

____

____

2. Next, list some follow-up actions. Ask yourself: "What will it really take for me to meet this goal?" List at least five ideas below:

____

____

____

____

____

____

____

____

____

3. Finally, translate any action you just listed into immediate steps—the kind of items that you would include on a daily to-do list. Think of tasks that you could complete in less than one hour, or start within the next 24 hours.

____

____

____

____

____

____

____

____

____

____

____

____

____

____

You can apply this three-step technique to any goal for your career or the rest of your life. The point is to move from ideas into action.

CREATE YOUR NEXT SEMESTER

This exercise offers a chance to celebrate your successes during the past term—and to think in specific ways about what you want to create next term.[6]

Part 1: Update your First Step

Looking back on this past semester, you might be surprised at how quickly it went by. You might also be surprised at how much you learned, both inside and outside the classroom.

In the space below, list three things that you did well during the current term. Perhaps you took the initiative to meet a new person or created an effective way to take notes in class. Write down any success that you find personally significant, no matter how small it might seem to others. Use additional paper as needed.

1. ______________________________

2. ______________________________

3. ______________________________

Now take a moment to write about three things that did not go as well as you wanted during the past term. Give yourself permission to explore whatever comes to mind—anything from a simple embarrassment to a major mistake. If you missed a class because you set your alarm for 7 p.m. instead of 7 a.m., you can write about that. If you failed a test, you might describe that experience as well.

As you practice truth telling, remember to keep it light. It's fine to acknowledge breakdowns and to laugh at yourself as you do.

1. ______________________________

2. ______________________________

3. ______________________________

Part 2: Determine what you want next

You've come a long way since first setting foot on campus. Now consider where you want to go next term. Brainstorm some intentions in several areas of your life and channel them into some new behaviors.

Do this by building on the writing you did in Part 1 of this exercise. Reflect on ways to maintain or expand on the successes you listed. Also consider ways to change or prevent some of the experiences you didn't like.

Determine what you want from academics. For instance, you could set a goal to raise your grade point average to a specific number, or to declare your major by a certain date. Complete the following sentence:

In my academic life, I want to . . .

____

____

Now consider your social life. Perhaps you want to resolve a conflict with an instructor or roommate. Or you might want to deepen a connection with someone you already know and make this person a friend for life. Put such goals in writing by completing the following sentence:

In my social life, I want to . . .

____

____

Finally, brainstorm a list of specific actions you can take to meet the goals you just wrote. Record these actions in your calendar or to-do list. For more suggestions on goal-setting, see Chapter Two.

journal entry 29

Discovery/Intention Statement

You've done a lot of writing during this course. To retain your key insights from this experience, review your responses to the Critical Thinking Exercises and Journal Entries in this book.

On a separate sheet of paper, summarize your key discoveries. List any intentions that call for further action. Write any new Discovery Statements or Intention Statements that seem appropriate.

power process

BE IT

All of the techniques in this book are enhanced by this Power Process.

To tap into the full benefits of this Power Process, consider that most of our choices in life fall into three categories. We can:

- Increase our material wealth (what we have).
- Improve our skills (what we do).
- Develop our "being" (who we are).

Many people devote their entire lifetime to the first two categories. They act as if they are "human havings" instead of human beings. For them, the quality of life hinges on what they have. They devote most of their waking hours to getting more—more clothes, more cars, more relationships, more degrees, more trophies. "Human havings" define themselves by looking at the circumstances in their lives—what they have.

Some people escape this materialist trap by adding another dimension to their identities. In addition to living as "human havings," they also live as "human doings." They thrive on working hard and doing everything well. They define themselves by how efficiently they do their jobs, how effectively they raise their children, and how actively they participate in clubs and organizations. Their thoughts are constantly about methods, techniques, and skills.

Look beyond doing and having

In addition to focusing on what we have and what we do, we can also focus on our being. While it is impossible to live our lives without having things and doing things, this Power Process suggests that we balance our experience by giving lots of attention to who we are—an aspect of our lives that goes beyond having and doing. Call it soul, passion, purpose, or values. Call it being. This word describes how we see ourselves—our deepest commitments, the ground from which our actions spring.

The realm of being is profound and subtle. It is also difficult to capture in words, though philosophers have tried for centuries. Christian theologian Paul Tillich described this realm when he defined faith as "ultimate commitment" and the "ground of being." In the New Testament, Jesus talked about being when he asked his followers to love God with all of their heart, soul, and mind. An ancient Hindu text also touches on being: "You are what your deep, driving desire is."

If all this seems far removed from taking notes or answering test questions, read on. Consider an example of how "Be it" can assist in career choices. In a letter to his father, a young man wrote:

> *We just went to see the Dance Theatre of Harlem. It was great! After the last number, I decided that I want to dance more than anything. I have a great passion to do it, more than anything else I can think or dream of. Dancing is what will make me happy and feel like I can leave this earth when my time comes. It is what I must do. I think that if I never fulfill this passion, I will never feel complete or satisfied with what I have done with my life.*

In his heart, this man *is* a dancer now, even before his formal training is complete. From his passion, desire, commitment, and self-image (his *being*) comes his willingness to take classes and rehearse (*doing*). And from his doing he might eventually *have* a job with a professional dance company.

Picture the result as you begin

The example of the dancer illustrates that once you have a clear picture of what you want to *be*, the things you *do* and *have* fall more naturally into place.

The idea is this: Getting where you want to be by what you do or by what you have is like swimming against the current. Have → do → be is a tough journey. It's much easier to go in the other direction: be → do → have.

Usually, we work against nature by trying to have something or do something before being it. That's hard. All of your deeds (what you do) might not get you where you want to be. Getting all of the right things (what you have) might not get you there either.

Take the person who values athletics and wants to master tennis. He buys an expensive racket and a stylish tennis wardrobe. Yet he still can't return a serve. Merely having the right things doesn't deliver what he values.

Suppose that this person takes a year's worth of tennis lessons. Week after week, he practices doing everything "right." Still, his game doesn't quite make it.

What goes wrong is hard to detect. "He lost the match even though he played a good game," people say. "Something seemed to be wrong. His technique was fine, but each swing was just a little off." Perhaps the source of his problem is that he cannot see himself as ever mastering the game. What he has and what he does are at war with his mental picture of himself.

You can see this happen in other areas of life. Two people tell the same joke in what seems to be the same way. Yet one person brings a smile, while the other person has you laughing so hard your muscles hurt. The difference in how they do the joke is imperceptible. When the successful comedian tells a joke, he does it from his experience of already being funny.

To have and do what you want, "Be it." Picture the result as you begin. If you can first visualize where you want to be, if you can go there in your imagination, if you can be it today, you set yourself up to succeed.

Be a master student now

Now relate this Power Process to succeeding in school. All of the techniques in this book can be worthless if you operate with the idea that you are an ineffective student. You might do almost everything this book suggests and still never achieve the success in school that you desire.

For example, if you believe that you are stupid in math, you are likely to fail at math. If you believe that you are not skilled at remembering, all of the memory techniques in the world might not improve your recall. Generally, we don't outperform our self-concept.

If you value success in school, picture yourself as a master student right now. Through higher education, you are gaining knowledge and skills that reflect and reinforce this view of yourself.

This principle works in other areas of life. For example, if you value a fulfilling career, picture yourself as already being on a path to a job you love. Use affirmations and visualizations to plant this idea firmly in your mind. Change the way you see yourself, and watch your actions and results shift as if by magic.

While you're at it, remember that "Be it" is not positive thinking or mental cheerleading. This Power Process works well when you take a First Step—when you tell the truth about your current abilities. The very act of accepting who you are and what you can do right now unleashes a powerful force for personal change.

Flow with the natural current of be → do → have. Then watch your circumstances change.

If you want it, "Be it."

career application

Duane Bigeagle earned his B.A. in Elementary Education and found a job teaching kindergarten in an urban public school.

To his surprise, the hardest thing about the job was not interacting with students—whom he enjoyed greatly—but interacting with his coworkers. Though Duane had heard of office politics, he did not expect them to be so strong in an educational setting.

Duane's greatest concern was a colleague named Reneé, a teacher with 25 years of experience. During weekly staff meetings, the school's principal asked teachers to share any problems they were experiencing with students and collectively brainstorm solutions. Reneé smiled a lot, offered suggestions, and freely offered praise for anyone who was willing to share a problem. During informal conversations with Duane before or after school, however, Reneé complained bitterly about other teachers on staff—including those whom she'd just praised during staff meetings.

Being new to the school and a first-year teacher, Duane decided that he wanted to avoid making enemies. His goal in relating to staff members was simply to learn everything he could from them. With that goal in mind, Duane adopted the habits of carefully observing the classroom strategies used by other teachers and listening without judgment to any coaching they offered him.

Reneé talked with Duane every day and, after gossiping about other teachers, freely offered her advice for managing his classroom. By the end of the school year, Duane had enough of this. He worried that Reneé was taking on the role of a self-appointed mentor to him, and he disagreed with many of her ideas about teaching. He also worried that other teachers would perceive him and Reneé as a "team" and that her reputation for backstabbing would reflect negatively on him as well. ☒

Reflecting on this scenario

1. Identify a transferable skill that Duane demonstrates.

___

___

___

2. What behaviors lead you to conclude that Duane has this skill?

___

___

___

3. Identify another skill that would be useful for Duane to develop.

___

___

___

4. List two or three suggestions for Duane that could help him cope with office politics and solve his problem with Reneé.

___

___

___

Name ______________________________ Date _____/_____/_____

quiz

1. The article "Use power tools for finding work" presents two approaches to job hunting. Briefly summarize both sets of strategies.

2. Compare the two approaches you summarized in the previous question. Explain how one can be more effective than the other.

3. Explain the meaning of the suggestion to "promote your boss."

4. According to the text, it is impossible to escape leadership. True or False? Explain your answer.

5. Summarize a three-part structure for writing effective cover letters.

6. List three strategies for keeping your career plan alive.

7. List three examples of information to *omit* from your résumé.

8. Explain the suggestion to "give yourself a raise before you start work."

9. Using the Power Process: "Be it" eliminates the need to take action. True or False? Explain your answer.

10. If your scores are lower on the Discovery Wheel the second time you complete it, that means your study skills have not improved. True or False? Explain your answer.

learning styles application

The questions below will "cycle" you through four styles, or modes, of learning as explained in the article "Learning styles: Discovering how you learn" in Chapter One. Each question will help you explore a different mode. You can answer the questions in any order.

what if *Consider this statement: "You are on the edge of a universe so miraculous and full of wonder that your imagination at its most creative moment cannot encompass it. Paths are open to lead you to worlds beyond your wildest dreams." If you adopted this statement as a working principle, what would you do differently on a daily basis?*

why *Consider your experience with this book and your student success class. Which of your attitudes or actions changed as a result of this experience?*

how *List one suggestion from this book that you would like to apply but have not yet acted upon. Describe exactly how you will implement this suggestion.*

what *List five suggestions from this book that you've already applied. Rate each suggestion for its effectiveness on a scale of 1 to 5 (1 is most effective, 5 is least effective).*

master student profile

RUTH HANDLER

(1916–2002) As a cofounder of Mattel, she invented the Barbie doll in 1959. After being diagnosed with breast cancer and undergoing a mastectomy, she designed a prosthetic breast that was later patented as Nearly Me.

When Ruth Handler first proposed the idea of a grown-up doll to the toy designers at Mattel—the company she and her husband ran—the designers thought she was crazy. Little girls want to pretend to be mommies, she was told.

No, said Handler. Little girls want to pretend to be bigger girls. And she knew this because she spent a lot of time observing one little girl in particular—her daughter, Barbara, nicknamed "Barbie."

All her life, Ruth has considered the word "no" just another challenge.

When Ruth graduated from East Denver High School and announced her intention to attend college, her family didn't give her a lot of encouragement. Marrying her high-school sweetheart—a broke-but-talented artist named Elliot Handler—was more traditional than going to college. But she ended up at the University of Denver. And she married Elliot anyway. When she took two semesters of business education at the University of California at Los Angeles, she was the only married woman in her class. And she became the first woman to complete the program.

Ruth fell in love with Southern California and was hired as a stenographer at Paramount Studios in Hollywood. The year was 1937. Ruth worked at Paramount until 1941, when she became pregnant

with Barbara, and stayed home until after the birth of her son, Ken, in 1944. Staying home made Ruth restless; she wanted to help [her husband] Elliot run his giftware and costume jewelry business. "You make something; I'll sell it," she told him.

In 1944, while the United States was embroiled in World War II, Elliot designed a new style of picture frame made out of the then-revolutionary new plastics. His partner, Harold "Matt" Matson, built samples and Ruth took the frames to a chain of photography studios and got a large order. The three celebrated, calling their new business "Mattel" after MATT and ELliot.

Soon after, plastic was needed for the war effort and became unavailable for civilian use. Fortunately, Elliot came up with the idea of making frames out of scrap wood. Ruth took the samples back to the photography studio and got an even bigger order. Mattel could continue operating. The leftover wood from the picture frames led to a thriving business making doll house furniture.

Worldwide, Mattel sold millions of Ruth Handler's Barbie dolls, boosting the company's sales to $18 million. Within ten years, customers had bought $500 million worth of Barbie products.

Over the years, Ruth moved up from cofounder of the company to executive vice president to president to cochairman of the board of directors. These titles were practically unheard of for women in the 1960s.

Handler remembers one episode that occurred despite her executive status. A brokerage house was holding a meeting with the investment community at a private club, and Handler was to be the keynote speaker. When she arrived at the club, the program planners ushered her into the club through the alley and kitchen. Later, she discovered that she was sneaked into the building because the club didn't allow women. ☒

From Ethlie Ann Vare and Greg Placek, *Women Inventors and Their Discoveries.*

photo and illustration credits

Introduction: p. xii: (finger/string) © Image Source/Corbis; (runner) © Masterfile Royalty Free; (piggy bank) © Darren Greenwood/Design Pics/Corbis; (clock) © Tetra Images/Corbis; p. 11: (money) © Don Farrall/Getty, (statue) © Ron Dahlquist/ Getty, (nurse, woman in pink) © Masterfile Royalty Free, collage by Walter Kopec; p. 13: © Tom Stewart/zefa/Corbis; p. 16: © Masterfile Royalty Free; p. 18: (juggler) © Masterfile Royalty Free, (clock) © George Diebold/Getty, collage by Walter Kopec; p. 22: © George Doyle/Getty.

Chapter 1: p. 24: © Masterfile Royalty Free; p. 34: (demonstration) © Michael Newman/PhotoEdit; p. 34: (girl practicing CPR) © Stockbyte Royalty Free/Fotosearch; p. 39: (man) © Tanya Constantine/Getty, (fern) © Tim Laman/Getty, (ballet shoes) © Scott T. Baxter/Getty, (protractor) © Vladimir Godnik/Getty, (meditating woman) © Meg Takamura, (easel) © Stockbyte/ Getty, (microphone) © George Doyle/Getty, (holding hands) © Doug Menuez/Getty, (music) © Gregor Schuster/Getty, collage by Walter Kopec; p. 42: collage by Walter Kopec; p. 47 (all): © Photodisc; p. 48 (all): © Photodisk; p. 51: © Masterfile Royalty Free; p. 52: © Wonderfile; p. 55: © Tao Chuan Yeh/Getty Images.

Chapter 2: p. 56: © Masterfile Royalty Free; p. 58: © ImageSource/ Fotosearch; p. 67: (teacher) © Comstock, (medical workers, construction worker, potter, woman in office) © Fotosearch, (lawyer) © image100/Wonderfile, collage by Walter Kopec; p. 69: © Alamy Images; p. 78: © Stockbyte; p. 79: © Wonderfile; p. 80: © 2006 Ben Loehrke, Youth Advocating Leadership & Learning, www.yallrelief.org. Volunteers from Indiana University working on a house damaged by HurricaneKatrina, Gulfport, MS. ; p. 84: (man) © Masterfile Royalty Free; (boy with remote) © Ron Chapple/Corbis; (plan) © Corbis; collage by Walter Kopec; p. 89: (both women) © Photodisc Blue, (illustration) Walter Kopec; p. 90: © Royalty-Free Corbis/Corbis; p. 93: © Bennett Raglin/WireImage/Getty Images.

Chapter 3: p. 94: © Tetra Images/Corbis; p. 102: © Deborah Jaffe/ The Image Bank/Getty; p. 104: © Jamie Grill/Corbis; p. 106: © image100/Corbis; p. 112: (top) © Image Source/Alamy, (bottom) © BananaStock/Alamy; p. 114: (woman's face, clock, folders) © Photodisc, (gears, "Stop" sign) © ComstockKLIPS, (hammock) © Artville, collage by Walter Kopec; p. 121: images © Masterfile Royalty Free; collage by Walter Kopec; p. 122: Photos.com; p. 125: © Bettmann/Corbis.

Chapter 4: p. 126: © Corbis/Royalty Free; p. 128: images © Masterfile Royalty Free; collage by Walter Kopec; p. 129: images © Masterfile Royalty Free; collage by Walter Kopec; p. 130: images © Masterfile Royalty Free; collage by Walter Kopec; p. 132: images © Masterfile Royalty Free; collage by Walter Kopec; p. 133: © Masterfile Royalty Free; p. 136: © Chris Pancewicz/Alamy; p. 138: © Brand X Pictures/Alamy; p. 139: © Graham Bell/Corbis; p. 141: © Masterfile Royalty Free; p. 145: © Digital Vision/ PictureQuest; p. 150: © Photodisc/Getty; p. 153: Courtesy Craig Keilburger.

Chapter 5: p. 154: © Brand X Pictures/Alamy; p. 156: © Rubberball/PictureQuest; p. 159: © Photodisc/Fotosearch; p. 165: © Digital Vision Royalty Free/Wonderfile; p. 167: Walter Kopec; p. 170: (people) © Photodisc, (illustration) Brian J. Reardon; p. 175: © Corbis/Royalty Free; p. 176: © BananaStock/ Alamy; p. 179: © Maiman Rick/Corbis Sygma.

Chapter 6: p. 180: © Robert Michael; p. 182: © Gaetano Images Inc./Alamy; p. 185: © Image Source/Corbis; p. 187: © Image 100/Corbis; p. 196: © Masterfile Royalty Free; p. 201: © Bloomimage/Corbis; p. 205: © Iconotec/Wonderfile; p. 207: © Royalty-Free/Corbis; p. 209: © Photodisc; p. 211: images © Masterfile Royalty Free; collage by Walter Kopec; p. 212: © ImageState/Wonderfile; p. 215: © Reuters/Corbis.

Chapter 7: p. 216: © Garry Black/Masterfile; p. 219: © Steve Cole/Getty; p. 229: (images) © Photodisc, (collage) Walter Kopec; p. 234: images © Masterfile Royalty Free; collage by Walter Kopec; p. 241: (rubbish on shoreline; volunteers with rakes) © Masterfile Royalty Free; (woman) PhotoAlto/Alamy; collage by Walter Kopec; p. 242: © Digital Vision Royalty Free/Fotosearch; p. 245: © Colin McPherson/Corbis.

Chapter 8: p. 246: © John Wilkes Studio/Corbis; p. 250: © Masterfile Royalty Free; p. 254: © Sven Hagolani/zefa/Corbis; p. 256: © Masterfile Royalty Free; p. 263: (people) © Photodisc, (lightbulb) © Comstock Klips, collage by Walter Kopec; p. 265: © Photodisc/Fotosearch; p. 267: © Photodisc/Getty Images; p. 269: © Masterfile Royalty Free; p. 275: (ladder) © Burke/Triolo Productions/Brand X/Corbis, (woman) © Simon Marcus/Corbis, collage by Walter Kopec; p. 276: © Ingram Publishing/Alamy; p. 279: © Bettmann/Corbis.

Chapter 9: p. 280: © Darren Greenwood/Design Pics/Corbis; p. 292: © Michele Constantini, PhotoAlto/Getty; p. 297: © Masterfile; p. 298: © Masterfile; p. 301: © Masterfile Royalty Free; p. 302: © Photodisc/Getty Images; p. 305: Photograph used by permission of Curtis Brown Ltd. Copyright © 2002 by Po Bronson. All rights reserved.

Chapter 10: p. 306: © Masterfile Royalty Free; p. 308: (man) © Photodisc, (group) © Corbis, collage by Walter Kopec; p. 311: (hand) © Photodisc, collage by Walter Kopec; p. 320: © Thinkstock/ Alamy; p. 326: © image100/Alamy; p. 331: collage by Walter Kopec; p. 332: images: (Jesse Owens) © Bettman, (Albert Einstein) © Alan W. Richards/Princeton, (Nelson Mandela) © Paul Velesco/Gallo Images/Corbis, (Golda Meir) © Reuters/ Corbis, (Aung San Suu Kyi) © Emmanuel Dunand/Getty, collage by Walter Kopec; p. 339: (images) © Photodisc, collage by Walter Kopec; p. 343: © Masterfile Royalty Free; p. 344: © Wendy Ashton/Stone/Getty; p. 347: © Bettmann/Corbis.

endnotes

Introduction

1. John Henry Newman, *Newman Reader*, "Discourse 5. Knowledge Its Own End," http://www.newmanreader.org/works/idea/discourse5.html (accessed April 26, 2007).
2. Fordcarz.com, "Quotations from Henry Ford," http://www.fordcarz.com/henry_ford_quotes.htm (accessed April 26, 2007).
3. U.S. Department of Labor, Bureau of Labor Statistics, "Working in the 21st Century," http://stats.bls.gov/opub/working/page6b.htm (accessed May 1, 2007).
4. William James, *Talks To Teachers On Psychology; And To Students On Some Of Life's Ideals* (Project Gutenberg e-book), http://www.gutenberg.org/files/16287/16287-h/16287-h.htm (accessed May 1, 2007).
5. Robert Mager, *Preparing Instructional Objectives* (Belmont, CA: Fearon, 1975), 23.
6. Robert Hutchins, "The Great Conversation: The Substance of a Liberal Education," *Great Books of the Western World*, vol. 1 (Chicago: Encyclopædia Britannica, 1952), xi.
7. Malcolm Knowles, *Andragogy in Action* (San Francisco: Jossey-Bass, 1984).
8. Deborah Davis, *The Adult Learner's Companion* (Boston: Houghton Mifflin, 2007).
9. Abraham Maslow, *The Further Reaches of Human Nature* (New York: Viking, 1971), 300.
10. Excerpts from *Creating Your Future.* Copyright © 1998 by Dave Ellis. Reprinted by permission of Houghton Mifflin Company. All rights reserved. Excerpts from *Human Being: A Manual for Happiness, Health, Love, and Wealth* by Dave Ellis and Stan Lankowitz. Reprinted by permission of Breakthrough Enterprises.

Chapter 1

1. Neil Fleming, "VARK: A Guide to Learning Styles," 2006, http://www.vark-learn.com (accessed October 30, 2006).
2. David A. Kolb, *Experiential Learning: Experience as the Source of Learning and Development* (Englewood Cliffs, NJ: Prentice-Hall, 1984).
3. Barry Reece and Rhonda Brandt, *Effective Human Relations: Personal and Organizational Applications* (Boston: Houghton Mifflin, 2002), 65–85.
4. Douglas A. Berstein, Louis A. Penner, Alison Clarke-Stewart, and Edward J. Roy, *Psychology* (Boston: Houghton Mifflin, 2006), 368–369.
5. Howard Gardner, *Frames of Mind: The Theory of Multiple Intelligences* (New York: Basic Books, 1993).
6. Mihaly Csikszentmihalyi, *Finding Flow: The Psychology of Engagement with Everyday Life* (New York: Basic Books, 1997).
7. Carl Rogers, *Freedom to Learn* (Columbus, OH: Merrill, 1969).
8. Richard Malott, "Self-Management Checklist," Counselling Services, University of Victoria, 2003, http://www.coun.uvic.ca/learn/program/hndouts/slfman.html (accessed April 26, 2007).
9. B. F. Skinner, *Science and Human Behavior* (Boston: Free Press, 1965).
10 William James, *Pragmatism and Other Essays* (New York: Washington Square, 1963).

Chapter 2

1. Adapted from Dave Ellis, Stan Lankowitz, Ed Stupka, and Doug Toft, *Career Planning,* Third Edition. Copyright © 2003 by Houghton Mifflin Company. Reprinted by permission.
2. Ibid.
3. From "Press Room—Answers to Frequently Asked Questions," National Association of Colleges and Employers, http://www.naceweb.org/press/quick.htm#qualities.
4. Adapted from Dave Ellis, Stan Lankowitz, Ed Stupka, and Doug Toft, *Career Planning,* Third Edition. Copyright © 2003 by Houghton Mifflin Company. Reprinted by permission.
5. Ibid.
6. Ibid.
7. Ibid.
8. Ibid.
9. Ibid.
10. National Center on Education and the Economy, *Tough Choices or Tough Times: The Report of the New Commission on the Skills of the American Workforce* (San Francisco: Jossey-Bass, 2007).
11. Frank Levy and Richard J. Murnane, *The New Division of Labor: How Computers Are Creating the Next Job Market* (Princeton, NJ: Princeton University Press, 2004), 47–48.
12. Adapted from Dave Ellis, Stan Lankowitz, Ed Stupka, and Doug Toft, *Career Planning,* Third Edition. Copyright © 2003 by Houghton Mifflin Company. Reprinted by permission.
13. Ibid.
14. Joe Cuseo, "Academic-Support Strategies for Promoting Student Retention and Achievement During the First Year of College," University of Ulster, *Student Transition and Retention*, http://www.ulst.ac.uk/star/data/cuseoretention.htm#peestud (accessed September 4, 2003).
15. U.S. Department of Labor, Bureau of Labor Statistics, "Computer Programmers," http://www.bls.gov/oco/ocos110.htm (accessed May 18, 2007).

Chapter 3

1. Alan Lakein, *Take Control of Your Time and Life* (New York: New American Library, 1973), 28.

2. Linda Sapadin, with Jack Maguire, *It's About Time! The Six Styles of Procrastination and How to Overcome Them* (New York: Penguin, 1997).
3. Stephen R. Covey, *The Seven Habits of Highly Effective People: Restoring the Character Ethic* (New York: Simon & Schuster, 1989), 152.
4. M. A. Just, P. A. Carpenter, T. A. Keller, et al., "Interdependence of Nonoverlapping Cortical Systems in Dual Cognitive Tasks," *NeuroImage* 14, no. 2 (2001): 417–426.
5. David Allen, *Getting Things Done: The Art of Stress-Free Productivity* (New York: Penguin, 2001).

Chapter 4

1. School of Information Management and Systems, University of California, Berkeley, "How Much Information? 2003," October 27, 2003, http://www.sims.berkeley.edu/research/projects/how-much-info-2003/execsum.htm (accessed October 13, 2006).
2. John Morkes and Jakob Nielsen, "Concise, Scannable and Objective: How to Write for the Web," 1997, http://www. useit.com/papers/webwriting/writing.html (accessed May 18, 2007).
3. From *Information Anxiety* by Richard Saul Wurman. Copyright © 1989 by Richard Saul Wurman. Used by permission of Doubleday, a division of Bantam Doubleday Dell Publishing Group, Inc.
4. From Ann Raimes, *Universal Keys for Writers*. Copyright © 2005 by Houghton Mifflin Company. Reprinted with permission.
5. Joe Barker, "Recommended Search Strategy: Analyze your Topic & Search with Peripheral Vision," University of California, Berkeley, http://www.lib.berkeley.edu/TeachingLib/Guides/Internet/Strategies.html (accessed May 18, 2007).
6. William Glasser, *Take Effective Control of Your Life* (New York: Harper & Row, 1984).

Chapter 5

1. Walter Pauk, *How to Study in College* (Boston: Houghton Mifflin, 2001), 236–241.
2. Tony Buzan, *Use Both Sides of Your Brain* (New York: Dutton, 1991).
3. Gabrielle Rico, *Writing the Natural Way* (Los Angeles: J. P. Tarcher, 1983).
4. Joseph Novak and D. Bob Gowin, *Learning How to Learn* (New York: Cambridge University Press, 1984).
5. Douglas Bernstein, Louis A. Penner, Alison Clarke-Stewart, and Edward J. Roy, *Psychology*, Seventh Edition (Boston: Houghton Mifflin, 2006), 605.
6. William Glasser, *Take Effective Control of Your Life* (New York: Harper & Row, 1984).

Chapter 6

1. Adapted from Linda Wong, *Essential Study Skills*, Fourth Edition. Copyright © 2003 by Houghton Mifflin Company. Reprinted with permission.
2. Joe Cuseo, "Academic-Support Strategies for Promoting Student Retention and Achievement During the First-Year of College," University of Ulster, *Student Transition and Retention*, http://www.ulst.ac.uk/star/data/cuseoretention.htm#peestud (accessed September 4, 2003).
3. Ibid.
4. Daniel L. Schacter, *The Seven Sins of Memory: How the Mind Forgets and Remembers* (Boston: Houghton Mifflin, 2001), 14.
5. American Foundation for Suicide Prevention, "Risk Factors for Suicide," 2007, http://www.afsp.org/index.cfm?page_id=5147440-E24E-E376-BDF4BF8BA6444E76 (accessed January 4, 2007).
6. This article incorporates detailed suggestions from reviewer Frank Baker.
7. U.S. Department of Agriculture and U.S. Department of Health and Human Services, "Dietary Guidelines for Americans 2005," http://www.health.gov/dietaryguidelines/dga2005/recommendations.htm (accessed May 18, 2007).
8. National Institute of Alcohol Abuse and Alcoholism, "A Snapshot of Annual High-Risk College Drinking Consequences," 9/23/2005, http://www.collegedrinkingprevention.gov/StatsSummaries/snapshot.aspx (viewed January 5, 2007).
9. Alzheimer's Association, "Brain Health," 2006, http://www.alz.org/brainhealth/overview.asp (accessed October 30, 2006).
10. David B. Peterson and Mary Dee Hicks, *Development First: Strategies for Self-Development* (Minneapolis, MN: Personnel Decisions, 1995), 22.
11. Adapted from "But They Did Not Give Up," http://www.des.emory.edu/mfp/OnFailingG.html. (Accessed January 6, 2007).

Chapter 7

1. Quoted in Theodore Cheney, *Getting the Words Right: How to Revise, Edit and Rewrite* (Cincinnati, OH: Writer's Digest, 1983).
2. William Perry, *Forms of Intellectual and Ethical Development in the College Years* (New York: Holt, Rinehart and Winston, 1970).
3. *Critical Thinking: A Statement of Expert Consensus for Purposes of Educational Assessment and Instruction* (Millbrae, CA: The California Academic Press, 1990).
4. Quoted in Alice Calaprice, ed., *The Expanded Quotable Einstein* (Princeton, NJ: Princeton University Press, 2000).
5. Arthur Koestler, *The Act of Creation* (New York: Dell, 1964).
6. Quoted in Donald Asher, *How to Get Any Job with Any Major: Career Launch and Re-Launch for Everyone Under 30* (Berkeley, CA: Ten Speed, 2004), 9.
7. *Setting the Standard*, Office of Ethics and Business Conduct, Lockheed Martin Corporation, 2003, http://www.itcilo.it/english/actrav/telearn/global/ilo/code/lockheed.htm (accessed May 20, 2007).

Chapter 8

1. National Association of Colleges and Employers, "Why Do Employers Want to Hire You—The New Graduate?" 2007, http://www.jobweb.com/joboutlook/2007/student2.htm (accessed May 31, 2007).
2. U.S. Census Bureau News, "Minority Population Tops 100 Million," May 17, 2007, http://www.census.gov/Press-Release/ www/releases/archives/population/010048.html (accessed May 31, 2007).
3. Carl Rogers, *On Becoming a Person* (Boston: Houghton Mifflin, 1961).
4. Thomas Gordon, *Parent Effectiveness Training: The Tested New Way to Raise Responsible Children* (New York: New American Library, 1975).
5. Sidney Jourard, *The Transparent Self* (New York: Van Nostrand, 1971).
6. Vincent A. Miller, *Guidebook for International Trainers in Business and Industry* (New York: Van Nostrand Reinhold, 1979), 46–51.
7. Maia Szalavitz, "Race and the Genome: The Howard University Human Genome Center," National Human Genome Center, 2004, http://www.genomecenter.howard.edu/article.htm (accessed October 5, 2006).
8. Diane de Anda, *Bicultural Socialization: Factors Affecting the Minority Experience* (Washington, DC: National Association of Social Workers, 1984).

9. W. T. Wilson, "The Dawn of the India Century: Why India Is Poised to Challenge China and the United States for Global Economic Hegemony in the 21st Century," 2005, www.keystone-india.com/pdfs/The%20India%20Century.pdf (accessed May 31, 2007).
10. U.S. Census Bureau, "Exports from Manufacturing Establishments: 2001," July 2004, http://www.census.gov/mcd/exports/ar01.pdf (accessed May 31, 2007).
11. Lydia Ramsey, "Minding Your Global Manners," 2005, http://www.mannersthatsell.com/articles/globalmanners.html (accessed May 31, 2007).
12. Thomas Friedman, *The World Is Flat: A Brief History of the Twenty-First Century* (New York: Farrar, Straus, and Giroux, 2005).
13. LaFasto and Larson refer to their book *When Teams Work Best* in their online article: "Center for Association Leadership: The Zen of Brilliant Teams," July 1, 2002, http://www.asaecenter.org/PublicationsResources/articledetail.cfm?ItemNumber=13295 (accessed January 4, 2007).
14. National Association of Colleges and Employers, "Why Do Employers Want to Hire You—The New Graduate?" 2007, http://www.jobweb.com/joboutlook/2007/student2.htm (accessed May 31, 2007).
15. Michael Motley, *Overcoming Your Fear of Public Speaking: A Proven Method* (Boston: Houghton Mifflin, 2003).
16. MySpace, "Safety Tips," www1.myspace.com/misc/safetyTips.html (accessed January 4, 2007).

Chapter 9

1. Saul Hansell, "Yahoo's Growth Being Eroded by New Rivals," *New York Times*, October 11, 2006, http://www.nytimes.com/2006/10/11/technology/11yahoo.html (accessed May 31, 2007).
2. David U. Himmelstein, Elizabeth Warren, Deborah Thorne, and Steffie Woolhandler, "MarketWatch: Illness and Injury as Contributors to Bankruptcy," Health Affairs, February 2, 2005, http://content.healthaffairs.org/cgi/content/full/hlthaff.w5.63/DC1 (accessed May 31, 2007).
3. Joe Dominguez and Vicki Robin, *Your Money or Your Life: Transforming Your Relationship with Money and Achieving Financial Independence* (New York: Viking Penguin, 1992), 55.
4. AlcoholPolicyMD.com, "Frequently Asked Questions About College Binge Drinking," http://www.alcoholpolicymd.com/alcohol_and_health/faqs.htm (accessed May 31, 2007).
5. Marie O'Malley, "Educating Undergraduates on Using Credit Cards," Nellie Mae, 2002, http://www.nelliemae.com/library/cc_use.html (accessed May 31, 2007).
6. "High Hopes, Big Debts," The Project on Student Debt, 2006, http://projectonstudentdebt.org/files/pub/High_Hopes_Big_Debts.pdf (accessed May 31, 2007).
7. Sandy Baum and Kathleen Payea, "Education Pays 2004: The Benefits of Higher Education for Individuals and Society," College Board, 2005, http://www.collegeboard.com/prod_downloads/press/cost04/EducationPays2004.pdf (accessed May 31, 2007).
8. M. P. Dunleavey, "Basic Instincts: Buying Online with a Brain That's Offline," *New York Times*, October 7, 2006, http://www.nytimes.com/2006/10/07/business/07instinct.html (accessed May 31, 2007).
9. O. C. Ferrell, John Fraedrich, and Linda Ferrell, *Business Ethics: Ethical Decision Making and Cases*, Sixth Edition. Copyright © 2005 by Houghton Mifflin Company. Reprinted with permission.

Chapter 10

1. U.S. Department of Labor, "Secretary's Commission on Achieving Necessary Skills (SCANS)"; March 9, 2006, http://wdr.doleta.gov/SCANS/ (accessed May 31, 2007).
2. National Association of Colleges and Employers, "Why Do Employers Want to Hire You—the New Graduate?" 2007, http://www.jobweb.com/joboutlook/2007/student2.htm (accessed May 31, 2007).
3. U.S. Department of Education, "Sexual Harassment: It's Not Academic," March 14, 2005; http://www.ed.gov/about/offices/list/ocr/docs/ocrshpam.html (accessed May 31, 2007).
4. U.S. Department of Labor, *Report on the American Workforce 2001*, http://www.bls.gov/opub/rtaw/pdf/rtaw2001.pdf (accessed May 31, 2007).
5. James Kouzes and Barry Posner, *The Leadership Challenge: How to Get Extraordinary Things Done in Organizations* (San Francisco: Josey-Bass, 1987).
6. Adapted from "Plan for Sophomore-Year Success," *Becoming a Master Student Athlete* (Boston: Houghton Mifflin, 2006), 319.

additional reading

Adler, Mortimer, and Charles Van Doren. *How to Read a Book.* New York: Touchstone, 1972.

Allen, David. *Getting Things Done: The Art of Stress-Free Productivity* (New York: Penguin, 2001).

The American Heritage Dictionary, Fourth Edition. Boston: Houghton Mifflin, 2001.

Bolles, Richard N. *What Color Is Your Parachute? A Practical Manual for Job-Hunters and Career-Changers.* Berkeley, CA: Ten Speed, updated annually.

Bronson, Po. *What Should I Do with My Life? The True Story of People Who Answered the Ultimate Question.* New York: Random House, 2003.

Brown, Alan C. *Maximizing Memory Power.* New York: Wiley, 1986.

Buzan, Tony. *Make the Most of Your Mind.* New York: Simon & Schuster, 1977.

Chaffee, John. *Thinking Critically.* Boston: Houghton Mifflin, 2003.

Conlin, Mary Lou, ed. *The Working Reader.* Boston: Houghton Mifflin, 2001.

Covey, Stephen R. *First Things First.* New York: Simon & Schuster, 1994.

Ellis, Dave. *Creating Your Future: Five Steps to the Life of Your Dreams.* Boston: Houghton Mifflin, 1998.

Ellis, Dave, and Stan Lankowitz. *Human Being: A Manual for Happiness, Health, Love and Wealth.* Rapid City, SD: Breakthrough Enterprises, 1995.

Ellis, Dave, Stan Lankowitz, Ed Stupka, and Doug Toft. *Career Planning.* Boston: Houghton Mifflin, 2003.

Engleberg, Isa N., and Dianna R. Wynn. *Working in Groups: Communication Principles and Strategies.* Boston: Houghton Mifflin, 2003.

Facione, Peter. *Critical Thinking: What It Is and Why It Counts.* Millbrae, CA: California Academic Press, 1996.

Ferrell, O. C., John Fraedrich, and Linda Ferrell. *Business Ethics: Ethical Decision Making and Cases.* Boston: Houghton Mifflin, 2005.

Friedman, Thomas. *The World Is Flat: A Brief History of the Twenty-First Century* (New York: Farrar, Straus, and Giroux, 2005).

Germer, Fawn. *Hard Won Wisdom: More Than 50 Extraordinary Women Mentor You to Find Self-Awareness, Perspective, and Balance.* New York: Perigree, 2001.

Gibaldi, Joseph. *MLA Handbook for Writers of Research Papers.* New York: Modern Language Association, 1999.

Golas, Thaddeus. *The Lazy Man's Guide to Enlightenment.* Layton, UT: Gibbs Smith, 1997.

Greene, Susan D., and Melanie C. L. Martel. *The Ultimate Job Hunter's Guidebook.* Boston: Houghton Mifflin, 2004.

Gross, Kim Johnson, and Jeff Stone. *Dress Smart Women: Wardrobes That Win in the New Workplace.* New York: Warner Books, 2002.

Higbee, Kenneth L. *Your Memory: How It Works and How to Improve It.* Englewood Cliffs, NJ: Prentice Hall, 1996.

Hill, Napolean. *Think and Grow Rich.* New York: Fawcett, 1996.

Hurtado, Sylvia, et al. *Enacting Diverse Learning Environments: Improving the Climate for Racial/Ethnic Diversity in Higher Education.* Ashe-Eric Higher Education Reports, 1999.

Kaminsky, Howard, and Alexandra Penney. *Magic Words @ Work: Powerful Phrases to Help You Conquer the Working World.* New York: Broadway Books, 2004.

Kolb, David A. *Experiential Learning: Experience as the Source of Learning and Development.* Englewood Cliffs, NJ: Prentice Hall, 1984.

Kreitner, Robert. *Management.* Boston: Houghton Mifflin, 2004.

Lathrop, Richard. *Who's Hiring Who?* Berkeley, CA: Ten Speed, 1989.

Levy, Frank, and Richard J. Murnane. *The New Division of Labor: How Computers Are Creating the Next Job Market.* Princeton, NJ: Princeton University Press, 2004.

Light, Richard J. *Making the Most of College: Students Speak Their Minds.* Cambridge, MA: Harvard University Press, 2001.

Manning, Robert. *Credit Card Nation: The Consequences of America's Addiction to Credit.* New York: Basic Books, 2000.

Metcalf, Allan. *Predicting New Words: The Secrets of Their Success.* Boston: Houghton Mifflin, 2002.

Nolting, Paul D. *Math Study Skills Workbook*, Second Edition. Boston: Houghton Mifflin, 2005.

Ober, Scott. *Contemporary Business English.* Boston: Houghton Mifflin, 2005.

Orman, Suze. *The Road to Wealth.* New York: Riverhead, 2001.

Pauk, Walter, and Ross J. Q. Owens. *How to Study in College*, Eighth Edition. Boston: Houghton Mifflin, 2005.

Peddy, Shirley, Ph.D. *The Art of Mentoring: Lead, Follow and Get Out of the Way.* Houston, TX: Bullion Books, 2001.

Pirsig, Robert. *Zen and the Art of Motorcycle Maintenance.* New York: Perennial Classics, 2000.

Raimes, Anne. *Universal Keys for Writers.* Boston: Houghton Mifflin, 2004.

Robbins, John. *Diet for a New America: How Your Food Choices Affect Your Health, Happiness and the Future of Life on Earth.* New York: H.J. Kramer, 1998.

Rothwell, J. Dan. *In Mixed Company: Communicating in Small Groups and Teams.* Belmont, CA: Wadsworth, 2004.

Ruggiero, Vincent Ryan. *Becoming a Critical Thinker*, Fifth Edition. Boston: Houghton Mifflin, 2006.

Schacter, Daniel L. *Searching for Memory: The Brain, the Mind, and the Past.* New York: HarperCollins, 1997.

Schlosser, Eric. *Fast Food Nation.* Boston: Houghton Mifflin, 2001.

Semler, Ricardo. *The Seven-Day Weekend.* New York: Penguin, 2003.

Strunk, William, Jr., and E. B.White. *The Elements of Style.* New York: Macmillan, 1979.

Tobias, Sheila. *Succeed with Math: Every Student's Guide to Conquering Math Anxiety.* New York: College Board, 1995.

Ueland, Brenda. *If You Want to Write: A Book About Art, Independence and Spirit.* St. Paul, MN: Graywolf, 1987.

U.S. Department of Education. *The Student Guide.* Published yearly. (Federal Student Aid Information Center, 1-800-4-FED-AID). Available online at http://studentaid.ed.gov/students/publications/student_guide/2004 _2005/english/index.htm.

Watkins, Ryan, and Michael Corry. *E-learning Companion: A Student's Guide to Online Success.* Boston: Houghton Mifflin, 2005.

Weil, Andrew. *Natural Health, Natural Medicine.* Boston: Houghton Mifflin, 1998.

Welch, David. *Decisions, Decisions: The Art of Effective Decision Making.* Amherst, NY: Prometheus, 2002.

Wurman, Richard Saul. *Information Anxiety.* New York: Doubleday, 1989.

Wurman, Richard Saul. *Information Anxiety 2.* Indianapolis: QUE, 2001.

Index

MONDAY ___ / ___ / ___ /

Monitor	Plan
7:00	7:00
7:15	
7:30	
7:45	
8:00	8:00
8:15	
8:30	
8:45	
9:00	9:00
9:15	
9:30	
9:45	
10:00	10:00
10:15	
10:30	
10:45	
11:00	11:00
11:15	
11:30	
11:45	
12:00	12:00
12:15	
12:30	
12:45	
1:00	1:00
1:15	
1:30	
1:45	
2:00	2:00
2:15	
2:30	
2:45	
3:00	3:00
3:15	
3:30	
3:45	
4:00	4:00
4:15	
4:30	
4:45	
5:00	5:00
5:15	
5:30	
5:45	
6:00	6:00
6:15	
6:30	
6:45	
7:00	7:00
7:15	
7:30	
7:45	
8:00	8:00
8:15	
8:30	
8:45	
9:00	9:00
9:15	
9:30	
9:45	
10:00	10:00
10:15	
10:30	
10:45	
11:00	11:00
11:15	
11:30	
11:45	
12:00	12:00

TUESDAY ___ / ___ / ___ /

Monitor	Plan
7:00	7:00
7:15	
7:30	
7:45	
8:00	8:00
8:15	
8:30	
8:45	
9:00	9:00
9:15	
9:30	
9:45	
10:00	10:00
10:15	
10:30	
10:45	
11:00	11:00
11:15	
11:30	
11:45	
12:00	12:00
12:15	
12:30	
12:45	
1:00	1:00
1:15	
1:30	
1:45	
2:00	2:00
2:15	
2:30	
2:45	
3:00	3:00
3:15	
3:30	
3:45	
4:00	4:00
4:15	
4:30	
4:45	
5:00	5:00
5:15	
5:30	
5:45	
6:00	6:00
6:15	
6:30	
6:45	
7:00	7:00
7:15	
7:30	
7:45	
8:00	8:00
8:15	
8:30	
8:45	
9:00	9:00
9:15	
9:30	
9:45	
10:00	10:00
10:15	
10:30	
10:45	
11:00	11:00
11:15	
11:30	
11:45	
12:00	12:00

WEDNESDAY ___ / ___ / ___ /

Monitor	Plan
7:00	7:00
7:15	
7:30	
7:45	
8:00	8:00
8:15	
8:30	
8:45	
9:00	9:00
9:15	
9:30	
9:45	
10:00	10:00
10:15	
10:30	
10:45	
11:00	11:00
11:15	
11:30	
11:45	
12:00	12:00
12:15	
12:30	
12:45	
1:00	1:00
1:15	
1:30	
1:45	
2:00	2:00
2:15	
2:30	
2:45	
3:00	3:00
3:15	
3:30	
3:45	
4:00	4:00
4:15	
4:30	
4:45	
5:00	5:00
5:15	
5:30	
5:45	
6:00	6:00
6:15	
6:30	
6:45	
7:00	7:00
7:15	
7:30	
7:45	
8:00	8:00
8:15	
8:30	
8:45	
9:00	9:00
9:15	
9:30	
9:45	
10:00	10:00
10:15	
10:30	
10:45	
11:00	11:00
11:15	
11:30	
11:45	
12:00	12:00

THURSDAY ___ /___ /___ /

Monitor	Plan
7:00	7:00
7:15	
7:30	
7:45	
8:00	8:00
8:15	
8:30	
8:45	
9:00	9:00
9:15	
9:30	
9:45	
10:00	10:00
10:15	
10:30	
10:45	
11:00	11:00
11:15	
11:30	
11:45	
12:00	12:00
12:15	
12:30	
12:45	
1:00	1:00
1:15	
1:30	
1:45	
2:00	2:00
2:15	
2:30	
2:45	
3:00	3:00
3:15	
3:30	
3:45	
4:00	4:00
4:15	
4:30	
4:45	
5:00	5:00
5:15	
5:30	
5:45	
6:00	6:00
6:15	
6:30	
6:45	
7:00	7:00
7:15	
7:30	
7:45	
8:00	8:00
8:15	
8:30	
8:45	
9:00	9:00
9:15	
9:30	
9:45	
10:00	10:00
10:15	
10:30	
10:45	
11:00	11:00
11:15	
11:30	
11:45	
12:00	12:00

FRIDAY ___ /___ /___ /

Monitor	Plan
7:00	7:00
7:15	
7:30	
7:45	
8:00	8:00
8:15	
8:30	
8:45	
9:00	9:00
9:15	
9:30	
9:45	
10:00	10:00
10:15	
10:30	
10:45	
11:00	11:00
11:15	
11:30	
11:45	
12:00	12:00
12:15	
12:30	
12:45	
1:00	1:00
1:15	
1:30	
1:45	
2:00	2:00
2:15	
2:30	
2:45	
3:00	3:00
3:15	
3:30	
3:45	
4:00	4:00
4:15	
4:30	
4:45	
5:00	5:00
5:15	
5:30	
5:45	
6:00	6:00
6:15	
6:30	
6:45	
7:00	7:00
7:15	
7:30	
7:45	
8:00	8:00
8:15	
8:30	
8:45	
9:00	9:00
9:15	
9:30	
9:45	
10:00	10:00
10:15	
10:30	
10:45	
11:00	11:00
11:15	
11:30	
11:45	
12:00	12:00

SATURDAY ___ /___ /___ /

Monitor	Plan

SUNDAY ___ /___ /___ /

Monitor	Plan

MONDAY	TUESDAY	WEDNESDAY	THURSDAY	FRIDAY	SATURDAY	SUNDAY

MONDAY	TUESDAY	WEDNESDAY	THURSDAY	FRIDAY	SATURDAY	SUNDAY

MONDAY	TUESDAY	WEDNESDAY	THURSDAY	FRIDAY	SATURDAY	SUNDAY

MONDAY	TUESDAY	WEDNESDAY	THURSDAY	FRIDAY	SATURDAY	SUNDAY

Name ____________________

LONG-TERM PLANNER ___ / ___ / ___ to ___ / ___ / ___

Week of	Monday	Tuesday	Wednesday	Thursday	Friday	Saturday	Sunday
___ / ___							
___ / ___							
___ / ___							
___ / ___							
___ / ___							
___ / ___							
___ / ___							
___ / ___							
___ / ___							
___ / ___							
___ / ___							
___ / ___							
___ / ___							
___ / ___							
___ / ___							
___ / ___							
___ / ___							
___ / ___							
___ / ___							
___ / ___							
___ / ___							
___ / ___							
___ / ___							
___ / ___							
___ / ___							
___ / ___							
___ / ___							
___ / ___							

Name ______________________

LONG-TERM PLANNER ___ / ___ / ___ to ___ / ___ / ___

Week of	Monday	Tuesday	Wednesday	Thursday	Friday	Saturday	Sunday
___ / ___							
___ / ___							
___ / ___							
___ / ___							
___ / ___							
___ / ___							
___ / ___							
___ / ___							
___ / ___							
___ / ___							
___ / ___							
___ / ___							
___ / ___							
___ / ___							
___ / ___							
___ / ___							
___ / ___							
___ / ___							
___ / ___							
___ / ___							
___ / ___							
___ / ___							
___ / ___							
___ / ___							
___ / ___							
___ / ___							
___ / ___							
___ / ___							

MONEY MONITOR

Date	Description	In	Out

MONEY MONITOR

Date	Description	In	Out